# COLLEGE TO UNIVERSITY
## THE HANNAH YEARS AT MICHIGAN STATE
### 1935–1969

## Paul L. Dressel

Michigan State University
University Publications
East Lansing, Michigan 48824

Library of Congress Catalog Card No.: 86-62900
ISBN: 0-940635-00-3

PRE Ref.

# Contents

# Preface

Much of the credit for the development of Michigan State University from a relatively small agricultural college to a university of world renown must go to John Alfred Hannah. For nearly thirty-four years the institution flourished under his direction, beginning in 1935 when he became secretary to the State Board of Agriculture—at that time the governing board of the college. Working closely with Robert Shaw, the college president, Hannah was effectively the second ranking administrator of the college until, in 1941, he became its president.

Hannah demonstrated his capacity for leadership by refurbishing the mission of the institution, specifying many of the steps necessary for its growth and improvement. He encouraged the development and activation of the ideas of others, and urged them to take advantage of changing circumstances and resultant opportunities to expand the programs and services of the institution to serve the people of the state, the nation, and the world. He vigilantly promulgated this mission until his retirement from the presidency in 1969.

This volume is not a biography of John Hannah. Neither is it a history of Michigan State during the years in which Hannah exercised leadership. Rather it is an attempt to portray the nature of the institution as it existed before Hannah's involvement as administrator, to indicate his expanding vision of the institution's role, and to discuss and evaluate the means by which he encouraged its transformation. Inevitably, there are elements of history and biography, but primarily this book is a case study in the transformation of a small land-grant college into a major university under the leadership of a man thoroughly committed to the land-grant mission. Hannah saw that mission as a mandate to the institution to provide the opportunities and services required to help people improve the quality of their living, increase personal satisfactions, and contribute to the improvement of their state, nation, and society.

In the years since his retirement, Hannah has viewed with concern the weakening of the commitment to public service at Michigan State and at other land-grant institutions as well. Thus a natural extension of this review of the Hannah years at Michigan State is a consideration of its relevance to all colleges and universities that accept the public service obligation as a mission rather than as a means of currying public favor and institutional support.

Whether or not I am qualified to undertake this task must be determined by the results. I certainly had the opportunity to peruse the institution and its mission. I joined Michigan State in 1932 as a graduate student and part-time assistant to the head of the mathematics department and served the institution in a variety of roles until retirement in 1976. During those four-plus decades I had the opportunity to observe Hannah in action on many fronts, to talk with him in depth about many of the innovations that he and others generated, and to discuss with him many of the studies and evaluations that I and my associates produced. I admired both his effectiveness and charisma in all of these circumstances.

Hannah did not simply order or demand change or improvement. He asked for studies of problems and for suggestions about how to alleviate problems if they could not be eliminated. Studies were sometimes disturbing to him even when he heeded them. I well recall a phone call one morning about 7:30 a.m. Hannah acknowledged and thanked me for a report sent the day before and then, after a brief pause, said, "Dressel, you should know it used to be a lot easier to make decisions than it is now when you send out these reports." We both recognized this as a compliment.

Dynamics at Michigan State in the Hannah years, arising always out of a sense of purpose and direction, made life interesting. As a result of the innovations and the studies that I made of them, I became extensively involved in consulting on higher education problems elsewhere and in writing about them. Thus, in retirement, it seemed natural to re-search and reexamine in greater depth the developments at Michigan State. One of the more satisfying aspects of this task has been the availability and readiness of John Hannah to discuss, read, and react to the materials collected and to my attempts to make of them a coherent discussion of the Hannah years at MSU—a good example of the continuing and lifelong education that Hannah so strongly supported. From it, I have reached the conviction that effective academic work and scholarly endeavor must be both satisfying in their results and enjoyable in the process.

If learning must be both satisfying and enjoyable, so also must be the processes that give direction and character to the nature of the learning experiences. And they can—indeed must—be so without eliminating continuous effort and rigor. But there must also be humility and humor. Despite the greatest sincerity and concentrated effort, much of what we humans propose and support verges on the ridiculous and only escapes it by wise and tolerant interpretation. Charismatic and intelligent leadership inspires individuals to step outside their own biases and selfish concerns for their personal welfare to address the broader concerns and values of our culture, nation, and of all people. This, I believe, characterized the Hannah years at Michigan State. Only with such leadership, can the faculty of an institution be brought to accept and promote the service mission. A re-search of the nature and obligation of that mission is overdue—especially in land-grant institutions.

*East Lansing, Michigan*                                    PAUL L. DRESSEL
*August 1986*

# Acknowledgments

Surely, some measure of the esteem in which an individual is held is found in the responses of those requested to provide comments and materials about that individual's contributions and impact. Though comparative norms do not exist, the materials, phone calls, and letters forthcoming in response to my request for materials and recollections for preparation of a statement of John Hannah's role at Michigan State furnished overwhelming evidence of the affection and respect accorded him by the faculty, students, and board members with whom he was associated at Michigan State.

Some reason for that esteem is found in the time and attention he gave to my questions and to reading of successive drafts of various aspects of the Hannah years at Michigan State. Because of this, I must acknowledge Hannah himself as the most helpful and completely forthright of all those who aided my efforts.

I am indebted also to Dean Myron S. Magen and his associates in the College of Osteopathic Medicine at MSU, who provided a convenient and congenial environment in which to work.

Acknowledgments are due to James Denison and William Combs, both of whom are now deceased, but who were long associated with President Hannah in various capacities and contributed greatly to the amassing of materials about Michigan State during the Hannah years. Professor Combs was the first director of the MSU Archives.

David Heenan, who was himself involved in International Programs, prepared the very extensive paper from which chapter twelve was extracted. He also read and critiqued many other chapters and provided additional background on several of them.

John Cantlon, Vice President for Research Development, was especially helpful in sharing with me his own writing and observations about development of the research program as well as commenting on many other matters.

Herman King and Frederic Dutton provided extensive materials and critical reactions to many others. John Useem gave the first rough draft a critical reading and provided numerous suggestions.

Ruth Frye, Evelyn Guiste, and Dora Marcus made extensive contributions in various ways and at various stages of the effort. Ann Shickluna carried the major burden of preparing typescripts, editing, and handling the many details involved in manuscript preparation. Dr. Holly Holdman's research in the MSU Archives and Historical Collections and selection therefrom of materials relevant to my task were invaluable. I also appreciate the assistance given to her by Frederick Honhart and his associates in the archives.

This project would have been impossible without the grant made by the Kellogg Foundation, which played a major role in supporting John Hannah's efforts. Although, as always, the foundation refrained from any criticism, Russell Mawby, Arlon Elser, and Laura Davis were helpful in many ways—especially in providing information on grants made to Michigan State.

The number of contributions forbids listing all of them, but to all I express my thanks.

As a final acknowledgment, I must state that this task has been an absorbing and gratifying cap of my many years of association with Michigan State. It enabled me to weather, with minimal grief, a relatively depressed period in Michigan State history marked by both financial exigency and uncertainty in institutional mission. Furthermore, the task enabled me to renew working relations with John Hannah, which had necessarily been severed when he retired from MSU in 1969.

# PRELUDE
## *A Man, A Mission, A Monument*

JOHN A. HANNAH

# John A. Hannah

John Alfred Hannah was born in Grand Rapids, Michigan on October 9, 1902. His grandfather, who had emigrated from England and settled in the Kalamazoo–Grand Rapids area, became involved in a market gardening business and later expanded this into a florist business. His father operated a hatchery and greenhouse on a small farm at the outskirts of Grand Rapids. In his youth John Hannah's life centered on agricultural activities. Hannah notes in his memoirs that at the age of five or six his father assigned to him the responsibility for the family's flock of chickens. This was the beginning of his interest and career in poultry breeding and raising. While still a young boy he gained recognition and a reputation for his Barred Plymouth Rocks and Black Orpington chickens, which he exhibited in poultry shows around the state and at the Michigan State Fair in Detroit. While still in high school he became the secretary of the West Michigan Poultry Association and later the secretary of the State Poultry Association, the superintendent of the poultry department of the Western Michigan State Fair in Grand Rapids, and subsequently a similar officer of the Michigan State Fair in Detroit.

At the age of nineteen, John Hannah changed vocation from the law, which his family had encouraged, to poultry science, in which he had already achieved leadership. Following two years at Grand Rapids Junior College and a third year in law at the University of Michigan, he entered what was then the Michigan Agricultural College in East Lansing.[1] Graduated in June 1923 at the age of twenty, he joined the extension faculty of the college as a poultry specialist. In

NOTE: For this prelude I have drawn extensively, including direct quotations, from a statement prepared by Madison Kuhn in 1966 at the close of Hannah's twenty-fifth year as president.

1. Since its founding in 1855, Michigan State University has undergone five name changes. Throughout this volume, I will use "Michigan State," "the college," or the title or abbreviation appropriate to the years about which I am speaking: 1855–61, Agricultural College of the State of Michigan; 1861–1909, State Agricultural College; 1909–25, Michigan Agricultural College or MAC; 1925–55, Michigan State College of Agriculture and Applied Science, or MSC; 1955–64, Michigan State University of Agriculture and Applied Science, or MSU; 1964–present, Michigan State University, also MSU.

a day when each farm hatched its own chicks, an extension poultryman spent much of his time teaching how to improve flocks by culling out the hens that laid fewer eggs. To teach more people, Hannah developed "relay" culling classes in which each farmer-student agreed to train neighbors and they, in turn, to demonstrate publicly their relayed learning.

People who watched Hannah in those years recalled that his six-foot one-inch height and his big shoulders gave him visibility in the groups that crowded around him. The rolling tones of his earnest, well-paced voice carried easily, clearly, and convincingly above any distraction. He impressed them with his quiet handsomeness, his modesty, his serious manner, and his quick understanding of the reasons that could prompt a listener's question.

Having helped the hatchery industry to give farmers better flocks, he struggled to rescue it in the harsh Depression years after 1929. Shrinking markets were prompting a few less-than-scrupulous companies to hatch little eggs into little chicks that would lay little eggs. They neglected health precautions and sold at "sacrifice" prices through misleading advertisements. To protect the honest hatcheries on which the future of the industry must depend, Hannah began to work on what became one of the hundreds of National Recovery Administration (NRA) codes. As president-elect of the International Baby Chick Association, he devoted its 1933 annual convention to the drafting and adoption of that fair trade code. The code prohibited exaggerated advertising, set a minimum size for hatching-eggs, established health standards, required that chicks be sold at or above the cost of production, and regulated hours and wages of workers. Approved by President Franklin D. Roosevelt in December, its test would lie in the firmness and the diplomacy of its enforcer. Hannah was assigned that task. With a year's leave of absence from Michigan State, he established his offices in Kansas City as Managing Agent of the National Commercial and Breeder Hatchery code authority.

Success brought other offers that Hannah had to weigh against a return to extension at the close of the year. Should he continue indefinitely with NRA, head the poultry department of one of the nation's largest universities, become an executive in the U.S. Department of Agriculture, or "pull chestnuts from the fire" in New Deal Washington for a leading meat-packing firm? Rejecting all of these, he determined to make a career at Michigan State. On President Robert S. Shaw's nomination, the State Board of Agriculture elected him as secretary to itself and to the college.

For the first six months of 1935, the new secretary commuted between Michigan, where he reasoned with legislators about the college appropriation, and Missouri, where he fought to keep the hatchery code viable. After the U.S. Supreme Court subsequently killed NRA in the Schechter case, the hatchery authority gradually dissolved, but the industry attributed much of its regained prosperity to the ethical habits that Hannah had enforced.

Previous board secretaries had remained silent in the monthly faculty meetings; but even at Hannah's first ones, in the winter and spring of 1935, he reported on legislative prospects, the budget, building plans, and the campaign to attract more freshmen. Soon he was sharing in every major decision in the president's office. When he succeeded to it, at the exceptionally early age of thirty-eight in 1941, there was no immediate revolution in policy.

Five months after Hannah moved from the offices of secretary to those of president, Japan attacked Pearl Harbor. To students, he discounted the pessimists who "tell us that civilization is going to be wiped out by this war." With ingenuity and reasonable intelligence, he promised, "we may be able to build again in our lifetime a world surpassing anything history has ever seen in individual opportunities and satisfaction, and in fair treatment for common people everywhere." In that spirit, he and the faculty accelerated the work of those who would shortly enter the armed services, continued the education of women so that they could assume the positions that men were leaving, and offered liberal and professional training to 10,000 air cadets, army engineers, language-culture specialists, and young reservists sent to the campus for a few months or a year. Research and extension staffs concentrated on stimulating food and industrial production. And President Hannah continued to plan an education for the world to which students would return after World War II.

In his third year in office, the University of Michigan, at its February 1944 commencement, conferred an honorary Doctor of Laws degree on the man who had not stayed there to receive a Bachelor of Laws. The citation recognized Hannah as "an educator alive to both the immediate problems and the ultimate purposes of teaching and research" and as "an administrator endowed with broad vision, resolute will, and the capacity to achieve."

Concern in 1944 that returning veterans be broadly educated was matched by a hope that they be properly housed. On the day that Paris was liberated, President Hannah asked the board to plan dormitories and apartments for the coming inundation. Borrowing $6-million at 1 and 2 percent, while capital was idle, the university awaited the lifting of wartime building restrictions. In five new residence halls and eleven apartment houses, in steel quonsets, in wheelless trailers and barracks apartments ("Fertile Valley"), and in all of the old residence halls, the institution sheltered 11,000 people in 1948. Few universities moved so fast or so far. In the 1960s there were 2,000 brick apartments scattered in three university villages. On the campus lived 20,000 students—more than on any other.

New buildings constantly nibbled at the agricultural frontier of the campus, forcing experimental fields, barns, and buildings to leapfrog over one another. In its first year of classes, Michigan State was two buildings and a barn in a small clearing and a square mile of forest. When Hannah came in 1935, he found it had grown to two square miles, and he added six more. Of the eight, two-thirds were in research fields and woodland; the remainder was devoted to instruction and residence. To an $8 million investment in land, buildings, and equipment in 1935, more than $200 million were added.

Hannah's repeated pleas for ethics in athletic competition won him not only a place in the Western Conference but, in 1951, the chairmanship of an American Council on Education committee to study abuses. In its report, that committee of presidents called for reforms that its chairman had long advocated. The Big Ten, for example, raised its eligibility requirements from a D average to the C essential for progress toward a degree. The Hannah report helped—for a time—to stem overemphasis on athletics in higher education.

Just as Hannah's concern for Michigan State's athletic stature followed him into the presidency, so did his dedication to the extension service's work with rural families. Home economics, youth club, and agricultural agents brought into their organized groups the people who were moving into the countryside, there to face problems long familiar to farmers. With the president's encouragement, they also carried extension programs into towns and cities where the traditional strength in consumer economics found a new audience.

In his early years in extension work, Hannah traveled rural Michigan with the embryo staff of what MAC President Kenyon L. Butterfield had introduced in the 1920s as "continuing education." The ideal of enlisting the entire faculty in the service of all of the people of the state had been quietly interred after Butterfield resigned in 1928. But twenty years later President Hannah revived both the concept and the title. He also named one of the newer residence halls for Kenyon L. Butterfield; it stands across the drive from the W. K. Kellogg Center for Continuing Education.

President Hannah's pioneering in general education, athletic integrity, and continuing education was recognized in 1949 by his election to a three-year term as president and executive committee chairman of what became, in part through his initiative, the Association of State Universities and Land-Grant Colleges. He offered the services of its members to every federal agency that could benefit.

U.S. President Harry S. Truman, in his 1949 inaugural address, proposed a fourth point in foreign policy: "to help the free peoples of the world, through their own efforts, to produce more food," clothing, housing, and power to "realize their aspirations for a better life." Hannah immediately volunteered "the full cooperation" of the land-grant schools. Here, he pointed out, was an opportunity to carry the extension service to the world's troubled areas. Appointed by President Truman to the Point Four Advisory Board, Hannah urged universities to accept their greatest opportunity in history. He asked business groups to see in this not another costly give-away program but a thrifty investment in helping underdeveloped areas grow by their own efforts. As chairman of the National Conference on International Economic and Social Development in Washington in 1952, he promised that "we can no longer admit the millions of oppressed," but we can "give them in their own homelands a chance to do for themselves what we have done here, and by so doing reestablish America as the symbol of hope."

One of Point Four's first university contracts, signed by President Hannah, was to send Michigan State staff to train counterparts in agricultural colleges of the National University of Colombia. Another sent experienced agents to demonstrate insecticides and steel-tipped plows in India. In Taiwan, faculty helped plan agricultural instruction and research for Nationalist China. And workers from a score of countries came to observe extension work among Michigan farmers. In all of this, President Hannah saw a new role for the institution: It must not only educate men and women who would guide the world; the university must itself guide the world. President J. L. Morrill of the University of Minnesota remarked in 1961 that the Hannah leadership was "acknowledged and relied upon by the United States Government, the leading private foundations, governments and institutions overseas and the whole American university community."

By 1965 Hannah had flown more than one million miles on university and federal matters. He was beginning to ask whether one university could afford to spread itself much thinner. For several years no other American school sent so many of its staff on overseas assignments. This was maintained at substantial cost—not in state-allocated dollars, for governments and foundations provided them—but in the loss to the campus of so many of its best people for a year or two at a time.

Yet President Hannah insisted that the university send its own experts rather than outsiders, and the best whenever possible rather than the second best or the expendable.

Whatever the cost, Hannah saw in this missionary work benefits to the university in knowledge of other peoples and cultures. It enriched teaching, broadened research, and strengthened the new foundation-supported institutes of African, Asian, and Latin American studies. And it contributed to the training of young people who, like the contingents of Peace Corps trainees, would soon go overseas themselves. As the international dimension grew, President Hannah remarked that "the returns to the university have been greater than its investment." In the broadest sense, including worldwide reputation and attraction of funds and scholars, he was undoubtedly right.

John Hannah could not with good grace refuse U.S. President-elect Dwight Eisenhower's request that busy people take their turn in Washington. In January 1953 he told a faculty meeting that, having been too young to serve in World War I and tied to the campus in World War II, he could not refuse a call to become Assistant Secretary of Defense for Manpower and Personnel. He had other reasons, too, for taking the position. "There is too much validity," he told a Senate committee, "in the statement that is often made that the sons of the well-to-do family go to college and the sons of some of the rest go to Korea." He hoped for a more equitable policy regarding the draft, but one that would not destroy the contribution that universities were making.

Entrusting his presidential duties to a committee of five, he promised to spend most of his weekends on the campus with his wife Sarah, their children, and the university's problems. His year of leave was extended, but only after Secretary of Defense Charles E. Wilson visited East Lansing to plead with the Board of Agriculture.

In Hannah's nineteen months in the Pentagon, the nation moved out of the Korean War into an uneasy truce, where it had to discover how to remain alert against future crises. As Assistant Secretary, Hannah developed a program of continuing military education for those who had served their minimal time; but his preference was for career personnel who would develop superior skills and remain on active duty. He asked for pay differentials for such people. To increase the dignity of the national service, he revised troop education to emphasize the importance of the individual in a democracy. He updated regulations to permit the sale of liquor in military clubs and messes. When liquor dealers around the post allied with temperance groups to lobby against the order, he told a press conference: "I haven't any intention of backing up." After he ordered integration of the remaining all-Negro fighting units and the all-white elementary schools on southern military bases, the Washington representative of the National Association for the Advancement of Colored People (NAACP) told a reporter: "When segregation ends in schools on military posts, it will be a tribute to the honesty and integrity of Dr. Hannah, who has tried to carry out the President's program against stubborn opposition from diehards within the Government."

Hannah returned to campus in August 1954 with the Medal of Freedom and with President Eisenhower's commendation: "we can ill afford to lose men with your foresight, integrity and judgment." But he was far from lost to the national defense effort. For ten years he would continue to serve as chairman of the U.S. Section of the Permanent Joint Board for the Defense of the United States and Canada. Since its creation in 1940, the board has met several times each year to explore the means of military cooperation between the two neighbors. Although the board was advisory rather than executive in character, members from the military services often implemented directly the ideas that developed in its discussions. Its inspection trips would take Hannah to the Pine Tree and DEW lines, far to the north of his favorite Ontario fishing spots. Later he was assigned to the Board of Consultants of the National War College, to the Cordiner Committee to study servicemen's pay, to the boards of visitors of the air force and military academies, and to the survey of off-post welfare and morale of military personnel throughout the world.

President Hannah returned from the Pentagon only a few months before Michigan State would mark the centennial of its founding on February 12, 1855. But he had planned for it from the day that he had accepted the presidency. Beginning with Founder's Day, when Michigan State was recognized by a U.S. postage stamp as the oldest land-grant tradition, the year's celebration was punctuated by scholarly symposia, conferences, concerts, the new musical *Michigan Dream*, and an outdoor centennial of farm mechanization. But the spirit of the year was summed up in the words chosen from U.S. President Abraham Lincoln: "It is for us the living . . . to be dedicated here to the unfinished work."

For its second century, Michigan State was assembling new assets. Describing the old library as the "single greatest barrier to the combined educational advancement of this institution," Hannah had repeatedly asked the legislature for a new one. When he insisted in 1953 that it must take precedence over a new building for animal industries, a Michigan editor attacked what he considered an unwise effort to convert the college into a university. But in 1955 the new library was nearing completion, animal industries were close behind, and the same editor welcomed the college's change in name to Michigan State University. But even President Hannah could not anticipate that in ten years the new library would have exceeded its million-volume capacity and that he would return to ask the legislature for another unit.

Other developments in the centennial year strengthened the university. To meet the impending scarcity of professors, the Depression-born retirement age of 65 was advanced to 68 and 70. The rather unwieldy monthly faculty meeting became a quarterly senate, and much of its legislative power was given to an academic council. A new College of Communication Arts realized the president's desire for a common curricular core in journalism, radio, and television. The university television station, on a rather inaccessible UHF channel, was replaced by WMSB that shared channel 10 in a unique arrangement with a commercial station.

In the university's second century, Hannah assumed another responsibility by accepting President Eisenhower's appointment as chairman of the new U.S. Commission on Civil Rights. He had participated in national movements for higher ethics in business, athletics, and military service; now he would test the moral code where it was most blurred. Michigan State University, created on Lincoln's birthday in 1855 and given economic viability by Lincoln's signing of the Morrill Act in 1862, was an appropriate institution to which to look to find particular obligation toward the unfulfilled implications of the Emancipation Proclamation.

How important the Commission on Civil Rights would become was scarcely apparent in December 1957. Unable to legislate or execute, it could only investigate complaints, recommend action by Congress or President, and expire in the fall of 1959. *Nation* magazine commented that a group whose six members were deliberately chosen for moderation that would invite a conservative Senate to confirm it was "not likely to break many lances crusading for civil rights." But that expectation was not borne out. With its life extended and its power enhanced, the commission exhibited moderation in its judicial attitude rather than any lack of zeal. "There are those who argue that we cannot outlaw prejudice and intolerance," its chairman remarked in 1961, "but we can make discrimination illegal."

Hannah's determination was apparent to many from the beginning. In 1957 the *New York Times* thought the commission had "a most distinguished chairman." As president of Michigan State, it recalled, Hannah had integrated dormitory rooms, struck racial identification from student records, refused to play athletic teams that discriminated against "Negroes," and rejected a "Negro quota" for the faculty on the ground that "it is not the policy or practice of the university to examine the color of a man's skin for the purpose of either qualifying or disqualifying him from employment."

The commission's integrity was tested when, following months of staff investigation, it went to Alabama for hearings on voting restrictions. The members included the distinguished J. Ernest Wilkins, a black man. Finding no unsegregated hotel in Montgomery, the group commuted each day from nearby Maxwell Air Base. Nothing could have emphasized more clearly the role of federal money in building islands of constitutional compliance within a state.

Hannah continued to serve on the commission under Presidents John Kennedy and Lyndon Johnson. Father Theodore M. Hesburgh, president of Notre Dame, was the only original member to remain with him on the commission throughout the years. But new members and new problems brought no major change in commission opinion, save for greater unanimity and greater determination. One factor contributing to this harmony was the chairman's decision to leave most of the public questioning of witnesses to members with legal training, while he directed much of his energy toward pressing the commission to make vigorous recommendations.

If President Hannah maintained better-than-average rapport with the changing college generations, it was in part because his office door stood literally open. Each month he invited to Spartan Roundtable twoscore student leaders for dinner and discussion of university affairs. Sometimes they caucused in advance to pace and barb their questions for "Uncle John," but he welcomed the opportunity to explain his point of view.

Hannah's sensitivity to student thinking softened more than one crisis. After a Communist speaker episode in 1962, he appointed a student-faculty committee, which, following the lead of a state college group, recommended a simple rule: any organization could bring any speaker to the campus so long as the speaker was identified in the routine registration of the meeting. Board and president supported the rule unequivocally. Extremist speakers ceased to be exciting martyrs, and the public recognized the courage of the policy.

Similarly, Hannah had stated in the early 1950s that members of the Communist Party would be dismissed from the faculty, but that former members who had renounced all allegiance to the Communist cause would be secure. The president's refusal to be intimidated preserved the integrity of academic freedom.

Again and again, Hannah would insist upon the right of a professor to inquire, teach, speak, and write in his or her area of professional competence, subject only to the judgment of academic peers. He not only rebuffed the outside censor but resisted any temptation to ask a faculty member to be more discreet. To a legislative committee investigating the School of Labor and Industrial Relations in 1962, he explained: "This freedom from harassment is a hard-won right, not to be surrendered lightly, and no university worth the name has any choice but to defend it."

Brighter, more sophisticated, and more involved students had come in unusual numbers to Michigan State after the opening of the Honors College in 1957. There, free of prerequisites, they could move quickly through the academic maze to their chosen area of study. Through honor sections, proseminars, and participation on research teams, they matured intellectually. They also developed an esprit de corps that took them into positions of leadership in major campus activities.

His support for new colleges within the state did not imply that President Hannah expected or wished enrollment at Michigan State to level off. In full-time attendance it had climbed from thirty-eighth nationally in his first fall term as secretary to twenty-third in his first presidential year to ninth in 1951. Ranking ninth again in 1964, it was led by the multicampus California and New York empires and by Minnesota, Wisconsin, Ohio State, and Illinois. With other universities expanding too, Hannah did not expect Michigan State to lose its attraction. Though accused of being enchanted with size, Hannah in fact could not bring himself to support the rejection of any qualified applicant.

At a time when mounting enrollment required more legislative funds for higher education, the demands of other groups left Michigan State with a declining share of the state's tax dollar. To those who would fill the gap by raising fees, Hannah replied that to turn away talented young people because they could not afford the cost of a higher education would deprive society of needed leaders. It would "create an upper class of the sort for which there is no place in democracy," and even generate an explosive situation among those refused admission. He objected as well to a public loan program that would only postpone the prohibitive costs to a time when the young graduate would be launching a career and family. Society, he thought, could well afford to invest in the greater skills and higher taxes that a college graduate would return.

When, in 1961, appropriations threatened to fall still farther behind anticipated enrollment, President Hannah presented a Seven Point Program to explore more effective use of faculty and facilities. A dozen years earlier he had remarked that "it is doubtful that we have yet achieved the ultimate of efficiency in the transfer of knowledge." Out of the Seven Point Program evolved the Educational Development Project with foundation support, a Learning Resources Center, and a number of far-reaching reforms. Courses with fewer class than credit hours not only released rooms and faculty, but encouraged those habits of independent study without which education may cease at graduation. Coaxial cables linked campus buildings to promote research into teaching by closed-circuit television. Hannah sought to enlarge the function of the residence halls, which tend to stand idle by day and to insulate residents from the intellectual centers of the campus at night. To new residence halls, gathered in coeducational complexes, he added classrooms, laboratories, libraries, auditoria, and faculty offices. There, in a single location, a student could find some classes, professors, library readings, concerts, and public lectures.

Autonomy had proved its worth in history of Michigan State's only branch. Alfred G. Wilson and Matilda Wilson—who, as members of the Board of Agriculture, had helped elect Hannah as secretary—gave $10 million in property and money. On their Meadow Brook estate in Oakland County, Chancellor Durward B. Varner assembled symposia to plan a liberal and scientific curriculum for engineers, business executives, and teachers. There the first freshmen came in 1959 to new buildings, alert young Ph.D.s, and overly demanding studies. Experienced persons on the East Lansing campus had predicted that difficulties would arise from the rigorousness of the enterprise. From its beginning Michigan State University-Oakland remained a completely separate institution under President Hannah and the board. In recognition of that autonomy, the diplomas of the first class bore its new name: Oakland University.

There were similar moves toward college autonomy in East Lansing. At Hannah's initiative, much of the authority over graduate study was transferred to the various colleges, under the coordinating hand of the graduate dean. Many of the university's budget decisions that had been centralized under president and treasurer were given to the new office of provost. The provost, in turn, delegated much of this to deans and department chairpersons. All of this was consonant with the long-standing autonomy of the Board of Agriculture—which in 1959 became the Board of Trustees—which is answerable to the voters, and of the president, who is the administrative officer accountable to the board for the quality of the university.

To preserve and extend autonomy in Michigan higher education, President Hannah sought and won election as a Republican delegate to the 1961–62 convention that wrote Michigan's fourth constitution. A member of the Education Committee, he defended the traditional constitutional independence of the governing boards of the major state universities. He successfully urged its extension to the others. But he also supported a stronger State Board of Education with power to articulate the work of all. His efforts were forward looking but premature in Michigan. A particular function of that board, he believed, would be to determine the location of new community and regional colleges. He had hoped that every major center of population would have such a college within commuting distance.

Although President Hannah had accepted many part-time assignments and two appointments of limited duration, he continued to refuse any that might sever his ties with Michigan State. He quickly but courteously rejected enquiries about his interest in becoming president of several other prestigious universities. President Truman had pressed him to become chairman of the Tennessee Valley Authority; President Eisenhower had wanted him for Secretary of Defense. In almost every election year of the 1950s and 1960s, leaders of both parties urged him to enter a primary for governor or U.S. Senator. More than once it was suggested that such positions would be only stepping-stones to something higher. His reception of these proposals was epitomized in his inquiry of one reporter: "Who is deader than last year's governor?" His chosen career was Michigan State University. In Hannah's more than forty years there, few colleges had grown as much in size and stature. By 1964 MSU became the forty-third member of the Association of American Universities. Believing that it was on the way to becoming one of the world's great universities, Hannah saw opportunity and immortality enough in MSU.

Despite his many absences from campus and his many interests, Hannah always maintained close contact with the faculty. His annual State of the University addresses set the course for the institution and provided guidelines for the faculty.

Hannah retired from MSU in March 1969 and accepted a presidential appointment in Washington as administrator of the U.S. Agency for International Development (AID). In 1974 he accepted a role in the United Nations in New York as deputy secretary-general concerned with the planning of the World Food Conference held in Rome in that year. In January 1975 he accepted the United Nations' assignment as executive director of the World Food Council with headquarters in Rome and continued in that post until retirement at the end of August 1978. He played a key role in organizing and launching the International Fund for Agricultural Development (IFAD), headquartered in Rome, with resources of more than $1 billion contributed from all the developed countries of the world and all of the Organization of Petroleum Exporting Countries (OPEC) countries. He continued as chairman of the board of directors of the International Fertilizer Development Center (IFDC) with principal headquarters in Muscle Shoals, Alabama. The IFDC has a worldwide mandate to deal with the problems of fertilizer manufacture and use in the worldwide effort to increase food production in the developing countries of the world, emphasizing first the food-deficient countries, most of which are in the tropics of Asia, Africa, and Latin Ameria. Hannah continues as a trustee of the International Agricultural Development Services and a member of its executive committee.

Hannah's interest in international development dates back to 1949 and the beginning of the Point Four Program of technical assistance to the less developed areas of the world. He served President Truman for two years as a member of the International Development Advisory Board, which formulated policies for the Point Four Program.

In 1979 he was chairman of the Citizens Advisory Task Forces on Civil Service Reform of Michigan. The comprehensive recommendations of that panel of fifteen distinguished citizens have been favorably received, and many of them have already been implemented through constructive action by the State Civil Service Commission actions given by the governor and other state officials.

Beginning in 1978, with the departure of MSU President Clifton Wharton for the State University of New York, Hannah assumed active leadership of the efforts to build a state center for the performing arts. Hannah's letters to MSU faculty, staff, and alumni and his personal activity resulted in major gifts to the campaign, helping keep the center's ground breaking on schedule. The fruit of Hannah's attention can be seen today in the Wharton Center for Performing Arts.

Hannah continues to be active in the personal management of his two farms in Michigan and on behalf of a wide variety of activities concerned with the improvement of the quality of life for all people everywhere. In 1983 he was appointed by Michigan Governor James Blanchard to serve as a member of the newly established Commission on Higher Education. Now, in 1984 he continues to appear regularly in his MSU office. The MSU campus is in itself a monument to John Hannah's vision and determination.

# PART I
## *Background*

# 1
# Founding and Formative Forces
## (1849–1930)

To understand Michigan State University under the leadership of John Hannah, it is first necessary to know what Michigan State was in 1935 and how it got that way. John Hannah himself took the time to assimilate that history and base his leadership thoroughly upon it. Hence the events of the Hannah years evolved out of a thorough knowledge of what the college had been and a conviction of what it should become. That conviction assumed a continuance of the land-grant philosophy and the adaptation of it to the changing needs of society in the nation. It assumed also that the land-grant institution had a unique mission in the total system of American higher education.

Colleges and universities in America have been influenced by many external and internal forces, and in combination these forces have helped to mold a system that is distinctive among similar institutions around the world. Colonial colleges such as Harvard, Yale, and William and Mary had little difficulty building a curriculum and developing a mission that was primarily concerned with advancing the cause of Christianity through the training of a literate and reasonably intelligent clergy. Early curriculum offerings were based on the trivium (grammar, rhetoric, and logic) and the quadrivium (arithmetic, music, geometry, and astronomy), courses of study that had their origins in the Middle Ages. Core courses included classical languages (Latin and Greek were required for admission), religion, literature, science, and philosophy.

During the late eighteenth century and throughout the nineteenth century, as religious denominations became more diverse and the needs of the country expanded, new educational approaches and missions were adopted that greatly affected the role and programs of American universities. Certainly one major change was the movement away from strict adherence to a particular religious doctrine. Greater emphasis was given to the natural sciences, English language and literature, mathematics, and modern foreign languages.

As the westward migration across the continent began and continued throughout the nineteenth century, colleges and universities multiplied and educational opportunities and efforts were widely disseminated. With the expansion of the American frontier, and the waves of immigrants that arrived in this country, came new problems that had to be faced. One result was a growth of awareness and a new enthusiasm for social as well as political democracy, unrestrained individualism, and a wholesale move away from a highly centralized nation. Individual communities sought to attract new settlers by advertising the availability of academies and colleges, which, augmented by a growing trend to support educational institutions through public funds, led to the establishment of all shapes and sizes of normal schools, technical institutes, and state universities. States were exceedingly liberal in granting licenses and charters to new schools. By the time of the Civil War, more than 180 permanent colleges and universities had been established.

Michigan attained statehood in 1837. In view of the widespread move to establish state universities, it is not surprising that one of the first actions of the state legislature was to enact a law calling for the founding of its own university. The state's institution was to be entitled to a Congressional grant of seventy-two square miles of land (nearly 50,000 acres), was to be located in Ann Arbor, and in keeping with the spirit of the times, was directed to maintain branches in other localities, each of which was to have courses in the field of agriculture. For want of funds, and perhaps for other reasons, the regents of this "University of Michigan" were either unable or unwilling to establish these branches, and the mandate to teach courses in agriculture was largely ignored.

At that time farming was neither highly regarded nor flourishing. A few concerned people attributed the problem to a lack of knowledge about agricultural techniques and the application of scientific agriculture. It was the persistence of this small group that led to a movement to establish a school or college where the science of agriculture could be developed and studied.

The Michigan Agricultural Society, founded in 1849, took the first overt step toward establishing an agricultural college. The executive committee of the society asked Bela Hubbard, a Detroit naturalist and farm owner, to draft a recommendation, called a "memorial," to the legislature requesting a college that would offer a liberal education related to farming. As the recommendation indicated, development of scientific agriculture required, beyond knowledge of practice and willingness to experiment, a knowledge of the fundamental laws of science. Also implicit in this recommendation were two considerations that became basic precepts of land-grant institutions. First, the sciences, both natural and social, were considered essential parts of a liberal education. This view was in marked contrast to some of the then current emphases on the classical languages and mathematics found in most Eastern colleges. Second, knowledge itself was regarded as having little value unless applied to the immediate concerns and problems of the workaday world. This second precept was even more radical than the first, for it involved the unresolvable differences between proponents of liberal education on one hand and of practical, vocational, or professional education on the other. The promulgation of these two viewpoints reflected an initial shift from an emphasis on strictly elitist education for intellectuals to more democratic opportunities for the general population. Concession to the validity of agricultural education was eventually extended to the mechanic arts, to home and family living, and to other aspects of human activity. Hubbard's memorial had also included the statement: "Nor should the claim of literature and the fine arts be wholly neglected, as tending to polish the mind and manners, refine the taste, and add greater lustre and dignity to life."

Presumably in response to the Hubbard memorial, the state legislature requested that Congress allocate 350,000 acres of federal land for the development of agricultural education. In subsequent years several unsuccessful attempts were made before such a support program was instituted in the Morrill Act of 1862. The state legislature seemed hesitant to move on its own, perhaps because both the University of Michigan and Michigan State Normal at Ypsilanti professed an intention to introduce some courses related to agriculture. However, by 1854, their interests appeared to have subsided, and the legislative committee of the Agriculture Society resolved that the agricultural college should be a new and separate institution. Michigan's second constitution contained a specific injunction to establish such a school.

John C. Holmes, acting for the executive committee, initiated a program of petitions addressed to the legislature requesting appropriations to provide land and buildings for the new independent agricultural school. Despite understandable resistance from the University of Michigan—for what institution can accept with equanimity a further dilution of funds already perceived as inadequate—a law creating the Agricultural College of the State of Michigan was signed by Governor Kingsley S. Bingham in February 1855.

Locating and acquiring land, agreeing on programs and courses, designing and constructing facilities, and hiring faculty all needed to be executed before the college could open. The original site consisted of 667 acres, largely forest, and was located three miles from the capitol. Defective construction delayed the college's opening, but finally, on Monday, May 11, 1857, the doors were officially opened. The initial staff comprised four professors, an assistant in chemistry, and the president, Joseph R. Williams, who had been an early proponent of establishing an agricultural college. The first applicants consisted of seventy young male candidates, of whom sixty-seven were admitted. Sixty-three students actually began their training on May 12. These students came to the college with diverse talents and backgrounds: some were required to make up deficiencies; others needed additional background in algebra, commercial arithmetic, and English grammar; and a third, more advanced group studied chemistry, advanced algebra, and grammar. The task of curriculum development was extremely difficult and lacked precedent. Scientific agriculture, despite claims for its importance, was at best undefined and, in fact, hardly existed—certainly not in any organized manner. Despite the obstacles, the staff moved boldly ahead.

The enabling legislation stipulated that a primary mission of the new college was to teach an "English and Scientific Course," which in the language of that day referred to a nonclassical assortment of courses including English language, literature, mathematics, geography, political economy, and history. Perhaps the "practice" of agriculture was more relevant than the theory because, as indicated above, the content of scientific agriculture was undefined and almost nonexistent. At the outset, the study of agriculture was relegated to laboratory and field work, although it was expected that students "would discover applications of principles learned in the classroom." Not until after 1896, when the long vacation was shifted from winter to summer, did required farm work begin to disappear from the curriculum.

One of the first field work assignments was to supply the necessary manpower to clear the 667 acres of forest (broken only by two small clearings) that constituted the original campus. Such field work enabled many students to earn most of their expenses during their stay in college. Among other things, the labor requirement made a physical education program unnecessary; and the spring, summer, and fall operation of the farm (and hence the college) certainly minimized the costs of heating the campus buildings. On the other hand, this schedule took farm youths away from their homes at times when they were needed most.

The experimental farm, in some respects, overshadowed other aspects of the college and resulted in confusion as to the college's nature and even its existence. One of the most serious difficulties concerned ongoing financing. Some legislators assumed that, having been provided with land and a few buildings, the institution would soon become self-supporting. The uncertainty of future attitudes of state legislators encouraged President Williams and others to renew the quest for a federal grant of land that would constitute an endowment for the college.

Uncertainty of financing was not the only threat to the college. Some people argued that an agricultural college should not have a four-year academic program—that only a two-year program of technical studies was needed. The existing governing board, at that time the State Board of Education, agreed that a two-year program was reasonable. This, in turn, brought an urgent appeal by the State Agricultural Society to the legislature to establish a separate governing board to be designated as the State Board of Agriculture.

Joseph R. Williams, first president of the college, later was elected to the state Senate and became president *pro tem* of the Senate in 1861. In effect, he wrote into law the specification of a degree program that "shall embrace not less than four years." Courses to be provided explicitly included English language and literature, mathematics, moral philosophy, history, civil engineerng, technology, and household economics. Seemingly, opportunity for a liberal education was thereby assured and the educational program was expanded to include homemakers and mechanics. Nevertheless, the issue of whether the college should be limited to agriculture recurred from time to time. The legislation of 1861 also provided legal authority for the development of extension and research functions and made the college president an ex-officio member of the Michigan State Board of Agriculture as well as the chief executive officer of the college.

Although finances continued to be a problem, the land-grant income beginning in 1869 provided a reasonably secure future that permitted the college to expand the faculty and improve its quality. Although the land-grant income rose to $30,000, that income was never adequate to support the gradually expanding programs of the college, as some legislators had apparently expected. Annual appropriations for operations and for new buildings were required. Past uncertainties, relatively small numbers of alumni, and the clientele being served made gift solicitation essentially impossible for many years. Ready access for students required that fees remain low. During the tenure of President T. C. Abbot (1862–85) students paid no tuition, and total fees for four years amounted to about $30.

Through the years after 1870 to the close of the nineteenth century, the college was able to acquire the services of such able professors as George Thurber (botany), Manley Miles (zoology, first course in economic entomology, principles of stockbreeding, controlled experimentation), Liberty Hyde Bailey (world authority on palm species), Perry G. Holden (field crops), Eugene Davenport (livestock), and W. J. Beal (botany). Some professors covered several fields or transferred from one to another. For example, Albert J. Cook, graduate of 1862, returned as a mathematics instructor in 1867 and after two winters of study at Harvard became professor of zoology and entomology. Cook later prepared a kerosene emulsion that was long a standard contact insecticide.

Robert C. Kedzie, a graduate of the University of Michigan Medical School, came to the college as a professor of chemistry and engaged in such varied and useful studies as effects of muck land on crops, deaths caused by use of Paris Green (arsenic) in coloring wallpaper, analyzing soils, and testing water samples. In 1875 he also made the first systematic attempt to bring college services to farmers—an initial provision of extension services.

Liberty Hyde Bailey demonstrated the beneficial effects of cross-breeding, hybridization, and chance growth of seedlings on hardiness of fruit and vegetables. William James Beal, under whom Bailey had studied, developed a wild garden, a grass garden, and an arboretum for instruction, observation, and research. Through these efforts he had a marked influence on programs and students. Perry G. Holden carried on studies on corn and potato cultivation and offered, in 1894, the first "short course," a practical course for farmers.

The brief and inadequate sampling suggests the quality and range of faculty contributions to the enhancement of the reputation of the college. Unfortunately, other developing land-grant institutions successfully lured such persons away from Michigan with offers of more money, prestigious administrative assignments, better research facilities, and release from vexing chores. Bailey, for example, in going to Cornell, was relieved of the odious tasks of supervising lawn mowing, leaf raking, gardening, fruit harvesting, ice delivery, and garbage collection. By 1895 college alumni were on the staff of twenty-five land-grant schools. Thirty graduates were professors (usually department heads) at land-grant schools.

By 1900 the college had gained a reputation as a source for recruiting good teachers, excellent researchers, and able administrators; but it suffered greatly because of the continuing turnover of faculty. Faced also with relatively modest enrollment growth, the institution again became uncertain of its mission. A rumor that the college might be turned into a prison farm to raise sugar beets did not help morale. Another nagging concern was that three presidents—Edwin Willitts (1885–89), Oscar Clute (1889–93), and Lewis G. Gorton (1893–95)— had arrived and departed within a decade and thus had had little influence on the college. Strict surveillance by the Board of Agriculture (even in regard to the use of textbooks), almost negated presidential leadership and infringed on academic freedom. Despite such campus problems, the college extension services were gradually expanding in, for example, summer programs for teachers and training for creamery managers.

The next president, Jonathan LeMoyne Snyder (1896–1915), brought a unique credential to his office—an earned doctorate in psychology and pedagogy. He came also with experience in the public schools and with a strong commitment to manual training, home economics, and agriculture. During the twenty years of his presidency, admission standards were gradually raised to require a high school diploma, enrollment quadrupled, staff increased fivefold, and extension workers and county agents increased to equal the on-campus faculty of 1896. Nine major buildings were added and the legislative appropriation increased from $16,000 to $560,000. A change in scheduling replaced the summer courses (and required field work) with a three-term school year (fall, winter, and spring) which, along with a new curriculum for women, foresters, and veterinarians, attracted a new clientele. A mail campaign to recruit new students, spearheaded by Snyder, publicized the college and was certainly a factor in attracting students to it. Excursion trips by train brought literally thousands of people to the campus—3,000 during one day in 1899 and 8,000 during an excursion week each August. The college's semicentennial observance of 1907 (celebrating the opening rather than the founding) brought 20,000 people to the campus to hear President Theodore Roosevelt pay tribute to the college. The Land-Grant College Association met in Lansing in the same week and elected Snyder as its new president. The college was by then widely and favorably known—a recognized leader among land-grant colleges.

Subsequent to his semicentennial address, Roosevelt appointed a Country Life Commission with Liberty Hyde Bailey as chairman and K. L. Butterfield (class of 1891 and later president of the college in 1924–28) as a member. That commission's report suggested the desirability of extension agents. The first formally designated extension worker was appointed at the college in 1908. By 1915 the extension staff numbered twelve in addition to fifteen county agricultural agents.

During the Snyder administration, authority and responsibility formerly exercised by the State Board of Agriculture and by the faculty were gradually transferred to the president. The state's third constitution gave the board constitutional status coequal with that of the University of Michigan Board of Regents, the legislature, and other government offices. In 1909 the legislature acted to modify the college organization, changed the name to Michigan Agricultural College (MAC), and directed the board to choose a chairman who would preside only in the absence of the president of the college. The president, legally at least, was now the responsible administrative head. The law also redefined the faculty as "the president, professors, and associate professors." This could have been (but was not) regarded as an infringement on the institutional autonomy conferred by the constitutional status.

By 1913 some people feared that engineering was eclipsing agriculture at the college, and this combined with and refueled the recurrent effort to save money by concentrating all engineering at the University of Michigan. A campaign to change MAC's name to "Michigan State College" was also instrumental in arousing concern about institutional developments. The continuing need for increasing the legislative support of the college generated a legislative move to restrict or destroy the engineering division by a rider attached to an appropriation bill to increase the mill tax. The board, believing the rider to be unconstitutional, appealed to the state supreme court. The court's ruling supported the invalidity of the rider and further asserted that the entire act was thereby invalid. Thus, the earlier inadequate tax remained in effect. In the end, the irritation engendered in the legislature by the appeal apparently focused on President Snyder. Rumor had it that, unless he resigned, the next legislature would be even more negative toward the college. Snyder resigned, opposition disappeared, and the mill tax allocation was doubled in 1915.

Despite many gains in the Snyder era, many problems went unresolved. Salaries remained inadequate, which contributed to the difficulty in recruiting and retaining able persons. Of the academic staff 60 percent were instructors, and only one-fifth of them had earned master's degrees. Loss of outstanding professors to other institutions and rapid turnover of instructors posed serious handicaps to attaining quality.

Following Snyder's resignation, Frank S. Kedzie was made acting president and, later, president (1915–21). Kedzie had grown up on campus, worked in his father's (Dr. R. C. Kedzie) laboratory, and succeeded him as head of the Department of Chemistry in 1902. The advent of Kedzie, who was well known and highly regarded by the alumni, was enthusiastically received and led to a fund-raising campaign for a Union Memorial Building.

In 1916, the engineering block of buildings was destroyed by fire and the threat of the removal of engineering to Ann Arbor was once again resurrected. By prompt action, Kedzie found temporary class accommodations and acquired, by appeal to Ransom E. Olds, a gift of $100,000 for a new engineering building. These accomplishments voided any further consideration of eliminating the engineering program and indeed brought public appreciation of the program and admiration for the prompt reaction to what could have been catastrophic. The appeal of funds for the R. E. Olds Hall of Engineering also set a precedent for seeking private donations for the college.

World War I brought disruption to the campus as adaptations were made to provide for training students for the army. After the war the expectation of an increase in student enrollments did not materialize. Enrollment in agriculture and veterinary medicine declined while that in engineering increased. Yet other colleges and universities were crowded. Why? An agricultural depression had caused declining interest in farming, and youth from rural areas generally lacked funds to meet even the low costs of attendance at MAC. Furthermore, students seemed to be less attracted to what then appeared as rather narrow, vocationally oriented programs. Programs in the liberal arts and sciences and in business, and flexibility in career and program development, seemed essential if the college was going to attract students and, in the spirit of the Morrill Act, educate people "for the several pursuits and professions in life." Expansion of the college program to provide majors in the arts and sciences required revision of existing courses, addition of new ones, and especially, a gradual improvement in the faculty originally hired to teach only elementary courses. A new science and arts program was added in the fall of 1921 but, in view of prior difficulties about departure from agricultural tradition, was designated as "applied science." Widespread concern regarding college program emphasis and enrollment decline led to the resignation of President Kedzie, who was shortly afterward appointed dean of the Division of Applied Science.

Some agricultural leaders were once again concerned that the college was veering away from its primary mission. Moreover, the emphasis in agricultural education continued to be on production, whereas the farmer had become concerned with selling surpluses. The State Board of Agriculture itself, by election and appointment, was reconstituted to reflect rural emphases.

Mission clarification and program revitalization were obviously necessary if confidence and continuing support by the legislature were to be achieved. After an interim during which Dean Robert S. Shaw served as acting president, David Friday, an economist, was selected as president with the expectation that under his leadership the college would shift emphasis from increasing production to marketing and increasing agriculture commodity prices. Friday resigned after one year (1922–23). Probably his major contributions were encouraging the development of the liberal arts, expanding engineering toward industrial management, and stimulating graduate study. Although he moved to strengthen horticulture, his personal involvement in research, writing, and speaking was regarded, both on and off campus, as indicative of a lack of concern for and neglect of the college.

For a second time, Dean Shaw became acting president after Friday's resignation. During the next several months various actions further broadened the college programs. Sociology was given departmental status. A Division of Liberal Arts was created in recognition of the increasing number of majors in English, economics, language, music, and history. Majors in political science, sociology, and mathematics, and shortly thereafter, in psychology and philosophy were also available. Two years of a foreign language were required for admission to the division, and an additional two years of college language study were necessary for the baccalaureate degree. Because Michigan Agricultural College now provided liberal arts and science degrees, its name was changed in 1925 to Michigan State College of Agriculture and Applied Science. The liberal arts and sciences had thus expanded their service role to include the provision of educational opportunity for a liberal education and for a variety of previously ignored occupations.

Both the Morrill Act of 1862 and the Michigan legislative act of 1863 sanctioned this broader interpretation of the college's mission, but the inclusion of "Agriculture and Applied Science" in the college name was deemed necessary by the sponsor of the name change bill to achieve support. Nevertheless, for most practical and popular usage MAC became MSC.

Kenyon L. Butterfield, in accepting the presidency in 1924, was returning to his alma mater. He had been president of Rhode Island State and subsequently Massachusetts University. Butterfield viewed the main purpose of the land-grant college as the development and provision of occupational or career programs, but he also strongly supported liberal education as a significant component of "liberalized occupational courses." In recognition of problems faced by students in a new environment and in making career decisions, a freshman counseling, advising, and orientation program was added. Butterfield strongly supported extension and other programs directed to improving the quality of rural life. He introduced the Continuing Education Program (1926) to serve urban Michigan, but it was premature because it lacked financial support and aroused suspicion that extension service funds might be diverted to nonproductive and urban-based programs. Butterfield made other proposals regarding centralization and control of experimental work, research, and finance. When Butterfield returned from an international conference in early 1928, the board, much disturbed by the previous year's deficit of over $100,000, asked for and received his resignation as of May 1. Apparently the board had concluded that Butterfield had moved too fast and too far into unnecessary and perhaps undesirable developments. Yet much of what Butterfield strove to accomplish came to fruition later under the presidency of John Hannah, who had been a poultry extension specialist during the Butterfield era.

Shaw, who had now served three times as interim or acting president, was chosen to succeed Butterfield. Shaw had three times reduced a deficit, and the deficit of June 1928 disappeared within a year after he took office. By June 1929 there was a reserve of nearly $100,000. But the Depression, engendered by the stock market crash of October 1929, brought stringent and continuing financial exigencies. Retrenchment and reluctance to add programs characterized the early years of Shaw's administration. It would have been easy and no doubt popular in many quarters to have cut back on or eliminate the recently added programs in arts and sciences. Shaw refused to consider this possibility and cautiously supported expansion of the liberal arts departments and the graduate program in fields supportive of the land-grant character of the college. Salaries were reduced, promotions postponed, and vacancies remained unfilled.

In August 1932 charges of financial irregularities resulted in a grand jury investigation of the college. The basis for this was in great part a result of the divided responsibility between president and board secretary. The first was responsible for educational policies, the second for financial decisions. The results of the investigation brought about legislation in 1933 that unambiguously established the president as the chief executive.

The college still was hampered by deficiencies in facilities and faculty, but its major character and basis for further development were fairly well determined and accepted. The gradual change from an institution oriented primarily to agricultural and rural concerns to an institution serving societal needs in the broadest sense was confirmed during the Shaw presidency (1928–41). This emerging institutional character was ably supported by John Hannah as board secretary (1935–41) and further developed when he succeeded to the presidency (1941).

# 2
# Programs, People, and Problems
## (1930–1943)

In the early 1920s Michigan Agricultural College (MAC) was entering a new stage of development and taking on a new character. It had achieved recognition and a reputation, especially among land-grant institutions, for instruction, extension, and applied research in agriculture, in home economics, and to a lesser extent in veterinary medicine and engineering. The institution was now beginning to develop majors in the liberal arts and sciences and new career programs based upon these disciplines. By the early 1930s the college had become a very different organization, in both program offerings and structure, from what it had been prior to 1900.

### CURRICULUM

Despite relevant research accomplished in Europe, especially in Germany, knowledge of scientific agriculture was rudimentary when instruction began at the Agricultural College in 1857. For many years thereafter, students attained most of their agricultural knowledge and skills largely by practical work in the fields. Student labor at low hourly rates, though barely adequate to cover housing and food, made the institution economical to both the state and the student. Faculty members were not highly specialized. Although students studied largely in the arts and sciences, courses were still taught principally by faculty members who were well acquainted with, if not actually involved in, the central activity of the institution—agriculture. Mechanics, surveying, and other aspects of civil engineering that were introduced to the curriculum in the early years were regarded as essential for the farmer of that day. The move in 1885 to expand the mechanic arts to include industry was attended with doubt. Only gradually did the mechanic arts expand to become a program in mechanical engineering. The women's program that was introduced as a department in 1896 had relied extensively on courses in the arts and sciences and even

31

required two years of instruction in piano, an instrument deemed essential to bring culture to the farm home. The professor in charge of the women's department, Edith F. McDermott, was also designated the "matron"—a forerunner of the dean of women, a position created in 1898. Although the first dean of women remained only three years, the designation became a continuing one in 1901 with Dean Maude Gilchrist, who served for twelve years and became also the first dean of the Division of Home Economics in 1909. The first dean of men, Fred T. Mitchell, was not appointed until 1935, when it was decided that the conduct and welfare of women required attention to, if not regulation of, the conduct and behavior of men. Neither the president nor the faculty had the time to deal with extracurricular matters or with occasional student indiscretions.

In 1896 the agricultural curriculum was reorganized, providing for a number of departments and a sequence of courses in each. Public speaking was introduced in 1898, apparently with the expectation that graduates might assume roles that called for facility in expressing ideas to the public. In 1902 forestry achieved departmental status after existing for many years as a single course. In 1906 electrical engineering became a department, drawing courses from the Department of Physics. The initial emphasis in physics was on the generation and distribution of electrical power and its use in rural areas. In 1907 an engineering division came into being. A course in dramatics was also added in that year. In 1908 a long-time concern with the preparation of teachers of agriculture and home economics led to the introduction of a Department of Education. Education programs and courses had become regarded as a specialized field in contrast to the earlier pattern in which an experienced professor might extend his or her range of responsibility to include courses in teaching methods and curriculum. Obviously, the college was expanding in many directions.

This broader concept of the college mission became more evident when, in 1908, the first dean of agriculture was appointed, preceding by one year the appointment of a dean for the Division of Home Economics. Heretofore, the president had also been dean, though not formally so designated.

Courses in veterinary science had been given for many years as part of the agriculture program rather than as a specialty. An epidemic of hog cholera, alleviated by a serum produced by Charles E. Marshall of the college faculty, led to a request by livestock owners that there be formal training in veterinary science. Thus in 1910 the Division of Veterinary Science, with Richard P. Lyman (MDV from Harvard) as dean, came into being. It offered the Doctor of Veterinary Science degree based upon a four-year program instead of the three-year program then common elsewhere.

At this point there were seven departments in agriculture: soils, farm crops, dairying, farm mechanics (later to be called agricultural engineering), animal husbandry, farm supervision, and poultry husbandry. Forestry continued as a department but was actually regarded as a separate speciality in the Division of Agriculture. The college, which had started on a spring-summer-fall program and a long vacation during the winter, had moved long since to a fall-winter-spring program. In 1914 a summer school was started to accommodate individuals desiring credit work in fields in which they had not previously studied, and for students seeking to make up work in their overloaded programs. An abandoned graduate program that had existed briefly in the late 1800s was revived offering a master's degree. It was intended largely to provide training for persons going as faculty members to other land-grant colleges, and thus its emphasis was primarily on the application of the disciplines to agriculture. In 1914 the Smith-Lever Act, which Kenyon L. Butterfield had actively promoted, established the Cooperative Agriculture Extension Service. This act recognized and supported the further development of activities already initiated informally by interested faculty members who attempted to meet the many requests coming to the college. Indirectly, the act also encouraged graduate study.

World War I, and the active involvement of the United States in it in 1917, brought a decline in enrollment in agriculture and in veterinary medicine, in great part because farms and rural areas were suffering from a collapse in prices. Additionally, courses offered by the college had become so technical in nature and so burdened by requirements that they had become unpopular with students. An effort in 1920 by alumni to attract high school students proved relatively ineffective; it became evident that something must be done to provide a more attractive program. Obviously, courses such as "Modern English for Engineers" and "French for Engineers" were not attractive to nonengineering students. Neither would such courses be acceptable to a faculty hired to develop strong programs in the arts and sciences. The subservience of the arts and sciences to agriculture, home economics, engineering, and veterinary science was coming to an end.

An applied science and arts curriculum presented by the faculty was approved by the State Board of Agriculture in 1921. In its first year this program attracted nearly 100 additional students, but many of them were more interested in history, literature, language, and the social sciences than in the natural sciences. In a sense, the recurrent issue of whether the sciences, pure or applied, are part of the liberal arts was being forced upon the attention of the faculty.

The inauguration of the Division of Applied Science and the apparent departure of the college from its primary emphasis on agriculture had already generated concern among agricultural leaders. They also viewed with alarm the lack of growth of the college, but saw this development as part of a tendency to emphasize nontechnical academic on-campus studies rather than focus on problems faced by the farmers. Indeed, it seemed to many of these leaders that the long-time emphasis of the college on increasing production and improving quality should be turned to dealing with falling prices and surpluses. The fact that the attractiveness of the land-grant institution and the support of it had been based on its contributions to a growing economy, and hence that a change in emphasis might generate problems in acquiring legislative support, seemed not to have been fully recognized. Nor did the critics of the existing system recognize that such a shift in emphasis would require the hiring of faculty members formally trained in those liberal arts and science disciplines that were being added in the program expansion. Evidently sociology, political science, and economics, along with their applications to business and industry, would be, in the long term, relevant to the issues raised in pricing, marketing, and utilization of surpluses. Those members of the faculty who had long supported the development of the arts and sciences also argued that the expansion of these offerings would result in better courses and instruction for students in the traditional land-grant fields. In a sense, the college, in responding to the apparent interests of students by adding degree programs in the arts and sciences, was setting the scene to prepare individuals who would be better qualified to deal with economic and sociological problems. Career-oriented students and faculty tended to prefer arts and sciences courses that had direct relevance to career development. However, these broader problems were and are heavily political and worldwide in nature; they do not yield as readily to alleviation or resolution as the problems of increasing productivity. Faculty members hired for competency in the social science disciplines often felt more at home in the discipline than in its applications. There was thus some reason for the concern evidenced by the agricultural leaders.

When the applied science division came into existence in 1921, the only majors available were in bacteriology, botany, chemistry, and entomology, four fields that had been deemed essential as background for students in agriculture. Only minors were available in such fields as economics, English and literature, history and political science, mathematics, French, German, Spanish, physics, and zoology. Almost immediately seventy-three new courses were added to change all minors, except foreign languages, into majors. Drawing and design was added as a major, and minors were developed in geology, music, physiology, and physical training.

The introduction of majors in the arts and sciences brought about a review of student load. For many years students had been faced with a requirement of twenty credits and at least twenty class hours conjoined with the expectation of sixty hours of homework. Even with a seven-day week this meant over eleven hours of work per day. On February 16, 1923, the faculty redefined the student load as sixteen credits and thirty-two hours of homework. The concept of three hours of effort, in or out of class, for one hour of credit had arrived.

Majors in social science and humanities proved attractive to students and, as a result, the Division of Liberal Arts was set up in 1924. The new division was not to become a unit solely concerned with liberal education. Although various people in the liberal arts departments objected to special courses for applied fields, others immediately saw that the liberal arts and science disciplines would provide new career programs. A business administration course was added in 1925. Public school music and a hotel training program were added in 1927–28. In 1929–30 the Department of Publications and Journalism appeared. Sociology and economics, having been opened to treatment of concerns beyond agriculture, separated into two departments. A social work series was added to sociology in 1930. The English department added courses in speech, which would eventually lead to a separate department in that area, and also courses on the impact of Christianity on literature and culture, which would lead to a department of religion. Initially, however, these courses were viewed as necessary for the training of service personnel in extension and for YMCA and YWCA secretaries. Joining the general emphasis on new career programs, the Division of Veterinary Science added a program in medical biology that would prepare students for careers as medical technologists, but were also appropriate for students aiming ultimately at medicine or other health-related fields.

Meanwhile, the applied science division added programs in physical education for men and women, primarily to provide teachers of physical education. The attractiveness of these programs for athletes and the observation that a strong athletic program would help to attract students were not unrelated. Previously the institution's atypical spring-summer-fall academic schedule had deterred any serious venture into intercollegiate athletics.

The development of arts and sciences majors placed emphasis on graduate work, particularly for those faculty members who lacked an advanced degree. Formerly, on-campus advanced study by faculty had been limited to vacation periods but the elimination of that rule encouraged faculty members to seek graduate study and an advanced degree.

Although most departments of the arts and sciences in the early 1930s still recognized their obligation to provide instruction and special courses as necessary to agriculture, home economics, engineering, and veterinary science, an increasing number of discipline-oriented faculty not only disliked to teach such courses but in some cases were completely unwilling to take responsibility for their development. Their contention that such "watered down courses" no longer adequately presented a discipline to the student or took into account the gradual increase in the quality of students admitted surely had some validity. But this did not decrease the problems of advisers and students who sought courses of interest and relevance to career plans. As the arts and sciences departments expanded their course offerings into majors, they tended to view their introductory courses as prerequisites for advanced courses rather than as offerings appropriate for nonmajors.

Even students and advisers in the liberal arts and sciences found difficulty in fulfilling distribution requirements and simultaneously seeking a major. Courses that provided an overview of each of the various disciplines were not available. Thus, the Divisions of Applied Science and of Liberal Arts found themselves confronted with providing a general education to their own majors at the same time as they were moving away from such offerings for students in technical fields. Yet much of the faculty teaching load still consisted of service to students enrolled in the original land-grant areas of emphasis.

### THE UNDERGRADUATE STUDENT

A Michigan freshman coming to the college might have had prior contact with extension workers of the college (county agricultural agents, home demonstration agents, 4-H Club leaders, or extension specialists). He or she might have attended one of the many conferences, short courses, or demonstrations offered by the college on campus and at various places in the state. Farmers Week, held late in January, attracted hordes of farm families with many of the younger visitors involved in 4-H Club activities. Some extension specialists like John A. Hannah had become so interested in young people that they personally became enthusiastic recruiters of students for the college—

and not solely for the programs in agriculture and in home economics. Career development for rural youth had become an accepted institutional responsibility.

By 1930 the student applying to Michigan State was expected to have completed three units of English; two in algebra and plane geometry; four or more in the sciences, mathematics, and history; and a language. The remaining six units of the fifteen required could be in courses accepted by the high school, although physical education, penmanship, military training, and spelling were unacceptable. Fewer than two units in a foreign language were also unacceptable. With thirteen acceptable units an individual might be admitted, but an additional four credits of college work were required for each missing unit. A person might also gain admittance by passing an entrance examination. An individual fifteen years of age or older, of good moral character, with fifteen acceptable units and a recommendation by his or her high school principal was admitted without examination.

The applicant had to specify a major or program. Agriculture offered, through its several departments, majors in agricultural engineering, animal husbandry, dairy husbandry, farm crops, farm management, horticulture, landscape architecture, poultry husbandry, soils, forestry, and agricultural economics. The latter was provided by the Department of Economics in the Division of Liberal Arts.

The Division of Engineering provided programs in chemical, civil, electrical, mechanical, and (in cooperation with agriculture) agricultural engineering. Special programs in sanitary, highway, and metallurgical engineering and in hotel training were possible.

Home economics offered a general course as well as majors in foods and nutrition, clothing, institution management, home furnishing, design and art, textiles, home economics teaching, and a five-year program in nursing. A program that prepared students to manage a cafeteria or coffee shop was also offered. No course in "wifery" was available to balance the three in "husbandry"! Neither was there a course in marriage, even though many young women of that day admitted that that was a major goal.

The Division of Veterinary Medicine offered a six-year program leading to a Bachelor of Science degree after four years and a Doctor of Veterinary Medicine degree after six years. There was also a four-year program leading to a degree in medical biology.

The Division of Liberal Arts emphasized a "very elastic" curriculum with the student advised to "decide upon his [sic] major interest at the beginning of the sophomore year." Prelaw, social work, business administration, hotel training, public school music, and applied music were also presented. Indeed, the programs looked much like those of a modern liberal arts college.

Preparation for secondary school teaching with particular emphasis on vocational teaching in agriculture or home economics was available. Preparation for a career in extension was also provided.

Men, with few exceptions, were required to take one year of physical education and two of military science. They were also required to demonstrate "the ability to swim thirty yards, using any stroke." Women, exempted from military science, were required to take equivalent credits in academic subjects.

In those years students were expected to acquire a college catalog and read it to inform themselves about opportunities, requirements, and regulations. If they did so, they would have learned that the college also offered a two-year winter course in agriculture (including some science and English) and short courses (of one or two weeks) in general agriculture in dairy, poultry, home economics, floriculture, pickle packing, bookkeeping, and rabbit breeding. Faculty members or students from urban backgrounds might be forgiven for initial surprise and amusement, but they soon found, by reading the catalog, that such courses provided real substance and met significant needs.

Four and one-half pages in the 1930 catalog were devoted to listing the staff of the Agricultural Experiment Station and to describing its purposes. Five and one-half pages were allocated to cooperative extension services in agriculture and home economics. By 1970, one page covered both. These services now addressed a distinctive clientele and involved only a small portion of the academic faculty.

Students and faculty, whether or not they were in agriculture, were almost certain to have classes scheduled in the agriculture building or one of the closely associated group of buildings devoted to dairy, horticulture, forestry, or botany. Classrooms in the engineering building provided instruction and office space for mathematics and for art as well as engineering. Both had been part of engineering for some years. Likewise, home economics classrooms were used by other disciplines. Thus, in the 1930s and 1940s students and faculty members from arts and science disciplines soon became aware of the volume of activity in and the value of the original land-grant units.

As freshmen in those years approached their advisers to develop a program, they quickly learned that the flexibility ("elasticity") of some liberal arts programs was not characteristic of all. For many majors and career programs, most courses or alternatives were required. Some programs still required as many as twenty credits per term and, because of an excessive number of two- and even one-credit courses, students might enroll in six to eight courses. Programs were definitely career oriented. Home economics was exceptional in decreeing that not more than 76 credits might be in "purely" home economics subjects. The number of credits required for a degree varied but were generally 200 or more and might run as many as 225. Moreover, credit totals did not reflect the often numerous laboratory or field requirements that characterized many courses of that day.

In selecting courses and sections, the student (and adviser) was likely to find options reduced because certain courses were restricted to certain groups of students, although such restrictions were gradually disappearing. There were special courses or sections for home economics students in chemistry, physics, and bacteriology. The mathematics department provided special courses for students in agriculture, business, science, and engineering. Women majoring in mathematics were likely to find the college's overall two-to-one ratio of males to females had changed to ten or fifteen to one in mathematics and science courses. The standing rule in mathematics class scheduling, as well as in several other disciplines, was that fifteen students per section was a maximum. When an enrollment of sixteen was reached at registration, a second section was opened. Other departments were not necessarily as rigid, but most adhered to the small-class concept of teaching with specific assignments made and attendance checked at each class section.

In home economics, a four-credit course in dietetics was offered for women, and a three-credit course for men. English and some other liberal arts departments had moved by 1930 to eliminate courses designed for specific groups. Thus, a course in literature exclusively for engineers was no longer to be found. A chemistry course in bleaching and laundering offered in the late 1920s only to home economics students had disappeared. Courses for women entitled "Religion in the Home," "Women's Place in Modern Religious Movements," and "Religious Callings for Women" were dropped when their proponent and teacher, a Miss Lovewell, departed. (The college was thereby also deprived of an intriguing name—no doubt to the relief of the dean of women.)

However, interesting courses still existed. Two courses on explosives for land clearance attracted many students (but fortunately disappeared long before the student activists of the 1960s arrived). Prospective teachers were offered a course in personal hygiene for their specific needs. Agricultural students could enroll in dairy chemistry, chemistry of nutrition, or agricultural analysis (chemical analysis of feeds and fertilizers). Courses in repair of farm tools and construction of farm conveniences were available. *Drainage, sewers,* and *sewage* were terms that appeared frequently in agriculture, bacteriology, and engineering. Topics and specifics covered in courses were then (and are even today) matters of very real concern, but the terms used at that time tended to be concrete in relation to specific problems. For example, civil engineering provided five concrete courses: sand, cement, and concrete; masonry and arches; reinforced concrete; advanced concrete design; and concrete structures. These provided a total of nineteen credits, which approached the dimensions of a minor in concrete. A few years later, a move to abstract nomenclature resulted in more sophisticated course descriptions dealing with "cementitious materials."

Courses in hippology and Military Science 313 were open to female students. The former consisted of instruction and stabling, feeding, grooming, breeds, and gaits of the saddle horse. A practical (short) course in horseshoeing, "Principles of Horsehoeing," taught by Dr. John Hutton, provided a series of lectures on principles for correct fitting, balancing, and application of shoes. Military Science 313, or equitation, staffed by military officers and advanced students, provided active experience in riding. Because no side saddles were available, the three courses offered rather more opportunity for bifurcated garments than the dean of women of that day approved. She ruled that if, of necessity, women wore these garments to classes other than riding classes, a full-length coat was required. The rules were not to be skirted with impunity.

Although the term *international* did appear, almost incidentally, in five course descriptions, the student who sought courses dealing with other nations and cultures had slim pickings—so slim, in fact, that he or she probably enrolled elsewhere. Latin America appeared as the focus of only four courses—three in history and one in geography. Other than the limited historical treatment necessitated by European exploration and domination, courses about Africa, Asia, Canada, China, India, Japan, and Russia appeared nowhere in the curriculum. These omissions were characteristic of the period rather than of Michigan State's curriculum.

A freshman, on going to class, was unlikely to find either a Ph.D. or a professor as a teacher. In 1935, there were but 46 professors out of a full-time faculty of 344 and only 61 Ph.D.s. Of the 46 professors, only 12 had the Ph.D. For many years a policy held that there be but one professor to a department; the few exceptions were made apparent by extraordinary titles. For example, since there could not be two professors of animal husbandry the second was called a professor of horse husbandry (a title that disappeared by 1930). Other unusual titles arose out of similar circumstances: professor of pomology (a second professor in horticulture), professor of sanitary bacteriology, professor of pathogenic bacteriology, professor of machine design, and research professor of institutional administration.

Whether a professor or a graduate student directed freshman classes or laboratories, the chances were very good that the individual took pride in his or her teaching. Faculty members tended to come from land-grant institutions (Michigan State particularly), and many of the graduate students came with some experience in public school teaching. Professors (there were no formally designated department heads as yet) not only dominated their departments but also played a major role in teaching assignments and in checking up on what went on in the classroom. One young instructor, noting that a professor had been watching and listening to his classroom from the hallway for several days, asked for comments. In return the professor recounted the story of a German Ph.D. professor who made great demands of his students, but when it was determined that none of them ever took any more mathematics, he was fired. The point was concisely and clearly made that there is more to teaching than covering content and forcing students to work. There was general insistence that at each class meeting attendance be recorded, that student completion of assignments be checked and recorded if not graded, and that a specific assignment be made for the next class meeting.

Instructors, particularly those who were city bred, were sometimes troubled by course content that had been selected in great part because of its relevance to students in agriculture, home economics, engineering, and forestry. For example, a section of the textbook in agricultural mathematics that dealt with the mixing of fertilizers used a number of terms, including "fish waste," that might have had no meaning to the city-bred mathematics instructor and that indeed might have provoked wonderment as to how such material was collected and processed. One instructor in mathematics faced with teaching differentiation and integration by graphical procedures found that he needed first to teach himself. He knew the theory but not the practice. Nevertheless, the service role still generally accepted by all of the departments of the sciences and the liberal arts required that each instructor do the very best possible with the students facing him or her. This commonly required that the instructor become sufficiently familiar with the various majors to demonstrate the relevance of a discipline to the various programs in agriculture, forestry, engineering, business, and home economics.

Most undergraduate students at MSU were serious minded, as students in the applied fields have generally always been. They sought an education they could use—they demanded relevance. In an elitist sense, standards used were not always high, but small classes, the sincerity of the instructors, and the pervasive demand that there be almost daily assignment of work, assessment of student activities, and progress certainly meant that the majority of the students worked and benefited from it. Grades of A, B, C, D, F were weighted 3, 2, 1, 0, −1, respectively, with a student's grade-point average determined by dividing the total number of points accumulated by the number of credits *earned*. This resulted in a quirk which puzzled many students and some faculty members for years. There were circumstances in which it was better to fail a course than to pass it with a D to maintain the cumulative two-point average required to remain in college. For example, ten credits of A and five credits of F gave a 2.5 average, but ten credits of A and five of D gave only a 2.0. For *sequential* courses in mathematics and sciences, it was wiser to get an F than a D.

Faculty commonly demonstrated sincere concern for their students by urging those in difficulty in their first quarter to remain in the same program for the first year with the hope of improvement. But such well-meant advice frequently backfired in that students having an average below C at the end of the first year were not acceptable for continuance or for transfer to other programs. The exception was in the liberal arts and applied science programs where it was possible to change a major while remaining in the same division. But, in general, administrators and faculty members of that day accepted the idea that students already had made a career decision. If not, then it was considered best *for them and the institution* that they leave. The implications of this view are clearly evident in the datum often quoted then that only one-third of the entering students completed their degrees, usually in four but sometimes five or six years later. Though it was known that some students, after two or three years, transferred to other institutions or professional programs, there were no data on this and there was no interest in collecting it. Even half a century later, few institutions know what happens to those students who transfer elsewhere.

No doubt in the tradition of emphasis on work that had characterized the early program in agriculture, laboratory requirements tended to be stringent. Even as late as 1950, laboratory requirements in sciences and technology courses at Michigan State and other land-grant institutions tended to be more demanding than in state and private colleges and universities. (John Hannah, reflecting on his own undergraduate years, commented that he found that many courses were scanty in content and loaded with busy work.) The time requirements were burdensome for both students and faculty. Nevertheless, for some students, particularly those who withdrew at an early stage, the number of detailed manipulative tasks apparently provided some satisfaction and generated some residual skills. There were also some benefits from transferring between the credit degree curriculum and the short-course noncredit certificate program. Students facing difficulty in the degree program or finding it too theoretical, could achieve a more meaningful experience in the short courses. A few students whose interests and ambitions were aroused by short course experiences were able to transfer to the degree program later and work their way through it, usually with some credit given for prior short-course experience.

Many of the social activities of undergraduates tended to revolve around the division or department in which they were enrolled. Students were identified by their divisional affiliation. Interest in intercollegiate sports perhaps played one of the major unifying roles. Peoples Church, an interdenominational church in East Lansing, which had developed a close but informal association with the college, provided religious and social experiences for students through its programs and the affiliated YM and YWCAs. Students and their organizations did not play any significant role in policy making at the college, even with regard to student conduct.

The dean of women, a professor of French, correctly interpreted her expected role as largely that of preserving high moral standards through rules of conduct imposed on students. The limited residential facilities for women were monitored by housemothers who received orders of the day (and night) from the dean of women. Men suffered relatively few restrictions although reported departures from the strict moral standards of the day could receive immediate and rigorous action. Drinking and smoking on the campus were prohibited, and interracial dating, although not definitely proscribed, was frowned upon. At least in Michigan, the 1930s and early 1940s were still a period in which many parents regarded state institutions as places where ethics, morals, and religious values of students might be weakened if not destroyed. John Hannah had become fully aware of this and was strongly concerned about it as an individual. Later as an administrator he became especially concerned about the relationship among student views and values and the public relations of the college.

On-campus housing facilities for students were definitely limited in the early 1930s. For men, there was only Wells Hall, which accommodated about 204 students. Mason Hall, accommodating 446 men, was not open until fall term 1938. There were two campus dormitories for women. The Women's Building accommodated 150 students and Mary Mayo Hall, opened in September 1931, accommodated 246 students. By the end of the decade Sarah Langdon Williams (258), North Hall (80), and the Union Building (80) were available. It was always carefully noted that these dormitories were under the supervision of trained and carefully chosen house chaperones. Rooms in private houses were available for both men and women, and the college expended great effort to review and approve all of these rooms. It was made explicit that men and women could not rent rooms in the same rooming houses. Rules of housing for married students and widows were nonexistent except that married women could not live in the residence halls. Sororities and fraternities played a significant role in student housing and were controlled by college rules.

Many students, especially women, were able to earn their room and board by working in the homes of East Lansing residents. Faculty households particularly enjoyed the opportunity for some inexpensive help. Amusing situations sometimes arose. One faculty wife, herself raised on a farm, had a succession of freshman women, usually home economics majors, residing in her home. When one such student arrived while the wife was canning, the student was instructed in detail how to go about the task. It was perhaps with a slight touch of embarrassment that the wife later learned that this young woman had been active in 4-H Club work for years and had received national recognition for her skill in canning. Although recollections are frequently false or biased, most students looked back fondly on their experiences in rooming houses and working and living with families. Indeed, in some cases, rooming house owners and families became major factors in the persistence of students in college. A few students may have been exploited by excessive demands on their time, but such cases must have been few because complaints were rare.

At that time there were many opportunities for men to work on campus. There were no unions to control the distribution of work, and students did much of the custodial work, ground work, and animal care. The major barns had upstairs living quarters for students, who earned their rent and a little more by caring for the animals in the barn. There were many *real* jobs for football players, but no feeling that athletes were given preferential treatment.

The deans of men and of women, particularly the dean of men, voiced recurring concerns about students' meals. In the women's residence halls and in the Union Building food services were controlled by the Division of Home Economics, thereby involving faculty directly in the operation of the institution and providing opportunities for practical experience for the home economics students. Wells Hall provided food service in the basement with menus occasionally reviewed by home economist dietitians. Although the early 1930s covered the depths of the Depression, meal charges still seem ridiculously low compared with those of the present day. One could purchase a weekly meal ticket for $2.50. The cost of food served on campus benefited from the fact that much of it was produced on the college farms. Cheese, milk, and heaping ice cream cones were available at very modest prices in the dairy store on the first floor of the dairy building. Especially in the spring, instructors might need to delay or slow the pace of their lectures to accommodate students whose attention was concentrated on their melting ice cream rather than on their notes. Of course, the instructor may well have been aided by the fact that he or she too had an ice cream cone in hand.

Although inflation over the years almost completely obscures the significance of particular charges in the 1930s, there were at least two aspects of tuition and fees that should be noted. First, there was a consensus that a land-grant institution should not charge in-state students for their instruction. In 1932 Michigan State charged a tuition fee of $15 per term for out-of-state students. Approximately $30 was charged to all students to cover laboratory, gymnasium, and health service fees. Additional fees might be charged to cover equipment breakage in science courses. Much was made of the fact that certain fees were imposed by the student body upon themselves but collected by the college. In more recent years, students have questioned whether they should be assessed fees on the basis of the authorization of students who preceded them, but the busy students of the day accepted faculty judgment and readily paid. The total of athletic, debating, and artist course fees, Union fee, Student Council, and Associated Women Students' fees, *State News* fee, and class dues was approximately $6.50. In recognition of the Depression, some other fees were reduced. The Student Council and Associated Women Students' fees were reduced from fifty cents to ten cents, and this was collected but once a year. Class dues of thirty-five cents were reduced to twenty cents. The fact that such small reductions were made suggests that the relatively small size of the fees and tuition could still be a significant financial factor for the students of that day. The reductions also reflect an administrative concern about student charges not evident in recent administrations.

Although the undergraduate had little opportunity for involvement in decision making, concern for the student's well being was amply evident in the policies and practices of the day. Most students recognized and accepted this. Student and faculty participation in governance in any systematic way was a matter of future development.

## THE GRADUATE STUDENT

In the early 1930s, graduate programs at the doctoral level were relatively recent at Michigan State. Ernst A. Bessey, the first graduate dean, presided over a program of somewhat limited scope. The doctorate was offered in bacteriology, botany, chemistry, economics, education, entomology, plant breeding, foods and nutrition, horticulture, physics, sociology, soils, and geology. Doctoral minors were available in a few other departments. Scholars in some of these disciplines at other universities as well as some of the doctoral students themselves at Michigan State expressed surprise that the Ph.D. was available in certain of the departments mentioned.

In that day these departments and their disciplines were still oriented toward the land-grant mission of the college. The programs were rather more practical but no less sound than degrees offered elsewhere, if one may judge by the later careers of the doctoral degree recipients. Besides the doctoral programs there were many master's programs in the sciences and arts departments. Disciplines such as geology, geography, history, political science, and mathematics provided strong programs and were signaling a desire to move ultimately to offering the doctorate.

The graduate student of the early 1930s was, on the whole, a scarce article and prized accordingly. In the fall of 1932 only 270 graduate students were enrolled, 56 of them being women. The graduate student of the 1930s at Michigan State faced a very different world from graduate students at major private and state universities. A number of the faculty members who offered graduate courses were at the level of assistant professor and relatively recent recipients of the graduate degree themselves. The student seeking a doctoral degree usually had a master's and would therefore find himself or herself educated beyond the degree of many associate professors and professors who held only the bachelor's degree. Students seeking a master's degree might find themselves more aware of recent developments in the discipline than some senior associates. Usually, however, these associates would be much more knowledgeable about practical applications.

Although graduate students were small in number, they were generally carefully selected. Thus, a graduate student was very likely to be regarded almost as a departmental project to be cherished and assisted in every way possible. Moreover, being in a college and department in which the major chore was undergraduate instruction, the graduate student tended to be viewed as a prospective teacher and student adviser. It was not unlikely that some part of a graduate student's experience would include these chores.

Although office space was limited and had been expanded in recent years largely through the installation of flimsy partitions in former classrooms, the graduate student, whether or not officially employed by the department, might be assigned a working space not markedly different from that available to a full-time faculty member. Private offices were privileges of deans and professors. Not infrequently, the professor shared an office with a secretary or with a graduate student accepted as his or her personal protegé. One graduate student who arrived in 1932 recalled sharing the office with the professor of the department for two years, an unusual but by no means unique experience. That graduate student learned, as did others, that in-coming phone calls from students, high school teachers, citizens of the state, or indeed from anybody asking questions, required a courteous and informed response so far as that was possible.

The graduate student employed as a graduate assistant or in other ways by a department was part of a collegial relationship not essentially different from that among other members of the staff. Teaching, participating in the development of course outlines, and making, giving, and grading examinations were viewed as normal experiences and as integral to graduate study for a career in higher education.

Although many of the professorial department heads of the day had a secretary, some found that the pressure of sharing an office with a secretary was intolerable. Professor Louis Plant of the mathematics department fell into the pattern of asking the graduate student in his office to do various clerical tasks. When asked why he had no secretary, Professor Plant replied that he had had one but that he had kept so busy finding things for her to do he eliminated the position. In due time the graduate student was asked to type all of the departmental examinations. When the student informed Professor Plant that he was obligated to take several of the examinations that he was to type, Plant responded: "Go ahead and type them. If there is any question that would cause you trouble, leave it out."

Graduate students, especially those enrolling in a master's degree program, were likely to have come from some distance and from a very different type of institution and thus were more likely than undergraduates to be surprised and somewhat impressed by the campus. Undergraduates, whether coming from rural or urban areas, were largely from the state of Michigan, knew the reputation of the institution, and very possibly had visited it at some time. The campus was entirely north of the Red Cedar River, and the buildings were spread around an oval. Home economics, a women's residence hall, the Union Building, and some faculty residences dominated the north side of the circle. The east end of the oval was dominated by an agricultural building and several immediately related structures. On the south were engineering, the power plant, a laundry, the gymnasium and football stadium, and the armory just south of the river. Immediately to the south of the river across the little Farm Lane Bridge was ample evidence that this was an institution founded to provide benefits to farms and rural areas and that it continued to do so. (See map on page 365.)

Individuals who had attended institutions in which liberal arts faculties had emphasized the liberal arts as ends in themselves felt a distinct earthiness in the approach to knowledge at Michigan State and were pleased to find that knowledge in mathematics, chemistry, physics, economics, and sociology was not only good in itself but was also good for something in reference to problems that concerned real life situations and many people. Even today, graduate students tend to be immersed in the particular disciplines and departments in which they pursue degrees, but the interaction among disciplines and departments at MSC was such that most graduate students became acquainted with the extended aspects of their disciplines into other disciplines and might even have become involved in some practical problem presented from the Divisions of Agriculture, Engineering, and Home Economics. Graduate students were assured that what they were doing was interesting and useful. Likewise, they had rapport with and trust in faculty members and frequent interaction with them. The faculty accepted the responsibility to help students, especially graduate students, develop as persons as well as scholars. Graduate students grew and glowed under this treatment.

### The Administration and Faculty

During the 1930s the dominance of agriculture was evident in the administrative organization of the college. President Robert Shaw had been the dean of the Division of Agriculture. The governing board was designated as the State Board of Agriculture. The secretary of the board was selected directly by the board and reported to the board. Committees were dominated by deans and professors with the latter being either department heads or having some administrative role by virtue of their professorial appointment. The person who effectively served as assistant to the president did so under the title of research professor of institution administration.

Departments were small, administrators on the whole were few in number, and communication was good. In the Depression period of the early 1930s, salaries were lowered, staff was decreased, and budgets were very tight. But the miseries and the uncertainties of the period no doubt in part created an institutional unity. Furthermore, after a period of difficulties with rapidly changing leadership there was a general confidence in the institution and an optimism about moving ahead in the future. A large proportion of the faculty had lived through days just as difficult, and the gradual improvement in programs and personnel was apparent even under financial stringency. Continuing financial constraints had forced the board to recognize that authority within the institution could not be divided among two or three officers.

Faculty meetings of the day tended to be relatively routine. With tight budgets there were no magnificent new proposals for expansion in degree programs or in research. The emphasis tended to be on routine announcements and perfunctory committee reports dealing with changes in such matters as requirements, substitution of one course for another, and the like.

Faculty meetings rarely excited much concern except when a proposal threatened competing departments or scholars. A few faculty members long recalled a lengthy argument between the professor of foreign languages and the professor of mathematics about the relative merits of these disciplines in training what one Harvard president had earlier referred to as the "muscles of the mind." Persons with some knowledge of the contemporary developments in theories of learning could walk away from such a faculty meeting with renewed insight into why and how the phrase "faculty psychology" had originated.

Despite the exigencies and uncertainties of the early 1930s, Michigan State in those years was a pleasant place. The campus was small. People were friendly and approachable. There was generally an open door policy, and students could talk with deans or even with the president. Interest in and concern for students were ever present. At some points, this concern may have been unreasonably intrusive as exemplified in the long list of rules and policies with regard to class attendance, but the underlying rationale was constructive rather than punitive. There were no distinctive lines, as there were later, between secretarial, academic, and administrative professional personnel. Not uncommonly, the effectiveness of a dean's office or a professorial departmental responsibility was dependent upon a highly efficient female secretary who worked many hours beyond the call of duty and very probably would have been dean had she not been of the wrong(ed) sex. One dean's secretary, of rather forbidding demeanor, apparently knew all of the divisional students by name and was so fully aware of their work and athletic involvements that each student's schedule was, in effect, tailor made.

The pervasive land-grant commitment to service was surely a factor in determining the approachable environment at MSC. Students who had extensive contact with the various arms of the extension staff not only felt that they were already acquainted with Michigan State faculty, but they may well have met on one or more occasions faculty members and administrators from the college. And, although the departments in the liberal arts and sciences had growing programs for their majors, many of these programs were still so small that departmental majors were well acquainted with each other.

Graduate course offerings were few in number, and faculty commitment to scholarly research, contrasted with the applied research of the experiment station, was rare. Indeed the typical faculty load—fourteen to sixteen credits—and a class hour and laboratory commitment running as much as thirty hours per week—left little time for research activity, with one exception. Individuals whose salaries in total or in part were defrayed through the Experiment Station were assigned to research and expected to produce results relevant to the area in which their efforts were directed. A reduction in load for administrative assignments or occasionally for a faculty member responsible for a number of graduate students was possible but uncommon. Deans regularly taught and generally seemed to enjoy it. Indeed, the dean of veterinary medicine insisted on teaching the first course in bacteriology and did it very well. In their instructional role, deans would continue to mingle with teaching faculty of their departments and play a role in their discussions and decisions. A teaching dean was particularly effective in arousing the willingness of various individuals and units to discuss and combine forces on an interdepartmental basis to meet the needs of students or deal with problems generated by the faculty in extension or in the Experiment Station.

Despite the heavy faculty load and the general expectation of an eight-hour work day and a five and one-half day week, faculty members found time for students and were available to them. The relatively few committees were dominated by individuals already involved in administration. Nevertheless, the problems of the institution were well known and were openly discussed. Faculty members, especially those in agriculture, home economics, and engineering, were involved in one way or another in the operations of the institution and felt that they had a voice in what happened. Salaries were low of necessity, but President Shaw's comment to the effect that he would prefer that salaries never be so high as to attract faculty members primarily for that reason made some sense. Strong personal commitment to a task and satisfaction in it may indeed conflict with ambitions that cause an immediate task to be regarded only as a step to something else of greater significance and higher pay. Although there were problems and discontent, that discontent was not so much with exigencies of the moment as with a perceived disparity between what the institution actually was and what it should or might become.

## A PERIOD OF FERMENT

In the 1930s the college appeared to be almost idyllic, rural, and intimate in great part because of its size, homogeneity, and commitment. Walter Mallman, professor of bacteriology from 1918 to 1965, retrospectively commented at retirement that for many years the college made "little attempt to serve the outside world except through the extension service. We were a world unto ourselves—happy with the knowledge that we were the first land-grant college in the Union. Being first, everyone knew we were the first, and being first, we were the best, and there was little need to broadcast our wares and little need to improve the quality of our product. Other land-grant schools had forged ahead of us in research and output of well-trained graduates. In our well-protected conclave, we lived to ourselves and were content." But stress and gradual, reluctantly accepted alterations were taking a toll.

Under President Kenyon L. Butterfield, 1924–28, there had been an attempt to wrestle with the issue of what a land-grant institution should be in an era in which to be completely preoccupied with the rural areas of the state and nation was clearly to ignore changes in the nature of agriculture and the family farm and home, on one hand, and urban and suburban problems, on the other. Butterfield was perhaps premature in his efforts, but his vision was sound and accurate, based upon both knowledge of the institution and experience in similar institutions. Butterfield's grandfather had assisted in founding the college, and his father had served as secretary of the Board of Agriculture from 1889 to 1899. Butterfield himself had been president of two land-grant institutions: Rhode Island State and, subsequently, Massachusetts University. In returning to his alma mater in September 1924, Butterfield expressed his view that the college should avow as its main purpose "the development of occupational courses." He saw the charge to the college under the Morrill Act as educating those "who worked in machine shops as well as those who worked on the farms." Further-more, this meant that the extension concept should apply to industry and labor and, hence, should involve the total institution, rather than relate solely to agriculture and home economics. It was not surprising that farmers of the state viewed such developments with some alarm, which was compounded when Butterfield alluded to the importance of providing cultural experiences in art and music. The latter sugges-tion represented a realization that the approach to agriculture and rural problems had been too strongly focused on the means and neces-sities of living and too little on cultural development. His ideas on broadening institutional responsibilities constituted a threat to existing extension and experiment station programs since expansion in new areas might well mean contraction in existing ones. Although the State Board of Agriculture responded to these alarms by expediting the departure of Butterfield, his ideas, although temporarily dormant, persisted. Hannah and others who had been exposed to them would resurrect them under more opportune circumstances.

The off-campus activities generated through extension, to which Butterfield had directed special attention, were continuing to grow; but several aspects relating to farming, to the home, and to individuals were not well coordinated. As technical knowledge increased in ag-riculture, course and credit offerings expanded, which tended to dis-place general education and to encourage demands that *all* courses have clear relevance to a chosen career field. Such courses as dairy chemistry and speech for prospective county agents had become all too common. Liberal education became limited and the courses increas-ingly narrow in focus.

In the early 1920s the development of courses in science and the liberal arts had provided justification for creating an applied science division and later a liberal arts division. Although the primary pur-poses in so doing were to coordinate nonvocational offerings and add a few majors, the latter were slow to develop because the enrollment simply did not permit large expansion in the major disciplines. There was no justification for offering advanced courses in physics, chemis-try, mathematics, and other disciplines with only a few students avail-able to take them. And it was not easy, especially when no direct effort had been made, to attract students whose primary interests were in the liberal arts and sciences. It was not yet politic to do so.

However, these new divisions did make it possible to provide career-related programs in secondary school teaching, business, hotel admin-istration, and nursing. Although it would be some years before agri-business became formally acknowledged as a major emphasis, many graduates in agriculture were already accepting positions in business or industry rather than returning to the farm. Strengthening of science offerings would soon lead to career-oriented programs (chemical engineering, for example) and demands for graduate degrees. These developments also raised the recurrent issue of whether the institution existed to educate farmers, to educate rural youth to a wider range of opportunity, or to provide career education for anyone desiring it.

The gradually increasing range of degree programs offered students the opportunity for choices that had not previously existed, but it still was the expectation of the majority of the faculty that the incoming student should have chosen a program before enrolling. Accordingly, the typical pattern of the day was that the entering student choosing engineering, agriculture, home economics, or veterinary medicine was encouraged to stay with that program for the first year despite possible poor performance or dissatisfaction on the student's part. Faculty advising was limited, and vocational counseling was not available. Butterfield had introduced a counseling program, but it quickly disappeared when he departed.

Thus, although the institution demonstrated a deep concern for individual students in many ways, the persistence rate was a lamentable 30 to 35 percent. Some people viewed this as evidence of high standards. Others took it as an indication that admission standards should be markedly raised. Other more perceptive individuals noted that many students coming to the institution were not originally committed to seeking a degree or even committed to a field in which a degree was available. Since the institution also offered a variety of short courses and one- and two-year certificate programs in agriculture, attendance at the institution for a year or two could be and was accepted in rural areas as a noteworthy accomplishment.

There were those who felt that the lack of counseling and a period of exploration combined with the difficulties of transferring from one program to another presented possibilities for improvement in student persistence. This possibility even suggested that transferability from nondegree vocational offerings to degree programs or vice versa might be appropriate for selected students. Occasionally it was permitted, but usually this was attended by great concern that how-to-do-it experiences neither be accorded degree credit nor displace usual degree requirements.

During the 1930s the college was growing, which precipitated other changes. Growth required additional faculty and brought a different type of young faculty member, often educated in the liberal arts and sciences. In 1931 the 302-member faculty consisted of 42 professors,

62 associate professors, 79 assistant professors, and 119 instructors. By 1941, the faculty had increased to 607, consisting of 67 professors, 82 associate professors, 256 assistant professors, and 202 instructors. The faculty had doubled in ten years with the major increase at the two lowest ranks—from 198 to 458. Departments increased in number from 40 to 46. Courses increased from 1,353 to 1,872, most additions being in the arts and sciences and some at the graduate level. The number of Ph.D.s on the faculty had increased markedly, but the percentage had not because of the coincident increase in total numbers of faculty members. At the professorial level, only 26 percent of the faculty possessed the doctorate. All department heads (a term which had been introduced by that time partly because there were now several professors who were not heads) were professors but only 16 of 46 heads were Ph.D.s. Of the 82 associate professors, 34 percent possessed the Ph.D., whereas 44 percent of the assistant professors and 32 percent of the instructors held the degree.

In 1931 the undergraduate student enrollment was 3,218, and there were 266 graduate students. By 1941 the undergraduate enrollment was 6,195 and the graduate enrollment 367; both faculty and students had essentially doubled.

It is also of interest to note that whereas by 1931 the original campus and adjoining land of 677 acres had been expanded to 1,613 acres, by 1941 it had further expanded to 2,455 acres. All of the later expansion had taken place from 1935 to 1941, when John Hannah had been secretary of the State Board of Agriculture.

As enrollments and majors in the arts and science divisions gradually increased, department heads, in filling vacated positions and adding new ones, tended to look for a different type of individual than in earlier years. In hiring someone in mathematics or chemistry it no longer seemed important to ascertain whether a candidate was interested in agriculture or engineering or had had any experience in traditional land-grant areas. This reinforced the tendency to eliminate those arts and sciences courses designed specifically for students in agriculture, engineering, or home economics.

The trend toward faculty specialization within a discipline was becoming evident. One young instructor joining the mathematics department in 1934 taught within the next three years such varied courses as mathematics for agriculture, mathematics for business, calculus for engineers, mathematics for finance, mathematics for insurance, several courses in statistics, synthetic projective geometry, and a course in alignment charts (used in those precomputer days to avoid time-consuming arithmetical calculations). In addition, this same individual became responsible for a course in teaching mathematics for prospective teachers of mathematics. This wide array of assignments was accepted enthusiastically by the instructor, who viewed the work as a rich and broadening experience in learning about a wide range of applications of mathematics.

New Ph.D. faculty members joining the staff within the next several years demanded and took pride in a narrower focus and made evident immediately their expectations that their superior preparation entitled them to teach advanced undergraduate and graduate courses immediately. Their own specialized interests rather than the interests of the public or of the students were to be served. For example, a young assistant professor whose primary commitment for five to ten years had been to the discipline of mathematics was unlikely to know or care about the specific applications of calculus to engineering and, lacking such knowledge, was likely to respond sarcastically to students asking about applications or relevance to their field. A young assistant professor in the sciences or mathematics engaging in conversation with professors in agriculture or engineering might soon learn that a large proportion of those faculties knew nothing about some of the topics being presented to their students. And this, in turn, could lead to a complete shift from close interdepartmental cooperations to closed departmental corporations, each pursuing its own interests.

The original expectation that students in all of the applied fields have experiences with philosophy, literature, and other areas of the liberal arts was no longer met. Development in the various career fields seemingly required the addition of more courses to an already heavy load or the displacement of less relevant liberal arts courses. The liberal arts departments, in adding more courses, sought to satisfy their faculties and attract majors. What might be a tempting array of courses to prospective majors was discouraging to nonmajors because there were no meaningful criteria for choice and no apparent possibility of relating courses offered to their own personal or career interests and concerns. For some faculty members and students, the curriculum in arts and sciences was becoming more timely and attractive, whereas for others it seemed to be an inappropriate and vain pursuit of liberal education or of a career program specifically based upon the social sciences and humanities and upon a single discipline.

A related and inevitable development was apparent in the dissolution of composite multidisciplinary departments. Economics courses first appeared in sociology. When a Department of Economics appeared, it offered economics as a general discipline and also special courses in agricultural economics. Ultimately, separate economics departments emerged. A few courses in speech were offered by the Department of English but, as such courses increased, speech became a subunit in the department. Later it was given departmental status and shortly became the Department of Speech and Dramatics, thereby forecasting still another division. For a time the Department of Chemistry included chemical engineering. Geography, first appearing in zoology in 1925, was later assigned to geology, and then became a separate department. The composite Departments of Philosophy and Psychology and of Publications and Journalism likewise divided. Drawing and design, a department in engineering, added courses in art and later spawned two departments.

Newer members of the faculty did not readily identify themselves with these disciplinary settees (they were more than chairs), and so pressures developed first for separating the courses within the department and providing alternative majors, and ultimately for separating a single department into two or more departments. More than one young assistant professor secretly cherished the hope of becoming a department head overnight.

At the same time, there were stresses in the relationships between operational and instructional aspects of the institution. In the early 1930s, a person in charge of college publications could also head the Department of Publications and Journalism. A separation between the instruction in journalism and the publication task for the institution soon led to a change in name from journalism to publications and ultimately to discarding publications as an instructional area. Newer faculty began to view the management of physical and campus facilities as an intolerable burden as they turned to scholarly rather than practical pursuits. Professor William G. Beal created the Beal Botanical Garden in 1873 and regarded its development and care as an essential aspect of his instructional, service, and research activities. His successors were less inclined to accept such operational tasks.

With an increase in programs and in students, there was an obvious increase in administrative and managerial operation. Deans could and did call upon faculty members to assist in various ways through informal arrangements, but deans simply were involved with too many details and too many committee meetings to have time to see students. "Assistants to" deans appeared on the scene to deal with students, a step taken very reluctantly, because both President Shaw and President Hannah preferred lean administrative budgets. The phrase *assistant to* was carefully selected to avoid any implications of delegation of authority or of administrative status. Indeed, such assistants would usually continue a three-quarter or half-time teaching load.

Newer staff members also tended to react negatively to the college's highly paternalistic attitude toward students. The necessity of checking and reporting classroom attendance each day was regarded as a clerical, time-wasting detail, and it could be a source of irritation and embarrassment for students who appeared after attendance had been taken. Likewise, insistence on making specific assignments each day and daily collecting of information on student performance were viewed as reducing lecture time and as interfering with more significant scholarly activity. The expectation of many professor-heads that their colleagues be in their offices when not in class became difficult to enforce, particularly because space shortages sometimes required that three to six persons share an office. One retired faculty member recalled a broom-closet office so small that conferences with students were held in the hallway.

In the developing liberal arts and science departments, the problem of placing graduating students in jobs became a major concern. For many years the placement of students had rested largely with the department and had presented little difficulty because of the specificity of student preparation. The well-known outlets and well-established contacts were limited. The placement problem was different for graduates in history, literature, and mathematics, and the typical faculty member or professor in those departments was likely to have little interest in or the contacts required for placing graduates in jobs. L. C. Emmons, who became dean of the College of Liberal Arts, very early recognized these problems and moved to have a member of the faculty released part time from teaching to engage in contacting possible employers and negotiating interviews with students. Fred Mitchell, the dean of men, was also instrumental in encouraging a more systematic approach to assisting students in career planning and in finding employment after graduation.

The longstanding and rather rigid approach with regard to dress, housing, and behavior of female students increasingly became a matter of concern and sometimes of ridicule. Young women coming to the college to study home economics or some aspect of agriculture were often from backgrounds that accepted the social mores and personal habits that were consonant with college rules. For some students the rules were merely minor irritations. But as young women increasingly came from urban areas and permissive families, more than irritation became apparent. The requirement that women going to play field hockey wear a skirt over their bloomers until reaching the field may have provided a picturesque scene, but its rationale became subject to more pervasive questioning. A changing of the guard in various quarters was needed. One wit suggested that perhaps the college should seek a dean of women who had either more worldly experience or a less vivid imagination.

Attitudes toward students from out-of-state were also changing. So long as the college was clearly oriented to serve the rural areas of the state, there was no great influx of students from outside of Michigan. But developing arts and sciences began to attract more out-of-state students. Ultimately, this was to become a matter of legislative concern, but at the time there was a general feeling, at least on the campus, that this influx was beneficial to the students and that it was helping to move the institution toward a national rather than a limited provincial perspective.

In appointing John Hannah as president effective July 1, 1941, the Board of Agriculture noted the progress made over recent years, while also voicing concern that the original institutional commitment not be lost:

> John A. Hannah has been associated with Dr. Shaw as Secretary of the State Board of Agriculture for the last six years. During this period he has had charge of the huge building program of the College. He has actively participated in all of the normal functions of the Secretary of the College and has had charge of the high school publicity program designed to promote greater cooperation and good will between high schools of the State and the College. His activities have resulted in the development of much credit and good will toward the institution.
>
> The Board is aware of the splendid progress that has been made in the fields of Engineering, Home Economics, Veterinary Medicine, Applied Science and Liberal Arts but feel that the President of the College should be a man with a keen appreciation of the importance of maintaining and increasing the effectiveness of the services of the College to the agricultural interests of Michigan. Mr. Hannah is a graduate of the Agricultural Division of the College. He served for ten years as an extension poultryman and is internationally known for his work in this field. He was engaged in special work for the U.S.D.A. when he was asked to become Secretary of the College and gave up a more lucrative position to take over that position where his conduct has made him a natural selection for promotion to the office of the presidency of Michigan State College.
>
> The Board feels that the best interests of the College will be served by the elimination of a period of uncertainty in the college's administration by the immediate appointment of Mr. Hannah to the presidency to be effective July 1, 1941, upon the retirement of President Shaw.
>
> State Board of Agriculture Minutes
> December 21, 1940

With board support Hannah immediately selected and appointed the new secretary to the board, Karl McDonel, who ably seconded Hannah's plans and goals. There could be no doubt of where influence and authority rested in this administration, despite the continuity of deans and department heads. Of eight deans on hand in 1931, only two had been changed by 1941. In agriculture, the department heads or professors were the same. In engineering, three out of four department heads were the same. In veterinary medicine they were the same. In the applied science division, six of eight were the same while, in liberal arts, seven of eight had been changed. Administrative tenure existed in practice if not in policy. The lack of change in most divisions reflects the satisfaction noted by Mallman. Changes in the heads of the liberal arts division reflect the large number of changes that had taken place in that division under the leadership of Dean L. C. Emmons.

Hannah, as secretary, also had a very significant role in some of these changes. Working with Emmons, he had developed a program of high school visitation which was certainly one of the major factors in bringing about a doubling of enrollment and the recognition throughout the state that Michigan State College offered something more than engineering, agriculture, home economics, and veterinary medicine.

In addition, by exploiting the self-liquidating pattern to borrow funds, Hannah broke free from the dependence on the legislature for campus residences. In addition to Wells Hall, which housed 204 men, a new men's residence hall, Mason-Abbot, housed 807. For women residents, Mary Mayo housed 246, Sarah Langdon Williams 258, North Hall 86, and Louise H. Campbell Hall 300. And in institutional managed cooperative houses 150 to 200 students were housed.

Obviously, by 1941, Michigan State was a different institution than it had been in 1931. The ferment over the years was beginning to show up in deliberations about liberal education for career students as well as for majors. Concern about student advising and counseling was also apparent. There had emerged an institutional consciousness that was something more than the composite of consciousness and pride in the various divisions. From his prior experiences as a student and extension worker, Hannah had become thoroughly familiar with the history and recent developments of the college. The new president had an agenda for action.

Hannah, in his first address to the faculty, outlined many developments that he hoped to see in the institution in the next several years. Shortly he also suggested ways in which long-time department heads and deans could retreat from administrative duties with dignity and dispatch. With the attack on Pearl Harbor, however, all of these aspirations and plans had to be laid to one side. Most of the younger faculty disappeared and existing programs had to be cut back markedly to accommodate efforts in support of the nation's military involvement. Yet, surprisingly enough, the problems raised and the insights generated were by no means forgotten. Time was found to consider and resolve many of them before the institution faced the postwar flood of returning veterans and its subsequent continuing growth as a university.

## A Period of Frenzy

Pearl Harbor was attacked on Sunday, December 7, 1941. The immediate impact on the campus was unsettling, all the more because it was months before any definite pattern began to emerge with regard to demands upon students and faculty. Signals and messages coming from Washington were, from time to time, inevitably confusing and contradictory. Senior men were first advised that they would be permitted to finish the school year. Then, in a complete reversal, those in ROTC were called into service some weeks before the close of the spring quarter of 1942. Hannah recommended, and the faculty and board approved, granting degrees to those who would normally have graduated at the close of the spring quarter.

It would have been interesting to know what went on in the classrooms on the Monday morning after Pearl Harbor. One young instructor in the mathematics department recalled that he took a few minutes at the beginning of each class that day to comment on the situation, the immediate uncertainties involved, and the longer-term certainties of all able-bodied young men being called into service including many of the instructional staff. Several students approached him for further comment. Since the fall quarter exams were to get under way almost immediately (Monday, December 15), the instructor's advice was that the best thing that each one could do at the moment was to concentrate on the task at hand, hoping that by the beginning of the new quarter in January some clearer indications would emerge. That instructor long remembered those few minutes he had taken with his students because three of those students took the trouble to make personal contact with him after the war and commented that his few words had indeed been timely and had helped many students in the class to adjust to the situation. Their truly stunning comment, however, was that that was their only class in which an instructor had deviated in any way from the usual classroom routine on Monday, December 8, 1941. Despite its earthy origins, the college had acquired some professors who did not permit mundane matters to perturb the pursuit of knowledge.

Hannah immediately began making Washington contacts, indicating the intent of the college to serve the war effort in every possible way. Initial actions included development of special programs for students remaining in college (flight training, safety skills, languages, navigation, photogrammetry, agricultural skills for women, home nursing, and first aid). The Extension Service initiated activities to assist in the war effort by increasing food supplies, despite the withdrawal of many workers from the farms. Possible use of the campus facilities for military programs was investigated, and a plan for reassignment of faculty members from areas of reduced enrollments to fields of mathematics, science, and other strategic areas was developed.

Faculty members organized to find land and arrange for victory gardens. Those involved long recalled one individual who announced that, since he was convinced that the war would be a long one, the wise thing to do in gardening was to concentrate on one or two crops each year. He asked to be allocated an acre of land and planted one-half acre in tomato plants and the other half in beets. Recognizing that he faced a major problem in preserving the anticipated yields, he scoured the state and finally was able to purchase a small commercial canning unit and what seemed like astronomical quantities of cans. The equipment was installed in his basement, and everything was made ready for an efficient operation involving his colleagues who would be permitted to do some canning of their own in return for assisting him. Meanwhile, like many others, he was exploring war-related jobs and found one which called for his immediate presence in Washington. Shortly, he wrote his colleagues that he would be unable to return to do any canning, sent the key to his home, and told one and all that they might feel free to harvest his produce and can it along with their own. A good many professors learned what their agricultural associates already knew, which was that half an acre of tomato plants can, under good circumstances, produce many tomatoes.

Unmarried younger male members of the staff approached the imminence of military service in a variety of ways. A few whose special competencies made their presence of some importance on the campus in dealing with the various military programs that were beginning to emerge were given reasonable assurance that they would be retained to work with military programs. One young married man with a child, who had been alerted to some responsibilities in a program to be started in the fall of 1942, received a call from the War Department asking him to appear in Chicago to be interviewed for a special assignment and probable commission as a captain. He was advised in a rather unsettling tone that if he did not appear he would very likely be drafted immediately. Over the weekend the young man sought out John Hannah, who indicated that, since the institution had already been advised that it could place several people on a priority basis for operating its programs, the greatest personal contribution would likely be that of remaining on campus. He told the young man that the implied threat might well be ignored. His accessibility and quick response to personal contingencies was typical of Hannah and endeared him to many deans, department heads, faculty, and students.

The college was soon involved in handling a variety of military programs. One for the Air Force involved young men taking a five-week program of courses, very much like those taken by any college freshman group, before entering preflight schools. A course in communications with emphasis on skills was included in the program. The conjunction of liberal education with military training, physical education, and flight instruction undoubtedly influenced the thinking of a number of faculty members about the development of general education, especially of the course in the Basic College first described as "Written and Spoken English." The attitudes and industry of these young men pursuing an intensive program at the very edge of possible catastrophe were revelatory.

Michigan State was one of several institutions to which a large number of young men with specialized talents were sent for interviewing, testing, and recommendations about appropriate placement in the military. This program, designated the STAR Program (Specialized Training and Replacement), brought 100 to 200 men per week to the campus, where they were first greeted by Colonel Dorsey R. Rodney, commandant of the ROTC staff, and placed in the hands of a somewhat augmented military unit, including a number of reserve officers. The servicemen selected were of high ability and possessed special talents in psychology and pesonnel work, engineering, or language competency. Most of them saw this as an opportunity for assignment to a task more interesting and suited to their talents. A few strongly resented severance from the military units in which they had already achieved some status and anxiously pulled on various strings to be sent back to those units. This element of discontent in the program was more than counterbalanced by the hope and optimism of others seeking a reassignment more to their taste. The young instructor already mentioned as being held for a key role in the military programs of the college was suddenly called to President Hannah's office and notified that in accord with the demands of the War Department he had been assigned to the War Department as a civilian educational adviser and was responsible for coordinating this program and defining the educational policies under which it operated.

The following week, in meeting the first group, the new civilian education adviser found his task complicated by a reserve major who gave orders about housing, food, drill, and other matters, intimating that the counseling, testing, and presumed major features of the program would be delayed and fitted into military requirements. An appeal to the colonel evoked scarcely concealed disgust and an immediate appeal to higher authority. The result was a letter specifying that the civilian educational adviser had the equivalent rank of colonel. Meeting with future STAR groups, the "equivalent rank of colonel" was so emphasized as to result in an undeserved respect heightened, if anything, by the fact that nobody seemed to know what the "equivalent rank" phrase meant. This was dramatized by an episode in which the civilian educational adviser returned to his desk to complete some details and started to leave the building by a door opening on a walkway girded on both sides by head-high bushes. On throwing open the door, the adviser was startled to find that the sergeant had, for unknown purposes, marched a group of approximately 100 men onto the walkway and successfully debarred access to it. Startled, the civilian educational adviser demanded of the sergeant, "What the hell are these men doing here?" The sergeant, also startled and undoubtedly overimpressed by the "equivalent rank" injunction, immediately shouted in his best military manner, "Into the bushes, men, and let the colonel through." Thus, a second major confrontation was decided in favor of the civilian educational adviser.

Another special program involved seventeen-year-olds who were permitted to start college under military auspices and assured the opportunity, assuming satisfactory grades, to complete one full year of college work before going into service. This group of young men started in the fall. It was required that their performance be reviewed at the end of the fall quarter by a review board composed of two officers and the civilian educational adviser. Immediately a problem developed. Both officers insisted that students whose grades fell below a 2.0 average should be summarily dropped from the program. On reaching eighteen years of age, they then would be immediately inducted into the service. The civilian educational adviser argued that first-term students were usually retained unless their grades fell far below a 2.0 average. Again the civilian educational adviser appealed to the colonel, who announced that thereafter in the review of individuals the judgment of the civilian educational adviser would be weighted as 90 percent of the decision and the judgment of each officer as 5 percent. During subsequent reviews the officers turned their backs to the individuals being judged, thereby emphazing their disagreement and disgust.

In July 1943 another military group appeared on campus for training in what came to be designated as area and language studies—in this case for service with occupation forces. The experiences in this program and the principles derived from it materially affected later development of language and foreign area studies at MSC. Though many of the participants ended up in assignments very different from those anticipated, the program surely had residual benefits for the college.

The maturity and the motivation displayed by both men and women students during the war years made it evident to Hannah and to the faculty that a return to the cloistered and controlled prewar programs was neither possible nor appropriate. Educational programs must be reshaped, and housing and student personnel programs must be expanded. A new breed of student must be accommodated.

Although the military could produce ridiculous situations on campus, it also moved expeditiously and with due concern for the needs and rights of individuals. Committees involved in lengthy discussions are not essential to reaching democratic solutions or even to teaching them democratically. Numerous administrators, including the president, found ways in the next ten to fifteen years of expansion to move expeditiously, wisely, and usually with humanity in facilitating and supporting change. Michigan State was different because of the war, and several individuals who played a prominent role during the war years remained or returned to apply their insights to remolding the college. Among those who did so was Colonel Dorsey R. Rodney, whose ability and even delight in cutting through either military or academic red tape to support individual and educational concerns were further evidenced in his tour of duty as first dean of the College of Business and Public Service.

# 3
# Development of Colleges

The two previous chapters have referred to the divisional structure of Michigan State as it developed and existed before 1944. In this chapter, this early structure is briefly reviewed and extended to treat the nature and rationale for the changing administrative structure of the Hannah years.

The Divisions of Engineering and of Home Economics, each headed by a dean, appeared in 1907. Maude Gilchrist, dean of women since 1901, became a double dean when she assumed the deanship of home economics. In 1908 a dean of agriculture was appointed, and in the following year a dean of the Division of Veterinary Science was added. These three additional divisions — engineering, home economics, and veterinary medicine — were elaborations of parts of the early program in agriculture. Some mathematics, physics, mechanics, surveying, and aspects of civil engineering had appeared in the curriculum from the beginning. All of these disciplines were addressed to farm problems, although their relevance to liberal and general education was also recognized.

### ENGINEERING, 1907

The land-grant act, in using the phrase "mechanic arts," had generated an obligation that had been recurrently ignored by those who perceived the mission of the college as serving the needs of agriculture. However, the argument that the acceptance of the federal land-grant funds required training in the mechanic arts resulted in the creation, in 1885, of a Department of Mechanical Arts. Its stated objective was to graduate liberally educated scientists who could apply their knowledge to economic production. Shop work (regarded as analogous to labor in the fields) was extensive, including woodworking, blacksmithing, and foundry experience. Although a total of 250 term hours was required for a degree, the shop work, like field work in agriculture, carried few credits. Mathematics, surveying, strength of materials, thermodynamics, hydraulics, electricity, and the steam engine were all included in the mechanical arts program. Thirty credits in composition, oratory, and literature were also required.

Surprisingly, a year of German was included so that the graduates would be able to read about current scientific developments in Germany.[1] Mechanical arts had actually been defined as a program in mechanical engineering, although it was not formally so designated until 1891.

The engineering program was augmented in 1901 by a program in civil engineering. In 1906 these were joined by a program in electrical engineering, which originated in the Department of Physics. In 1907 these three engineering programs became the Division of Engineering. Chemical engineering (initiated in chemistry) joined the division in 1932 and metallurgical engineering in 1948. From the "mechanical arts" originally introduced as courses related to agriculture and expanded in 1885, presumably to serve factory and industrial needs, an engineering division had gradually emerged—not without resistance from the legislature and the agricultural interests who viewed these as unwarranted deviations from the original charge. The accusation of duplication of the engineering program at the University of Michigan would be repeatedly made.

The early program in agriculture had included two courses in veterinary science, and by 1883 a full year's program was offered. A four-year degree program became available in 1910, but veterinary medicine remained subsidiary to agriculture, and its future remained uncertain for many years.

## HOME ECONOMICS, 1896

Although the college was obligated by state legislation (1861) to offer household economy, neither the facilities nor the funds were available for more than thirty years. In 1870 ten women were admitted to the State Agricultural College, but not until 1879 did a woman acquire a degree (in agriculture). Twenty-two women had graduated by 1895 from the Agricultural Course, having completed the same programs as the men. In September 1896, forty-two women were enrolled in the Women's Course which, in 1898 became the Women's Department.

In 1899 the legislature appropriated $95,000 for the Women's Building. It provided rooms for 120 residents and for some faculty members,

---

1. It is amusing to note that, for some years after the Ph.D. was offered in several sciences, the test for German proficiency was translation from a German volume on the steam engine.

a dining room, cooking laboratories, sewing facilities, faculty offices, and a two-story gymnasium. A music room was also included since the Women's Course required two years of piano study. Thus, the Women's Course was the first of what later came to be called residential colleges.

Sewing and cooking constituted the first formal course experiences in home economics. Home economics was as yet undefined, and only after about twenty years were home economics courses expanded to require 25 percent of the degree requirements of the women's curriculum.

In 1909 the Division of Home Economics was established. Since the women students were now learning about many aspects of the home, a "practice house" was established in 1915 in which twenty seniors each term carried on the life and work of the home. Later a home management house for eight women was created in one of the old faculty houses that had been built in 1857.

Some type of practical experience long continued to be evident in many of the programs. The original program for women was viewed as scientific training for farmers' wives, although no courses in marital relations were included and premarital field work was effectively discouraged. By 1915 cooking, sewing, woodworking, and gardening (both flowers and vegetables) accounted for the required practical experience, paralleling the earlier field experience required of the men in agriculture. Courses in household management, home nursing, house architecture, dietetics, color and design, food processing, and institutional management appeared. Vocational preparation for home economics teaching (authorized by the Smith-Hughes Act of 1918), hospital dietitians, tea room managers, milliners, and florists was added. The program gradually took on an aura of vocational preparation; attention was focused on intern experiences.

In 1923 the food service facility for the 180 women living in the Women's Building was transferred to the Division of Home Economics and managed as the women's commons. As of 1932 the institution administration (IA) program in home economics was responsible for all food service management on campus. During the 1920s and early 1930s the Division of Home Economics was also responsible for the laundry (located in the Women's Building) and for the selection of dormitory furnishings for new residence halls. Institutional management experience for students was also facilitated by assigning those in the advanced course in management the responsbilities for the East Lansing High School lunch from January to June. Students planned the menus, bought and prepared all foods, handled the money, paid the bills, and kept accurate accounts.

An early report on management of the women's commons indicates that the primary function was to provide clean, wholesome, properly chosen food for the women students at a reasonable price. Secondary functions were to demonstrate home economics standards of food habits and theory, instruct students in proper social behavior at meals, introduce a type of food service worthy of the dignity of a college dining room, and provide a laboratory for instruction in institutional management. The staff consisted of four cooks and twenty-five students. Foods cooked in the institution classes were also used. The students also served, cleared the tables, and washed the dishes.

In 1936 the Division of Home Economics formally delegated management of food services in the Union Building to the Department of Institutional Administration. With acceptance of full responsibility by the department, students were provided with an opportunity to acquire actual experience in commercial food service catering. At about the same time, B. R. Proulx, who had been assistant dean of liberal arts and headed the hotel training program, was made Union Building manager and head of the Department of Hotel Administration. This move again confirmed the close relationship of home economics and hotel administration and the cooperation between campus service units and the training of students in related fields.

As new women's residence halls were constructed, members of the institutional administration department were involved in planning the food services and also a new laundry. But the burden was heavy, and confusion as to responsibilities increased. On June 2, 1936, the State Board of Agriculture clearly delineated the various responsibilities. Operations of all dormitories or living quarters for women, off or on campus, were placed under the dean of women. All dormitories, facilities, and financial statements were to be available to the Division of Home Economics for the purpose of observation and study. Responsibility for the food services in Mary Mayo and the Women's Building was placed with the dean of home economics. Thereafter, responsibility for the purchase of furniture, fixtures, and decorations and the determination of room rental prices were assigned to a dormitory committee composed of the board secretary (John Hannah), the comptroller, and Deans Fred Mitchell (men), Elizabeth Conrad (women), and Marie Dye (home economics). Management and business staff representation and influence became prominent; that of academic staff was becoming less so.

The move toward separating home economics from responsibilities for food services continued. In 1942 the food services in the Union were made independent of institutional administration; but Katherine Hart, supervisor of the food services, remained a member of the department staff. A few other members of the food services staff retained faculty status, and the services and staff were available for class work in institutional administration. Three women's dorms and North Hall were organized as a unit for food service and housekeeping, under the supervision of Mildred Jones and others, who also continued as members of the institutional administration staff. Facilities for laboratory work in the department were still available for all persons with faculty status. Changes in personnel and realignment of departments gradually eliminated these interrelationships.

The courses and programs in home economics were undergoing extensive change. In 1920 home economics provided four areas of specialization: foods and nutrition, clothing and textiles, vocational home economics, and general home economics. In 1923 related arts and a five-year combined home economics and nursing program appeared. Program statements continued for some years to exhibit a decided slant toward homemaking. By 1929–30, the catalog statement refers to study of the problems of the home and family and to the value of technical training as well as of liberal education.

A departmental structure was introduced in 1935: foods and nutrition; home management and child development; institutional administration; and textiles, clothing, and related arts. In 1943 a program on child development in the early years was added to prepare nursery school teachers for children of working mothers.

The 1940 catalog asserted that home economics dealt with the problems of home and family in a community setting, including working and living together, care and guidance of children, nutritional needs, clothing, housing, family income, health, comfort, and beauty. Home economics had come to be viewed as based upon an understanding of social, biological, and physical sciences and of the humanities. The emphasis was still on the home and family, but the curriculum was no longer selected to prepare a farmer's wife.

The first male graduate in home economics was a 1948 major in institutional administration. Males had been permitted to take courses but had been denied admission until Hannah, on behalf of that first male graduate, had intervened directly with the dean.

By 1949 the goals of home economics included preparing individuals for professions. By 1953–54 there were sixteen programs within the department and four interdepartmental programs. Over the space of years from 1929 to 1953, expansion of courses, programs, and course requirements had resulted in inflexible programs that included burdensome science requirements and extensive laboratory time.

The core course requirement came under recurrent review and change. That requirement was a residual attempt to ensure that each home economics graduate had contact with all aspects of the expanding field. The core requirement of fourteen courses and forty-seven credits in 1929–30 held until 1940–41, and then, after extensive curriculum restudy, was decreased to nine courses and thirty-five credits in 1953–54, and still further to five courses and fifteen credits in 1960–61.

In 1969 another reexamination of the nature and mission of home economics resulted in a fundamental rethinking of both the mission and the designation of "home economics," and in 1970 the name was changed to "human ecology." Four departments were formed: human nutrition and foods, human environment and design, family and child science, and family ecology. The latter department was regarded as an integrative department and was assigned responsibility for the new core composed of five new three-credit courses: nutrition and man, design for living, human development in the family, and management and decision making in the family. A three-credit integrative senior seminar completed the fifteen-credit requirement. The focus of the core was no longer on coverage of fields but rather upon values, problem-solving processes, and concepts applicable in all fields. The function was integrative rather than distributive. In addition, twenty-four credits in supporting disciplines were required.

The initial theme of home economics had been the improving of the quality of farm and rural life by improvements in methods of farming, food processing, sanitation, communication, clothing, housing, and transportation. Gradually the emphasis had changed to providing vocational or occupational courses, but still with much attention to practical experience and the perfection of skills. For example, home management had just appeared as a single course about 1911. By 1935 it became a department. It included courses in economic problems of the household, family relationships, home management practices, and standards of living. In 1938 a volume on home management by Irma Gross and Mary Lewis was the first of fifteen books published by the department. A later volume in 1947, *Home Management in Theory and Practice*, and revisions in 1958 and 1963 had a major impact on the development of the management concept. Research in home management and in consumer and family economics gradually shifted attention from skills to decision-making processes and practices in relation to outcomes desired and values underlying them.

The new designation as "human ecology" broadened the earlier mission of the college and also brought it into clearer focus by directing attention to the human organism and to its interrelationships with other organisms and with the environment. This field of study required an integrated pattern of scientific knowledge relevant to attaining and maintaining better and controllable environments. Human ecology was thus defined as the study of individuals, families, environments, and communities as integrated wholes and included the interactions among them. Field experiences with individuals and groups such as low-income families, social agencies, and community service agencies became important aspects of the learning experience for students in the college.

Over the span of years, especially from the early 1930s to the early 1970s, this division, school, and college at Michigan State was almost continually reexamining its objectives and its curricular structure. The breadth of its concerns and hence of course content, which bridged the arts, humanities, social sciences, and natural sciences, forced a search for unifying concepts and principles. Like agriculture, home economics was also involved in extension activities and in the interaction between extension workers in home economics and faculty members in research and instruction on the campus. For many years home economics was also vitally concerned in the operation of related services in the college itself. Like agriculture, too, home economics provided fertile ground out of which many departments, disciplines, and career programs arose including art, music, industrial arts, dietetics, teaching, nursing, retailing, physical education, and institutional management. Undoubtedly the presence of home economics was crucial in the development of the liberal arts and ultimately in enabling young women to move into the science, engineering, and business programs.

Unlike the College of Agriculture, however, home economics was continually faced with the task of defining an appropriate education for women. The curriculum was originally and inevitably oriented to the white, middle-class female. Despite the opening of many careers in the liberal arts, sciences, and health, the changing role of women in our society and the uncertainties of preparation for these changing roles constituted a continuing challenge for the college. In addition, the home and family itself have undergone changes that are partially implied in the change of designation from home economics to human ecology. In all of these changing pressures and curricular revisions, one thing has remained constant: the continuing emphasis on the vital importance of a general liberal education and of the values underlying the liberal education philosophy.

Although home economics did not become human ecology until 1970—the year following the retirement of John Hannah—there is clear evidence in his various memoranda and comments of his continuing interest in the search for a new concept of the home economics mission. The gradual change from home economics to human ecology is a story of changing values and roles—the kind of change that was endemic at MSU under John Hannah.

VETERINARY MEDICINE, 1910

The profession of veterinary medicine, which originated with the farrier, who shod horses and developed some skills in treating animal ailments, has, from its beginnings, faced problems of recognition and support. It has never been accorded the prestige granted to human medicine. Presumably, the patients of the veterinarian have no souls, and they cannot easily voice their complaints in specific terms.

The early program in agriculture at Michigan State included some attention to the veterinary art or science. In the first published four-year curriculum, a course in animal physiology was listed for the third year, and a course in "veterinary" was listed for the fourth year. In 1883 a full-year course in veterinary science was offered. The following year a request for a veterinary hall was included in the list of building needs. The resulting building sufficed until 1938 when, largely through Hannah's activities, a grant for $59,850 was received from the Public Works Administration toward a veterinary clinic. The total cost was $133,000.

A four-year degree program in veterinary medicine appeared in 1910. It was housed on the top floor of Agriculture Hall in what were, even for that day, inadequate and unacceptable quarters. As tractors replaced horses, veterinary medicine underwent a major change between 1915 and 1925. A joke of the 1920s was that there were fewer horses than veterinarians in Michigan.

In 1929, only thirty-one veterinary students were enrolled at MSC. The future of the program came into question as it had earlier in 1919–20, when a major drop in enrollments in veterinary medicine and agriculture had raised some doubts about the future of both programs. But by 1936, 226 students were enrolled in veterinary medicine. Increased interest in the field was due, in part, to finding new opportunities in the treatment of pets. The dog was substituted for the horse in the study of gross anatomy, thereby somewhat easing refrigeration requirements, which had indirectly limited enrollment.

In 1949, at a meeting of the Board of Agriculture, the veterinary school needs generated by increased enrollment were discussed and characterized as acute. The facilities were once again recognized as inadequate for the number of students and for research and service activities.

Some part of the difficulty with the program in veterinary medicine was perhaps due to the rapid change in the dean's office. After Ward Giltner retired in 1947, Dean Claude S. Bryan was in office for only four years before he died in 1951. Chester Clark succeeded him as dean and in turn had a relatively short tenure of six years. Willis Armistead became dean in 1957 and remained until 1975. During the period from 1947 on, the institution was rapidly developing on a number of other fronts, and the needs of veterinary medicine were perhaps not adequately emphasized, although they were recurrently discussed. In 1954 deficiencies were reported in space and in staff. Although granted continuing full accreditation by the American Veterinary Medical Association in 1960, problems and deficiencies continued to accumulate.

At the request of President Hannah, Dean Armistead made a detailed study of the needs of the College of Veterinary Medicine and presented them to the Board of Trustees in 1962. Armistead's study clearly revealed that because of inadequate space, low salaries, heavy service emphasis, and no research funds, the college was in serious difficulty. The study also reported that time wastage and irritation were caused by the trivial, menial, and repetitive tasks imposed upon the faculty. The college lacked the clerical and technical staff required to back up faculty instruction, research, and service obligations. Extension services were characterized as poor, largely because of lack of funding. But by that time much of the attention of the administration and board had been turned to the possibility of a medical school on campus. Despite the study and weaknesses revealed by accreditation visits, veterinary medicine did not receive the resources that it needed.

Another serious problem—and a source of difficulty with the legislature—was that approximately 50 percent of the four-year enrollment was from out of state. The preference given to Michigan applications enforced selectivity on out-of-state applications, which resulted in a predominance of out-of-state students beyond the freshman level. Lowering admission requirements to accommodate more Michigan residents would have resulted in increasing failures or lowering standards.

The 1910 four-year program had gradually been upgraded by requiring increasing amounts of preveterinary study, which provided better prepared students, facilitated the selection and admission process, and upgraded the program quality. In 1966, a Doctor of Veterinary

Medicine program was authorized and the first six terms of the program approved. The advent of this program was once again an occasion for underlining the noncompetitive salaries, the lack of research space, and the substandard quarters for animal care and treatment. The program was no longer competitive with other schools. The steps to improvement and catch-up were specified but largely ignored.

Service and practical studies had long been a strength of the college. For example, the 1935 annual report listed studies directed to Bang's disease, horse parasite control, spoilage of frankfurters, and restaurant and swimming pool sanitation. Indeed, reading the annual report suggests that practical research, rather than the production of veterinarians, was the primary goal. Faculty quality was also a problem; published research brought progress and recognition while low salaries encouraged the departure of the best faculty members to other institutions.

Over the years, departments evolved in veterinary medicine. Anatomy and pathology appeared in 1915. Bacteriology appeared in 1900 and, after several name changes, emerged in 1954 as microbiology and public health. The surgery and clinics department, first appearing in 1917, became surgery and medicine in 1921. It contained separate sections for large animal surgery and small animal surgery and medicine. The basic science departments that served veterinary medicine also offered undergraduate majors and graduate degrees by 1930. They were thus able to serve both human medicine and osteopathic medicine when these colleges were established in the 1960s and 1970s. The basic science departments were strengthened by the addition of professors involved in research and oriented to human rather than to animal physiology. This staff expansion brought additional strength to veterinary medicine but also tended somewhat to divert the departments from their long-time focus on veterinary medicine and agriculture. Clearly, the financial demands of the medical schools did not aid veterinary medicine, although their existence certainly helped to emphasize its inadequacies.

The veterinary clinic, which had been constructed in 1930, and the anatomy/pathology building, which had been built in 1914, had long since proved both inadequate and poorly located. The urgent facility needs presented in 1948 resulted in an addition to the clinic. In 1965 a veterinary clinical center was built on the south side of the campus. Although the veterinary program had long carried on extensive service activity, it was not until 1976 that a special state appropriation was made for the diagnostic services provided. The veterinary staff was also caught up in the necessity of planning for a university-wide laboratory animal resources unit while its own operations remained underfinanced. New external program demands, institutional expansion in both graduate and undergraduate programs, downgrading in influence because of the arrival of two medical schools, and lack of statewide and national support combined to divert attention from the needs of veterinary medicine. The too-ready assumption that the advent of the Colleges of Osteopathic and Human Medicine would strengthen veterinary medicine proved incorrect. Basic sciences were improved but in ways that were of limited help to veterinary medicine. As this is written, the program deficiencies and needs are again being reviewed.

THE DIVISIONS OF APPLIED SCIENCE (1921)
AND LIBERAL ARTS (1925)

The Division of Applied Science appeared in 1921. Records indicate the faculty's intent to combine all of arts and letters, social sciences, natural sciences, and mathematics into a new division that would eventually offer majors in all of the "liberal arts and sciences," thereby tapping a new and badly needed source of students. The implications, at that date, of a Division of Liberal Arts and Sciences were more than the board members could accept—no doubt because they anticipated strong objections from the agricultural clientele and their legislative representatives. Within the institution itself, the faculty opposed the fragmentary disciplines, introduced primarily to serve the needs of agriculture, engineering, home economics, and veterinary science, becoming part of an autonomous unit offering majors. The Division of Applied Science was shortly (1925) joined by a Division of Liberal Arts. Neither of these units offered liberal education courses that American liberal arts colleges of the 1920s, or even of the 1960s or 1980s, would have recognized. Yet majors in the disciplines became available and advertisable, although most courses continued to be related by content and even by title to one of the original four programs. The mathematics major could lead to either an arts or a science degree. Considering the extent of teacher preparation, the career approach to arts and music, and the origins and continuing emphases of the social sciences, the Division of Liberal Arts could readily have been designated the Division of Applied Arts. The inclusion therein of business administration and hotel administration contributed to that character.

The antecedents of the departments that appeared in the Divisions of Applied Science and of Liberal Arts are instructive. Art history had appeared before 1921 in home economics. Art was offered in the Department of Drawing and Design, which served both engineering and liberal arts. Music originally was introduced in the Women's Course. Sociology and economics had appeared in agriculture. Education first appeared for teacher training in agriculture and home economics. Political science was part of the history department until 1949, and psychology was part of the philosophy department until 1946. Modern languages, speech, drama, journalism, and religious studies had originally appeared in the English department. In addition, it is relevant to note that nursing first appeared as a program in home economics and hotel administration as a program in engineering. Both business administration and social work originated in the Division of Liberal Arts, the first as an extension of economics and the second of sociology. Health and physical education courses arose first out of concern about the health of women students, and the courses were provided in the Women's Building.

From this review of events, it is evident that several factors operated to increase the scope of course offerings and ultimately the number of major and degree programs.

1. Certain courses in the natural sciences had been introduced originally into the agricultural programs because they provided a necessary basis for developing and understanding scientific agriculture.

2. Courses in aspects of sociology and economics were provided because of the applicability of certain concepts and principles to agricultural development and to the improvement of rural living.

3. Courses in foreign languages had been introduced because of their relevance (usefulness) in scientific careers rather than as contributions to liberal education.

4. Arts and music appeared as contributions to the quality of home life rather than as liberal education majors.

5. History, philosophy, composition, literature, and other fields were regarded as essential for producing liberally educated individuals who would also be better farmers, engineers, homemakers, or scientists because of this background.

These expansions in courses and programs were, in part, a response to internal institutional concerns although they were always interpreted and justified in terms of elaborating the college's land-grant mission. After World War I, decline in enrollments in agriculture and in veterinary medicine and some evidence of an undue, or at least unpopular, emphasis on technical studies had led to highlighting the responsibility of the land-grant institution to educate people "for the several pursuits and professions in life." Clearly the institution sought to sustain or expand its enrollment. The addition of the Department of English (1923), the separation of sociology from farm economics, and the strengthening of horticulture (1922) to give more attention to fruit growing were all part of a response to the dual concern of meeting needs and attracting students. The Divisions of Applied Science and of Liberal Arts were inevitable if the institution was to grow.

### INSTITUTIONAL CHANGES

A number of overall changes in the institution both influenced and were influenced by these additional divisions and programs. Requirements for admission were strengthened, and some students were required to spend a year of extra preparation before admission.

In 1896 the agricultural curriculum had been reorganized and a department structure introduced that included agriculture, livestock management, horticulture, poultry, dairying, and agronomy, including soils and farm crops. Agriculture was again reorganized under Robert Shaw, who became its first dean in 1908, into the Departments of Soils, Farm Crops, Dairying, Animal Husbandry, Farm Supervision, Poultry, Farm Mechanics, and Forestry, which apparently was recognized by that time as a separate specialty. By 1911 it was recognized that the credit load placed upon students was heavy. It was reduced from twenty-five to twenty credits, largely by reduction of the science and arts components. Despite reduction in overall credit requirements, each student was required to have exposure to all departments, and the general expansion of knowledge in agriculture by that time seemingly justified more time spent in agriculture and less in science and arts. This was simply a recurrence of the repeated trend in applied fields toward an imbalance which, now arising in a number of divisions, was unlikely to be corrected unless the move was made at the college rather than the divisional level.

Expansion in courses and programs made it essential to improve the quality of the faculty. Emphasis on graduate work, originally initiated in the late nineteenth century and briefly revitalized in 1914 as an institutional obligation to prepare faculty members for land-grant college faculties, was once again declared important. By the mid 1920s, the master's degree was definitely an earned degree requiring a year of planned study, and the Ph.D. was emerging as a degree of stature well beyond the master's. The graduate school as a distinctive unit headed by a dean appeared in 1929. Faculty graduate study, long limited to vacation periods, was encouraged. Faculty members returned to graduate study, recognizing that bachelor's and master's degrees might in the future be overshadowed by increasing attention to the doctorate. But institutional growth was not yet such that potential requirements posed a serious threat. Few deans or department heads had earned a doctorate.

This overview of the development of the six undergraduate colleges and of the graduate school, all of which were in place by 1930, provides a background for a more detailed examination of the development of those colleges that emerged thereafter by splitting departments or units into new units and recombining them in various ways. The review of the growth of additional colleges and programs and their redefinition and restructuring during the Hannah years provides some basis for understanding the maturation of Michigan State from a small agricultural college into a large university. In viewing that development, it becomes evident how difficult it is for an institution, as it grows, to maintain and strengthen the unique aspects of its originally assigned mission and to support and extend it by expansion into new areas rather than weakening or abandoning it.

## THE SCHOOL OF SCIENCE AND ARTS, 1944

In 1944 the Basic College (which will be discussed in chapter five) was introduced to provide a common core for all undergraduate programs. Former divisions could now be designated as schools and encouraged to give primary attention to majors and career programs in the junior and senior years. The original career schools seem generally to have favored this move in that the new general education program offered a readily identifiable and available set of courses to meet the liberal education requirement, long supported by the college as an essential aspect of all programs. The "liberal arts and science departments" were less favorably inclined toward the Basic College because many professors disliked the interdisciplinary course (then a new and dubious entity) and viewed with concern the apparent loss of students and credit hours from their own courses. They did not recognize that their own concentration on majors had virtually destroyed their service function for the original "land-grant" divisions. Many observers of the discussions and the vote to create the Basic College were convinced that only the strong support of President Hannah and of the faculties of the original land-grant units carried the day.

The combination, also in 1944, of the Divisions of Applied Science and Liberal Arts into a School of Science and Arts gave the liberal arts and science faculties some assurance that their voices and concerns would be prominent in the new organization. Furthermore, the new

School of Business and Public Service relieved science and arts of the responsibilities for business administration, physical education, health and recreation for men, health and recreation for women, hotel administration, journalism, police administration, public administration, and social service. The School of Science and Arts still included the sciences, education, and the career emphases of the departments of music and art. In addition, premedical, predental, and prelaw programs permitted the first year of the professional degree program to be counted as the fourth year of the baccalaureate. The Wildlife Management Services was a career-oriented program in zoology.

The School of Science and Arts was not synonymous with the liberal arts. Furthermore, the immediate postwar years brought large numbers of career-oriented veterans. Those faculty members who had hoped to see the institution become one in which students pursued "knowledge for its own sake," in the well-known but meaningless phrase of the idealists, were disappointed.

The School of Science and Arts was organized into six divisions: biological science, education, fine arts, language and literature, physical science, and social science. Under Dean Lloyd C. Emmons, these divisions were essentially nonfunctional, for the dean sought to achieve unity in pursuit of liberal education goals, although both the divisional and departmental statements of purpose made evident the various career prospects offered. Size, details, and increasing paper work discouraged global college planning and encouraged divisional responsibility. Department chairpersons reported that college meetings were nonfunctional and largely a waste of time. So, in 1962, after eighteen years, the single College of Science and Arts was broken into three colleges: natural science, social science, and arts and letters. The avowed purposes were to increase efficiency, to attain a clear focus on the common problems of divisions, and to strengthen the thinking and planning for liberal education.

The College of Business and Public Service, partly because its departments were spread widely over the campus, had never been able to give effective direction to its diverse units. Journalism was transferred to the College of Communication Arts as a school along with the Department of Advertising. The Department of Health, Physical Education, and Recreation was shifted to education.

At the time when the three colleges were created, Professor Harry Kimber, a long-time supporter of general and liberal education, commented that he would predict a switch back to a single college within ten years. Why? "Why, of course," said Kimber, "to strengthen liberal education in the university!" Kimber was wrong, but in the spring of

1984 the provost and president urged just such a change and for that very reason. Not surprisingly, the faculty generally and those in the three colleges specifically exhibited skepticism and reluctance. One is inevitably reminded of an amused cynic's explanation given in 1962 for the Division of the College of Arts and Sciences into three colleges: that it had become very difficult to find a dean capable of directing the single large college, but having split that one college into three, the problem of finding three capable deans would be impossible. In subsequent years, he and other faculty members viewed the prediction as validated.

The creation of the three "liberal arts" colleges hardly strengthened liberal education. The College of Natural Science included the School of Nursing and soon began emphasizing research and graduate programs. The College of Social Science included the School of Labor and Industrial Relations, the School of Police Administration and Public Safety, the School of Social Work, and the School of Urban Planning and Landscape Architecture. The College of Arts and Letters, with majors in the Departments of Art, English, Foreign Languages, History, Music, and an interdisciplinary program in comparative literature, was perhaps best able to pursue the liberal education goal of educating the whole person, but was not immune to emphasizing careers and increasing attention to research and graduate instruction. Moreover, colleges were beginning to become preoccupied with their own problems and missions and give less attention to the mission of the university as a whole. Centers, institutes, and other units were coming into existence to deal with some of the broader issues that transcended colleges and departments.

## THE COLLEGE OF BUSINESS ADMINISTRATION, 1944

The origins of the College of Business Administration can be traced to a State Board of Education statement in 1856 that bookkeeping should be offered at the State Agricultural College. Starting in 1861, such a course was offered. By 1895 a course in farm management and accounts appeared. In 1916–17 courses in corporate finance, marketing farm products, and general accounting for agriculture and forest majors appeared under economics, which was then a part of the Department of History. Economics became a separate department in 1917–18 and, although lacking any faculty members especially trained in accounting, offered courses in accounting for agriculture, forestry, home economics, and engineering. In 1923 the first faculty member formally trained in accounting was hired.

The School of Business and Public Service was assembled in the academic year 1944–45 with the following departments drawn from the School of Science and Arts: business administration; physical education, health, and recreation for men; physical education, health, and recreation for women; hotel administration; journalism; police administration; public administration; and social service. The new school was created to administer a group of applied fields apparently on the assumption that business and public service were in some way involved in all. However, the disciplines were actually unrelated and provided no basis for association. It was widely assumed on campus that the business school was created simply to purify the offerings of the School of Science and Arts. The public service portion of the college designation was generally regarded as reflecting Hannah's commitment to service.

In 1949 the Department of Economics was moved to the School of Business and Public Service with the head of economics becoming the dean. Political science was severed from history and joined with public administration as a department in the School of Business and Public Service. These moves were freely interpreted as a step in upgrading the School of Business and Public Service to a respectable academic level. By 1963–64, the nonbusiness-related departments, including the Department of Urban Planning and Landscape Architecture, were moved elsewhere. The School of Business and Public Service became the College of Business.

The major goal in upgrading the School of Business and Public Service by the addition of the Departments of Economics and of Political Science was to attain membership in the Association of American Collegiate Schools of Business, which was accomplished by 1953. With the designation of Michigan State as a university in 1955, the schools became colleges. Hotel, restaurant, and institutional management, police administration and public safety, and social work became schools. The Graduate School of Business Administration was also created, including a Bureau of Business and Economic Research. At the same time, 1959, the Bureau of Social and Political Research was created.

When the School of Business and Public Service was created in 1944, Colonel (retired) Dorsey R. Rodney was selected as dean, perhaps on the theory that his long experience with military discipline as well as his acknowledged administrative abilities equipped him to manage the difficult task of conjoining these diverse fields. Dean Rodney knew the situation well since he had served two tours of duty with the college ROTC program. However, three deans and twenty years were required to separate the public service concept from the management concept and bring the college to an emphasis on business and hotel administration.

As the business administration and accounting programs expanded, specific service courses were combined or discarded. Such changes (as is almost invariably the case) had unanticipated consequences. The combining of the previously separate accounting courses for home economics and engineering students was a convenience and economy for the faculty. It was also deemed advantageous by the students, because the commingling of engineering and home economics students, as described in the memoirs of Professor A. J. Ruswinckel in the MSU Archives, constituted an informal dating bureau.

Like many other units of the college, the several departments and programs of the College of Business and Public Service had over the years been housed in a variety of places and had held classes in an even greater variety of places. Until the mid 1930s, economics was housed in a frame house originally erected as a faculty residence. When Morrill Hall was classified as a "firetrap" and declared unfit to be longer used as a residence hall for women, the Department of Economics was moved to the third floor. Only when eight or nine war surplus Meade buildings were erected was it possible to bring together most of the faculty. Classes, for a time were held in such diverse places as Peoples Church and Jenison Field House, or indeed, wherever there was a vacant space to serve as a classroom.

In 1962 the Eppley Center, constructed as a gift from the Eppley Foundation to house the School of Hotel, Restaurant, and Institutional Management, formerly located in Kellogg Center, was opened. Since the hotel school was part of the College of Business, the building became the administrative center for the graduate program of that college and was designated as the Graduate School of Business Administration. Later some questions would be raised as to whether this usage was fully consistent with the conditions of the foundation grant, which specifically related to the hotel programs.

The program in hotel administration attained a worldwide recognition. Faculty members could often receive special attention from graduates, as did one professor and his wife registering in a new, American-style motel in Killarney, Ireland. Likewise, an empty room might suddenly appear in a full hotel if the manager or an assistant was a Michigan State graduate.

Over the years, the College of Business developed extensive and widely known programs. But perhaps with the push to academic respectability, an overemphasis developed in *all* colleges of business on research and graduate instruction rather than on close cooperation and extensive communication with business, the basic constituency of a college of business. William V. Muse, in an article in *College News and Views* in the spring of 1983, raised the question: "If all the business schools in the country were eliminated, would anyone notice?" As vice-chancellor for academic programs for Texas A & M University System and formerly dean of the College of Business Administration, Muse expressed the point of view that, in moving toward a liberal arts or academic model, these colleges may have lost sight of the necessity to develop communication skills and other marketable skills in sales and computer usage essential for success in business. It is worth noting that Dr. Muse writes from the vantage point of administration in a land-grant institution and asserts, ". . . we need to strengthen our position by emphasizing the quality of our programs rather than the quantity and by forging a relationship with the business community that will work to the ultimate advantage of our schools' reputations, our faculties' sense of self-worth and our students' ability to find employment."

The College of Business at Michigan State has been sensitive to this problem. A service orientation is surely reflected in the establishment of the Troy Advanced Management Program for Detroit area executives in cooperation with Ford Motor Company, Chrysler, and General Motors. Furthermore, the involvement of the college in the 1950s under Dean Herman Wyngarden in developing a business school program in Brazil was widely regarded both locally and nationally as one of the best foreign projects sponsored by Michigan State, or indeed by any university in the United States.

However, the free service tradition of the extension aspect of the land-grant college has certainly not carried over to the College of Business either here or elsewhere. Moreover, to a more than desirable extent, the onrush of students into business programs has limited the college's services to other colleges and to nonmajors. Class size and faculty load limitations necessary for accreditation and required for retention of a quality faculty have effectively limited the cooperative interrelationships existing among programs in earlier years. Undergraduate majors and graduate students in the College of Business have first call on its courses and programs.

Emphasis on involvement in the operation of the institution, which gave rise to some of these programs, and the practical experiences for students prominent in the early stages of program development have disappeared. Muse's musings are not irrelevant.

## THE COLLEGE OF EDUCATION, 1952

The preparation of teachers of agriculture, home economics, and vocational education provided the initial justification for courses in education and the development of teacher education. Agricultural education appeared as a department in 1908, and by 1924 a Department of Education was created. Early ventures in the offering of education courses may have been most effectively related to the disciplines when individuals such as E. H. Ryder, professor of history, taught the history of education and pedagogy.

The incursion of the college into teacher preparation on a broader basis came in 1941, when a shortage of elementary teachers for rural areas was identified. Although "normal" colleges (or schools) existed, they prepared an inadequate number of teachers. Moreover, the extension program of Michigan State had established a linkage with rural areas and an awareness of need that justified response. A two-year certificate and a four-year certificate and degree program developed which included, as a primary feature, practice teaching in a rural, upgraded school. From 1941 to 1945 students in this program resided full time in a rural community for half of a quarter.

In 1943 financial support was provided by the Kellogg Foundation for a full-time, rural, community-oriented, student-teaching experience. From 1944 to 1946, scholarships of $100 per student teacher plus travel and living expenses were provided from the grant. Half of the salary of a professor was paid to provide for supervision and evaluation. In 1946 a field representative of the college was appointed to work with the State Department of Public Instruction in assisting local schools. Off-campus credit courses in child growth and development were offered at Harrison Lake and St. Mary's Lake, and counselor training in business and industry was offered in Detroit. The college was moving beyond the noncredit extension offerings in agriculture and home economics to provide graduate courses in education anywhere needed in the state.

The substantive or disciplinary courses in the elementary certificate programs were taught by the education department staff, who received the arrangement favorably because it permitted courses to be geared to the needs of the elementary classroom. It was less satisfactory to the disciplinary departments and probably would not have been tolerated except for Hannah's support. That program of balancing content and method is yet unsolved.

A Department of Elementary Education was created in 1951, confirming the commitment of the college to the field of elementary teacher preparation and not solely in the rural areas. Education was then a division of science and arts (1917–51). It became a school in 1952 and a college in 1955.

Secondary school teaching had developed in close cooperation with science and arts, home economics, and business. The college offered programs in preparation of teachers, administrators, couselors, and specialists at the elementary, secondary, and community college, and higher education levels. Manual training or industrial arts education had been shuffled from home economics to engineering (1916) and then to education (1953). Health, physical education, and recreation had moved from home economics to applied science to business and was transferred to education in 1959.

Education, which had had no departments until 1952, underwent a series of reorganizations in the next decade on the basis of various groups and departmental structures. The results only served to confirm that, in dealing with teaching, administration, and special services at all grade levels, all ages, and all types of individuals, it was impossible to find an organizational pattern that accommodated the diverse interests and activities of the education faculty and its relationships with other colleges and units in the university. It was also evident that, although a single budget for the entire college provided more flexibility and power for the dean, a department without a budget is not a "real" department and must watch its deportment if it would thrive. Whatever the rationale for the organization of the moment, many faculty members rejected it.

Hannah saw teacher preparation and other aspects of education programs as closely related to agriculture, home economics, the disciplines, and generally to the continuing concern for service in the state and nation. Clifford Erickson, the first dean of education, had been long committed to full-time community experience for all student teachers. He rejected the campus laboratory school approach and supported the operation of student teaching centers in various communities. Teachers lived in the community for one term and gave full time to student teaching and related activities—PTA meetings, supervision of extracurricular activities, church attendance, and Sunday school class teaching. Although the idea was stimulating and the programs generally successful, they were not the harbingers of the future. A single quarter, though it provided extensive involvement, was a brief period, and some doubts were thrown on the quality of the fifteen credits thus acquired, even with continuing supervision by an itinerant pedagogue or a resident professor. Campus professors were not pleased with the absence of majors for a term—especially those in mathematics and the sciences. Unionization and an oversupply of teachers effectively ended the full-time intern community experience.

In 1954 an effort was made by the College of Education to involve the other colleges more extensively in the training program for secondary teachers. Representatives of the various colleges were appointed by the governing board to a Committee on Teacher Education (so renamed in 1963). The members of this committee visited schools, observed, and met with administrators. For years (until 1982), the committee played a significant role in relating the professional and substantive aspects of secondary teacher preparation.

Another distinctive program of the college was the TTT Program—Training Teachers of Teachers, which over five or six years developed a clearer and more distinctive role for the college than that of other teacher colleges. As so frequently happens, the institutionalizing of a new idea proved to be elusive.

In 1968 10,500 students were enrolled in teacher training, 8,500 of them in the undergraduate program. The possibility of limiting enrollment was raised, as it had previously been for other programs, but Hannah, as always concerned with somehow meeting needs, rejected the idea and undertook to find additional funds. He retired before this was accomplished, however. It was left to Acting President Walter Adams and Provost Howard Neville to find transferable dollars in a tight budget.

THE COLLEGE OF
COMMUNICATION ARTS AND SCIENCES, 1955

On May 20, 1955, a School of Communication Arts with Gordon A. Sabine as its first dean was authorized by the State Board of Agriculture. This school, so it was announced, was to include journalism, radio skills, television skills, audiovisual aids, "et cetera." The "et cetera," in retrospect, clearly indicated some uncertainties about what additional programs might be added to this new school and was perhaps a recognition that a new vocabulary—"mass communications," "telecommunications," et cetera—was on the way. Journalism (then in the College of Business and Public Service) and speech (then in the College of Science and Arts) were also transferred to the new college. The change was so abrupt that it came as a shock to many persons and was not altogether well received. The rumor of the day was that an enterprising candidate for an administrative post had demanded a deanship. Later review of circumstances revealed that the idea originated on the campus well before the new dean was selected. In fact, the concern that brought about the School of Communication Arts was directly related to John Hannah's long-time intent to interrelate and thereby reinforce the obligations of the college to provide educational services to the state not only through the existing extension program but through a much broadened program using the full resources of the institution. His vision included such a school and placement in it of the various publication and communication facilities of the institution. He emphasized the advantages of involving both faculty and students in the operation of educational services, research, and instruction. These views had been formed over his many years of association with Michigan State.

Courses in speech and dramatics had been introduced into the Department of English in the early years of the twentieth century. By 1930 there were four men in the Department of English offering courses in public speaking, acting, play production, oral interpretation, debate, and parliamentary procedure. One term in public speaking was required of all students in agriculture, engineering, and home economics. An advanced course in acting was open only to those students selected for roles in the term play. In part, this specification reflected an attempt to provide some "play" time for students in heavily loaded programs, but it also reflected the view that students learned by such experiences. Hence credit for them was fully as appropriate as credit for field work or laboratory exercises. Two courses in public speaking, one in interpretation and a first course in acting, were also required for students enrolled in physical education, teaching, or coaching. As was not uncommon in those days, the initial action imposing this requirement on students was taken without informing the faculty. The sudden increase in speech enrollment posed some problems.

A two-credit course in news writing appeared in 1919. By the mid 1920s, a major was available in English composition and journalism. This major was provided in cooperation with the Department of Publications and Journalism, headed by James B. Hasselman, who was professor of journalism, extension editor, editor for the Experiment Station, and publicity director for the college. To these responsibilities the next head of the department, A. H. Nelson, added those of directing the summer session and supervision of the radio station.

In 1932 the name of the department was changed to the Department of Journalism and Publications and to it was assigned responsibility for mimeograph and photographic services. Courses included journalism, extension writing, and college bulletin writing. By 1937 work in advertising, copywriting, editorial writing, history of journalism, farm and home writing, and bulletin writing were listed. And in 1937, a Department of Speech emerged from the Department of English. Its first designation as Department of Speech, Dramatics, and Radio caused it to be confused with the campus radio station, WKAR, and the name was thus changed to the Department of Speech, Dramatics, and Radio Education.

The combination of the war year pressures and the creation in 1944 of the Basic College brought temporarily a combination of the Department of Speech and the Department of Written and Spoken English in the Basic College. Audiovisual aids were extensively used, and for a time the department also provided these services for the entire institution. Speech correction was added as a formal part of the program. Subsequent discussions of such possible complex and lengthy titles as "Speech, Rhetoric, Public Address, Theater, Radio and Speech Correction" were finally resolved by calling the unit the Department of Speech with sectional or functional subtitles.

The theater program developed slowly over the years. Indeed, for many years there were no theater facilities on campus. Plays were produced in one end of the inadequate college gymnasium or perhaps in a theater in Lansing or East Lansing. The Peoples Church facilities occasionally provided space. By 1932 the Little Theater, the top floor of the Home Economics Building, served as a place for term plays. Later, the Student Union Ballroom and still later the Fairchild Theatre and Auditorium were available. None of these facilities were adequate in size or in equipment.

As theater developed into a formal area of study, credit courses in acting and participation in plays were completely separated. Academic distinctions between theory and practice, service and instruction, student activities and credit courses, and work and play were becoming ever more evident.

The Department of Speech originally was extensively and intensively involved in continuing service activities, which included annual extemporaneous speaking contests, development of fifteen-minute programs by speech department staff for radio WKAR, and, for a time, a one-week dramatic show over the radio. At the same time, the department provided assistance to the engineering and agricultural programs by offering individual coaching or courses for the improvement of oral performance.

Play contests were carried out in cooperation with rural agricultural organizations, and the three best in a given year were brought to the campus for Friday of Farmer's Week. 4-H Clubs developed pageants with the assistance of the speech department. Members of the department developed parliamentary procedure courses for short-course enrollees and served as parliamentarians for many types of meetings.

In 1937 Donald Buell of the Department of Speech developed a weekly review of Broadway plays and later provided a weekly television program. In the late 1940s the department was responsible for a children's theater program produced in the Lansing area under sponsorship of local organizations. Some of the plays produced through this program toured the state.

For many years, the Department of Speech was the major source of speakers at campus clubs and at lunches, banquets, and various group meetings of local and statewide organizations. In the 1940s the department sponsored a Student Speaker's Bureau, largely created through the initiative of Paul Bagwell, who developed a selection procedure and a brochure to publicize the program. Later, the department also sponsored many of the conferences for the Continuing Education Program and provided speakers for others. A speech clinic and a hearing clinic, developed as part of the service program of the department to the college, expanded to become both a professional degree and a clinical service program.

Thus, from about 1910 until 1955 courses in speech, play production, acting, parliamentary procedure; courses or services in speech and hearing correction; the development of work in journalism, publication, advertising; and the writing of extension publications and college bulletins presented opportunities and problems that suggested the need for new organizational structures. Television and film added new dimensions.

The development of services such as audiovisual aids and speech therapy and the inclusion of mimeograph and photographic services in the Department of Journalism and Publications presented administrative and budgetary complications. Furthermore, the combination of department head, extension editor, experiment station editor, publicity direction, and supervision of the radio station, which had for several years been associated with the publication and journalism department, placed an unreasonable burden on a few individuals who might work for twenty hours out of twenty-four. This burden interfered with the development of undergraduate academic majors and of graduate programs. It became inevitable that the generalist professor, covering theory and practice and involved in service as well as instruction, had neither the time for research nor for the development of a specialized curriculum. Nevertheless, Hannah persisted in his vision of a facility and an organizational structure that would bring together all institutional communication facilities and all departments involved in the various aspects of communication.

When, in 1955, the School of Communication Arts was authorized, it represented an attempt to bring together all instructional departments connected with the communications process. Immediately this new school inherited a number of problems associated with this long development. To what extent in a growing program can there be integration or even close liaison between operating services and academic units? To what extent can special courses directed to particular groups be maintained in a unit designed to study and develop an integrated program in mass communications? And, finally, to what extent can graduate programs and research activities be developed with a faculty also heavily engaged in extension and continuing education activities?

By 1958 a partial answer was provided to some of these questions. A Division of Mass Communications, including the Departments of Advertising, Television-Radio, and Film, and the School of Journalism, coupled with a new core curriculum for all communication arts majors, brought some unity to the program. In addition to the Division of Mass Communications, the College of Communication Arts included the Department of Speech, which in turn, included theater, rhetoric and public address, radio and television, speech pathology and audiology, interpretation and speech education, and an area of general communication arts. The introduction of a Ph.D. degree in communication arts provided a broad-ranged doctoral program in which each of the communication areas could make contributions.

The Communications Research Center began operating in 1958–59 and immediately drew national attention by completing a study of Michigan newspapermen. In addition, it initiated an analysis of the effectiveness of educational telecasting. Apparently the research was to have an applied orientation, in part perhaps because no all-embracing theories of communication were yet available.

In the 1957–58 "Annual Report of the College of Communication Arts," presumably by Dean Gordon Sabine, is this statement:

> The original decision to separate the teaching program from the operation of the campus media grows in importance, significance and wisdom. We are blessed in having the campus media available as important laboratories for our students but in being permitted to concentrate the talent and energy of our faculty and staff in an academic program unhindered by the vast detail necessary in media operation.

Eventually, the burden on operational personnel and their concern for excellence of performance coupled with vast increases in the numbers of students involved in the communication field brought complete separation of instruction and operation. Student internships could be both a burden and a threat to program equality. Sabine's statement was incorrect on one point. The original decision was to keep teaching and operations together. But when the Communication Arts and Sciences building became available in the 1980s, it was at once obvious that physical contiguity had little to do with coordination of teaching and operations. It is ironic that in emphasizing the unity of communications—the common factor underlying public service and instruction—the two functions should become so clearly separated.

### ESTABLISHMENT OF THE MEDICAL COLLEGES

In 1956, another medical school for Michigan was advocated by various individuals and groups. (Medical schools already existed at the University of Michigan and Wayne State University.) A study by MSU Professor of Sociology C. R. Hoffer provided documentation of the need for more doctors, especially in rural areas. Hannah had been waiting for an opportune moment to add a medical school. In 1959 he appointed a committee to investigate and make recommendations about the desirability and feasibility of seeking authorization for a medical school. A meeting held with state legislators to discuss MSU's future role in the medical service area opened the way to further deliberations.

On December 9, 1959, John Hannah wrote a letter to Emory Morris of the Kellogg Foundation exploring the possibility of the foundation's assisting in the funding of a medical school. On December 22, 1959, a letter from Morris to Hannah indicated that MSU goals paralleled those of the foundation. Meanwhile, on December 16, 1959, Hannah presented a proposal for a medical center to the MSU Board of Trustees, which suggested, as a first step, that the new college of medicine be conjoined with the College of Veterinary Medicine and with the programs in medical technology and nursing education. The proposal suggested that a college of dentistry should be added later, that a curriculum in public health should be developed, and that a medical research institute should be formed.

The administrative structure and physical plant were to be innovative, and a medical library would be the center of this development. The clinical areas would be planned to handle rural and urban needs, to decrease the specialization and isolation of physicians, to share research among groups, and to focus on the problems of aging. An analysis of the reasons why this should be done at Michigan State was presented and a tentative time table suggested. The need for a vice president for medical affairs was indicated, but for the interim an institute of biomedical services would be responsible for coordination of nursing education, medical technology, veterinary medicine, and parts of the curriculum in medicine. The proposal was approved by the board.

On October 20, 1961, Hannah requested a grant from the Kellogg Foundation to initiate a two-year preclinical program in medical education at Michigan State. The proposal included the creation of a biomedical institute to develop the basic medical sciences using currently existing and additional health-related programs. Students would complete their clinical training at Wayne State University or at the University of Michigan. The foundation indicated that the proposed project could not be supported at that time because the planning thus far had been inadequate and indicative of an apparent lack of interaction with medical educators. In addition, formal approval by the legislature would be necessary.

On November 21, 1961, the Board of Trustees established the Institute of Biology and Medicine as the coordinating unit for the anticipated medical center. The institute was to provide expanded advanced degree programs, strengthen health-related professions at the university, provide a two-year preclinical medical school, and establish an integrated health curriculum at undergraduate and graduate levels that would permit the students to choose their careers at the last possible minute. A unit for promoting and conducting research was included. The biological sciences and professional health-related areas would be attached to the institute with no duplication of existing departments. Human medicine would have a director with an adequate budget.

On December 1, 1961, Hannah wrote to Morris indicating that the National Institutes of Health had made a grant of $2 million for facilities and that the Kellogg Foundation grant was needed before the January legislative meeting. It was anticipated that the prestige of the grant would assure the location of the medical school. Morris's response of December 11, 1961, indicated that the grant would not be made until final plans were presented and that the proposal was to include legislative approval. His response also expressed some concern that the Michigan State planning group had not made extensive contact with or sought advice from the Wayne State and the University of Michigan medical schools. In effect, such contact had been deliberately avoided.

The MSU faculty hoped to so define and limit medicine that it would be controlled by the general faculty.

Obviously support from the Kellogg Foundation was not forthcoming as rapidly as had been anticipated. Several issues were involved. One clearly was whether or not the state was ready to support a third medical school. Neither the Wayne State University nor the University of Michigan administrators and medical faculties was supportive of a third medical school or of locating it in East Lansing. Lack of hospitals in the Lansing area and the consequent lack of an adequate range of clinical cases argued against that location. In addition, it was clear that Michigan State wanted a complete medical school program rather than a two-year school. The third factor was that Michigan State was inclined toward a program that would interrelate the several health sciences and provide common experiences for them. To do this, it was proposed that the medical program begin with the junior year so that students in the medical program would have two years of common experience with students in other health specialties—nursing science, veterinary medicine, and medical technology. There were many problems with this approach and much dissatisfaction, but it was viewed as the only immediately acceptable way to relate undergraduate health programs and the postbaccalaureate medical program. As it turned out, that proposal provided a talking point but did not affect the actual medical program as it developed.

By June 4, 1962, Hannah was able to report to Emory Morris that a two-year medical school had been approved but that the four-year proposal must come back before the legislature at a later date. The Michigan Coordinating Council for Public Higher Education recommended that a cooperative program of graduate education and basic medical sciences be established involving Michigan State University, the University of Michigan (U of M) and Wayne State University (WSU). The recommendations suggested that a two-year graduate program in human biology leading to either a Ph.D. or M.D. be established and that the Ph.D. could be done wholly at Michigan State, but that the medical students must transfer to the U of M or WSU. This was certainly not what Hannah sought.

Not until June 4, 1964, was William Knisley, assistant provost and director of the Institute of Biology and Medicine, able to report to Emory Morris that a dean, Dr. Andrew Hunt, had been hired for the medical school. Hunt apparently had accepted many of the ideas that had been developed and had expanded them in an attractive manner. His additions and elaborations were undoubtedly instrumental in gaining Kellogg support.

The proposal from Michigan State to Kellogg Foundation for support of a preclinical human medicine program, as of May 1964, incorporated a new approach based upon planning done with a grant from the Commonwealth Foundation. Among other things the proposal included social science representation among the basic disciplines supporting human medicine and included research in medical education as an integral part of the program. A request was made for $5,993,920 for projected facilities. A request was also made for $1,006,100 for immediate operating expenses for five years. On September 10, 1964, Kellogg Foundation made a five-year grant of $1,250,000 for a preclinical college of human medicine. The College of Human Medicine began instruction in the two-year preclinical program in the fall of 1966.

On May 25, 1967, Hannah wrote a memorandum to Howard Neville, the provost, indicating that the Kellogg Foundation was probably open to requests for $1,500,000 for a physical facility for a four-year medical school. Negotiations were successful, and the groundbreaking for the new Life Sciences Building took place on June 23, 1969. Hannah had retired in March of that year. As one of his last acts he sent a lengthy letter to Governor William G. Milliken in which he reviewed the history of the medical college and urged sympathetic attention to it. It had required about fifteen years to move from acknowledgment of need for a third medical school to the actual addition of one at Michigan State. But the complete fruition of the idea did not come until the first four-year doctor of medicine degrees were granted by the college in 1972.

In the years since 1969, the original vision of a coordinated health sciences program has not been entirely lost; but financial problems, changes in key administrative personnel, and perhaps some hesitancy or even resistance have effectively delayed, if not permanently derailed, the idealistic plans for an integrated program of health sciences. The association between the College of Social Science and its Departments of Anthropology, Psychology, and Sociology and the College of Human Medicine has had limited benefits and has not significantly affected either the social sciences or human medicine. The College of Osteopathic Medicine chose not to follow the pattern. Attempts to attach the Medical Technology Program to the medical colleges were unsuccessful and eventually abandoned. Nursing, having attained college status, pursues its own destiny.

There are several features of the original deliberations and developments that continue to cause some difficulties with the three medical colleges. The decision to have but one department in each of the basic sciences was wise in many respects; but staffing departments of anatomy, biochemistry, microbiology, pharmacology, pathology, physiology, and zoology in such a manner as to meet the needs of three medical schools as well as advance the disciplines poses complex problems that—thus far at least—have not been solved to everyone's satisfaction. The basic science departments have not acquired the research support for which they had hoped, and the medical schools find a changing faculty handling the basic science courses for medical students. The problem of relating basic science, clinical science, and clinical experience, which is always difficult, is further complicated at MSU. Yet there is no evidence of desire to abandon the existing pattern.

Although many of the proposed distinctive features of the College of Human Medicine were discarded, the college did retain some of the features explicit in its original planning. One was the emphasis on the use of community hospitals for observation and for clerkship and intern experiences. The College of Human Medicine provides clinical education, research, and service programs in seventeen hospitals located in six Michigan communities.

The Michigan Public Act 162 of 1967 established a state school of osteopathic medicine to be assigned to the campus of a state university "already having a school or college of medicine." Since the University of Michigan exhibited no interest and Wayne State University imposed unacceptable conditions, the choice fell to Michigan State, where, following Hannah's long-established view, there existed willingness to discuss and develop any worthy program desired by the state. Obviously, however, the College of Human Medicine would have to become a four-year M.D.-granting college to fulfill the terms of the act. The Michigan College of Osteopathic Medicine, started in Pontiac in 1967 with the assistance of the Michigan legislature and the city, moved to the Michigan State campus and opened classes there in 1971. It was the first college of osteopathic medicine to be located on a university campus. In subsequent years additional colleges of osteopathic medicine have appeared throughout the country. The MSU college has had marked and beneficial impact on their development and on that of osteopathic medicine.

At Michigan State the two colleges of medicine have developed mutual respect and some cooperation. Both emphasize a community approach and use many hospitals around the state for student clinical experiences. There is not and there is unlikely to be a university hospital, but a clinical facility on campus adjacent to the medical college's offices and instructional facilities provides some opportunity for practice with ambulatory patients by medical students and faculty from both colleges. The presence on the campus of the Colleges of

Veterinary Medicine, Human Medicine, and Osteopathic Medicine gave MSU the distinction of being the only university in the United States (and perhaps the world) to be blessed or encumbered by three college's of medicine.

The original land-grant emphases on agriculture, engineering, home economics, and veterinary medicine were dominant at Michigan State when Hannah became secretary of the State Board of Agriculture in 1935. However, the Divisions of Liberal Arts and of Applied Science had been in existence for a decade. They were attracting students and altering the image of the mission of the institution. Although many of the liberal arts and science departments still accepted service course teaching as their primary responsibility, attention was being diverted away both from service courses and from liberal and general education by aspirations for graduate programs. The increasingly burdensome requirements in agriculture, home economics, engineering, and veterinary medicine in a sense supported this development. Thus, despite the apparent attention to the liberal arts and sciences, Michigan State had simply expanded the scope of the career education emphases. As new colleges were created this career emphasis continued.

Public service and applied research were still generally accepted as an obligation of the institution, but it was becoming apparent that new structures or new approaches were required if this emphasis were to be maintained and extended. The College of Communication Arts and Sciences ultimately emerged as one such attempt.

Concern for general and liberal education, for developing graduate programs, and for educating a larger and broader segment of the people also required new structures and organizations transcending the colleges. Subsequent chapters consider these coincidental developments.

# PART II
## Instruction and Academic Programs

# 4
# Programs and Courses

Essential to the evolution of the colleges and, ultimately, to the development of Michigan State University was the development of departments on the basis of disciplines. Initially disciplines existed solely to provide service courses for students in agriculture, engineering, home economics, and veterinary medicine, and thus organizational structure (departments, division, etc.) was largely a matter of administrative convenience and contiguous space assignment. Courses were offered and programs served on an institutional rather than on a disciplinary basis.

### PROGRAMS

The Divisions of Applied Science and of Liberal Arts first emerged, out of an expanding array of courses, largely to attract and accommodate more students. The divisions and their existing programs and courses immediately became breeding places for new courses and programs that further affected the school and college structure. John Hannah, as a student, had seen the Division of Applied Science take form. As an extension employee, he saw another division, Liberal Arts, created. This immediate past history of new programs, new majors, increase in numbers and quality of faculty, along with changing missions and emphases promoted organizational and structural change during Hannah's subsequent tenure as president. The evolution of these new courses, new majors and departments, and new or reorganized divisional schools was thrilling, providing unique opportunities for faculty and administrative creativity, recognition, and advancement. Ineffective performance, so long as sincere effort was apparent, was seldom overtly criticized; an individual would instead be given another assignment. As Hannah's long-time secretary remarked, "Dr. Hannah would never knowingly hurt anyone if he could avoid it." A result beneficial to the university was that new units were headed by individuals committed to a unified institution rather than to the empire building so often demonstrated by imported administrators. By 1969, when Hannah retired, there were 15 colleges, well over 100 departments, and many centers, institutes, and other units.

With Hannah's continuing emphasis on extending institutional services and meeting new needs thereby, it was relatively easy to add new courses and programs. Much later it became evident that course proliferation in some departments added to costs by contributing to small classes while serving no real need—except professional ego. Whims, fads, and the "my course" syndrome ultimately had to be curtailed. Similarly recurrent external pressures for new programs were considered and sometimes explored but rejected when evaluation proved such action appropriate. A degree program in mobile homes that briefly existed at Michigan State in the 1950s is a good example. The program was as flimsy as many of the mobile homes of that date, and it was abandoned. Such programs demanded both additional resources and substantive content. Tourism, on the other hand, as a major source of income in Michigan, did deserve attention and later received it through MSU's Extension Service and a degree program in the College of Business.

*Police Administration*

The program in police administration, appearing first in 1937, offered a total of eight courses and twenty-three credits. Most of the course work was provided voluntarily by staff members of the state police who offered a series of lectures and extensive, closely supervised field work. The program was realistic and practical in the land-grant pattern.

By 1969, the School of Police Administration and Public Safety listed six professors, two associate professors, three assistant professors, and four instructors. Among them were four Ph.D.s, nine master's degrees, and two law degrees. The curriculum offerings included 39 courses and 187 credit hours. The available programs included several career possibilities and offered master's degrees. Practical experiences were still emphasized, but the State Police were not explicitly involved. Thought and theory had replaced most of the action.

By 1983, the program had become the basis for the School of Criminal Justice and had further expanded to ninety-nine courses and included a Ph.D. program. The offerings had become obviously more impressive by including courses in "criminalistics." The baccalaureate program included twelve courses in chemistry (thirty-four credits), six courses in physics (twelve credits), and four courses in mathematics and statistics (seventeen credits)—a far more rigorous program than that of 1937.

*Hotel Administration*

In 1929–30, a hotel training program was an option in each of the Divisions of Engineering, Home Economics, and Liberal Arts. There were no courses specifically directed to hotel matters, but a summer training program in hotel facilities was required each year. By 1950, the Division of Hotel, Restaurant, and General Institutional Management was a unit in the School of Business and Public Service. It offered twenty courses. Institution administration, a department in the School of Home Economics, listed many courses dealing with good service, menus, laundry, housekeeping, equipment maintenance, and administration in hospitals, school cafeterias, dormitories, and commercial situations. The practice course in institutional administration provided management experience in the college food services, residence halls, and laundries. "Hotel" was carefully avoided in course names and descriptions except for the phrase "menu pricing for restaurants and hotels." Engineering's attention to hotels had shrunk to a single course on hotel architecture. By 1969, the School of Hotel Administration and Restaurant Management offered thirty-eight courses. The close association between hotel and restaurant management and campus operations (the residence halls and Kellogg Center) had gradually disappeared, although some type of field work continued to be possible in some programs.

*School of Packaging*

The program in packaging technology first appeared in the 1952–53 catalog as a major in the Department of Forest Products of the Division of Conservation. By 1958, packaging was separated from forest products. Only three courses (wood and fiber containers, container padding, and container handling and loading) were specific to packaging, but that deficiency was remedied by 1960–61, at which time the courses available included nine undergraduate and three graduate courses. The School of Packaging was created that year, started at least in part by a $100,000 grant from the Packaging Fund of East Lansing. By 1980, a master's degree was added, and the expanded course offerings included six at the graduate level. In 1980, one of the packaging courses focused on environmental quality: water, air and water quality, laws, economics, energy considerations, and resources conservation. Employment opportunities for packaging majors expanded to include purchasing, production, quality control, packaging development, research, sales, marketing, testing, and technical service jobs. The school is now housed in its own building. The purist may sneer at a "packaging" major, but the land-grant philosophy recognizes that conservation, preservation, and distribution of food have become as important as production.

Our civilization and our culture may, in future generations, be characterized by their packaging more than their monuments. The pyramids of Egypt were in fact packages and preserved much about Egyptian culture. Indeed, packaging is a fundamental human concern, beginning with the womb and extending to the tomb, with clothing and housing packages in between. Current packaging courses deal with various concepts that appear and reappear in many courses and programs: motivation, attractiveness, materials, properties, economic and social issues, automation, permeability, durability, measurement, and evaluation. The recently added Willed Body Program of the medical colleges completes the packaging spectrum offered at Michigan State.

Of the four programs in mobile homes, police administration, hotel administration, and packaging, the first was too narrowly defined and was dropped. The three successful continuing programs have undergone marked change. Initially, these three emphasized practical experience. Over time, they developed many specialties, subspecialties, and courses, and tended to deemphasize practical experience. In so doing, they reflected the pattern already established in earlier career-oriented programs that had severed connections between academic courses and campus operations.

## COURSE DEVELOPMENT

Course development, when viewed over time, is a major factor in developing degree programs, departments, and colleges. Review of the early steps and further developments of a number of courses illustrates the process.

The advent of the Divisions of Liberal Arts and Applied Sciences solemnized the transition of Michigan State from an institution devoted primarily to agriculture to one providing a broad undergraduate education, although the departments, for some years, consciously continued to meet the needs of the older units as well as developing programs of their own. Thus, economics in liberal arts continued for some years to provide courses in agricultural economics before the latter appeared as a separate Department of Agricultural Economics.

For some years, courses in speech, debate, and dramatics were offered in the Department of English. In 1933, a two-credit course, practical public speaking, "designed for advanced agricultural students who expect to engage in Smith-Hughes or county agent work" appeared. Emphasis was placed upon preparing speeches suitable for farmer's organizations. Later, as the Department of Speech developed, service courses disappeared.

The program in advertising is another example of how a department emerged gradually from a few courses. In 1929–30, the Department of Publications and Journalism (of which the head was also director of publications) offered a two-credit course in advertising copy. In the course, students analyzed the advertising appearing in newspapers and journals and wrote their own copy on the basis of this analysis. In that same year, the Department of Drawing and Design and Art offered a course called fundamentals of advertising display—a two-credit course offered as a four-hour laboratory primarily directed to business administration students and covering such topics as lettering, composition, color, and practice in advertising layout. These two courses, although offered in different departments, were to be taken together or sequentially. Although the departments were reorganized, the same courses appeared in 1933–34: art 244F was still a two-credit course dealing with the fundamentals of advertising diaplay and was correlated with journalism 202M which still involved analysis of advertising and the writing of copy. By 1936–37, the Department of Journalism had become the Department of Journalism and Publications and offered a three-credit course on current practices, Journalism 202A. This course was to be followed by 202M. The Department of Art still continued the course 244F in advertising display. By 1939–40, the three courses were renumbered to be taken at the junior level.

A combination major in English and journalism had existed in the English department for some years but not until 1938 was a major in journalism recognized. By 1943, a course in radio advertising, Journalism 303H, had been added. The following year, four courses appeared in journalism for majors in the area of advertising, the fourth course being newspaper and advertising management. This emphasis was underlined by the disappearance of the course in advertising layout formerly offered in the art department. By 1949, the list of courses was expanded to a total of nine, plus a course in psychology of advertising in the Department of Psychology. The nine courses covered introduction to advertising, principles and practices of advertising, radio advertising, advertising copy and layout, advertising research, advertising campaigns, direct mail advertising, retail advertising, and newspaper and advertising management. In 1951, a course in advertising production was added to the list. Leaflets on the advertising programs appeared but no course on advertising programs was added. In 1952 still more courses appeared: copy editing for advertising majors, advertising workshop, field practice, and retail advertising problems; the course in radio advertising disappeared. A number of other courses also disappeared including advertising research, advertising campaigns, direct mail advertising, and retail advertising. However, a new course for five credits appeared, journalism in public relations, that discussed organizational relations with mass communications media. By 1961, the list of journalism courses was twenty-eight in number, including five graduate courses. The involvement of the university in international projects resulted in the addition by 1968 of a four-credit course in international advertising. A student now might take as many as fifty credits in an undergraduate advertising specialization. Advertising appeared as a department in 1960, after having appeared initially (as had journalism, speech, theater, and religion) in the Department of English.

*Geography*

Geography must certainly have been a significant factor in many early course offerings, but its recognition as a distinct discipline for study must be credited to the zoology department which offered it as a course in 1925. By 1927, a Department of Geology and Geography existed and continued until 1955, when the two were separated into distinct departments. The new Department of Geography was first in the College of Science and Arts and later in the College of Social Science when that college was formed in 1961. The first full-time geographer was added to the faculty in 1929. Geography emerged as a social science, heavily descriptive, but also including the study of the surface (climate, landforms, and biogeography) aspects of the earth—a physical science approach.

By 1943–44, partly because of war demands, the program was extended to include cartography, aerial photography, and photogrammetry. Geography also gradually expanded to include topics such as geographical relationships to settlement, recreational land use, urban geography, and climatology. By 1945, geography offered nineteen courses and by 1952 had expanded to thirty-two courses. By this latter date, international involvements of the college and the growth of faculty numbers were affecting the departmental program, made evident by courses dealing with the geography of the Soviet Union, Western Europe, Eastern Europe, the Far East, the Near East, Latin America, and Africa. By 1956–57, the Department of Geography was offering thirty-one undergraduate and ten graduate courses, and its program description pointed out the existence of courses dealing with the human, historical, economic, political, urban, recreational, and physical aspects of geography as well as techniques and methods, eastern and western Europe, the Soviet Union, the Far East, the Near East, the Caribbean, and Africa. By 1958–59, course offerings were further expanded to six courses in physical geography, six in economics and land use, two in history, two in politics, three in population and settlement, fifteen in regional geography, and thirteen in technical and methodological research. During the 1960s, the new faculty, who were added at the rate of one to three per year, brought new ideas from major graduate departments and permitted additional under-graduate and especially graduate courses. The faculty of six had grown to twenty by 1970, by which time it was recognized that the nature of geography as a discipline should be covered more thoroughly, and quantitative methods were added to the existing emphasis on cartog-raphy, remote sensing, field methods, and writing ability.

By 1962, the department asserted that geography was concerned with areal differences and similarities of the world in their relevance to human affairs. Geography was to be regarded as a bridge between the social and the natural sciences—as the spatial science of the earth and its life. Department chairperson Lawrence M. Sommers, in 1977, noted that "introduction of quantitative techniques and greater em-phasis upon theoretical methodology . . . make research and teaching strategies in the discipline more rigorous, scientific, and predictive."[1]

A Master of Arts in Geography was begun in the early 1950s, and the Ph.D. degree was approved in 1957. In number of graduate stu-dents and number of degrees granted during the 1970s the MSU department was second only to that at the University of California at Los Angeles.

From 1957 to 1969, the Department of Geography granted 24 Ph.D.s and 98 master's degrees. From 1969 to 1976, 80 Ph.D.s and 103 master's degrees were awarded. The department began giving special regional attention to Latin America and Africa in its program, areas too fre-quently ignored in American colleges and universities. As the graduate program evolved, increasing emphasis also was placed on systematic or topical research and courses.

The development of this department well reflects John Hannah's views on the national and international obligations of institutions, although he had no extensive direct interaction with it.

---

1. Lawrence M. Sommers, "Some Characteristics, Problems, and Trends in the Evolu-tion of Geography Graduate Study in the United States: The Example of Michigan State University," paper presented at the First International Conference of Latin Americanist Geographers at Paipa, Colombia, August 8–12, 1977.

## Botany and Plant Pathology

In 1859, the Department of Botany and Vegetable Physiology was created as one of the five original departments of the college. The Department of Zoology and Animal Physiology supplemented the former to cover both the vegetable and animal kingdoms. Geology had not yet appeared, but some attention was paid to the mineral kingdom in courses on soils and in chemistry.

After a few years vegetable physiology was moved into agricultural courses. Botany continued as a department until 1931–32, when it became the Department of Botany and Plant Pathology. Botany achieved maturity much earlier than other sciences and acquired a capable staff of Ph.D.s. By 1940, its head, Dr. E. A. Bessey, had attained a degree of international renown. Graduate programs were introduced and a definite emphasis on research and graduate education (due in great part to Dr. Bessey, the first graduate dean) became evident by the 1930s. In 1940, the department offered forty-five courses at the undergraduate level. By 1970, there were twenty undergraduate and thirty-seven graduate courses.

Plant pathology was a relatively new science in 1940. Its staff included converted traditional biologists or individuals educated in a land-grant institution. The plant pathology faculty was a minority in the department but was highly visible in extension and Experiment Station activities. Course titles in 1940 reflected this extension emphasis: forest pathology, diseases of shade and park trees, general plant pathology, fruit diseases, diseases of field and garden plants, diseases of ornamental plants, methods in plant pathology, and general principles of disease control. By 1970, this group of eight three-credit courses was replaced by five courses: introductory plant pathology, diseases of forest and shade trees, advanced plant pathology, plant disease control, and plant diseases in the field. The last three were graduate courses.

Plant pathology was not the only aspect of economic botany to appear. The study of weeds, long traditional in botany, developed in the late 1940s into chemical weed control, with tremendous economic impact. Mycology (study of fungi) had come, likewise, to have great significance for health, especially in the study of tropical diseases.

## Chemistry

Instruction in chemistry began in 1857, and two years later agricultural chemistry was one of five departments. In 1870, elementary chemistry was taken by freshmen, analytical chemistry by sophomores, and agricultural chemistry by juniors. Ten years later, 1880, organic chemistry and chemical physics were added. The latter was not the chemical physics of the mid twentieth century but rather an incursion of physics into the curriculum by courtesy of chemistry. All courses were directed to agricultural students.

With the addition of a mechanic arts program in 1885, blowpipe chemistry and metallurgy were added to the Department of Chemistry offerings. In 1895, with the addition of the degree program for women, elementary chemistry (with a special laboratory), analytical chemistry, and organic chemistry were designated as required for women.

By 1905, the department had expanded from two to six faculty members and offered nine courses specifically and respectively designated for agriculture, women, and mechanical students. Domestic science chemistry and chemistry of animal nutrition were also offered.

In 1909, the chemistry offerings increased to sixteen, each designed specifically for majors in agriculture, forestry, women's course, and engineering. Chemistry of wood products and preservatives for forestry students and chemistry of beet sugar manufacture for agricultural students reflect the specificity of offerings.

By 1915–16, the chemistry staff increased to twelve and the courses to thirty; the majors for which each course was designed were specifically indicated. Eleven courses (a total of more than fifty credits) were designated as required or elective for home economics. Course titles such as animal nutrition, chemistry of wheat flour, physiological chemistry, chemistry of fuels, textile chemistry, pyrometry, and power plant chemistry reflected breadth in one sense and narrow specificity in another.

By 1925, with the approval of an applied science degree program, a major in chemistry became possible. In 1930, the department listed some forty-five courses, of which twelve were clearly intended for majors other than chemistry. The determination of course requirements for programs was removed from the department offering courses to the major or program requiring them. Course content was negotiated. Degree programs and requirements were gravitating to departments rather than being college-determined.

Specialty courses gradually disappeared over the next thirty years. Titles such as water and sewage analyses, bleaching and laundering, and application of dyes had disappeared by 1935. Textile chemistry, steel and alloy analysis, plant chemistry, dairy chemistry, chemistry of nutrition, and electrometallurgy continued at least until 1950. The special interests of individuals, the dates of their retirements, and the addition of new majors or departments were determining factors in continuation, transfer, or elimination of these special-purpose courses.

The appearance of synthetic fibers brought dramatic changes to the textile industry and hence to the knowledge of chemistry required. Similar developments in other fields made it possible for the chemistry department to organize the subject into logical sequences in general, inorganic, organic, physical, analytical, and theoretical chemistry. Chemistry majors might readily acquire the comprehensive and well-rounded training required to become professional chemists, while students majoring in other disciplines could acquire the background in chemistry appropriate to their own interests. Chemistry provided the fundamental courses, but instructional staffs in these various majors assumed the responsibility for applied courses dependent upon chemistry. The chemistry department became dedicated to the discipline rather than to its applications in other areas.

The development of biochemistry as a department indicates one way in which highly specific chemistry courses were assimilated into courses dealing with broader principles and concepts applicable to a wider range of problems. Nutrition and plant chemistry, for example, became parts of courses in biochemistry. Courses in steel and alloy analysis, electrometallurgy, plastics, metallurgical analysis, and electrodeposition of metals dealt with emerging technologies such as chrome plating, latex paints, and development of plastics. As the basic chemical concepts involved were included in courses in analytical chemistry, polymer chemistry, and so on, the technological aspects were taken up by departments such as metallurgy and chemical engineering.

In summary, when chemistry first appeared it was both totally service oriented and, by necessity, oriented to agriculture. As new majors appeared, many new chemistry courses were added and directed to specific user groups. This process reached a peak in 1925, when forty service courses were added, each designated as required or elective for certain groups. By 1969–70, the department was concerned almost entirely with its own undergraduate and graduate majors and with providing course sequences for the Bachelor of Science in Chemistry for careers in chemical industries, government laboratories, or graduate study in chemistry, and the Bachelor of Arts for premedicine, predentistry, high school teaching, technical positions (secretaries, librarians, sales), criminology, etc. Study of chemistry surely may contribute to a liberal education, but it is evident that the appearance of chemistry in the curriculum at Michigan State was originally, and continued to be, based upon career implications. Basic courses in chemistry have continued to be open to nonmajors, but other departments or programs have been expected to provide instruction in applications of chemistry.

*Zoology*

Zoology is the study of animal life, including domestic animals, wild animals, humans, and invertebrates such as insects. Zoology courses tend to be of two types: (1) descriptive-taxonomic courses describing the distribution, habits, and relationships of the animal kingdom or some portion of it; and (2) developmental courses concerned with some phase of animal development, such as embryology, genetics, or reproduction. Introductory courses are usually organized on an evolutionary-taxonomic basis, but also include an introduction to the more important developmental concepts.

Zoology, in a land-grant institution, found its domain threatened by the missions of other departments. The culture of domestic animals became a responsibility of agriculture. The diseases of domestic animals were the concern of veterinary medicine. Fish and game have been assigned to various units. Insect study is so important to agriculture that it early appeared as a separate department—entomology. Ecology, behavior, genetics, evolution, and comparative physiology are illustrative of the general concepts or problems of concern that are relevant across mammals, birds, reptiles, amphibians and fish.

In 1930, there were eleven courses that could be considered descriptive-taxonomic in nature, and there were four courses in genetics that were developmental in nature. In 1980, there were still eleven descriptive-taxonomic courses, but fifty-two developmental courses, including such graduate courses as developmental genetics (mechanism of gene action), ultrastructure, neuroembryology, analysis of hormone action, and cellular morphogenesis. The rapid increase in developmental courses may be attributed to the availability of National Institutes of Health grants for medical research, a shift from undergraduate to graduate emphasis, the development of medical schools at MSU, the expansion of faculty with medical interests, and the absence of direct responsibility for agricultural problems.

The ready availability of funds for medical research, the recruitment of faculty who could capture those funds, and the development of courses related to the interests of those faculty resulted in a collection of excellent, high-level courses indicative of a curriculum in its formative years. Since zoology has become increasingly related to the medical schools, it is not surprising that zoology is still experiencing growth.

*Entomology*

Although entomology is seldom given departmental status in the traditional university, in the land-grant college concern with the economic problems of insect control made it expedient to establish a department of entomology. This was done at MSU in 1906. The department's responsibilities included research in insect control, through the Agricultural Experiment Station; transmitting information to the public and responding to requests from the public; teaching service courses for such fields as forestry, horticulture, and animal husbandry; and teaching basic courses in insect biology and developing a curriculum for majors.

In 1950, the department could still be described in terms of these four responsibilities. Most of the staff members had at least a part-time appointment in the Experiment Station or Extension Service. The introductory course in basic biology and taxonomy of insects served as a prerequisite to all other courses. The courses in economic entomology were classroom versions of insect field problems. The department chairman emphasized responsibility to the taxpayers of Michigan but discouraged federal grant applications for fear of federal intervention. All members of the department were expected to share in answering the daily bundle of letters asking for information about "the enclosed bug." Failure to respond was likely to come to Hannah's attention and result in a low-key inquiry from him about the lack of response.

Professor Herman King recalled an experience that the department had with DDT. Before the development of DDT, there was no practical method of controlling mosquitoes, flies, fleas, bedbugs, and lice. Louse-borne typhus in the trenches and mosquito-born malaria in the swamps had long been major hazards of war. Both were readily controlled by the use of DDT. When the war was over, DDT was released to the public with no precautions about its use. Supplies were plentiful. In general, the pesticide laws of that time provided no precautions or controls—DDT was offered in various forms and with virtually no instructions. The Department of Entomology was swamped with calls from purchasers and dealers asking how to use the DDT already purchased.

With military manuals as printed references, many phone calls to colleagues in other states, and some guidance from greenhouse experiments conducted during the winter, Extension Folder F 93, "How to Use DDT on Vegetables," was published in March of 1946. The research published in it was inadequate, but it served as a stop-gap measure to prevent misuse and perhaps unfortunate consequences. As it turned out, DDT was highly effective and, for a time, the publication seemed to be an unqualified success. This and its quick publication, coupled with similar experiences in other states, led to an impression on the part of many people that universities could supply instant answers—that there could be an extension service without research—an impression that caused many headaches in subsequent years.

The success of DDT led to the development and marketing of many competing materials—lindane, chlordane, toxaphene, parathion, malathion, and many others. As these materials became more and more widely used and extension services continued to outdistance research, scientists became more and more uneasy about the possible hazards of the use of such substances but seemed unable to find funds or to organize the teamwork that would be required to do the appropriate research. Not until 1962, when Rachel Carson published *Silent Spring*, did the public become seriously concerned. *Silent Spring* marked the turning point from the euphoria of the 1950s, when a chemical was proffered for every problem, to the near panic of the 1970s, when every chemical posed a problem. Reacting to the changing mood of the public, Congress appropriated funds and newswriters anticipated instant answers. But tracing a pesticide from its application to its appearance in the shell of a robin's egg or a fish stomach involved many disciplines. In 1968, the Pesticide Research Laboratory, involving more than a dozen departments, was organized, which made possible a systematic approach to the problems of pesticide and other toxic residues. It also made possible the purchase of sophisticated equipment, leading to the discovery of "micro" amounts of chemicals in places where they had formerly been thought to be absent.

The persistent problem of pesticide residues has led to a new strategy of pest control. In earlier years pesticides were used as insurance by applying a full set of controls for all the pests known to be present. Now, use of pesticides is pin-pointed at the exact time to be most effective and applied in conjunction with cultural methods designed to minimize pest problems. This strategy, known as "integrated pest management," provides specific recommendations for each of many small areas, and is made possible by computerized observers in many parts of the state. Changes in control strategy have been reflected in curricular changes, since new graduates must be able to use the new systems and to do the research necessary to improve them.

In summary, it may be noted that, from its inception, this department and its curriculum have been shaped by the needs of the taxpayers as reflected by the Experiment Station and the Extension Service. The history of the department illustrates a close interrelationship of instruction, research, and extension, as well as some of the difficulties that can arise when extension is not supported by the appropriate research.

The review of the development of MSU's colleges in chapter three and of the creation of courses and programs in the departments forming the colleges in chapter four summarizes the growth of the academic programs and structures over a century. Several significant observations are apparent.

1. For approximately seventy years, the sciences, social sciences, and the arts existed primarily as service courses for the basic four land-grant units.
2. Home economics demonstrated a much clearer commitment to liberal education than did the other programs and maintained this commitment despite an increasing vocational or career orientation.
3. The gradual elimination of arts and science service courses for the various career programs in agriculture, engineering, and home economics was widely regarded by the arts and science faculties as an improvement, but students and faculty in those career programs found increasing difficulty in selecting liberal education courses of interest and relevance to career programs.
4. The appearance of undergraduate majors and of graduate programs in the disciplines quite naturally turned the arts and sciences faculty and departmental attention to disciplinary instruction and research and away from service activities either inside or outside the institution. As faculty quality increased and as the institution sought status among universities, its entire character gradually changed.
5. John Hannah himself remained committed to public service but on a much broader base than formerly—urban as well as rural and international as well as national and state.
6. Hannah was the central figure in encouraging and enabling the complete transformation of the land-grant college of the 1920s and early 1930s into an internationally known university, but, in so doing, he endeavored to maintain the institution's tripartite and integrated commitment to instruction, research, and service (especially the latter), which had long been the distinguishing characteristics of the land-grant college.

The following chapters in Parts II and III report on the more specific aspects of the developments and of various issues that arose as the institution underwent the metamorphosis reported in chapters three and four. The last two chapters (Part IV) constitute an analysis of what was learned in this experience about leadership, techniques for changing an institution, and implications for the future of universities committed to public service.

# 5
# General Education and the Basic College

No one can say with complete assurance just when general education appeared at Michigan State College. The curriculum of the Agricultural College of the State of Michigan in its early years was, with the exception of the classical languages, much like the programs of the Eastern colleges, but with added practical field work in land clearing and agriculture. Indeed, as we have seen, the institution depended upon the labor required of its students, and it was fortunate that that labor could be regarded and accepted as relevant to their education.

The first term of the new college began May 11, 1857, and ended October 28, 1857. The following year this term ran from April through October. Not until 1896 was the long vacation shifted from winter to summer, with the labor required of students diminished accordingly. Whether the replacement of outside labor by inside *labor*atory was greeted with enthusiasm by the students of that day is unknown. Laboratory experiences can be routine and dull even when well planned.

The mandate of the Morrill Act of 1862 "to promote the liberal and practical education of the industrial classes in the several pursuits and professions of life" was further broadened by a specific injunction that scientific and classical studies were not to be excluded from the curriculum. However, as a science of agriculture gradually developed and a program of courses in agriculture was introduced, science, social science, mathematics, and even literature came to be viewed in the context of their significance for study of agriculture, home economics, engineering, and veterinary medicine. One result was a decrease in the number of general or liberal education courses or credits. Another was the tendency to require that such courses have direct relevance in context and even in title. Thus, there emerged such courses as mathematics for students of agriculture, physics for home economics students, agricultural economics, and literature for engineering students. Even when course titles remained noncommittal, specific sections might be designated and adapted to curricular groups.

From the beginning, it had been recognized that in order to serve its purpose and attract an adequate number of students the institution should—indeed must—accept students with apparently deficient backgrounds. Such students could be admitted either by passing an examination or by taking remedial or "make-up" courses. For example, individuals who had not taken or had not adequately benefited from high school mathematics or English were required to take make-up courses. Thus, in 1931, English 102d was required "for students whose insufficient preparation in fundamentals of composition *handicaps them*" (italics mine). Though credit was given for the course (despite many objections), it had to be taken in addition to the three terms of English required for all students. No credit was given for plane geometry or for the remedial course in arithmetic required of some students.

Agriculture, engineering, veterinary medicine, and applied science programs all required study of the sciences, usually with some adaptations to the several programs involved. Thus the increasing number of students (women especially) who were entering the liberal arts division established in 1924 led in the 1930s to course adaptations or introduction of new sequences more appropriate for general education. In 1929–30, the physics department designated one sequence as "applied science or liberal arts physics." In 1936, there appeared in the Department of Zoology a three-term survey of biology staffed by two department heads (S. G. Bergquist and H. R. Hunt) and a dean (Ward Giltner). It is of some significance that two department heads and a dean accepted responsibility for developing and teaching such courses.

In 1937 the Department of History and Political Science offered a three-term survey of social science taught by Assistant Professor Walter Fee. In the next year, 1938, Stanard G. Bergquist introduced, in the Department of Geology and Geography, a three-term survey of physical science.

In 1938–39, the art department added a three-term sequence, introduction to the arts, treating successively art, drawing, and music. Much of the credit for development of these survey courses goes to Lloyd C. Emmons who became dean of the Division of Liberal Arts in 1934. These courses in the arts, social science, physical science, and biological science formed a general education program available to, but not required of, liberal arts students. Because it offered these courses and was committed to the general and liberal education generating them, Michigan State College joined the Cooperative Study in General Education supported by General Education Board Funds and directed by Dr. Ralph Tyler of the University of Chicago. The study also included the University of Chicago, University of Minnesota, Syracuse University, and Kansas State University along with numerous other state and private colleges and universities, which collaborated in an effort to clarify the concept of general education and to determine the criteria and procedures for developing general education courses.

In 1942, Dr. Chester Lawson joined the zoology department and took over responsibility for the survey of biology in the following year. Also in 1942, a three-term existing sequence in history of European civilization became the responsibility of Dr. Harry Kimber. This course was the nucleus of a more comprehensive history of civilization that was developed by 1944.

In 1942, the Department of English introduced a three-term survey course entitled "Great Masterpieces" covering, in successive terms, art, drama, and music. There also appeared a two-term course sequence, general college writing laboratory, followed by a third-term speech and English laboratory. The "general college" referred to in the course title was a unit established informally by John Hannah shortly after he became president of the college on July 1, 1941.

In 1936, a study made at the request of Dean Emmons had showed that only about one-third of the students entering Michigan State received a degree from the college. Another study indicated great variation among high schools in the preparation of their graduates. A program had been launched by John Hannah (as board secretary) and Dean Emmons in which college representatives visited high schools to interpret the opportunities available at the college, which had increased the number of applications, including some with less than fully admissible backgrounds. Having stimulated applications, what should be done with them? The response was—had to be—multifaceted. The long-existing availability of entrance by examination was refurbished, publicized, and made more readily available. Some individuals were offered a "summer school trial" admission, with assurance that a C-average performance would be recognized for full admission by fall. This procedure was facilitated by S. E. Crowe, who became director of the summer session in 1942, and by R. S. Linton, the registrar and admissions officer.

## The General College

John Hannah was well aware of these events and trends when he became president. Appeals from students (or their parents, state representatives, or senators) quickly convinced Hannah that some "dropped" students and rejected applicants deserved a second chance. A program of selectively admitting students or readmitting them as "unclassified" was instituted. Their number increased from thirty-two in 1940–41 to eighty-eight in the following year. Some of the individuals admitted under the new policies were also uncertain about a major. A two-year terminal program that could lead to either a career or to transfer to a four-year degree program looked promising to Hannah, Crowe, Linton, and Dean of Men Fred Mitchell. On May 21, 1942, Crowe was made director of the general curriculum. Direct admission of two-year students to the General College was formally approved. The anomaly involved in having both a general curriculum and the General College was resolved the following year by changing the title of director of general curriculum to dean of the General College.

The 1942–43 catalog stated that "students may be admitted to the two year General College, regardless of credits or grades, if the high school principal so recommends." Transfer from the two-year General College to a degree-granting division was permitted "if a satisfactory record is accomplished in the General College." Students in the General College were required to complete at least four of the following courses:

| | |
|---|---|
| Introduction to the Arts | 6 credits |
| (Art 101, 102, 103) | |
| Survey of the Physical Sciences | 9 credits |
| (Geology 101, 102, 103) | |
| Introduction to the Social Sciences | 9 credits |
| (History 101, 102, 103) | |
| Survey of Home Economics | 12 credits |
| (Home Economics 140a, 140b, 140c) | |
| Writing, Speech, and English Laboratory | 9 credits |
| (Speech 151; English 152, 153) | |
| Survey of Human Biology | 9 credits |
| (Zoology 101, 102, 103) | |

A year of mathematics, or foreign language could be substituted for one of the survey courses. Requirements in physical education and military science had also to be met. All additional courses were electives. Upon completion of ninety-two credits with a C average, a certificate was granted. Transfer to a degree program would be possible if grades were acceptable. This program was somewhat like that of the University of Minnesota General College.

The survey course in home economics dealt in successive terms with family life, clothing and home furnishings, and food for the family. Being limited to General College students, it was regarded as general education. Credits could be acquired in typing by demonstration of a speed of 60 words per minute. Shop mathematics was planned but never offered. The three-term survey in great masterpieces appeared as an elective, as did the sequence in history of European civilization. A number of orientation courses, providing information on careers in various fields, also appeared.

| | |
|---|---|
| Development of Agriculture | 1 credit |
| (Agriculture 101) | |
| Introduction to Conservation | 2 credits |
| (Conservation 201) | |
| Dairy Husbandry | 3 credits |
| (Dairy Husbandry 101) | |
| Orientation for Men | noncredit |
| (Education 101) | |
| Introduction to Hotel-Keeping | noncredit |
| (Hotel Administration 105) | |
| Personal Hygiene | 2 credits |
| (Hygiene 225a) | |
| Elements of Engineering | noncredit |
| (Mechanical Engineering 101) | |
| Methods of Effective Study | 1 credit |
| (Psychology 101) | |

In 1942–43, the General College enrolled 385 men and 95 women, a total of 480 students. The unit had resulted from concerns about student retention, opportunity for borderline students, and program rigidity that discouraged and even prevented interdivisional transfer of students enrolled in programs for which they lacked motivation or ability. The Orientation Office, initiated in the spring of 1940 at the instigation of Dean of Men Fred Mitchell, was given responsibility for the orientation program for new students and immediately launched a program of interest and aptitude testing accompanied by vocational and educational counseling.

Several experiences of the new Orientation Office reinforced much of the thinking that had already resulted in the establishment of the General College and the general education survey courses. Divisional deans became aware that a student making poor records in one division might do well elsewhere in the institution. For example, in the fall of 1940, the dean of agriculture called the Orientation Office at the close of review of academic performance and remarked that a young man from the Bronx enrolled in the forestry major had failed all of his work and would be dropped. However, the dean said, "I noted that on some of the tests which were given as part of orientation, this young man showed up with high ability and I would be glad to retain him or transfer him elsewhere if you work out what you think is an appropriate program for him." The young man in question was a victim of parental solicitude. Raised in the Bronx, five feet and five inches in height, and rotund if not actually obese, the young man was obviously misplaced in the crowd majoring in forestry, who averaged nearly six feet in height and were obviously inured by their dress and appearance to extensive outdoor activity. The young man explained that his major was a last-minute compromise between his mother and father. The former had wished him to be a physician and the latter an engineer. He was told on the night before his departure to East Lansing that they, his parents, would resolve the matter that night and inform him in the morning. As it turned out, each abandoned the original demand and settled on forestry after leafing through the college catalog. His mother felt that taking care of trees and tree surgery must have some things in common with medicine and his father felt that "one could not handle those big trees without knowing basic engineering principles." Transferred to a program in the arts and sciences that included chemistry, German, physics, and mathematics, the young man supplemented his all-F fall quarter record by all-A performance. Only some time later, with Hannah's support, did the faculty permit cancellations of Fs under such circumstances.

Another year a young woman presented herself at the Orientation Office indicating great unhappiness with her program in home economics. Her Canadian father, who felt that money spent on the education of young women was wasted, agreed to support her education only if she would undertake a major in home economics, which he thought must surely have some practical value for a woman. Extensive testing and counseling revealed that she had no particular disability for home economics, nor indeed for any program offered in the university; in fact, she evidenced some clear aptitude for a science program. When, after weeks of irresolution, she sought her father's approval to change fields, he paid a stormy visit to the Orientation Office and, although he roundly denounced the college for interfering, agreed to approve the change if the Orientation Office would certify that another program would better suit his daughter. In her next session at the Orientation Office, the young woman enthusiastically explored various alternatives. At the end of a few weeks, however, she rather shamefacedly declared that "now that I don't have to be in home economics I find that that's what I really want."

The response to summer counseling clinics aimed at students not entirely certain about a major also made it obvious that the long-time conviction of the faculty that students should know their major when they entered college was no longer valid. The expanding offerings in the liberal arts, sciences, and business attracted a broader array of students and presented them with more options. Hannah, because of his own early experiences in shifting from law school to a bachelor's program in agriculture at Michigan State, and because of his extensive contact with young people during his poultry extension days, viewed this as a natural state of affairs. As enrollment increased at what seems a precipitous rate to about 8,000, the number of applications rejected also increased. At one point Hannah personally reviewed all rejected applications and out of several hundred selected some students that he directed should be given an opportunity. When, two years later, it was reported to him that only four or five of these students were still in school, his immediate and quite serious comment was, "Just as I thought; some of these people can make it if you let them in."

Hannah was also much aware that increasing pressure from the faculties in agriculture, home economics, and engineering for more technical courses and for increased amount of work in science as a background for these technical courses tended to reduce the amount of student time available for liberal and general education courses. In addition, as the liberal arts and science programs developed, it was obvious that faculties in those departments who had formerly accepted an entirely supportive role now wanted to develop their own majors and move toward offering graduate study as well. It may not have been ideal, but in the 1920s an engineering professor could readily plan the program of a freshman or sophomore engineer by using courses in physics, chemistry, literature, and other disciplines designated as specifically planned for engineering. An increasing range of courses in the various arts and science departments presented advisers and students in the technical fields with difficult choices. Moreover, it led to the selection of courses on the basis of convenience rather than of course content or quality of instruction. Hannah viewed the establishment of the General College and the various related developments as moves on a wide front to deal with complex, interrelated problems. The composite impact of Emmons' interests in liberal education and Crowe's General College had produced a series of courses that formed the nucleus for a full-fledged program of general education. Just where these developments might have gone is uncertain. December 7, 1941, brought a whole new set of pressures when students and faculty were almost immediately assimilated into the war effort. By the fall of 1943, the institution was heavily involved in a variety of military programs and had reassessed its faculty talents to accommodate these programs.

## BASIC COLLEGE ORIGINS

In 1943, Emmons, looking to the close of the war, appointed a committee to formulate a program of general education for the Division of Liberal Arts. Its report in the winter of 1944 proposed that each student be required to take four of eight courses, including English composition, biological science, physical science, literature and fine arts, history of civilization, social science, and a composite course drawing upon logic, philosophy, and psychology. Meanwhile, as general education had become diminished by pressure for more specialized courses in agriculture and engineering, President Hannah, who had already expressed concern about rethinking the undergraduate program, had been listening to Dr. Floyd Reeves, who excelled in raising questions and providing insights.

Hannah asked Dean Emmons to hold up action on the general education recommendations that had been presented in winter 1944. Hannah also invited Dr. Reeves to meet with the entire college faculty to speak to problems that would shortly arise with expanding enrollment and to suggest some ways to deal with them. Reeves predicted major postwar enrollment increases at Michigan State based in part on location and programs as well as on returning veterans. Fresh from observing general education developments at the University of Chicago and at the University of Florida, he suggested consideration of a required, rather than elective, core. He also stressed the importance of counseling and reinforced Hannah's own support of a program of credit by examination. The latter idea, never very attractive to faculty members ingrained with traditional classroom and lecture approaches, was made slightly more so by emphasizing the importance of an acceleration option for the returning veteran.

At Hannah's request, action on the liberal arts division proposal was tabled and an institution-wide committee with Dr. Reeves as consultant was then appointed to formulate the general and liberal requirements for the entire institution. The chairman, Howard Rather, head of the Department of Farm Crops, was in many ways an unlikely but very fortunate choice. Five of the eight committee members could be regarded as representing the traditional land-grant units. The need for general education was certainly more evident to faculty in agriculture, home economics, engineering, and veterinary medicine than it was to the liberal arts faculty. A required general education core was also more attractive to them in that it eliminated the ever-increasing complexities of advising students in selection of appropriate liberal arts and science offerings from an extensive array of courses designed to attract majors.

The committee moved rapidly to develop the framework for a basic college and for changes in the organization of the institution that would promote this development. In March 1944, Dr. Reeves made a presentation to the State Board of Agriculture that was very favorably received by board members and also brought immediate attention from the press. Hannah was interviewed extensively. He remarked that, for some time, many of the freshmen entering the institution could neither speak nor write forcefully or intelligently. Many, too, possessed only rudimentary knowledge of mathematics, history, and the basic sciences; others had no conception of their place in nature or in society. In short, too many students were unprepared to become citizens in the broadest sense. Hannah then emphasized the importance of both common and individualized educational experiences for students and of the need for student counseling. At the same time as the idea of a basic college was introduced, the college's divisional structure was reorganized. The appointment of a dean of students brought together the previously separated personnel services for men and women, a new student counseling service was established under the dean of students, and a board of examiners (also under the dean of students) was designated to be responsible for the comprehensive examinations in the new courses and, generally, for an institution-wide examination program for credit.

### The Basic College, 1944

The Basic College started with seven courses, each with nine credits: Written and Spoken English, Physical Science, Biological Science, Social Science, Effective Living, History of Civilization, and Literature and Fine Arts. Every student was required to take Written and Spoken English, one of the two sciences, one of the two social sciences, either History or Literature and Fine Arts, and finally, any one of the three courses not already taken. This pattern followed very closely that which had already been developed for the General College and later included (with some alterations) in the recommendations for the liberal arts division. There were those who would have preferred a common core rather than permit options, but many thought it impossible to combine Biological Science and Physical Sciences, and there was little or no precedent for it at the time. Effective Living was not regarded highly by many social scientists oriented to courses in the several social sciences. Nevertheless, the interest in personal development and personal problems seemed to some persons sufficiently important to be included. In a similar fashion, although on somewhat different grounds, historians and literature and fine arts professors regarded their areas as completely separate. Many persons expressed the hope that most students would take all seven courses, and early statements of the Basic College included this expectation. However, forty-five credits had been demonstrated to be about the maximum that could be required of students in all of the various divisions. As it turned out, even requiring a fifth course to make up the forty-five-credit total was criticized by those in some of the vocational areas.

The names of two of the courses also became matters of concern almost immediately. The origin of "Written and Spoken English" as a title was uncertain and rather curious in that there wasn't any other kind of English. Despite its focus on skills of reading, writing, speaking, and later, listening, it was met with considerable skepticism among faculty members and ridiculed by some students, who shortly renamed it "splitten and broken English"—thereby unwittingly and aptly characterizing some of their own performances. "Effective Living," which emphasized affective outcomes, was also seen as lacking in substance, and its attention to dating, family, children, creation, and recreation soon earned it the popular designation "effective loving." It turned out to be neither effective nor loved. It is worthy of note that both Written and Spoken English and Effective Living suffered from the fact that few if any such courses had been offered in the past. There was no precedent and no available group of faculty members with relevant experience.

The combination of literature and the fine arts also brought problems, even though a survey course in literature and also one in the arts area had existed for general college students. But few faculty members had extensive experience in all of the three fields covered— literature, art, and music—and the attempt to interrelate them around certain common concepts and values later led, as one faculty member put it, to teaching art, literature, and music separately in consecutive terms in an attempt to "achieve a more thorough integration." The jargon of general education meant different things to different people.

The course in Written and Spoken English may have suffered somewhat in the eyes of some faculty members because it was seen as a successor of the sequence English 152, 153, and Speech 151 which had been introduced to remediate student deficiencies. It was often remarked that the 150 sequence should not have been accepted for credit for students seeking a baccalaureate degree. Though there is no record of credit being specifically denied, a handwritten note in the registrar's personal catalog of 1944 said "credit for English 152, 153 and Speech 151 should not be allowed in upper school since it is lower than freshman English." Others thought that nothing could be lower than that. The credit problem for remedial work had previously arisen with regard to English 102d, which had been added for students not ready to begin the 102e, f, and g sequence. It would arise again in dealing with the disadvantaged students after World War II.

When the Basic College opened in the fall of 1944–45 with 1,613 students enrolled, the faculty immediately found a great range in English facility. Some students felt that Written and Spoken English was a waste of time. They asked to take the comprehensive examination at once. An equal or greater number of students, perhaps 10 percent, were simply not ready for it. By 1946, three clinics were created in the Department of Written and Spoken English: reading, writing, speaking. Work with students in the clinics was necessarily highly individualized, and very quickly the principle was stated that any clinics offered in a class mode should include no more than fifteen students. By 1947, the total enrollment in the college was more than 9,000. The problem of deficient students became an increasing irritation for both professors and other students.

*Comprehensive Examinations*

Credit in the Basic College was based on a grade in each course determined entirely by a comprehensive examination required after three terms. The full implications of this were only beginning to dawn upon the faculty by 1947. As the faculty expanded, it was generally found that incoming faculty members had never heard of comprehensive examinations operated on this basis and were quite antagonistic to them. Originally, approval to take the comprehensive examination before completing three terms in class was granted by a counselor. Faculty reactions forced transfer of this authority to the dean, and ultimately to the department and the dean jointly. With large numbers of students involved, procedures had to be routinized.

Mature veterans were generally delighted with the idea of acquiring credit by examination and took advantage of the opportunity. In the early years of the Basic College when veteran student enrollment was high, a C performance on the comprehensive was accepted for credit; many acquired credit thereby. Soon the faculty and department heads insisted that an A or B based upon student performance for three terms be required. A C+ remained acceptable for the occasional older student. Many faculty members resisted the departure of outstanding students from their classes and soon moved to introduce honors sections to retain these students.

Some faculty members found it difficult to deal with students whom they could neither fail nor reward with an A. Temporary grades given at the end of the first and second term were replaced by the comprehensive examination grade. A few students, and occasionally very able students, demonstrated by their absence from class or by failure to fulfill assignments that they were quite confident of passing the examination and would therefore ignore the professors. Faculty became so irritated by this attitude that they voted for and the dean approved a policy stipulating that a grade of F would bar the student from the examination. Thus, little by little, the significance and impact of the comprehensive examination were being destroyed. First, the various ways in which to get the permission to take the comprehensive examination had been tightened. Second, the performance criteria required for credit had been raised. Finally, individual instructors were given the right of failing a student taking the examination. The significance of this is most vividly illustrated by the case of a brilliant individual enrolled in the first term of the biological science course who decided it was a waste of his time. With permission he took the comprehensive at the end of the first term and received an A. The instructor had given him an F based on his lack of class attendance. It was decided that this F took precedence over the A for performance, and the individual in question withdrew from the institution. As a side light it may be noted that, although some felt that President Hannah would too readily intervene and change faculty decisions, his reaction in this case was that it was an unfortunate situation but not one in which it was appropriate to override a dean and the faculty.

Another problem generated by the comprehensive examination was the amount of time required to make up new ones. With students entering every quarter, it became necessary to prepare a new examination each quarter of each course and still maintain the security of the examination. The early practice of allowing students to keep their copy of the examination after taking it raised violent objections on the part of the faculty, who found students coming to them with examination in hand to raise questions about items. Instructors who had not been on the examination review and development committee might not have seen the test items in advance and were embarrassed by their inability to answer a student's queries immediately. Obviously, in those circumstances, an instructor might maintain that the item in question was faulty, thus adding fire to student criticism of the test.

In presenting an examination draft to a departmental committee, the author of the exam ran the risk of losing the best questions. Simple factual questions survived because everyone knew the answers. Items that required a student to think also required faculty members to think. Review committee members uncertain about an answer could be mollified only by the elimination or rewriting of such an item. In the science courses, the cultivation of critical thought processes was paramount and faculty were hence more willing to tolerate exam items that required thought. But even though attempts were made to keep science examinations secure so that most of the items could be reused from time to time, faculty members became intrigued with certain thought-provoking questions and proceeded to use them in their lectures and classroom discussion. Obviously, once presented in class, the best thought-provoking item, especially if identified as a comprehensive examination question, no longer served the purpose for which it was written.

Faculty were also opposed to the giving of temporary grades that were then obviated once the comprehensive was taken. Disparities in instructor and examination grades generated dissatisfaction. The student with the higher examination grade criticized instructors, and the instructors criticized the examination. The student with the lower examination grade complained that the examination was unfair. So did his or her instructor. Parents, too, might become involved, especially when a child failed the comprehensive. Complaints from parents, high school principals, teachers, and members of the legislature found their way to the president's office, naturally generating on his part a concern about the fairness of the whole procedure. The accuracy and fairness of instructors' grades were seldom addressed.

The validity of performance on the examination as an indication of a student's actual ability relative to course objectives was also of continuing concern. In Written and Spoken English, in which writing, speaking, and later, listening were emphasized, the comprehensive examination of necessity included an essay, a speech performance, and a lecture or oral presentation as a basis for testing listening comprehension. The time required to read essays and to listen to student speeches (the last two weeks of the course were taken up with speeches given by all students on a relatively narrow range of topics) was exorbitant. Listening was tested separately for a time, but was never fully accepted as a goal. Time-consuming effort and tension also existed in testing students in the literature and fine arts course, which emphasized comprehension, understanding, and insight with regard to various works of art. The introduction of surprise works of art on exams was particularly irritating to students (and some faculty members), who complained that they did not know how to respond if a work had not been discussed in class or covered in lectures. Attempts to assess students' judgment by objective means were also controversial. Some members of the faculty objected to the fact that comprehensives in areas other than Written and Spoken English did not require written essays as test answers, but few would entertain the challenge to prepare, read, and grade essay material. As numbers increased, most faculty members frankly admitted that they did not in their own assessments use questions requiring oral or written responses but rather test items that required choosing from among multiple choice responses.

Another aspect of the examination program was the security problem. With thousands of individuals taking the same examination, it was necessary to print them. This was done under reasonably secure conditions by a local printer who had long handled secure materials for governments. Yet any student could start a rumor that a comprehensive examination was "out." Occasionally faculty members serving on a review committee might give way to an impulse to talk about a "cute" test item to a class or a student. One professor serving on a review committee gave the correct answers to all questions on a comprehensive examination to a group of athletes whom he was tutoring. The professor's rationale was confused, but apparently he felt that such a fiasco would force the college to eliminate the comprehensive examinations. Although the faculty member was summarily discharged, the event unquestionably had some continuing impact. In another incident, a student, irritated by his own experiences with comprehensive examinations, dropped out of college, obtained a job in the printing company, and the next year became an instrument for smuggling out and selling parts of several comprehensive examinations. Warned by rumors, the college and printer took appropriate steps.

The use of the comprehensives in validating the completion of general education requirements raised several issues. One was in regard to transfer credits from community colleges. The Basic College faculty, the dean, and President Hannah were favorably disposed toward the community colleges of the state. Some community college faculty members were interested in the interdisciplinary courses, but most community colleges offered the traditional disciplinary and more readily transferable courses. Thus the Basic College had to evaluate transfer credits in relation to its general education requirements. A proposal requiring that junior college transfers must first pass the comprehensive was rejected as unfair to students. Inevitably, traditional science, social science, and literature courses came to be evaluated as equivalents of the Basic College courses, despite the fact that similar traditional courses were not acceptable as substitutes for students enrolling as freshmen at Michigan State.

The issue of "double credit" appeared. Should a student transferring to Michigan State be permitted to use a history sequence for a basic course requirement and also have that history sequence counted as part of a major? Although not really double credit, the credits would count in two different categories. Within Michigan State, a similar problem arose in that students could spread Basic College course requirements over two or three years. Thus, a student might, in the first or second year, take several courses in history or in literature and art and then also seek credit by taking the comprehensive examination for history of civilization or literature and fine arts. This possibility was ruled out as a clear case of double credit. Although students were permitted to take certain departmental courses on a noncredit basis to prepare for the comprehensive examination for credit, no one ever did.

Since many other institutions in the country were interested in general education programs, the program at Michigan State, especially the evaluation aspects of it, received national attention. Members of Michigan State's Board of Examiners staff found disparity between the interest in and deference for their work nationwide and their exposure to frustration at home.

Generally, the department heads were favorably inclined toward the comprehensive examination. A common examination provided a strong incentive for a professor to hold closely to the course syllabus. At the same time, professors chafed at the limitations this imposed. Those professors who had not shared in the development of the basic courses and who neither understood nor accepted the service role of the Basic College heavily criticized the system. The fact that one department head regularly used the examination performance of students to decide on promotions and salaries of faculty did not endear him to the staff of that department.

Hannah, sensitive both to internal and external criticisms of the comprehensive examinations, addressed his concerns both to the dean of the Basic College and the head of the examining staff. The latter, already on the receiving end of much of the dissension was, to some extent, insulated from its impact because he reported to the dean of students rather than to the dean of the Basic College. At the same time, as long as Dean Howard Rather was adamant in refusing to consider any change, the system continued to operate. Large numbers—more than 2,000 students in some examinations—forced the use of less-than-satisfactory examination facilities. Hannah, observing one of these sessions complimented the efficiency of the procedure but expressed horror at the regimentation and probable student discomfort. The proctoring and identification checking procedures required of the Basic College faculty were regarded as demeaning by many proctors. Pressures for change increased.

To the pressures emanating from the core courses and comprehensives were added certain other developments that brought the situation to an explosive pitch. As a result of the university's rapid growth in the late 1940s, many faculty members lacking the Ph.D. were hired. This was not particularly startling because only a minority of the existing faculty possessed the terminal degree. But Hannah was expressing his intent to upgrade faculty quality, and it became evident that tenure was unlikely without a doctorate. Thus, to the continual change in courses, the accommodation of large numbers of students, and the growing concern of the Basic College faculty that they might become second-class citizens in a developing institution, was added the pressure for completing a doctorate. Many faculty members would have to pursue course work and write a dissertation while employed full time by the institution. Faculty of Written and Spoken English, who labored on a course regarded with grave doubts by the rest of the institution, found such pressures especially acute. The head of the course and department (also acting head of the speech department for some time) was able and dynamic but had strong political aspirations that increasingly took him away from the campus. Both faculty and students disagreed about the teachability of the skills (reading, writing, speaking, listening) stated as the goals of that course.

The physical science course also had serious problems. Students in fields requiring chemistry, physics, and mathematics were advised to bypass the course. Its expansive content discouraged many students. Women students favored the biological sciences, in which the faculty was much more successful in producing a course consistent with the general education aim of teaching an understanding of the nature of science rather than teaching many facts.

The Effective Living course, struggling under a cloud generated by its title, had never achieved acceptance by faculty or students. Many of the course's original faculty left in mild disgust. Social science—an alternative to effective living—benefited.

The literature and fine arts faculty had developed a good but tough and time-consuming course avoided by many students. The course faculty interacted little with the rest of the Basic Course and preferred to deal with an elite student group. History of Civilization, more traditional in content and method, attracted the larger number of students.

Pressures had been generated to eliminate the requirement of the fifth core course. The choice of paired courses in science, social science, and history and literature gave credence to the view that four courses were sufficient to sample the major areas of knowledge. If so, a student could use the remaining nine credits toward a major or career program. Proponents carefully avoided implying that this would reduce general or liberal education.

### PRELUDE TO CHANGE

So long as Howard Rather remained dean of the Basic College, his commitment to the existing pattern and his prestige served to negate, if not refute entirely, all of the questions and dissension that had grown up around the Basic College. As dean, he continually enunciated that the role of the Basic College was to serve the rest of the institution, and he leaned heavily on an advisory committee drawn from the various schools. But illness and death deprived the Basic College of Rather, its first and most able administrator. Dr. Walter Fee, head of the Department of Social Science, served briefly as an interim dean but wisely recognized that his was simply a holding operation until a new dean was chosen. The choice fell on Dr. Clifford Erickson who served as Basic College dean for two years from 1951 to 1953.

Erickson came to the deanship from education, where he had developed and served as director of the Institute for Counseling, Testing and Guidance, a service to the schools of the state. The choice of dean must have been a difficult task for Hannah. He continued to be strongly committed to general education and to many of the features of the Basic College. He was also sensitive to its difficulties and pressures for change. Though many aspirants would have debated the point, there was no one involved in the Basic College or so strongly committed to general education that the leadership mantle could readily be transferred. Within the Basic College, there were already numerous tensions and marked divisions and views. As important as it was to maintain the acceptance of the Basic College by the traditional land-grant units of the institution, the developing strength in the arts, sciences, and social sciences made the appointment of an individual from agriculture, engineering, or another wholly vocational unit inappropriate. Erickson, who had been far removed from the Basic College, conveyed to the Basic College faculty the impression that he was interested in general education but knew relatively little about it. His initial questions and his relatively abrupt actions also gave the impression to the faculty and the department heads in the Basic College that, in accepting the job, he had also accepted some presidential suggestions for immediate action. It was not in character for Hannah to appoint a dean and give him or her definitive instructions, but those who knew Hannah well knew also that he must have voiced his concern about an early resolution to internal and external problems.

Those who participated in early discussions with the new dean saw clearly that changes were to be quickly made. It was also shortly evident that the changes struck most of the Basic College faculty with consternation. Many faculty members subsequently attested that they had been ignorant of imminent action and that the faculty meeting in which specific recommendations had been quickly approved was prematurely called and inadequately informed. The seven basic courses were eliminated and replaced by four. Communication Skills replaced Written and Spoken English, a reflection of the view that Written and Spoken English lacked substance and that its title was a handicap. A new twelve-credit course, Natural Science, combined biological science and physical science. Since the physical science enrollment and faculty had been decreasing for some time, this decision forced the biological science staff to develop a new course quickly covering both physical and biological science. The reaction was less than enthusiastic. A new social science course (twelve credits) replaced the Social Science and Effective Living courses. The substance (if any) of Effective Living was to disappear and its staff would be absorbed into social science. A new humanities course (twelve credits) replaced History of Civilization and Literature and Fine Arts. The history emphasis was to be predominant. In fact, no member of the literature and fine arts department moved to the new course.

In these new courses, an examination would be given at the end of each term, and the grade on that examination would count toward 50 percent of the student's grade, the grade assigned by the instructor making up the other 50 percent. In effect, the comprehensive examination was discarded and replaced by a common term examination. The Board of Examiners, to that date based in the dean of students' office, was moved to the Basic College, which somewhat appeased those Basic College faculty members who had regarded the independent status of the Board of Examiners as demeaning and insulting. They would continue to press to acquire complete control of grading.

Erickson also arranged for the Counseling Center to be assigned to quarters in the Basic College building. Although this move was advantageous in that most of the center's clientele were Basic College students, the status of the Counseling Center as a university-wide service was somewhat weakened. Erickson evidently also felt that the Counseling Center should be tied closely with counselor training. Recalling that Erickson had originally established himself at Michigan State through the Institute of Counseling, Testing, and Guidance, there could be no doubt of his intent to increase both the quality of counseling provided to Basic College students and the quality of the counselor training program. Although the Counseling Center remained under the dean of students, some individuals viewed the purpose of these changes as centralizing control of the Basic College and matters immediately related to it in the Basic College's dean's office.

One additional change was made that permitted a substitution for that basic course nearest to the student's major. In effect, majors recaptured twelve credits; the general education requirement was reduced from forty-five to thirty-three credits. Thus, these changes accommodated the major criticisms that had accumulated during the initial seven years of the Basic College. Although they at first generated anger and lowered morale, more because of haste than lack of rationale, in retrospect it appears that most of the changes were justified and worked well. Quite certainly, Hannah did not expect all these changes to be made with such great rapidity, and he surely did not realize that the faculty had not been involved. It became apparent to Hannah that improved communication was a necessity and that faculty involvement in decision making must result.

Comparison of the haste in change with the deliberation in the original action was inevitable. The idea of the Basic College had been presented to the total college faculty by Hannah and Reeves on March 9, 1944. By March 14, an all-institutional committee selected by divisions was at work. After thirty-three sessions, the committee report was adopted by the faculty on May 22 and approved by the State Board of Agriculture in July. The new unit and its program were in place by September 1944. Speed there was, but everyone was fully informed—and almost everyone was supportive. Communication was clearly the key. Moreover, most of the features involved had already been worked through by the liberal arts faculty.

## BASIC COLLEGE, 1953–1969

In 1953, Erickson became dean of the School of Education. He was succeeded in the Basic College by Thomas Hamilton, a University of Chicago Ph.D. and former vice president at Pennsylvania College for Women (PCW—now Chatham College). Hamilton originally joined the faculty to coordinate the Ph.D. and Ed.D. programs in higher education. A former student of Floyd Reeves, he was familiar with the general education program at the University of Chicago and had been actively involved in the PCW program. Since the major immediate problems of the Basic College had been resolved, the three-year term served by Hamilton was uneventful.

Though, like Erickson, regarded as an outsider by the Basic College faculty, Hamilton successfully restored morale and direction by informal interaction with faculty, by listening to them, and by acting on their suggestions. For example, one lecture hour for listening training had been retained despite much skepticism as to its worth. Hamilton joined a group of communication skills faculty over coffee, as he often did, where one professor argued cogently that the hour should be returned to the primary instructor. Shortly thereafter, that change was formally proposed and approved, apparently because of Hamilton's presence and tacit approval.

Hamilton also pointed out that, despite early commitments to relate the Basic College programs to the total campus operation, there had been no effort to relate the programs to the residence halls, student personnel activities, or the lecture-concert series (as had been done at PCW). In fact, an effort had been made to relate certain basic courses to scheduled events, but the problems of coordinating the scheduling and requiring attendance at any evening event proved to be objectionable to both faculty and students. Nevertheless, Hamilton's comments were appropriate and undoubtedly contributed to later deliberations regarding living-learning residence hall facilities. Hamilton also assisted in developing a new sense of unity by encouraging the writing and publication of a book on the Basic College.

When Hamilton became the first academic vice president of Michigan State, he was succeeded as dean by Edwin A. Carlin. Carlin had joined the faculty in 1947, was well acquainted with the background of the Basic College, and was quite impatient with the continuing need to justify its existence. There had been no overt attempt to eliminate the Basic College, because it was amply apparent that Hannah supported the idea completely. Changes and adaptations had already been made and would be made, but for the foreseeable future the Basic College would continue. It had amply justified itself in accommodating the large numbers of returning veterans and in providing for acceleration. It had introduced honors work for the able, while at the same time offering those with weak backgrounds or learning disabilities opportunities for improvement.

Subsequent to the reduction from seven courses to four, the natural science program, headed by Chester Lawson, acquired a national reputation as a general education offering in science. It had also attained the respect of students and faculty on campus. The social science program under Walter Fee and the humanities program under Harry Kimber had developed interesting and challenging courses in which numerous distinguished members of the faculty, no longer in the Basic College, had participated.

The course in communication skills was the focus of most of the specific criticism still directed to the Basic College. Its emphasis was on the skills of reading, writing, and speaking. The attention to listening, which had been the butt of much humorous and cynical comment both within and outside the department, had gradually disappeared. The professors themselves were more adept at speaking than at listening. The course suffered by its lack of a defined content and of formal standards of achievement. In the very first year of the Basic College, Hannah had repeatedly commented that communication was an institution-wide problem both within Michigan State and between it and its constituency. To be effective citizens and workers, students must learn to communicate. But he insisted that assigning this responsibility to a single course or department was self-defeating. Students would feel no compulsion to improve their communication skills in other cases. Faculty members heard and assented, but only a few responded.

The Department of Communication Skills had been assigned a task it could not fulfill. The load carried by faculty members in reading student themes was arduous and little appreciated. The task of listening and reacting to student speeches generated no sense of exhilaration. The improvement services in writing, speaking, reading, and arithmetic, all at one time attached to that department and providing a necessary service, could lead the casual observer to see the entire department as operating at a subcollege level. The department tried to perform its assigned but impossible task, but the rapidly increasing enrollment, the acquisition of additional faculty members, and the increasing section size further complicated its problems. Although Paul Bagwell had given effective leadership in the development of the program, his interests had turned outward and his ambitions apparently were elsewhere. On entering the political scene, Bagwell resigned as department head, and Carlin took this opportunity to bring about a major change in the nature of the course.

Edward Blackman, who had been in the humanities department, became head of the Department of Communication Skills in 1958. Blackman was a very pleasant, intelligent, and highly regarded individual, but he was cast in a role he did not want. He undertook the task because he shared with Carlin and others the conviction that this course must be reshaped. In 1959, Communication Skills was changed to American Thought and Language and now described as a substantive course. In term one, it dealt with the American enlightenment and the influence of the American frontier. In term two, the course focused on American literature, the Transcendental Movement, and the collision of ideologies leading to the Civil War. In the third term the focus was on science and the crises of the first half of the twentieth century. The last part of the course attempted to develop a perspective, providing the student with insight and understanding about the nature and origins of American culture.

The continuing search for a better course in communication skills and the planning carried on up to that date were simply set aside. Many of the faculty members, hired for a course emphasizing communication skills, were not only antagonistic to the change but saw themselves facing the impossible task of acquiring sufficient scholarship in this new area. Twenty-five faculty members departed. Although the name had changed, the department had escaped, more or less unscathed from the earlier shakedown that had reduced the seven courses to four. The impact on the faculty of this change was more cataclysmic than the earlier change because the latter change was focused on a single department and amounted to an abrupt rejecting of its efforts since 1944. Moreover, it appeared both to those in the department and to much of the institution that communication skills (specifically writing, which was the only skill to which the majority of Michigan State faculty gave much credence) were being de-emphasized. In fact, they were, but the intent, the perception of that intent, and the actual result were undoubtedly at variance.

Critics of the department had seen the lack of substance in the course as committing the faculty and students to communication about drivel, thereby discouraging any significant experience in valuing and judgment. Accordingly the department lacked any criteria for appraisal of improvement. Communication, after all, must deal with significant ideas to justify attention in a college. By focusing students' attention on aspects of American heritage, reading about them, discussing them, and finally writing about them, those who proposed the change saw the course as assuming a more significant role in the education of the student. First, the subject matter itself would provide significant background for living and contributing in American society. Second, various aspects of communication would be put into a context that would be significant to the student and would provide a foundation on which all the rest of his or her education for participation in American society would rest.

Integrating writing skills with significant subject matter was by no means a new problem, although the attempt to separate writing as a skill from substance did not clearly appear until the course-credit system took hold of American higher education. Until that time, teachers of English composition had frequently been less experienced members of the English department. They have always faced the same problems faced by the staff of Communication Skills. Reading papers and providing significant feedback to the students are emotional and time-consuming experiences for both student and teacher. By providing a substantive basis for a course, it was hoped that the focus of reading, writing, and speaking could be shifted from individual feelings and personal problems to the issues and concepts involved in the course substance. Similarly, courses in English composition in English departments have frequently become courses in literature, with the intent that writing assignments would be based on the literary material rather than on direct personal experience. The difficulty, as was soon found in American Thought and Language, is that if the focus is on content, it becomes necessary to seek professors who have a background in that field, who, in turn, believe that coverage of content in class and knowledge of content on the part of the student often supersede the skills of reading and writing. Such a course may maintain, as did American Thought and Language, that through the use of selected American documents it provides training in reading and writing, emphasis on structure and development of ideas, and frequent writing assignments. However, particular instructors may regard specific knowledge of the American documents as the only matter of importance. Writing that is read only for accuracy of factual content does little to improve students' writing or thinking, and thus many faculty members ceased to require it.

The shift of title from Communication Skills to American Thought and Language was regarded by many university administrators and faculty members, including many who had regarded the Basic College with favor, as denial of the department's obligations to the rest of the university. The change in name from Basic College to University College in 1961 also suggested that the general education faculty no longer accepted the basic role originally assigned to it. For some years, there had been recurrent discussion of the possibility of a general education baccalaureate degree, but there was no enthusiasm for it in the rest of the university; if anything, there was a deep-seated antagonism toward it. Clearly, the University College no longer served the central role that it had in its earlier years. Although it had provided the other colleges with an opportunity to develop their advanced courses for undergraduates and their graduate programs, all departments and colleges had come to realize that credit hours had become a significant factor in the budget. They also wanted more time for the major and supporting courses. Hence, the University College course most clearly related to the major had already been waived.

The University College courses eventually became unknown entities to the faculty in the rest of the institution, although Hamilton and Erickson, because of their prior service as deans of the Basic College, continued as bulwarks in defense of it. After their departure, there was no one in central administration, except Hannah himself, who asserted the significant role of general education in the institution.

By the 1960s, the University College was no longer a prestigious or influential unit in directing university decisions and developments. In an attempt to restore the University College to its central role in the university, the Committee on Undergraduate Education issued a report in 1967 that dealt with this issue in explicit terms. It recommended that the content of the American Thought and Language sequence be immediately modified to ensure greater emphasis on writing skills. It also recommended that committees be established for each of the University College departments that were to be consulted on curricular planning and development, on changes in textbooks or teaching materials, and on changes in teaching procedures. This was essentially a recommendation for return to the advisory committee pattern of earlier years. Another statement by this committee indicated in no uncertain terms the general deprecatory attitude of the faculty toward American Thought and Language:

> American Thought and Language is a successor to the original Written and Spoken English Course instituted at the inception of the Basic College and later renamed Communication Skills. Throughout its several changes in content and title, its role in the general education program and its primary obligation have remained unchanged in the eyes of the entire university faculty—to teach writing as well as it can be taught in a 3-hour course of 1 year's duration. Neither the difficulty of the task nor the failure of other departments to insist upon high standards in writing can justify the withdrawal of American Thought and Language from this primary obligation.[1]

There was much chafing under the criticism, and many individuals in the University College regarded these comments as an invasion of the autonomy of the unit. There were some changes, but, with a faculty selected to achieve a high percentage of Ph.D.s and engage in scholarly productivity, there was no return to the earlier service role.

In 1967, the Department of Humanities added a course, Humanities 250—Traditions of the Orient, to its basic three-term courses. In 1968, each of the four University College departments offered an independent study course numbered 300 at the junior level. In 1969, Humanities 250 was expanded into four courses dealing with China, India,

---

1. "Improving Undergraduate Education," report of the Committee on Undergraduate Education, Michigan State University, 1967. In the MSU Archives and Historical Collections.

Japan, and Islamic civilizations. Student unrest and criticisms of required courses, along with aspirations of the faculty, became the basis for developing alternative tracks to the original three-term courses. In 1970, American Thought and Language provided a 100-level course in comprehensive English, partially countering the criticisms of the immediately previous years. In its basic course first term, two tracks were offered, regular and honors; in the second term, four tracks; and in the third term, four tracks. Humanities offered four tracks, Natural Science five, and Social Science four. In addition, Humanities offered a 341 course entitled "Humanities in the Contemporary World." Multiple tracks eliminated common examinations. This was inevitable, although there had been some discussions emphasizing the idea that the fundamental objectives could be the same despite different selections of content. Old hands on the faculty knew very well that neither students nor faculty would accept examinations that departed in any significant way from the actual content of a particular course. With multiple tracks and no common examination, the University College departments, in effect, had achieved freedom to develop courses at the whim of individuals. By 1979, courses were being offered at all levels in University College departments. But the baccalaureate degree programs and the graduate programs that some University College faculty members had aspired to add were not there. The University College was eliminated in 1980 and its various departments transferred to the other appropriate colleges. There were many who felt that this should have been done at least ten years earlier when the college had clearly rejected its original mission.

The lessons to be learned here will be more explicitly stated in chapter sixteen.

# 6
# The Honors College

The creation of the Honors College in 1958 was one of the most significant events in the Hannah administration. The seeming long delay in this action is part of its significance, for it (with other changes) reflected a broadened mission and a commitment to providing a challenging education for everyone.

The State Agricultural College was founded with a primary obligation to develop a practical educational program for rural youth. Students lacking a high school diploma were admitted by examination or by completion of some remedial work. Later regarded as a desirable forward step by many colleges, such admissions practices were suspect in the nineteenth century. Not until extensive evidence of the college's academic standards had been collected and presented to various national bodies by L. C. Emmons was the college fully recognized. In 1931, it was granted an "A" rating by the Association of American Universities. Michigan State graduates could then for the first time continue advanced study elsewhere without questions or loss of credit. The institution became eligible for membership in certain selective national honoraries, although it already had more than a dozen local and national honorary societies. In 1933, recognition was granted by the American Association of University Women.

The initial stimulation for discussion of various forms came with the increasing enrollments and the appearances of majors in the sciences and arts in the mid 1920s. Departmental honors programs existed in several departments by the late 1920s and early 1930s. Before that the only apparent institution-wide recognition of scholarship was that based upon grade-point average.

Before the 1930s, it had not really been strategic to make a special appeal to attract able students, since every move to develop the liberal arts and sciences generated suspicion. But when John Hannah and Emmons launched, in 1935 and subsequent years, the high school visiting program, able students were sought and attracted. By 1940, Michigan State was widely recognized as having solid programs, but high school counselors, teachers, and principals still urged excelling students to go elsewhere. The idea of an Honors College had been discussed by 1940, and had it not been for the attack on Pearl Harbor in December 1941, Hannah very likely would have launched or at least proposed an Honors College in 1942 or 1943. Indeed, the policy of credit by examination highlighted in the Basic College was seen by Hannah and others as especially appropriate for able and mature students. It had been so since 1910; Hannah himself had benefited thereby. So did many World War II veterans and adults in 1949 and after. Until well after the war there was neither pressure nor time or funds to develop honors programs.

In 1956, the College of Science and Arts reopened the honors issue and inaugurated a departmental and college honors committee, and in 1957 Hannah and Vice President Thomas Hamilton joined in naming a committee to formulate ideas for an honors college. At that time, an honors college was viewed solely as a vehicle to attract outstanding students in sufficient quantity to create a new image for the university. Neither the science and arts faculty committee nor the Basic College faculty saw it as a means for accelerating enrolled students.

In discussing an honors college, the first issue was its appropriateness. Some persons objected to it on the grounds that it seemed to be an elitist turn in a land-grant institution. Costs were also a concern. Decades-old questions were also resurrected about the lack of challenge in classes out of which the ablest students had been channeled. A projected waiver of general education courses was disturbing to some, although honors sections within general education courses were proposed to alleviate faculty concern.

The policy of extra expenditures for remedial work for inadequately prepared students was readily turned into an argument for providing education experiences appropriate to student preparation and need. Special education, whether for the gifted or the disadvantaged, tends to be costly. In a sense, it may be undemocratic and unfair because it subtracts from the funds available for the "average." On the other hand, a common program for all is also undemocratic because it ignores individual differences in interest and ability.

Hannah believed that a land-grant institution had an obligation to provide education for all who desired it and could profit from it. Funds were not and never would be adequate, but restriction of admission to any one type of student would be detrimental to all in a democratic society. The presence of gifted students would attract superior professors, indirectly improve the quality of all programs, and add luster to the degrees of all students.

Implicit in his appointment of and charge to the honors college study committee was Hannah's recognition that Michigan State's traditional commitment to the rural areas and to practical programs in agriculture, engineering, and home economics was in marked contrast to the University of Michigan's dominance in the learned professions. Moreover, the U of M's influence among public school administrators contributed to a view that superior students should attend that school, or even some other school, but not Michigan State. The Basic College, with its emphasis on general liberal education, career development, and counseling, had generated contacts with secondary schools and community colleges that helped to change this view. Nevertheless, Hannah felt that a more dramatic—perhaps even more drastic— change was required to arouse faculty enthusiasm and support, to direct student attention toward academic excellence, and to convey to the educators and public a new image of the institution. Perhaps both a special unit such as an honors college *and* a scholarship program were needed to attract talented high school graduates and community college transfers. Out of such considerations came the deliberations and the ultimate decision to establish the Honors College.

During the academic year 1957–58, the committee worked on its charge and came up with a recommendation leading to the establishment in the academic year 1958–59 of an Honors College charged with special responsibility for students of superior ability and achievement.

The committee began its deliberations with a document that apparently was the first formal statement about a university-wide honors college program. Dated September 30, 1956, it was distributed to various administrators by Thomas Hamilton, vice president for academic affairs. The document reflected the earlier thinking of the Instruction, Curriculum, and Research Committee and was no doubt influenced by the developments in science and arts. Subsequently, the document (slightly revised) was sent to the academic council and became the basis for further deliberation and action.

The essential elements of the original proposal were:

- Academically superior students should have highly flexible, continually challenging, individualized opportunities for learning.
- Both intellectual and personal development were to be fostered, and narrow specialization was to be avoided.
- Specific requirements should be few to assure maximum individual flexibility.
- Time acceleration in completing the baccalaureate should not be an objective, but coverage of more content material in a manner

conducive to depth of understanding and to integration across disciplinary lines should be.

- Breadth and depth should not be viewed as conflicting alternatives, but as interrelated and essential to individual comprehension and application.
- The Honors College, cooperating with the other colleges and departments, should be the university agency through which the needs of "genuinely able students" could be met and their potential stimulated and cultivated.
- The Honors College should also become the agency for publicizing institutional honors commitments and accomplishments.
- Honors College status for students should strengthen rather than weaken or displace the relation of majors with their academic departments and colleges, their professors, and their advisers in these units.

The Honors College began operation in fall 1958. The reputation of expeditious action had been maintained.

### Admissions and Requirements

For admission to the Honors College, students were required to have achieved a 3.5 average (based on a 4.0 scale) during their freshman year at Michigan State. Transfer students with comparable performance could also be admitted. Exceptional circumstances might also justify admission. Students had to apply, but admission (initially) was not dependent upon submission of a detailed honors program.

Consistent with the initial insistence on flexibility, all requirements other than the 180 quarter credits required for graduation were waived. Although the student's faculty adviser was to recommend to the Honors College Committee a student's readiness for graduation, a total of 180 credits were required and university and departmental rules and requirements were followed. Thus, a student could not acquire an engineering degree while "ignoring all requirements." In fact, waivers were first applied primarily to the Basic College general education requirements. These very liberal admission and program requirements underlined the Honors College Committee commitment to flexibility and individuality. When it was found later that a few students used the Honors College to avoid demanding study, these requirements became a matter of concern.

The committee's early deliberations dealt with many issues, resolved some, agreed to ignore others for the time being, and foresaw several that would recur later. It was anticipated that some honors students would be unable to maintain the required 3.5 average and would have to be dismissed from the Honors College. This was not seen to be a serious problem, since the Honors College enrollment was a second or additional affiliation that could be withdrawn with no immediate impact on the student and no public announcement of the fact. Credit for atypical Honors College experiences would be available. Some majors were recognized as rigid but would probably change with time. The extent to which students would ignore Honors College opportunities was not foreseen. The awesome size of the honors group, which quickly climbed to more than 1,000 students, was not anticipated. The 1955 study of freshman performance on which the 3.5 requirement was based suggested that a pool of fewer than 200 freshmen would finish their first year with a 3.5 average, but class size increased and grades became inflated. An all-university faculty advisory committee was recommended to facilitate coordination with other units and to discuss and make recommendations about such problems. Review and approval of special applications and of projected student courses of study were mentioned as possible problems for the committee to resolve.

## DEVELOPMENTS

The Honors College was initially housed in the MSU Library. Honors College students were given graduate student privileges in study access, withdrawal of journals, and graduate course enrollment. Certain prototypes of students were soon in evidence. There were those who enrolled in nineteen to twenty-three credits when fifteen or sixteen was a normal level. Others avoided honors work lest their point average suffer. Professorial grade distributions in honors courses and seminars were sometimes unduly rigorous for such a select group. There were a few students—fewer than anticipated—who took advanced work with much independent study and engaged in individual research projects. It was also apparent that not all advisers were imaginative, stimulating, and demanding in advising students. Furthermore rigid adherence to college and department requirements and suggestions could void Honors College opportunities and expectations.

The Honors College began to attract National Merit Scholars, which renewed the desirability of scholarship funds to attract able students. In 1962, funds were set aside to make awards to 150 National Merit Scholars who indicated intention to attend Michigan State. This immediately expanded the number of outstanding students at MSU and in the Honors College. In 1962, Michigan State enrolled more freshman Merit Scholars than any other institution, which attracted national attention and much criticism (and envy) from other universities. MSU was not the first institution to use money to attract able students, but the magnitude of the program spawned accusations that the university was "purchasing" students and that the reputation and quality of the National Merit program was being diminished. Other institutions were, of course, free to do the same, and others did.

In 1963, the Honors College was attracting prominent speakers, holding colloquia in the Honors College lounge in the main Library, and attracting 98 percent of the 5 percent of the total MSU student body qualified to join—775 students. The greatest number of enrolled students were from the Colleges of Natural Science (152), Social Science (145), and Arts and Letters (131). Additionally, 40 percent of the student leadership positions on campus were held by Honors College students. Sixty percent of the Honors College graduates went to graduate school, most with some financial assistance and most frequently at the University of Michigan, the University of California at Berkeley, Harvard, Massachusetts Institute of Technology, the University of Chicago, Yale, and the University of California at Davis. One third of these students pursued graduate study in the basic program areas of the land-grant college, a fact that was highly gratifying.

On June 15, 1963, President Hannah, who had served on the Michigan committee for the selection of Rhodes Scholars, reported to MSU deans that no nominations for these scholarships had been made from this institution during his period of service, and he suggested that MSU identify prospective candidates in their freshman year and follow through with them. Responsibility for selection of such students was placed with the Honors College. Under the directorship of Frank Blackington (1970–74), the Honors College produced its first Rhodes Scholar, followed by three more in a four-year span.

In 1966, John Wilson of the Office of the Provost reviewed the Honors College and presented an evaluation and recommendation to the provost. He noted that deferral of Honors College membership until the sophomore year posed some problems in program planning but that he found little support for change. In fact, not until 1974 were selected freshmen invited into Honors College membership, although honors sections and courses had been available to freshmen for some years. Wilson also expressed concern about the large numbers of Honors College students who made no use of its program-planning feature, and he suggested some required changes.

1. Specification of admission requirements beyond point average
2. Projection or plan of use of Honors College membership
3. Planning a schedule of honors courses in advance

4. Improvement in quality of honors student advising
5. Reduction in students by points 1 and 2

Wilson also argued that flexibility and individuality in planning should be balanced by some required small class or seminar groups of gifted and articulate students, which he felt were essential features of good honors work. Formal honors courses, sequential in nature, carefully planned and scheduled in advance, and central to the major (although not completely displacing interdisciplinary seminars or courses) were strongly recommended. Wilson also enthusiastically espoused one or more culminating experiences: a final comprehensive examination conjoined with a reading list, an honors research project, or a senior thesis. He insisted that the vision of honors students and their advisers should exceed the simple goals of course and project completion and credit accumulation still too apparent in much Honors College work. In fact, Wilson had himself been a Rhodes Scholar from Michigan State.

The 1969 recommendation of the University Honors Program Committee for revision of policies governing the Honors College dealt with and supported many of Wilson's ideas. It asserted, however, that at least one term of residence at MSU should be required before admission to the program and that to remain in the Honors College a student must have a program of study and demonstrate annual progress with it. Flexibility and individualization were not rejected but were controlled by goal definition and recurrent evaluation. No longer could a student take course work in many disciplines and no advanced courses in any. No longer could an honors student be content with the traditional program available to or required of the average student. Although a senior thesis (or similar project) was rejected as a requirement for all, the Honors College program took on many of the characteristics of graduate study. Freedom was to be used in a responsible manner by both student and adviser.

Faculty advising emerged from these reviews and revisions as being of tremendous importance—and also as requiring tactful collaboration with departments in selecting and training. The adviser who encouraged narrow, specialized, advanced study in a discipline was—according to the Honors College philosophy—as detrimental to student development as one who adopted a laissez-faire stance. From the Honors College view, the advising problem was complicated by a new university policy requiring that the student see an adviser *at least once a year.*

By 1969 Honors College graduates were regularly achieving recognition in many ways. In a memorandum to President Hannah dated

March 25, 1969, Dr. William Kelley, director of the Honors College, reported forty-seven graduate fellowship or scholarship awards. In another memorandum, Kelley reported the presence of 684 National Merit Scholars, more than any other institution in the country—a nice badge of success, indeed, for a retiring president.

### FROM PRIVILEGES TO OPPORTUNITY, OBLIGATION, AND INTEGRATION

Originally students with no interest in pursuing the opportunities of the Honors College were attracted to it by its privileges: graduate library privileges; early registration like that for varsity athletes; admission to special programs and seminars; access to a lounge, study space, and advice in the Honors College facilities; and recognition in various listings and commencement programs. A privilege not publicized but fully recognized was easy, ready contact with some of the most intelligent students in the institution. Class visiting privileges and easy access to faculty were also attractive. There was much to gain and nothing to lose by joining the Honors College. Initially, such privileges may have been viewed by faculty and Honors College staff as means of attracting students and institutionalizing the program. Basically, however, these privileges were facilitating features that enabled Honors College students, advisers, and faculty to plan and carry out distinctive programs, untrammeled by irrelevant matters of time, space limitations, and closed sections. After the program revisions of 1969–70, their facilitating role became evident.

A review of six selected and successful Honors College graduates is interesting and instructive. All entered with a prestigious scholarship award. All had multiple competencies and interests and astonishing programs: philosophy, engineering, and music for one; mathematics, English, and creative writing for another; computer science and theater for a third. All demonstrated the capability of handling more coursework than traditional undergraduate (or graduate) students. One student completed twenty-one credits in mathematics and chemistry (honors sections of several courses) two terms in a row and attained all As. Another successfully completed graduate-level coursework in three disciplines consecutively. The undergraduate years of these six students demonstrated that the Honors College had successfully provided the opportunity to experiment with various disciplines. The integration and specialization that led to career choices came only at a graduate level. For these remarkably talented students, an undergraduate goal statement specifying a discrete senior project or thesis would have been delimiting rather than stimulating. Flexibility and individualization do have merit. But examination of the programs of earlier students had also demonstrated that freedom undirected and uncontrolled can become a license to mediocrity or worse.

The Honors College, consistent with the original recommendations on which it is based, has not encouraged acceleration in completion of degree requirements. In fact, undergraduates have generally seemed more likely to take excess credits than to attempt early program completion. As indicated elsewhere, the general attitude of the faculty, once highly favorable to credit by examination and expeditious completion of degree requirements, has gradually come to regard acceleration as undesirable. In effect, the option of credit by examination is in abeyance. Thus, the Honors College faithfully reflects faculty and student preference in successfully providing educational experiences.

The Honors College has continued to be a vital, attractive, flexible program for individual students, a challenging experience for advisers, and a highly respected program on the MSU campus. In the early 1980s, when budgeting pressures forced cutbacks and the elimination of some programs, there was campus-wide unanimity that the Honors College must continue, a strong indication of the success of the program. In great part, faculty support of the Honors College has been forthcoming because the college has never been a competitor of degree-granting colleges, but rather a stimulator and a strengthener of college and departmental efforts to challenge individuals of high potential.

The actual institutional costs of the Honors College have not been determined. Director, secretary, office, and material costs may be identified, but such costs as faculty time, the difference between regular and Honors College undergraduate instruction, seminar time, and so on, are not easily determined. The benefits of the college have been regarded as well worth the effort and the costs. Students of exceptional academic quality were attracted to MSU in larger numbers. For many years Michigan State led the nation in recruiting National Merit Scholars. Locally, statewide, and nationally, the institution has been recognized for its honors program. Various grants and other awards to the university have been given, in part, because of Honors College activity. At the state level, the recognition and number of Merit Scholars has been perceived as reinforcing the academic soundness and quality of MSU's program.

Former Honors College directors have moved on to major administrative assignments elsewhere, indicating the prestige attached to the program and the university sponsoring it. The frequent change in directors has, in itself, been more advantageous than otherwise in that it has preserved and strengthened the function of the Honors

College as a facilitating university unit responsive to faculty and student concerns and to institutional mission. It also remains flexible in adjusting to changing circumstances. The Honors College has been a success in large part because of its flexibility and responsiveness. Its presence and success surely aided in acquiring the Phi Beta Kappa chapter which appeared in 1968. This was gratifying to Hannah, all the more because it was by then a recognition of merit rather than a means of acquiring it.

# 7
# The Living-Learning Theme

The phrase *living-learning* did not originate on the Michigan State campus, but it dominated much of the thinking about undergraduate education there from 1935 to 1975. For many users of the phrase, *living-learning* implied a four-year, full-time, integrated, educational experience in a small and excellent liberal arts college. The meaning imparted to the phrase has varied with time and personnel, but it has always included the concept of a continuing effort to relate formal learning and life experience. At Michigan State emphasis was on using residence hall space to improve learning, on making better use of available space, and on improving the quality of residence hall living. The rapid growth of MSU made such concerns urgent.

The combination of learning and living was not new at Michigan State. In its earliest years, faculty and students alike had interacted in performing practical work in the fields and barns as well as in the classroom. Students learned as they earned by that practical experience. Their more formal classroom learning took on added meaning from the demonstrations and practice in field performance.

The Woman's Building (later rechristened Morrill Hall), built in 1900, included a gymnasium, laundry, and home economics laboratories. The food service was managed by home economics faculty members and provided practical experiences for students. For a time, the dean of home economics was also the dean of women. Living-learning was a twenty-four hour task for students and faculty. In time, the availability of other buildings and facilities resulted in removal of the instructional program from the building. By the mid 1930s, the Woman's Building was declared a fire trap. The resident students were moved out and faculty with their heavy desks, files, and bookcases were moved in. Weakened by extensive prior remodeling, further remodeling was required to prevent collapse. Wooden stairs were replaced by steel stairways at a cost of $23,500. As of 1985, the building still stands, having undergone much additional remodeling, and still provides offices for many faculty members.

John Hannah, during his years as secretary to the State Board of Agriculture (1935–41), frequently remarked on the lack and the deficiencies of facilities. He could do so readily and at length because, almost from his first day as secretary, he was faced with construction and replacement problems. Farm Lane Bridge, first condemned as unsafe in 1895, had to be replaced. Arrangements to resolve the indebtedness on Mary Mayo Hall had to be (and were) made at once to avoid difficulties with the legislature. With self-liquidating loans, work was begun on Sarah Langdon Williams Hall (1937), Mason and Abbot Halls for men (1938), and Louise H. Campbell Hall (1939). Hannah, as chairman of the Committee on Dormitories, became fully aware of problems of operation and the quality of living. In particular, he was dissatisfied with the system of housemothers selected and directed by the dean of women, but he recognized that changes must wait for the opportune moment.

In the new Mason-Abbot halls for men, Hannah arranged that the manager of the halls be responsible to the dean of men for social and educational matters, but to the business office for managerial ones. A special apartment was planned for a faculty couple who acted as host and hostess for hall events and as advisers and counselors to the residents. No longer was the residence hall completely devoid of academic context. These changes set a new direction and served well for some years. The space available for social and recreational activity in these early dormitories was limited and relatively inflexible and unattractive by comparison with the multipurpose space of later residence halls.

On October 6, 1941, Hannah addressed his first staff meeting as president. In broad terms, he outlined institutional developments for the future in regard to facilities, programs, and faculty. Those present who had not known Hannah and had intimated some skepticism about his speedy selection and the lack of faculty involvement in it, quickly realized that this man knew the institution well and had definite ideas about its future that fairly well coincided with the hopes and aspirations of most of the faculty. Hannah demonstrated that he was aware of both large and small issues. For example, in remarks about some immediate concerns, he noted, "This is a campus of long distances with only ten minutes between classes. Start your classes on time and stop them on time." At that time, the maximum distance between buildings on the campus was about three-fourths of a mile. In the interval from 1935 to 1941 Hannah had, as secretary, brought $5 million in new construction to the campus. From his own earlier perspective as a student, Hannah could well view the 1941 campus as one "of long distance." By 1969, the maximum distance between classes would be as much as two and one-half miles. Time, distance, and learning space (square feet, character, and location) continued to be problems.

During the early years of World War II, regular enrollment dropped and military units of various types took up the slack on a revolving basis. Adjustments were made both in staff and facilities to accommodate these programs. By 1945, the first veterans were returning to campus. Speaking before the Economic Club of Detroit on January 12, 1948, Hannah remarked:

> So today, 93 years after it was established, Michigan State College is trying to cope with the problem of teaching 15,000 students to be useful, effective citizens. Like the University of Michigan, Michigan Tech, the teachers' colleges, and Wayne University, Michigan State entered the postwar period with seriously inadequate facilities. For example, when the first veterans returned to our campus in 1945, they found that the State of Michigan had not authorized a single classroom or laboratory there since 1929 when the student population was only 3,000. Not one single building had been added to our plant at state expense while the enrollment was increasing from 3,350 in 1932 to more than 7,000 in 1941, and the end of the war brought a deluge of new students to be educated through the expedients of doubling up, extending the college day far into the night, and increasing the size of classes.
>
> It would be unthinkable to establish an arbitrary limit on enrollments, thereby selecting a comparative few to attend our public colleges and saying to those we shut out: "We're sorry there is no room for you in college. It is too bad your parents can't afford to pay all your expenses and send you to some private college or university, but we just can't afford to educate at public expense everyone of intelligence and ability." If we did that [impose limits], there eventually would be no democracy under which to educate any one.
>
> As America grows in stature and importance as a world power, it is mandatory that colleges and universities, too, shake off their isolationism. It is essential, if our citizens are to make the enlightened decisions by which government is guided in a democracy, that they know their relationship to each other, and to their fellow men in other lands, to the natural order, to the developments of science, and to the higher law which governs all things.

To accommodate the increasing horde of students, temporary structures of various kinds were sought and placed on an extended campus. By 1951, these temporary structures included 12 classroom buildings, 267 apartment buildings, 450 trailers, 50 faculty houses, 104 quonset huts, and more were yet to come. New residence halls had been completed in 1947 (Phillips-Snyder for men), 1948 (Gilchrist for women), and 1951 (Shaw Hall for men). Only Shaw Hall, in design and location (south of the Red Cedar, which for years had been the south boundary of the campus proper) differed markedly in design from previous halls. Use of the residence halls during the summer by conferences and workshops had brought realization that extensive space went largely unused for many hours of the day. But the nature of that space and the access to it were not conducive to use by other than hall residents during the regular academic year.

Thomas Hamilton, on becoming dean of the Basic College in 1953, noted the failure of the college to use the students' total environment to attain its objectives. Having served previously as the vice president of a liberal arts college for women, he was convinced that significant learning should be both generated and reinforced outside of the classroom. He noted that neither the Lecture Concert Series nor the residence halls (still called dormitories) had been used for such purposes, although there had been some discussion between the student personnel staff and the Basic College about such a possibility.

The next residence hall venture for men extended the campus westward by adding Rather, Bryan, and Brody Halls in 1954, and Emmons, Armstrong, and Bailey Halls in 1955. Brody contained the meal service, recreation space, and meeting rooms for the complex. Observation of the operation of this complex again underlined that there was, indeed, a large amount of underutilized space associated with residence halls. A campus visitor strolling into Brody between meals was impressed by the great open spaces where few, if any, students were in evidence. Such impressions tended to undermine the continuing requests for facilities that Hannah made to the legislature and the public.

Long distances and travel time from residence halls to instructional facilities also became obvious to the students in the Brody area complex and to anyone observing the hourly trek to and fro of hundreds of students. Some of this mass movement was later eased by a campus bus service and by arranging that students residing in the complex could eat lunch at any convenient hall. Creating study spaces in the hallways of classroom buildings and using vacant classrooms for study eased the burden on the library and made it unnecessary for students to return to their halls when gaps between scheduled classes occurred. Meal times were also extended to accommodate travel time and students with noon-hour classes and to reduce crowding. Recurrent attempts to organize language tables or special discussions with invited faculty members in the large residence hall dining facilities were largely unsuccessful because of scheduling problems and noise, confusion, and the informality of the eating arrangements.

At some point in these recurrent efforts it was realized that the space problem was rather different than it had first appeared. Departments had tended to regard contiguous space as their own. At any given hour, a room might be unused or underused by a small class. Counting all available campus facilities, rooms, and chairs, it was found that there were at least five times as many spaces available for use as there were students to use them. Special and limited-purpose space (research facilities), however, combined with the task of matching class size to room size and equipment and faculty and student class-hour preferences greatly reduced the options. Central scheduling of classroom space became a necessity, and distribution of class hours over the full day became a requirement for each department. Faculty members, as well as students, might have to travel to a class across the campus. In 1957, the new Office of Space Utilization and Assignment began to correlate facilities planning and remodeling to needs rather than to desires and to assign space to obtain maximum usage. The concept of multipurpose space was applied more extensively than ever before.

On March 3, 1959, a special Committee on the Future of the University was appointed to analyze the existing status of the university and develop plans for the next ten to fifteen years. Among its many recommendations was included a call for increased emphasis on liberal education and a suggestion that a small residential college be created. The original and overly optimistic (as it later became apparent) statement was that "this college might experiment with novel approaches to learning and influence others by sharing." Another recommendation called for exploration of new developments in liberal education for women. Still another called for closer coordination of residence hall living with the academic programs. The inadequacy of instructional space and of faculty offices was noted. Data collected by the Office of Evaluation Services to identify and clarify the problems made such an impression on the committee that it also recommended the creation of an Office of Institutional Research.

The recommendations of this committee quickly and profoundly affected the university, in part because the committee chairman became the new provost and one of the committee members became director of institutional research. A Committee on the Education of Women was immediately created. Its recommendations, made in 1961, included one calling for the establishment of a small liberal arts college based in a residence hall. A tentative curriculum emphasizing the humanities and functional use of a foreign language was developed and included in the recommendation. The provost and president, who enthusiastically accepted the suggested program, would have moved immediately to create the new college, but several circumstances intervened:

1. The announcement of a new residential liberal arts college could generate public reaction that necessitated board discussion and authorization.
2. Faculty reactions indicated the desirability of processing the idea through the faculty committee structure.
3. No suitable space was immediately available in any residence hall.

Justin Morrill College did not open until 1965 in Phillips-Snyder, one of the older residence halls. Remodeling, at a cost of $64,000, provided offices, conference rooms, and classrooms. In retrospect, the college may have been launched at an unfortunate moment. Dissatisfaction with the status quo was amply evident among its students and faculty, and agreement on program features was not easily achieved. As the first of the residence-hall-based small colleges on campus, it was constantly viewed, reviewed, and criticized by all segments of the campus, including the Board of Trustees.

The authorization of Justin Morrill aroused interests in the initiation of similar colleges with distinctive emphases. In 1967, James Madison, with a social science policy theme, and Lyman Briggs, in the sciences, appeared.

## Brody Hall

The Committee on the Future of the University had remarked that campus growth seemed designed to maximize inconvenience, which led to a review of space with particular attention on Brody Hall, a central facility providing food services, recreational space, and group meeting space. In all, Brody Hall provided more than 100,000 square feet of multipurpose space. The increasing pressure for space led to the scheduling of some classes in Brody starting in spring term 1961.

Departments and faculty were asked to volunteer to hold class in Brody, and, although there were no special benefits or incentives to attract faculty members, many individuals did volunteer. Courses from a number of disciplines, including foreign language, were arranged in Brody on short notice. Though Brody was convenient for students residing in that area, faculty members generally were inconvenienced by the time involved in walking, driving, and parking there. Unless a professor customarily ate lunch at the Kellogg Center Dining Room located just across the street, he or she found no advantage to a class in Brody Hall. Noise from those entering or leaving the building around lunch time was a distinct disadvantage.

Students enrolling in these classes were not necessarily from the Brody complex of residence halls. Time, convenience, instructor preference, and errors by students or advisers brought students (often belatedly) from far parts of the campus. The first venture was unsatisfactory for all concerned.

After some remodeling, and with emphasis on the University College courses, Brody provided an effective instructional program for University College courses. The facility contained four classrooms, three science laboratories, an auditorium or kiva, thirty offices, and a small library or reading room containing materials related to the courses taught there. A faculty conference room was also available. In total, 725 individuals could be accommodated. Faculty members with offices assigned there usually held all of their classes there. In addition, representatives of the University College and of the Counseling Center were available so that Brody Hall became, in effect, a branch office of both units by 1967. All matters such as changes of major, academic actions on scholarships, changes of grades, and program planning could be handled. Similar patterns prevailed later for the Case, Wilson, and Wonders hall complex as well as for the Hubbard, Akers, Fee, Holmes, and McDonel hall complexes.

The effectiveness of this conjunction of academic and residence hall programs was a result of four characteristics of the institution in the period 1955–69. First, almost all freshmen and sophomores were required to complete the four University College courses. Second, most freshmen and sophomores lived in the residence halls. Third, the University College faculty was so large that department staffs could not have been housed together. Finally, both offices and classrooms in the residence halls were newer and more attractive than the original central facilities. The faculty members in these living-learning situations found the environment more relaxing, the opportunity for interaction with students attractive, and the opportunity to interact with advisers, counselors, and professors from other departments and disciplines mutually beneficial. An unanticipated attraction was that parking spaces were easier to find. Faculty members found that the major problem in teaching at Brody was their separation from their department and the attendant fear of being passed over at critical decision points regarding promotion, salary, and task assignment.

At its peak, the University College had three co-curricular programs in coeducational residence halls. Case Hall, the first coeducational residence hall, was almost finished in spring 1961 when forecasts for new students for fall 1961 made it apparent that finding enough space to house students would be a very serious problem. Some modifications were quickly made in Case's multipurpose space to provide offices, classes, and laboratories, so that by fall 1961 the University College was operating a branch in Case Hall. A student living there could complete all of the general education requirements without exposure to rain, snow, or fresh air. Wilson (1962), Wonders (1963), and Holden Halls (1967) were completed with central facilities conjoining two residence wings. The central facilities contained food services, classrooms, offices, laboratories, and a small library. McDonel (1963), Holmes (1965), Fee (1964), Akers (1964),and Hubbard (1966) Halls formed an east campus complex. Each complex contained Counseling Center staff, a director of student academic affairs, a director of extracurricular activities, and academic advisers. In total these various living-learning centers provided:

- 64 classrooms seating 3,884 individuals
- 26 laboratories accommodating 1,090 individuals
- 8 kivas and auditoriums seating 2,464 individuals
- 296 offices accommodating 296 faculty members, counselors, and advisers
- 4 small libraries seating 378 individuals
- 16 conference rooms seating 284 individuals

At its peak, living-learning space in the residence halls, including the three residential colleges, provided space for more than 7,500 students and more than 300 faculty members. No legislative appropriation had been requested or received for any of this space.

In addition to the University College branches and the three residential colleges, opportunity was provided for the College of Social Science and the College of Arts and Letters to develop a program of cultural activities in Fee and in Akers Halls. Although office and classroom space was made available, these ventures were not very successful. There were no courses in these colleges that involved the numbers of students that were in University College courses. Not many upperclass students remained in the halls. Faculty members of the degree colleges tended to be oriented to majors rather than students generally, and they were much more attached to their departments. Dr. Harry Kimber accepted the coordinating role in Akers Hall and developed an impressive schedule of speakers and discussions. These programs attracted so many students from elsewhere on campus that Dr. Kimber reluctantly had to restrict the program to students in Akers. In commenting on his task some years later, Dr. Kimber said that he did not feel that there was any real support for this program either in the residence hall or in the College of Arts and Letters. He pointed to complete abandonment of the idea after his retirement as evidence of disinterest. However, it should be recognized that the instructional loads in many departments, lack of purpose and clarity connected with this type of residence hall/college affiliation, and the scarcity of resources made assignment of college funds for residence hall programs a dubious operation from the view point of college faculties.

## THE RESIDENTIAL COLLEGES

### *Justin Morrill*

By the time Justin Morrill College opened in Snyder-Phillips Hall in 1965, its program plans and prospects had been examined and reviewed on and off campus. The facts that this was to be an *autonomous* degree-granting college and was named in honor of Justin Morrill, progenitor of the land-grant act, encouraged widespread publicity and continuing scrutiny. The purpose of the college, as it emerged from extensive deliberations, was to provide a rigorous liberal education integrating the theme of international understanding and service.

The first-year curriculum, in 1965–66, was to include extensive foreign language; a block of required courses to meet University College requirements—humanities and social science (twenty-eight credits each), natural science (thirty credits), and writing tutorials; a field of concentration from outside the college (a minimum of twenty-four to thirty credits); electives (a minimum of thirty credits); a senior independent study (four to eight credits); and a summer abroad. The specification of the elective credit minimum underlined a rather prescriptive approach to program definition. The faculty enjoyed *great* freedom; the students had *some*.

An entering class of 400 students was established, and a goal of 1,200 total students was set. Although study was to be rigorous, Justin Morrill was not to be an honors college. Justin Morrill was responsible to the provost and was to have administrative and budgetary autonomy. The hope voiced by the 1959 Committee on the Future that such a college might be an experimental unit for the entire university had been rejected. Justin Morrill had emerged as an autonomous unit attuned as much to its faculty's concerns, needs, and views about education as to students' needs and interest. Initially it was intended that a Justin Morrill student would be trained to have an inquisitive mind with a broad understanding of world citizenship skills and demands.

Each Justin Morrill student was expected to "perfect a functional use of one of the languages offered." Languages were offered in intensive courses of five, six, or eight credits per term. Inquiry and Expression (American Thought and Language equivalent) required twelve credits. The other general education requirements—arts and humanities, social science, and natural science—required twenty credits, eight more than the university at large. The major or field of concentration could be a traditional or an interdisciplinary one.

Students might choose as possible majors foreign languages, social sciences, humanities, natural sciences, and English composition (taught in tutorials) and were encouraged to sample extensively from courses available before choosing a vocation. A senior seminar was required.

Special courses available to Justin Morrill students included Mathematics in Western Culture; Human Development: Personality Patterns and Dynamics; and Economics of Property, Power, and Progress. These titles reflect the attempt to relate disciplines to problems or themes and suggest the dissatisfaction with existing departmental courses that led to these new offerings. Faculty and students soon found that an inspired course title does not necessarily produce a new and inspired course. Some emerged without substance and quickly vanished.

In the 1967 catalog, the independent study option was expanded to include a term on campus apart from formal coursework, off-campus community service, or a term of study overseas. Small classes were considered an important part of the Justin Morrill experience and hence instructional costs rose. Students seeking a broad liberal arts education, especially those considering teaching, law, and medicine, were encouraged to consider Justin Morrill.

In 1968, the college description emphasized the necessity of students' personal and intellectual maturity and identified faculty as "senior partners" in the student's quest for knowledge. Entering students were assigned an upperclass "academic assistant" to help with orientation and integration into the "community of learning." Language requirements in French and Spanish were reduced.

In 1969, four tracks (instead of three) of five to eight credits per term were available for foreign language study in French and Spanish. These tracks provided some flexibility, depending on a student's background, but also contributed to small classes and costs. The arts, humanities, and social science general education requirements were met through three term courses of three credits each plus one credit of supervised independent study each term. All the other requirements remained the same. Evidently the concept of independent study had been attractive but, in practice, it was not a significant program factor. A single-credit independent study requirement in the arts, humanities, and social science disappeared in 1970. In that year the inquiry and expression course focused on one term of expository writing and two terms of creative writing.

The original intent that students attain a functional use of one foreign language to be used in other courses and in study or travel abroad was not realized. By 1974–75 the foreign language requirement disappeared.

Pass-fail rather than traditional grading became extensively used. Justin Morrill developed the first and probably the most experimental of the three residential college curriculums. It may well have tried too much and changed programs too frequently to acquire a clear identity. It was at once overly flexible and overly rigid.

A competency-based program for adults and an evening track were developed in Justin Morrill's last years that attracted and deserved attention nationally. Eventually the college lost favor among administrators and the faculty generally. Students tended to transfer to other programs to complete their degrees. The college had never established distinctive character and, although it might ultimately have done so through its competency definition of the baccalaureate, this was widely regarded within the university as both educationally dubious and unreasonably costly. When, under the name of financial exigency, Justin Morrill was designated as a unit for termination in 1980, few dissented. Justin Morrill still remains a hallowed figure memorialized by Morrill Hall and the Justin Morrill Intercollege Program, but no longer by Justin Morrill College.

*Lyman Briggs*

Lyman Briggs College was established in 1967 and housed in Holmes Hall on the southeast side of the campus. The 1968 catalog stated its mission as: "to provide its students with an education in the sciences characterized by excellence and balanced by the inclusion of an unusually large segment of the components of a liberal education." Like Justin Morrill and James Madison, this residential college offered the benefits of membership in a collegiate community that focused on the intellectual, ethical, and social developments of its members and increased contact with the faculty and co-curricular activities related to students' educational goals, while providing the cultural and extracurricular benefits of university membership.

Lyman Briggs students included those seeking preprofessional training for medicine, dentistry, patent law, scientific writing, the history or philosophy of science, supervision and management in science-based industries, business or government services; those anticipating graduate work in either single or interdisciplinary fields for which the study of mathematics, physical, or biological sciences would provide an appropriate base; those who wished to be secondary-school science teachers; and those who desired a solid base or simply enjoyed the study of mathematics, physical, or biological science, but wished to defer their choice of specialization.

For admission to the Bachelor of Science degree program, a student had to meet general university admission requirements and have completed three years of high school mathematics and two years of high school natural science. The Lyman Briggs core program was ninety-nine credits and included fifteen credits of mathematics, three of computer science, eight of chemistry, twelve of physics, ten of biological science, and nine of senior seminar. The university general education requirement was met through twelve credits of social science; twelve of humanities; twelve of logic, history, and philosophy of science; and six of third culture rhetoric (a two-term writing requirement). The Lyman Briggs major, called a "field of concentration" in order to distinguish it from the traditional natural science major, was to contain thirty-two credits selected from one of five areas: the physical sciences (chemistry and a selection of courses in chemistry, mathematics, and physics); the biological sciences (a selection of genetics, developmental biology, comparative physiology, ecology, and population biology); the environmental sciences (statistics and probability and a selection of biology, geology, meteorology, and engineering); the mathematical sciences (a selection of mathematics, philosophy, statistics, and physics); and earth sciences (meteorology, astronomy, geology, and a section of geology, oceanography, fisheries and wildlife, and soil science). In 1969, a sixth field was added: history and philosophy of science, including philosophy and history in addition to the core program in physics, biological science, and astronomy.

Lyman Briggs offered an intensive yet intimate opportunity to undergraduate students interested in mathematics and natural sciences, and the college quickly earned the reputation of providing rigorous programs. The physical setting for Lyman Briggs was somewhat similar to the other two residential colleges, although more advanced planning was possible since construction of Holmes Hall, in which it was housed, was still at a stage where some adaptations could be made. Nevertheless, remodeling charges against the college amounted to more than $90,000.

Although Lyman Briggs College was extended the same autonomy and status as the other two residential colleges, its first dean, Frederic B. Dutton, chose to maintain a close working relationship with the

College of Natural Science. Dr. Dutton had long been affiliated with the chemistry department, and he had founded and directed the nationally recognized Science and Mathematics Teaching Center. He tended to regard the college as providing concentrations beyond departmental majors. Since Lyman Briggs College offered no science courses above the freshman level, many Briggs students ultimately sought majors in and a degree from the College of Natural Science. Thus, when the college was redefined as a school in the College of Natural Science in 1980 and the title of dean replaced by that of director, reaction was minimal. In fact many had concluded that such status would have been preferable in the first place.

*James Madison*

James Madison College admitted its first class of 225 students in 1967. The curriculum was based on the social sciences and focused on major social, political, and economic policy problems of the modern world. This residential college, like the others, provided a small-college atmosphere within the larger framework of the university and offered extracurricular activities, closer relationships between faculty and students, and student involvement and input.

Perhaps forewarned by the problems in Justin Morrill, the first James Madison dean, Herbert Garfinkle, enlisted prestigious faculty members from the various social science departments to define the college program before students arrived.

The core curriculum included University College general education requirements in American thought and language, humanities, and natural science. Students were to take a three-course sequence, introduction to the study of policy problems. Writing competency was required and was to be demonstrated by a twenty-to-thirty-page documented paper each year. Either a two-year foreign language competency had to be demonstrated or a one-year proficiency and nine credits in related areas such as history, geography, and political science. At least one course in quantitative research methods was required, as well as one term (junior year) of field experience in government, unions, political parties, and so on.

In 1968, the catalog stated that James Madison students would explore courses in their early years and make a major commitment later. Major study areas included war and peace, economic poverty and opportunity, racial and religious intolerance and discrimination, urban problems (of blight and delinquency), and constitutional democracy. An additional or coordinate major (complementary major) was encouraged. The supervised field study of fifteen credits was to take place over six months. James Madison acquired from its beginning the reputation of offering a sound and demanding program.

In 1969, coordinated preprofessional programs evolved, including journalism, prelaw, secondary-school social science certification, television and radio, and industrial relations.

Housed in Case Hall, Madison was assigned space on the third floor, which had to be extensively remodeled to provide offices and instructional facilities at a cost of more than $100,000, a figure that caused some consternation centrally although it was not unreasonable. President Hannah's view was that individuals agreeing to take on an innovative task must be given support.

### The Residential Colleges in Review

When John Hannah retired as president of MSU in 1969, the three residential colleges, Morrill, Madison, and Briggs, were flourishing, although Justin Morrill College was already suffering from some of the problems that ultimately led to its demise. James Madison, with its emphasis on public policy, had started with a clearer mission than Morrill by focusing on a concern common to many social scientists of that period and was thus able to draw a broader segment of faculty from the various social sciences and give rein to their interests in the policy problem. Lyman Briggs, in the beginning, had defined its role as providing programs for the variety of students who were interested in the broad field of sciences. In its concern about the impact of science on society, Lyman Briggs also opened the possibility for students interested in the philosophy of science, the history of science, or the impact of science on modern culture.

Each of these colleges faced the common problems of adapting its program to residence hall facilities and of cooperating with the management and student personnel staff of these residence halls. Morrill, having been placed in one of the older residence halls, faced such problems first and may have overinterpreted the extent to which it could use and direct activities in the hall. Student personnel representatives and management in Morrill were for the first time facing the problems involved when an academic unit with dean and faculty appeared on the scene. Justin Morrill was also established at a time when numerous students and faculty members were generally unhappy with existing patterns but did not have a very clear idea about what they really wanted. Other factors worked to undermine Justin Morrill. Originally, a great deal of emphasis was placed on the humanities and the use of foreign languages as a means of study as well as a set of skills for general reading and conversation. The Board of Trustees was unwilling to impose a language requirement on all students entering Justin Morrill, which, in effect, destroyed the significance of foreign language in the program. Early course listings include approximately a dozen courses offered in Justin Morrill that would be occasionally offered in one of the foreign languages. In fact, no course other than the foreign languages themselves was ever offered in a foreign language. Thus perished the hope that foreign language could be restored as a significant aspect of undergraduate education—not just as a set of developed skills but as a means of learning more about other cultures and of developing the ability to interact with them.

Each of the residential colleges was also dissatisfied with curriculum requirements. The existing general education courses were not regarded as satisfactory by any of the three residential colleges; they either demanded special sections of these courses or developed their own. Some faculty members in the University College resented and fought this individualism, correctly concluding that if these three colleges could break the long-standing general education requirements applied to all students, it was only a matter of time before such requirements would disappear.

Each college was concerned about the type of students entering its program and the type of faculty attracted to it. Having had the opportunity to note troublesome developments in Morrill, Briggs and Madison defined their programs more specifically. Students and faculty were attracted to the latter programs by the substance and directions specified rather than by the opportunity to "do one's own thing" that seemed to be implicit in the initial lack of specificity in the Morrill plan. The first year of each of the residential colleges was certainly the most interesting, because students and faculty were able to plan that year's program together as well as develop outlines and courses for the future program. Students and faculty joining the program thereafter would never have quite the same experience. Each college had something of a core faculty, but increases in the college enrollment and expansion in courses reinforced the anticipated need for many joint appointments with other departments. These posed some serious financial problems for the residential colleges. The department releasing an individual to teach a course in a residential college was inclined to argue that if a faculty member taught two courses for two quarters and was freed for research the third, then the involvement of that faculty member in two courses in one of the residential colleges called for payment of half salary. Furthermore, such joint appointments were apt to result in a greater flow of faculty through the unit with resulting problems of continuity and sequence. One of the attractions of a faculty member to a residential program was the potential to develop new courses, but late-comers were required to teach existing courses, which lessened their enthusiasm.

Each of the colleges faced problems with regard to facilities planning. Justin Morrill had to alter space in an older residence hall that had far less adaptable space than later ones. The other two residential colleges, coming at a later date, benefited by that earlier experience. They were located in residence halls that had already taken into account the desirability of merging living and learning. In actuality, Lyman Briggs was the only college to benefit from preplanning because it required laboratory space. When putting laboratory space into facilities connected with residence halls, problems such as air pollution, special plumbing, and special controls had to be confronted. It was fortunate that the Briggs faculty had had some prior involvement in the problem through using space contiguous to a residence hall for the Science and Mathematics Teaching Center.

All three colleges created additional costs for the university. Although many of the individuals who had originally discussed the idea of the residential college had viewed the university as having such a wide variety of undergraduate courses that a new unit would require only a few sequential core courses to establish the identity of the college, the faculty and deans in these new units promptly undertook to develop extensive curriculums. By 1969, Justin Morrill College had ninety-five courses, although fifty-four of them were special courses in foreign language. As the foreign language emphasis faded, those courses disappeared but, by 1975, courses numbered sixty-three.

By 1969 Madison College had fifty-three courses, later expanded to sixty with most of these requiring fewer hours in class than credit granted—perhaps because Madison students were expected to do some writing outside of courses and also to engage in extensive independent reading and study.

Briggs offered twenty-two courses in 1969 and these increased to thirty-nine by 1975 and sixty-one by 1983. The Briggs program included a core requirement of ninety-nine credits and specialization in biological, environmental, mathematical, and earth sciences, and in history and philosophy. Madison offered five concentrations: international relations and policy problems, ethnic and religious intergroup problems, and three others dealing with welfare, urban problems, and justice and morality. These colleges, while drawing on other departments and disciplines, tended to require special courses in mathematics, science, language, or philosophy.

Costs were apparently of little concern to the faculty or students in these units. In authorizing these units and the Honors College, the university had recognized the appropriateness of setting up some programs that would cost more than average, just at it had recognized the necessity of establishing special programs for poorly prepared and disadvantaged students. However, the multiplication of offerings in these colleges led to many small classes. Even though the colleges were finally required to open their classes to other students, such classes remained costly, especially at the advanced level.

The residential colleges also suffered from lack of identity in the general community of higher education, even though many other universities in the United States and elsewhere were experimenting with new units and organizations of subject matter. A student enrolled in one of the residential colleges found that few of his or her compatriots at other universities understood the significance of such a learning situation or its relationship to a major in a discipline. Other professional and graduate schools had difficulty interpreting the nature of a residential college student's course of study when such a student applied to transfer. Whereas the director of the Honors College might have ready entree to a deanship of even a presidency at another institution, faculty members staying overlong in an interdisciplinary program such as the University College or in one of the residential colleges might also suffer a loss of identity and find difficulty in returning to a disciplinary department at MSU or in going elsewhere.

All three residential colleges had problems of structure and governance both internally and in respect to the institution as a whole. University committees automatically acquired one or two more members with each residential college. In many cases, the issues of concern to these committees were almost irrelevant to the residential undergraduate colleges. As students were added to university committees, students from the residential colleges again increased in numbers. Within the colleges themselves, students naturally expected a greater voice in requirements because of the size and nature of the program, as did part-time and new faculty members. The original requirement in Madison College for extensive writing was not supported by many newer faculty members, and thus students and faculty conspired to eliminate the requirement. Students who were in the third or fourth year of a program were more likely to support certain "traditional" features of the program that newer students and faculty might wish to modify or eliminate.

When residence hall living ceased to be a requirement for enrollment, many students lived in their "residential" college for only a year or two. The colleges' problems in projecting meaningful identities for themselves caused many students to transfer to majors in one of the other colleges of the university. Eventually it became apparent that the retention rate of students from admission to final degree was significantly lower in the residential colleges than in the traditional units of the university, which came as a surprise to those who had maintained that the close interaction between students and faculty in the smaller residential units would actually increase retention rates within a college. In retrospect, many supporters of the residential college idea began to wonder whether it had been wise to set up independent colleges and whether it might have been more appropriate to identify residential college programs as special programs within existing colleges.

Interpreting such units to the supporting public was and is a difficult job. Why do these colleges exist? What evidence do we have that they provide a different or superior education than other units on campus? Is this a deliberate attempt to attract students that might otherwise go to liberal arts colleges? How can one in a public university justify the obvious additional costs of administration and the higher costs of instruction resulting from small classes? These questions arise within a faculty and administration as well as externally. An attempt was made to shift the Justin Morrill program to one particularly suited to adults and based on competency assessment and carefully planned individual educational experiences. Although an excellent program in theory, it was difficult to carry out and was never seriously considered for continuance after the grant supporting the program was expended. Flexible alternatives to traditional courses and credit requirement were no longer enthusiastically received.

As of fall 1984 Lyman Briggs continues as a program in the College of Natural Science and James Madison continues as a college, but with its own faculty rather than being dependent on part-time or short-term faculty from other colleges.

The experiences of Michigan State University with residential colleges support the conclusion that a faculty may readily agree that living is a prerequisite to learning, but they are also confident that new courses are essential to improve it. New colleges bring unanticipated problems and costs. They are likely to change character with time. They are not easily eliminated.

# 8

# The Development of Graduate Education

A Michigan statute of 1861 empowered the governing board of the State Agricultural College to grant degrees equivalent to those at the University of Michigan. With this authority, the college began to confer a Master of Science degree on graduates who were still actively pursuing "serious scientific study" three years after graduation. This was neither unique nor uncommon at that time. By 1871 there were a few "resident graduates" pursuing study with professors Robert C. Kezdie, Albert J. Cook, William J. Beal, and Manly Miles. Such study was essentially collaboration in laboratory investigation rather than formal graduate study involving requirements, courses, and credits. As Madison Kuhn reported in *Michigan State: The First Hundred Years, 1855–1955* (MSU Press), by 1879 one third of the living alumni who had been out of college for three years or more had received the master's degree. As increasing awareness of the German Ph.D. led all American colleges to reappraise graduate degrees, the requirements for the graduate degree at the college came under review. Rapidly increasing knowledge in the sciences caused some conscientious seekers after knowledge, as well as prospective contributors to it, to seek continuing study with eminent scientists. By 1881, an alternative path to the master's degree involved a year of study at the college, a thesis, and a final examination. A committee on the M.S. degree provided coordination and made all decisions. There was much flexibility in interpreting requirements—for example, the Committee on Advanced Degrees in 1905 declared that the Master of Agriculture could still be granted on the basis of approved practical experience and a thesis.

With formalization of graduate study, the disappearance of the earlier practice of automatic degree granting was inevitable. Graduate study expanded so that in the early 1890s one student of every ten enrolled sought a master's degree. However, not all succeeded, and increasing insistence on one year of full-time study greatly reduced graduate enrollment. For faculty members, graduate study now required unpaid leave.

On May 4, 1908 the faculty approved the recommendation made by the Committee on Advanced Degrees "that the professional engineering degrees, Civil Engineering (C.E.), Mechanical Engineering (M.E.), and Electrical Engineering (E.E.) be conferred upon graduates of the engineering course of this college, or other institutions giving a similar course, only upon completion of a prescribed course of study including the chosen branch of engineering as a major and one of the following subjects as a minor: viz; mathematics, physics, modern languages." It apparently was the intent that this professional "degree" become, in requirements, equivalent to the Master of Science. The action was premature, for granting of experiential professional recognition without formal study continued. The catalog of 1929–30 carried the statement: "Graduates who 'make good' may, under conditions stated elsewhere in this catalog, apply for and receive professional degrees: Ch.E., C.E., E.E., M.E., Met.E." The possibility of award of these professional degrees was continued into the 1950s but was then discontinued as meaningless in comparison with an earned Master of Science degree.

In 1913 a graduate committee was appointed to define and monitor a formal graduate program. In addition, the State Board of Agriculture created half-time graduate assistantships with stipends at about 40 percent of an instructor's salary. The graduate program that developed was especially appropriate for potential or present faculty members of land-grant institutions, including those at Michigan State. The master's degree was to be granted in one of the technical areas: agriculture, forestry, horticulture, veterinary science, engineering, or home economics. It was offered also in six of the natural sciences and in economics. A candidate whose baccalaureate was not in a technical field equivalent to one offered at Michigan State was required to complete one-half of the Michigan State baccalaureate requirement to qualify for admission to the master's program. Although it was expected that this program would revive the postgraduate program of the 1880s and 1890s that had trained applied scientists for the nation's land-grant colleges and experiment stations, it did not do so.

When David Friday arrived as president in March 1922, the graduate program was virtually nonexistent and had only twelve students enrolled. By rule, graduate study by the staff was limited to vacation periods; most of the staff, however, had twelve-month appointments because of extension or Experiment Station duties. Since many staff members desired to acquire the master's degree, the rule was abrogated so that the staff could pursue degrees on a part-time basis. Enrollment increased to 151 by 1925–26 (Kuhn, p. 282). The first M.S. in Home Economics (in nutrition) was granted in 1927.

During Friday's tenure, doctoral programs were authorized in seven departments: bacteriology, botany, chemistry, entomology, horticulture, soils, and farm crops. The first Ph.D.—in botany—granted by the college was to Edward J. Petry in 1925, a reflection of the rapid program expansion, since the Division of Applied Science had only been organized in 1921, and had then, for the first time, offered baccalaureate majors in bacteriology, botany, chemistry, and entomology. In contrast, the Ph.D. was not authorized in home economics until 1933 and first granted in 1947.

President Friday also stimulated development of graduate programs by urging the development and approval of distinct graduate courses, and by obtaining board approval for increasing the number of graduate assistantships from four to twenty-three. Much of the graduate program, however, was informal by modern standards, as evidenced by the graduate offerings in the 1929–30 college catalog (chosen because this was the year in which E.A. Bessey was named the first graduate dean). Of twenty-four departments listing graduate courses, nineteen did not assign credits to them and fifteen listed only five or fewer courses, suggesting that level rather than credit was the motivating factor in listing graduate courses. One department (electrical engineering) indicated that each of its eleven courses was normally offered for four credits. Botany listed but four courses and indicated that the student could enroll in up to fifteen credits per term in each. English, with twelve graduate courses listed, offered three courses of two credits, three courses of four credits, and two courses of five credits. Degree credit requirements were not specified but included a minor of twelve to sixteen credit hours and a major of thirty-two to thirty-six, implying that a minimum residence time of one academic year was equivalent to sixteen hours per quarter, a total of forty-eight credit hours. A thesis was required.

A graduate faculty was named in 1929 that included those actually involved in supervision or carrying out of graduate work. The graduate faculty comprised sixty-two persons, of whom only twenty-four had the Ph.D. A significant number (at least ten) had only a baccalaureate.

In the 1929 catalog statement of graduate degrees, it is also stated that "at the student's option he may elect to become a candidate for one of the following professional degrees [C.E., M.E., E.E., Chem.E., and Met.E.] on the same basis as for the M.S. degree, with the addition that Doctors of Veterinary Medicine may also become candidates for the corresponding professional degree." These professional degrees were also available to nonresident graduates under previously specified conditions and regulations. By the following year, the professional degrees were available only through nonresidence study and were restricted to graduates of the engineering division.

Recalling that the master's degree, when first introduced, was not based on residence at the college and later, in 1881, was made available either by on-campus study or nonresidence study, and, finally, was restricted to formal on-campus study of not less than one year, the professional degree can be viewed as an attempt to recognize the accomplishment of what has come in recent years to be regarded as nontraditional study. Then, as more recently, it was evident that although some individuals could achieve in informal ways the same results achievable by formal, systematic study, the definition and maintenance of standards constituted a formidable, if not an impossible, task. Ultimately (by the mid 1950s) the professional degrees in engineering succumbed to formal master's and doctoral programs in engineering.

## GRADUATE EDUCATION AFTER 1935

In 1935–36, the Ph.D. programs offered were still limited in number. In the physical sciences, only chemistry and physics offered Ph.D. programs. In the biological sciences, the doctorate was still available in bacteriology, botany, entomology, and zoology. Farm crops, soils, and horticulture were approved for doctoral study. In home economics, only the food and nutrition area had received approval. In the social sciences, economics, sociology, and education offered doctoral programs closely related to the still pervasive land-grant origins and orientation. MSC also offered a wide range of master's programs, some of which, as vouched for by students of that day, were very good indeed. Then, as now, disciplinary departments offering a master's program but not offering a doctorate were inclined to give much attention to their master's-level students, to regard them as colleagues, and to involve them in the total range of departmental problems rather than solely in graduate courses. Master's students in some departments had ready entrée to doctoral programs at other institutions. In 1938, a recipient of the Michigan State master's in mathematics seeking the Ph.D. at the University of Michigan was told that although residence credit requirements must be met a dissertation was all that was really necessary to receive the Ph.D. That was not typical at that time. The presence at Michigan State of an internationally known researcher in mathematics made the difference.

Departments not approved for graduate study sought to offer a few courses that might be approved as minors for master's or doctoral study. After attaining recognition as offering a minor for a master's program, departments would then progress to a master's degree in a limited segment of a discipline, to providing a minor cognate for doctoral programs, and ultimately to approval for offering a doctoral degree. Gradually self-imposed restrictions were eliminated. For example, in 1936–37 the restriction that the Ph.D. in farm crops be restricted to plant breeding was dropped. In 1939–40 dairy husbandry and forestry (restricted to wood technology) were added as doctoral programs in the Division of Agriculture. Mathematics was also approved for doctoral work in that same year, although prematurely so considering the mathematics staff of that day. In 1941–42, silviculture (forestry) was added to the Ph.D. roster, and/or the following year, animal pathology and chemical and metallurgical engineering were added. These programs were added despite the onset of World War II, which effectively eliminated further graduate developments for several years. As the war wound down and the institution began to grow, development of graduate programs was again given high priority. President John Hannah strongly favored and supported the growth of graduate study, although he may not have fully recognized the weaknesses that existed in many departments.

In the early days of graduate program development, only a limited number of faculty members were qualified to teach or supervise graduate students, and some of them were minimally qualified by rank and limited research. Teaching loads were heavy and, not infrequently, teaching responsibilities at the graduate level added to that load rather than reducing undergraduate teaching chores. The North Central Association (NCA) of Colleges and Universities which had for some time been concerned with the development of standards that would discriminate among institutions qualified to offer graduate programs, conducted a survey in 1945 that suggested that Michigan State College was barely qualified to offer master's programs at that time. The criteria used involved such factors as percentage of faculty holding the Ph.D., library holdings, publications, and the like. Although some department heads and deans had been concerned with these matters, the financial situation of the college had not really permitted it to seek or acquire faculty members of established research status. Indeed, the college had not infrequently lost individuals whose scholarly development had been fostered there to other institutions that could offer more money. A later 1955 survey of departmental standards conducted by John Zimmer at the request of Dr. Milton Muelder, the dean of science and arts, revealed low admission standards in many departments. This was a long-standing problem.

In 1935, when John Hannah first became involved in college administration, committees were generally few in number and were dominated by administrators. In 1935–36, for example, the Graduate Council, in addition to Graduate Dean Bessey as chairman, had as members two additional deans, four professors, and one associate professor. Actually, that configuration was a considerable improvement in faculty representation in comparison to the 1933–34 council on which there had been six deans, one department chairman, and one associate professor. By 1937–38 the membership of the Graduate Council was exactly the same as in 1935–36 except that the associate professor had been promoted to full professor. It is also illustrative to note that one of the deans (engineering) on the Graduate Council did not possess the doctorate. The membership of the Graduate Council remained unchanged until 1941–42 when the number of deans on the council was reduced to one, the graduate dean. Professor members for the next fifteen years tended also to be assistant deans or department heads.

After Bessey retired in 1943, Dr. Ralph C. Huston, previously dean of the discontinued Division of Applied Science, was appointed graduate dean and continued through 1949. He was succeeded by Dr. Thomas Osgood, who continued also as director of the Division of Applied Science and Mathematics in the School of Arts and Sciences. Attempts by Osgood to define graduate programs more carefully, raise standards, and institute control over them quickly caused difficulties. Departments and schools accustomed to independence resisted both the mode and the substance of the intervention.

Although impossible to verify by existing records, several retired professors recalled that rejections of graduate degree applicants by the graduate dean after they had been accepted by departments and colleges was a critical point, especially when several rejectees completed graduate degrees at a sister university with presumably higher standards and subsequently called on Hannah to report their experiences. Hannah listened and acted. In 1956 the School for Advanced Graduate Studies was described in the college catalog as a "coordinating agency for programs leading to master's degrees, which are administered by the deans of the various colleges." Doctoral programs remained in the School of Advanced Graduate Studies. An effort in that year to rigorously define "graduate faculty" failed to acquire support.

By 1960 the college catalog was emphasizing the functions of the departments, divisions, and colleges in administration of graduate programs, with doctoral programs determined by guidance committees "subject to policies approved by the Graduate Council of the University." Dr. Milton Muelder, vice-president for research development[1] and graduate dean in 1959, vigorously and eloquently supported this approach, asserting that the right of inquiry and review provided adequate basis for maintenance of high scholarly standards. This view apparently assumed that the efforts to improve faculty quality generated by the NCA survey had been successful. Others then and later would disagree and assert that quality concerns and standards continued to be something less than uniformly satisfactory across the university because of the unwillingness or inability of departmental faculties to critically evaluate the performances of their faculty members in accepting students, in planning doctoral programs, and in directing dissertations. There were many who thought that inquiry and review were never entirely successful in identifying or correcting these weaknesses.

The Graduate School and the Graduate Council had been charged, in 1956, with central planning, program implementation, and degree approval at the doctoral level. In 1961–62, however, under the leadership of Dean Muelder, the Graduate Council took on a more representative character through having four ex-officio members, fifteen elected members from the several colleges, and three appointed members. This pattern continued until 1969 when, for the first time, a student member appeared on the Graduate Council. Within the next two years student membership increased from one to three to five, and the Council of Graduate Students appeared in 1970.

From a small group of six to eight people, the Graduate Council had moved during the years of Hannah's involvement in administration to a group of twenty-eight to thirty people, with the elected faculty membership clearly dominating. The role of the Graduate Council has changed little since then, though its position in the committee hierarchy has. Until 1972, the Graduate Council and Academic Council had equal status, each reporting to the provost or president. Originally, this pattern was thought advisable to avoid tampering by the general faculty with graduate school standards. In 1972, in recognition of the improved quality of the general faculty, the Graduate Council began to report through the Academic Council and, in 1978,

---

1. Despite objections from the School of Agriculture and the Experiment Station, Muelder had been designated as director of research development in 1951 while head of the Department of Political Science and Public Administration.

it became a standing committee of the Academic Council. In a sense, the entire faculty now had a say about graduate education. It had taken many years to reach that stage.

President Hannah's tactics in faculty improvement had been successful. He had been greatly troubled by the 1945 NCA survey, which was perhaps the first clear signal to him that problems in faculty composition and graduate program coordination must be resolved if the institution was to move in the directions that he had already discussed with faculty. It was not an auspicious time to launch an alteration in faculty quality. The advent of veterans in large numbers forced faculty expansion at a time when Ph.D.s were in short supply in most disciplines. Furthermore, it was obvious that the college did not have the dollars required to attract outstanding faculty members. Moreover, the immediate need was for faculty in the Basic College.

The initial commitment made in this era of expansion was to seek able young faculty members, to encourage and even support their development, and to rigorously eliminate those who did not demonstrate progress. Extensive involvement of the deans and of the president himself in interviewing and screening of candidates was required. Paid leaves (equivalent in all but name to sabbaticals) were granted to instructors (and occasionally assistant professors) who did not have the doctorate so that they could acquire one as a condition of continued appointment and possible tenure. Previously, individuals employed in the college who had given evidence of interest in their work and had applied themselves dutifully were usually retained and promoted. Department heads, deans, and junior faculty were forced to recognize that those days were gone. After serving for a pretenure period, an individual might be given an additional year to complete a doctorate, but further extensions were unlikely. Given such a policy, the number of individuals who were able to combine a full-time job and successful pursuit of the doctorate (perhaps with a leave or two) was surprising— and, in some ways, disturbing, since some persons acquired doctorates in the department in which they were employed.

The large number of faculty members seeking doctorates brought about some modifications and innovations within the institution. The Doctor of Education (Ed.D.) offered in the College of Education had originally been restricted to individuals with public school experience who expected to return to administrative positions in the public schools. This degree did not require foreign language competency, and it also permitted a practically oriented dissertation rather than the theoretical dissertation of the Ph.D. It was an attractive possibility for mature individuals who had family responsibilities and a full-time job and were also seeking a degree. The Ed.D. came to be used as an alternative to the Ph.D. and was taken by many members of the early Basic College faculty, although the extent of disciplinary content in it was severely limited. The degree remained controversial, but it served a purpose.

The Doctor of Business Administration (D.B.A.) had a history somewhat like that of the Ed.D. Introduced in 1961 as an alternative to the Ph.D. to avoid the foreign language requirements, the degree disappeared after the Ph.D. requirements were modified. Both the Ed.D. and the D.B.A. took a somewhat broader approach to definition of content than the strict disciplinary orientation of the Ph.D.

At Michigan State, graduate education from its origins had included a definite orientation to the practical and hence to a transdisciplinary approach to study and research. The distinction between "purely academic" and "applied" degrees never carried much significance except in the cases of veterinary, human, and osteopathic medicine. When the Ph.D. requirements were liberalized to provide various alternatives to the foreign language requirement, and as the interpretation of the dissertation requirement likewise became more flexible, the use of the Ed.D. and the D.B.A. as Ph.D. alternatives virtually disappeared. Hannah took no position on these developments, although it was always evident that he did not favor nonfunctional requirements imposed by tradition or by maintenance of standards.

Faculty members primarily interested in undergraduate teaching found the rigorous requirement to conduct research in the discipline to be a major obstacle not entirely relevant to their interests or their anticipated teaching careers. Flexible interpretation of the Ph.D. degree in education permitted individuals to take substantial portions of their doctoral work in the teaching discipline and related fields. Furthermore, the education courses for the degree and the dissertation itself could be so modified as to have immediate relevance. Accordingly, the Ph.D. in education, with its emphasis on college teaching, took on the characteristics of what at other institutions was later (1970) called the Doctor of Arts for College Teaching.

Some individuals preferred to seek a Ph.D. in a substantive discipline. Heads of the departments in the Basic College, who were also either department heads or influential members of the various departments of the sciences, social sciences, and humanities, inaugurated discussions that led in 1949 to the introduction of a Ph.D. for college teachers. This degree was developed to provide a broad foundation for prospective college teachers without sacrificing necessary competency in the disciplines. The programs were seen as particularly appropriate for teachers of general education courses, but were also described as excellent preparation for college teaching in the traditional disciplines or specialized areas. The Basic College created a favorable situation for the establishment of programs of graduate study for prospective teachers by combining its teaching facilities and curricular tasks with those of the School of Graduate Studies. Advanced study in broad content areas, a teaching internship in the relevant general education course, and an adequate foundation in a special field were the major factors defining the doctorates in selected disciplines in the three general areas—biological science, physical sciences, and social science.

The Ph.D. for college teachers was hailed as an innovation, but it was not successful for two reasons. First, the degree, as designed, could be regarded as the traditional Ph.D. in a discipline *plus* an internship in the Basic College. For individuals interested in college teaching but not involved in the Basic College, the degree added an additional requirement, more time, and double jeopardy. Second, the internship requirements included stringent evaluation, perhaps by close colleagues, of those teaching in addition to the evaluation already required for promotion and salary increases in the Basic College departments. Although few, if any, persons sought or acquired the degree (existing records show no such degree recipients), the degree itself lingered on for a number of years in various formal statements within the catalog. About 1970, the Ph.D. for college teachers apparently disappeared through lack of use rather than by formal action. Nevertheless its formulation and acceptance was symptomatic of the widespread concern for the quality of undergraduate teaching at that date.

The number of Michigan State faculty members with degrees from Michigan State became an issue. During the institution's rapid growth, no concern was voiced about such inbreeding. Its potential for deteriorating quality was outweighed by the shortages of qualified faculty nationally. Since many of the faculty members involved had experienced mid-career excursions into military service that had slowed or altered their career plans, the university was disposed to be helpful and even lenient toward their degree pursuits. Furthermore, despite the rapid increase in the faculty numbers, deans and department chairmen, urged by the president, had made every effort to seek out individuals of ability and promise. On the whole, there was no disposition to believe that graduate degree standards had been compromised by the extensive enrollment of junior faculty in the degree programs of the college. Indeed, not infrequently, doctoral advisers and committees found some of these candidates imposing on themselves requirements not specified by rules or committees.

By 1960 the college had become a university in name as well as in fact, and the Graduate Council and graduate dean asserted that "a faculty member with the rank of assistant professor or higher may not earn an advanced degree from Michigan State University. He may, however, enroll for graduate study on a non-degree basis." It was a wise and timely move corresponding to a new policy to require the Ph.D. for appointment as assistant professor. By 1974–75, instructors in the tenure track were also barred from pursuing the doctorate at Michigan State. Faculty members, however, were permitted to pursue a master's degree program in another discipline or do work on a nondegree basis. The expanding interest in interdisciplinary studies led numerous faculty members to seek a master's degree in a field of interest relevant to their research or teaching.

Following the policies stated in 1956, master's programs of study were administered by the major department or division, subject to approval by the dean of the college. All-university requirements had been adopted and master's programs remained subject to policies approved by the Graduate Council with the possibility of review whenever that seemed desirable. By 1960–61, the master's degrees offered included Master of Arts, Master of Arts for Teachers, Master of Music, Master of Science, Master of Business Administration, Master of Fine Arts, Master of Landscape Architecture, Master of Social Work, and Master of Urban Planning. The last five degrees required credits beyond the minimum of forty-five. The Master of Fine Arts, at that time regarded as the terminal degree, required ninety credits.

In an effort to assure and maintain quality in all graduate programs, the Graduate Council spelled out program types with respect to course work and research, minors, collateral courses, examination standards, transfer credit, language, residence requirements, and the role and composition of the guidance committee. The development of these criteria did not necessarily reflect a concern about the low standards in the past but simply recognized that, with increasing numbers of graduate students and graduate faculty, some specific statements were required both to give guidance to graduate committees and to provide bases for review and enforcement by the Graduate Council and the graduate dean. Master's degrees, however, were becoming routinized, and, because many departments offered a nonthesis alternative, they became little more than another year of education beyond the baccalaureate. Attention and concern about graduate education had shifted to the doctorate.

### FOREIGN LANGUAGE AND STATISTICS

Consonant with widespread concern about competence in a foreign language, requirements for graduate students were spelled out in detail in 1960–61 in a manner that recognized the increasing number of foreign students seeking graduate study at Michigan State and the necessity for some flexibility. The former requirement of a reading knowledge of two languages (French, German, or Russian) was altered to include a reading knowledge of two languages in addition to those in which the student had been educated. Germanic, Romance, Slavic, Classical, and Oriental languages were indicated as appropriate. If two languages were selected from one of these groups, the student was expected to demonstrate speaking as well as reading proficiency in one of them. Another alternative permitted reading knowledge in one foreign language plus a program of study totaling not less than twelve credits directed to broadening the student's cultural, scholarly, and scientific background through courses not related to the major or minor fields. Alternatively, the twelve credits might be directed to development of the student beyond normal proficiency in areas related to major or minor fields. Statistics and computer technology shortly became specific alternatives under this second category. As another liberalization, foreign language examinations passed at another institution were accepted toward the requirement subject to the approval of the foreign language supervisor of the MSU Graduate School. Yet a fifth alternative was to complete a second year of a foreign language with a grade of B within two years before admission to a doctoral program. These changes took place only after much concerned discussion about precedents and standards. The enthusiastic embrace of innovation was now tinged with concern about reputation.

The Diploma for Advanced Graduate Study (DAGS) appeared in 1960. Approved by the Academic Senate in 1959, it offered planned graduate programs beyond the master's level that provided a unified sequence of graduate study for persons who desired proficiency beyond the level of the master's degree in their field but did not necessarily plan to obtain a doctoral degree. The programs included essentially the same course work and comprehensive examinations required of doctoral students but did not require a dissertation. Admission and grade requirements were the same as for doctoral students. One foreign language (or, in education, statistics) was required. The DAGS was available in Science and Arts and in Education. Curiously, a similar degree, Ed.S. (educational specialist), did not appear in education until 1967. The DAGS was a response to the needs of community college faculty and, to some extent, of individuals preferring to teach at the undergraduate level who desired to avoid the research requirement. It recognized the "all-but-dissertation" type of education as a legitimate and useful aspiration and provided what was later designated by some other universities as an M.Phil., or a Candidate Degree. The educational specialist program was designed for persons who wished to achieve, by a planned program of graduate study, proficiency beyond the level of the master's degree but not necessarily at the doctoral level. The program consisted of two full years or ninety term credits of graduate study beyond the bachelor's degree. Both the DAGS and the Ed.S. were regarded as terminal degrees, although the educational specialist program emphasized a more practical approach in response to state legislation specifying requirements for certification of public school teachers in curriculum, evaluation, counseling, and other skills at a level beyond the master's degree. Both of these intermediate degrees have continued to serve a small but significant group of individuals, primarily teachers in secondary schools.

Both programs have posed certain not entirely resolvable problems. Though designated as degrees at Michigan State, they have elsewhere been regarded as certificate programs. Neither degree was to be used as an "all but dissertation," but some such instances have occurred. Although it was not anticipated that many Ed.S. or DAGS recipients would continue or return to seek a Ph.D., since their degrees were defined as practical rather than research in nature, they could do so with the understanding that their current degrees were not in sequence and that not all prior work might be accepted at the doctoral level. The relation of these degrees to the master's also turned out to be uncertain and has depended on both individual circumstances and departmental views. Neither "degree" has lived up to its expectations, perhaps because the faculty orientation was moving further from the service orientation to attention to research and the Ph.D. programs.

## GRADUATE DEGREES CONFERRED

Four master's degrees were granted in 1882–83, and one or more (with a high of seven in 1893–94) were granted each year through 1910. By 1910, a total of 79 master's degrees had been granted—fewer than three per year in 28 years. During the same period, a total of 1,314 degrees (baccalaureate and master's) were awarded, of which 6 percent were master's. No master's degrees were granted in 1910–11 or 1911–12 but 30 were granted in 1912–13. Thereafter, one or more were granted each year with gradual increments bringing the number granted in 1932–33 to 91 and in 1968–69 to 2,572.

The first Ph.D. was granted in 1925. By 1935, a total of 62 Ph.D.s had been granted, with 14 being the maximum in any one year (1934–35). In 1952, the number granted (136) exceeded 100 for the first time. In 1969–70, a total of 676 Ph.D.s were granted.

The Diploma for Advanced Graduate Study, authorized in 1959, was first granted in 1960–61 and was most productive in 1964–65 (54), and in 1965–66 (24). It has continued to be awarded to a few individuals each year, reaching a total of 174 by 1982–83. The Educational Specialist (Ed.S.) first appeared in 1965–66 and has been awarded to between 40 and 60 students per year, reaching a total of 856 by 1983. Since 1969, the total of graduate degrees granted has exceeded 10,000. In 1982–83 degree totals since the founding of the college were:

| | |
|---|---:|
| Baccalaureate | 195,521 |
| Master's | 56,583 |
| Ph.D., Ed.D., & DBA | 12,298 |
| DAGS | 174 |
| Ed.S. | 856 |
| DVM | 3,627 |
| M.D. | 968 |
| D.O. | 813 |
| Total | 270,840 |

As the graduate program grew, many changes came about. In the early 1930s, a department of fifteen professors and instructors could absorb three or four graduate assistants and regard them as junior faculty, with office space and prerogatives not markedly different from those of the full-time faculty. In the post-Hannah 1980s, the same department might have nearly 200 names on the roster, with half of them graduate teaching assistants carrying much of the instructional burden for freshman and sophomore courses. Not infrequently, lack of adequate mastery of English by a teaching assistant was a problem for the students.

In 1932, the graduate student was charged a course fee of $10 and out-of-state tuition of $15 per quarter. The course fee for undergraduates was $32.50, with out-of-state tuition an additional $15. By 1969, regular fees for graduate students were $194 and for undergraduates $184. Additional out-of-state fees were $430 and $420. A doctoral student by 1959 paid a $504 dissertation research fee and, if he or she were going to be using campus research facilities, an additional $54 per term for 0 credits. If not using campus facilities (there was no good check), but using faculty for guidance, the doctoral students paid nothing for as long as it took to finish the dissertation. In time, the differentials between costs of graduate and undergraduate education increased. The university, having asked the legislature for increased funds because of the high cost of graduate education was, in turn, pressured to reflect this in increasing charges to graduate students. Differential charges related to program costs represented a threat to freedom of program choice. Hannah opposed differential charges, but some differential had to be introduced for graduate and medical students. The issue would continue to arise in later years.

Graduate teaching assistantships, graduate research assistantships, graduate tuition grants, and graduate office scholarships were expanded, often from research grants and contracts. Fellowships and tuition scholarships requiring no formal service also became available, thereby easing, for some graduate students, the burden of increasing charges. Exemption from out-of-state tuition became a significant cost factor, and the protocol for determining state residence and change in it expanded gradually to take up nearly a page and a half in the college catalog.

Both office space and living quarters for graduate students became sparse. Departments with large numbers of graduate assistants and other graduate students could assign only a desk, perhaps for specific hours, rather than an office to these students. Married student housing that had been provided for veterans of World War II was used for the many married graduate students. Housing space was still an important factor in attracting graduate students as a result of Emory Foster's meetings with the Graduate Council. In 1959, Dean Muelder had been able to announce special housing for graduate women students in Mary Mayo Hall and for men in Armstrong Hall. In an innovative move, graduate women were provided with keys and under no restrictions.

Owen Graduate Hall, completed in 1960 and expanded in 1965, provided the first really adequate housing for single graduate students. Two seven-story wings provided 422 double rooms with lounge, dining rooms, laundry, baggage storage, and office space.

Graduate students were still prized in 1969 and later, but as their numbers increased and programs proliferated, there was a trend toward loss of individualization.

### SUMMARY AND CRITICAL COMMENTARY

In the development of graduate education at Michigan State aspiration, at times, exceeded academic stature—a not uncommon characteristic in colleges and universities. The State Board of Agriculture approved on December 16, 1925, a faculty committee recommendation that the Department of Education, along with those of Economics and Sociology, be authorized to offer work leading to the Ph.D. degree. Although these degrees, like the degrees in the sciences and the departments of agriculture, were undoubtedly then viewed as based in agriculture and rural problems, the college was hardly ready to launch quality programs in these disciplines. In fact, the first doctorate in education was not awarded until 1947, demonstrating remarkable and appropriate restraint. The year 1947 was significant in that graduate enrollment reached 1,004. In that year also, master's programs in various foreign languages were approved, signaling a move into graduate programs in disciplines not necessarily part of a land-grant commitment.

In the rapid development of graduate programs, there were some difficult moments. Disciplines and departments that were admitted to offer graduate programs largely because of their strengths in interactions with agriculture, home economics, and veterinary medicine, were soon offering much broader programs. When steps were taken by Thomas Osgood, who became dean of the Graduate School in 1950, to establish policies, exert controls, and enforce standards, the resistance of departments and colleges, supported by the president, resulted in the replacement of the graduate school by a School of Advanced Graduate Studies. The factors in this change were threefold. Graduate committees, departments, and colleges were simply not accustomed to having their decisions scrutinized. When their decisions about admissions requirements and procedures were not only questioned but rejected, they found such actions simply unacceptable. With the creation of the School for Advanced Graduate Studies, responsibility for master's degree programs and requirements was vested in the major department (or division) subject to approval by the dean of the college.

The School for Advanced Graduate Studies retained a coordinating role which, in fact, quickly became virtually meaningless simply because of numbers and varieties of master's degrees. At Michigan State, as elsewhere, the master's degree in many disciplines was becoming little more than a fifth year of study. Faculty tended to focus their attention on the Ph.D.

On May 12, 1959, Dean Milton Muelder announced that the Graduate Council and dean of the Graduate School "will exercise the right of inquiry and review." The memorandum was explicit in placing responsibility on the faculty. For some time the system of inquiry and review was systematic and regular. Alan Tucker, assistant to Dean Muelder, maintained a complete file of departmental statements describing in detail the requirements for graduate study as developed by the departments and approved by the respective deans. Each quarter a printout was prepared listing each of the graduate students in each department, the date of admission, credits earned, grade point average for each term, date of qualifying exam, dates of language examinations, and so on. Each entry not consistent with the department's stated standard was marked in red. Such discrepancies were repeatedly checked until action was taken. Departments and professors tend to be remiss about stringent actions, preferring to leave them to others, and after Tucker left the system of inquiry and review became somewhat irregular.

Although Dean Muelder repeatedly and persuasively asserted the power of inquiry and review as a means to control the quality of graduate programs, effective use of inquiry and review must either be systematized and regularly conducted or foregone entirely. The occasional exertions of such power only upon the appearance of laxity become highly emotional events. Unless information and data on procedures and operations are regularly collected, there is no adequate basis for conducting a meaningful review. Furthermore, effective inquiry and review requires staff, and President Hannah, wisely and even necessarily, in view of rapid growth and financial strain, preferred a lean administrative staff.

When departments are essentially autonomous in controlling graduate programs, the criteria for membership on doctoral graduate committees and for chairing committees or directing dissertations tend to be lacking. Lacking formal requirements and procedures for recognition of graduate faculty status, it becomes difficult to assure that individual graduate programs are developed, monitored, and completed with due attention to standards, task requirements, and equity to the individual in time and supervision given. The potential for long-term peonage to a major professor and the difficulties attendant on individual student's efforts to appeal inequities or neglect continue to bring into question the decentralization of graduate program authority to the extent evident at Michigan State—and elsewhere.

On the other hand, when professors of ability and integrity are truly interested in their students and are fully responsible for graduate programs, flexibility has its advantages. Formal departmentally developed and graded preliminary examinations can be detrimental to individual programs and student development by forcing detailed study and review of inconsequential details. Specific credit requirements can enforce time serving and credit accumulation and displace the joy of intense accumulative scholarly effort. The inclusion in a graduate program of appropriate courses from other disciplines or the conscious development of a dissertation with practical implications for undergraduate teaching are not threats to quality, but can be so interpreted when rigid rules and procedures are insistently applied to every graduate student, every professor, and every committee.

Michigan State, like many other institutions, may have erred in misreading the departmental disciplinary concentration of the Ph.D. as requiring departmental and professional autonomy, when, in fact, the potential for variation in requirements and standards at the departmental and professorial level required (at least in the early stages) strong and continuous direction and reasonable means for enforcing it—both for the integrity of the institution and the fulfillment of the obligations to individual study and society. At Michigan State, the increasing strength and maturity in the departments gradually overcame most of the developmental problems and weaknesses. And, as of 1985, there is still a graduate dean, a position that has disappeared in many institutions.

# 9
# The Changing Character of Research

From its beginnings, the faculty of the Michigan Agricultural College was concerned with research although, for many years, the approach was one of experimentation by trial and error rather than of scientific research, for which both equipment and method were lacking in the United States. In its earliest stages research emphasis was on increasing productivity of crops and of various animals: horses (work and transportation power), cows (milk, butter, meat, and leather), sheep (wool and meat), pigs (lard, meat, leather), fowl (eggs, meat, and feathers or down). Productivity dependent on animals required, among other things, keeping them healthy. Even the cats and dogs, which later would be regarded primarily as pets by their owners (and a nuisance by others) were, in the nineteenth century, expected to serve such utilitarian purposes as guarding or driving animals and controlling pests. Until replaced by the automobile and the tractor, the horse was the major focus of veterinary medicine, although the health and productivity of cows, goats, sheep, pigs, rabbits, and fowl also received attention. Forests, cultivated bushes, and vines provided fuel, construction materials, animal shelters, and game areas as well as fruits, nuts, flavors, syrup, and medicines. Studies of soils and research on improvement of crops and forage also promoted productivity.

By the 1900s, extension and research activities were expanding to include farm and rural living with specific attention to food processing and preservation, nutrition, health, child rearing, and clothing. Aesthetic and humanistic concerns became evident in respect to beauty and convenience in the home and its furnishings. Music, religion, human aspirations, and emotions were viewed as needs to which the Extension Service should contribute, although hygienic human waste disposal was also regarded as a fundamental need worthy of attention.

In the 1920s, as exporting to Europe declined after World War I, problems of surpluses were replacing those of deficiency. Concentration on production was superseded by attention to marketing, distribution, pricing, and to seeking new crops or attaining better quality in existing ones.

Such changes created three major problems. First, individuals already in extension and research did not readily adjust to the changes. Distribution and pricing required different training and experience than increasing productivity. Faced with the long-run increase in production as well as the economic survival of farmers, a planned decrease in productivity was neither an immediate nor a long-term solution. Second, increased mechanization and greater profits of large-scale operations resulted in consolidation of farms. Mechanical improvements in distribution of weed killers and pesticides, as well as in planting and harvesting, increased efficiency and required less manpower. During the 1950s farm output increased slightly more than 25 percent, while farm population decreased by a little less than 25 percent. Concomitantly, growth of jobs in manufacturing, service industries, and government attracted many former farm workers to cities. Rural progress contributed to urban problems that fifty years later are not yet resolved. Finally, the complicated and far-reaching nature of these changes made them political issues of major importance. Views and values about their ultimate resolution have continued to differ markedly. Proposed and often controversial solutions to problems bred still other problems. Human reactions to the most rigorous and objective scientific research findings are often highly subjective depending upon who pays, who benefits, and who decides.

Before 1930, almost all research done at Michigan State was supported by the Experiment Station and directed to quick resolution of practical problems. Agriculture, veterinary medicine, home economics, and engineering dominated the research programs, while the natural sciences and social sciences contributed concepts and developed research methodologies. Heavy teaching loads, lack of funds, and the emphasis on teaching, advising, and service militated against disciplinary research. Research Ph.D. faculty were not yet present in numbers.

An altered vision of the future of the institution after World War II, in part a response to a broader range of federal support, made it evident that research must be encouraged and supported throughout the college. The first step was the establishment, at President John Hannah's recommendation, of an All College Research Committee by the State Board of Agriculture in June 1945. The committee was charged with encouraging and assisting the development of research in *all* departments and divisions. Committee membership was significant and included the division deans, the dean of the School of Graduate Studies, and the director of the Agricultural Experiment Station. The dean of agriculture was named chairman—a wise choice in view of the institution's traditions. The committee agreed immediately that its functions should center on policy and program matters. Administrative matters were to be handled by the chairman. Thus the continuing priority of agriculture in research seemed assured.

Although to many faculty members outside the School of Agriculture, this committee seemed to be a step forward, it was not welcomed by all. Some viewed the action as a deemphasis of teaching and public service. Hannah saw it as a necessary step to improve both.

The staff of the Agricultural Experiment Station was threatened. Its director pointed out that 90 or 95 percent of the on-going research at Michigan State was supported by funds from the Experiment Station. He feared that expanded research activities would mean a sharing of resources which, up to this time, had been restricted to agriculture. The idea of another research group was also repugnant (and even illegal) as far as the Experiment Station staff was concerned. They noted that the station's existence was authorized by the Hatch Act of 1887, which, in providing for their establishment, had stipulated that "these are not over-all miscellaneous research institutions; they are *Agricultural Experiment Stations.*" The Hatch Act stipulated that the Agricultural Experiment Station was to be *a department of the College of Agriculture.* The station staff concluded that any research work to be conducted with the support of federal funds appropriated by the Experiment Station must be under the auspices of the School of Agriculture and the director of the Experiment Station.

Implicit in this resistance to the All College Research Committee (even though chaired by the dean of agriculture) was the view that agriculture should remain the major and central focus of all research, and hence all research funds should be channeled through the Experiment Station. Consonant with this concept was a proposal that an assistant (or associate) director be appointed to the Experiment Station to encourage and assist the faculty of each of the schools in developing research proposals and submitting them for support. The Experiment Station staff and its director asserted that this approach would facilitate interdisciplinary problem-oriented research, but would ensure that research and extension in all departments and disciplines would be related to agriculture—the crucial issue upon which the future character of the land-grant college depended.

A decision that the new committee would refrain from intervening in Experiment Station programs or funds somewhat eased the strain.

Its primary responsibility would be to administer an *annual appropriation from current expenditures* of the college in the form of grants-in-aid to faculty members requesting them. At the outset the program received modest funding. From 1946 to 1951, the committee's budget was $10,000 per year. This was increased from $15,000 in the years 1952–54 and to $25,000 in 1955. A new policy in support of research had been established. Obviously there were severe limits on the extent to which current operating funds could be drawn upon to support research.

In 1951 Dr. Milton Muelder was appointed director of Research Development (reporting directly to President Hannah) with the charge to seek and assist others in seeking funds for research. The committee had proposed such efforts, but it was not in a position to seek funds or counsel others to do so. Meantime the faculties in the several original land-grant units agreed to refrain from seeking grants from the All College Research Committee. The natural sciences, which had access to other sources of funding, also exercised some restraint.

The committee and director Muelder struck up an effective working relationship. Muelder's efforts, however, were limited by the scope of his responsibilities, which included serving as head of the Department of Political Science and Public Service. Nevertheless, the implications were clear: research was to be encouraged throughout the institution using funds obtained from a variety of sources.

In 1955, a study commissioned by Vice President Thomas Hamilton of the effectiveness and accomplishments of the All College Research Program during its nine-year existence provided some interesting insights and better understanding of the implications of the grants. Most of the grants had gone into the support of "research," as commonly perceived, but the program was broadly interpreted. Funds had been made available to train a faculty member to use an electron microscope, to pay the expense of a prominent scholar to come to the campus, to assist musicians to write scores, and to help artists create works. In short, the program aided and encouraged "creative activity."

Tabulation of research grants by departments and schools indicated that, as anticipated, the School of Science and Arts (261), the Basic College (157), and the School of Education (84) had received the larger number of grants. The awards to disciplinary groups were:

| | |
|---|---|
| Natural sciences | 167 |
| Social sciences | 158 |
| Humanities | 96 |

The departments taking most advantage of the grants were:

| | |
|---|---|
| History and folklore | 76 |
| Natural science (Basic College) | 50 |
| English | 48 |
| Botany | 34 |

The grant program had been especially advantageous for Basic College faculty members working toward the doctorate in education and engaging in a dissertation project related to their department. There were 84 research projects on educational problems. Half were the dissertations of Basic College faculty members. One-third of the research projects were directly related to a concern or problem of Michigan people: agriculture (43 projects); industry (14); social, economic, political problems (20); Michigan history and folklore (9); and education (84). Clearly the long-time land-grant service orientation still played a dominant role in these research projects.

Analysis of the views and experiences of those receiving grants were also instructive.

- The typical or average grantee was a junior faculty member (instructor, assistant professor) in his or her mid thirties.
- The grants were relatively small ($200–$300), but proved essential both in motivation and support.
- Excessive teaching loads interfered with research and resulted in about 20 percent of the grants made going unexpended.
- Many grantees spent considerable additional personal funds for travel and maintenance in research-related traveling.
- Many grantees emphasized that their research contributed to the improvement of their teaching.
- Scholars in the humanities (English especially) were particularly appreciative of the grant funds since no prior support of research had been available to them.

Presumably the Hamilton report had a significant impact. In the next year (1956) the allocation for the All University Research Grants jumped from $25,000 to $75,000. By the year 1969, in which Hannah retired, the annual grant budget had increased to more than $212,000. More than 500 grants were made; a few were over $1,000. The grants were small even at that date. Retrospectively they seem insignificant, but their impact on the faculty was profound. Both scholarly research and educational or institutional research became expectations in all of the academic units of the institution. Recognition for research depended upon deans and departmental chairs, and the availability of funds gave the administrator an additional basis for urging faculty research.

In 1959, when Muelder became vice-president for research and development and dean of the School of Advanced Graduate Study, the committee was attached to that office with Muelder as chairman. The grant precedent established by that committee had markedly influenced the development of educational and institutional research across the campus, especially in the social sciences and humanities, as funds became available from federal and foundation sources. In 1959, the Office of Institutional Research was created, reporting to the provost and to the president. That office was provided with some funds to support institutional research studies by faculty members and departments.

From very small beginnings indeed, research had spread to become a way of life in scholarship, problem solving, and decision making in the university.

## Unanticipated Results of Research

Many problems that had been studied early in the land-grant institution continued to be studied at increasingly complex levels, and the attendant circumstances had changed as well. Small-scale trial-and-error solutions that were momentarily effective could, when applied on a larger scale over time, create new and more complex problems.

The unanticipated side and residual effects of large-scale (sometimes in excessive amounts) distribution of fertilizer, weed killers, and pesticides on the environment, on people, on domestic animals, and on wildlife soon brought realization that attempts to increase efficiency and productivity by this route were limited. Attempts to *eliminate* pests and weeds soon brought genetically altered pests and weeds that were immune to the treatments. Meanwhile the chemicals dispersed could start a long-term chain of events affecting soils, soil organisms, insects, birds, animals, and people. Drainage of chemicals into nearby streams created an alphabet soup of PCB, DDT, PBB, and DDE destructive of all life.

Through carefully controlled feeding and management animals became feed processors to produce food. Modern animal agriculture for meat production took on many of the aspects of an assembly line. Light, temperature, and the availability of food and water could be controlled to modify animal behavior. By improved packaging, storage, and distribution facilities, foodstuffs can today be made available in prime condition independent of season, weather, and climate. Collection, treatments, and storage procedures also contribute to taste enhancement, attractive appearance and texture, uniformity in size, increased nutritive value, and tenderness. But the animal feed, including additives that improve efficiency of meat production, may leave unhealthy residues in the food we eat.

The undesirable long-term chains of events affecting soils, people, or animals have forced a change in objectives. The concepts of resistance to and balance among the many destructive and beneficial impacts of various factors necessarily replaced the concept of elimination. For example, pest management, which involves the development of both plant resistance and the balancing of beneficial and destructive factors, has replaced the former optimistic but vain hopes of pest eradication.

The realization that fortuitous genetic modification could defeat pest eradication opened the door to the development of improved species through genetic modification by design. By separating genetic traits and multiplying them in bacteria or by replacing one chromosome with another, new plants can be created almost to order. Thus resistance to disease, insects, weeds, and cold can be attained and so can greater efficiency in use of water and fertilizer.

Research became an important activity for industry as firms sought to improve product quality and increase sales—always to the end of maintaining or increasing profits in competitive markets. However, business and industrial research directed to increase profit and research carried on in the tradition of academic freedom differed markedly in practicality and secrecy. Hence some early expectations that business and industry might support academic research were doomed to disappointment. Governmental support of Experiment Station research and extension work had been effective because interference had been minimal. Hence, when the "cold war" following World War II engendered extensive funds and opportunities for sponsored research, they were quickly seized upon by Michigan State and its increasing numbers of young Ph.D.s.

Although Michigan State was not a major research university that easily attracted research grants and contracts, with President Hannah's urging and his contacts and involvements with the federal government the institution moved rapidly to establish its credibility and performance in various research areas. By 1955, Michigan State was receiving funds from the National Science Foundation (NSF), the Atomic Energy Commmission (AEC), and the National Institutes of Health (NIH). Encouraged by Hannah, the Department of Physics began to move into nuclear science in 1950, and a cyclotron became a goal in 1957. With assistance from the Atomic Energy Commission, now the U.S. Department of Energy or DOE, the MSU/DOE Plant Research Laboratory was created in 1964 to conduct basic research on the biology of plant cells and tissues. The Pesticide Research Center, funded by a combination of state and federal dollars, appeared in 1968.

When the National Science Foundation program of grants for development of Centers of Excellence in Science became available, Michigan State immediately formed a university-wide committee to develop a proposal. Initial discussions leaned toward the inclusion of all sciences, natural and social. When it became apparent that the grant ($4.037 million) would not support an advance to excellence across the university, the proposal was directed to strengthening the departments and research programs in chemistry, physics, and mathematics. The grant was received, and in 1972 was supplemented with another award of $1.8 million.

The wisdom of the narrower focus became apparent later as the credibility of the work in nuclear high-energy physics paved the way to procuring federal funding for a cyclotron laboratory equipped with a large superconducting heavy ion accelerator. The 1979 award of the National Superconducting Cyclotron Laboratory grant to MSU brought to fruition efforts that had been initiated in 1950.

From 1955 to 1965, federal dollars at MSU increased to $15.7 million and by 1969 to nearly $30 million, nearly a four-fold increase in less than ten years. This rapid increase in funds brought problems as well as benefits both nationally and locally.

Successive vice-presidents for research at Michigan State, Milton Muelder and John Cantlon, reported little response from the humanities faculties to encouragement in seeking grants. There was a disinclination to develop projects in sufficient detail and with sufficiently widespread implications to attain support. Proposal writing itself appeared to be distasteful. The success of the All-University Research Fund in the humanities area indicated that for many humanities faculty members research emphases were highly individual and required only limited support.

As with research in the natural sciences, the question arises whether humanists, artists, musicians, and social scientists should be supported in doing what they individually prefer to do or whether projects that promise benefits for laypeople and the nation should be supported instead. Although the social sciences, specifically sociology and economics, and their applications (home economics) in rural life appeared early in the service and research program at Michigan State, research support was much less readily available for them than for the natural sciences and continued to be so even when natural science research vastly increased.

Research in the social sciences presents far different problems than that in the physical and biological sciences. Social science deals with the behavior, values, and motivation of individuals and collections of individuals. Each individual and each group possesses some capacity for setting and seeking personal and social goals. Group behavior is, under some circumstances (and with some error), predictable and predeterminable even in a democratic society. Behavior of each individual is not, except as restraints or incentives are imposed and enforced. Indeed, heterogeneity and individualism are often prized, although homogeneity and conformity are desirable in some circumstances. Conflict resolution takes up considerable energy and resources, and social scientists are in conflict about how to accomplish it.

Repeated attempts of social scientists to attain a separate foundation for support of the social sciences have not been successful. The National Science Foundation has maintained a separate division for the social sciences which has, at various times, identified several areas for support including social indicators research; municipal systems, operations, and service research; criminology; social data and community studies research; and evaluation methodologies for social programs. A quantitative approach is apparent in several of these areas, but the use of statistical analysis has not been regarded as a necessary part of a research project. Indeed the early confidence that sophisticated statistical analyses would provide social science research with the rigor of the physical sciences has been proved an illusion. What emerges from statistical analyses are generalizations, typologies, and methodologies that increase the complexities of relating fundamental social policies to individual differences. Mainstreaming of the handicapped in our schools, though desirable for some, may inflict upon teachers and other students inappropriate limitations. Deinstitutionalization of the mentally disturbed or deficient as an antidote to inappropriate institutionalization is not evidently a greater good for all.

The role of the social sciences in contributing to individualization and democratic socialization is still uncertain. Any proposal for public action emanating from social science research is always based on values not equally shared by all individuals. Social policies are always value-based and therefore subject to political resolution or radical action by constituencies of various persuasions and alliances. In their recognition and documentation of group and individual differences and in their analysis of processes and networks whereby action is attempted to achieve individual or group goals, the social sciences make their greatest contribution. In attempting to provide or become proponents for generalizations supporting a particular value-based choice to alleviate or resolve social problems, the social sciences may undo their more significant contribution to national, society, and personal development. The social sciences as sciences can provide data, analyses, and criteria for better understanding and strategy and tactics of human problem solution and methodology for evaluation and modification of proposed solutions. The most rigorous analyses and recommendations of academic social scientists cannot replace the political processes that must remain our societal value-balancing mechanism. The insight generated by social science research is often only a better understanding of why a problem is not readily resolvable. That understanding may change the problem.

### DIRECT AND INDIRECT COSTS OF SPONSORED PROGRAMS

Until after World War II, most institutionally sponsored research on the MSU campus was related to agriculture or to veterinary medicine and was supported in part by Experiment Station funds, which paid the salary of research professors, made allocations to project accounts in their departments, or made available research stations and other facilities. Most research, such as that on undulant fever in dairy cows, grew out of problems identified by the agricultural enterprise. The few gifts or grants to the college for research assistance were limited in amounts ($100, $500, etc.) and directed to particular problems and professors. Professor Harrison Hunt's long-time research on dental caries on rats was supported regularly at this level. Such funds went largely to pay for student assistance, travel, typing, and so on. External gifts and grants were regarded as expediting research that an individual would have undertaken anyway. Indirect costs or overhead, not yet fully recognized as such, were absorbed by the institution.

Research other than that in or related to agriculture was not directly supported. In 1932, V.G. Grove, the one mathematics professor who was doing research, had a twelve-credit teaching course schedule (three or four classes) compared with fifteen or sixteen credits for others. So tight was the budget that the use of writing materials such as "faculty pads" was restricted. Since Professor Grove's research required much calculation, he and his graduate students procured and used the backs of the discarded, not reprocessed, engineering drawings. Research today requires more extensive, sophisticated, and expensive equipment which, unfortunately, is seldom used efficiently. Indeed, for creative fundamental research, availability of equipment can be more important than creativity.

As demands and opportunities for research and support of it increased, grants and contracts had to cover labor, supplies, special equipment and services, and travel. Since the instructional burden and other chores had to continue, partial defrayment of faculty salary was required in some cases. Eventually it became evident that space requirements, library usage, general administration, departmental administration, contract administration, utilities, plant operations, and maintenance were also significant and always-increasing charges that the institution could not absorb and that the state legislature would not knowingly support. Direct costs—salaries and benefits, permanent equipment, expendable equipment, supplies, computer services, travel, and publication—were relatively easy to estimate and include in research support requests, since they could be directly related to project activities and requirements. Indirect costs—departmental administration, general administration, contract administration, accounting services, purchasing services, library expenditures and services, and plant operation and services—involved activities and services for the entire institution and were more difficult to determine. They were approximated either as a standard percentage of total costs added to the request or as a percentage of salaries and wages. Indirect costs or overhead, starting at 15 percent in some early contracts, rose to 40–60 percent of salaries in later ones.

Negotiation of indirect costs caused difficulties with both the external contracting agencies and institutional departments. Inflation assured that indirect costs would increase, but more extensive federal government regulations and requirements imposed additional costs. Institutions also became more adept at inclusiveness and, encouraged by the apparent success of several prestigious research universities, tended always to increase the indirect cost rates. Departments and faculty researchers became concerned that this might decrease the number of grants and encourage awards to institutions with lower rates. External agencies regularly questioned an institution's proposed indirect cost rate, especially when they saw new buildings arise, paid for by recovered overhead. The Michigan legislature balked at providing funds for their maintenance. Departments wanted all of the indirect cost funds attributed to their sponsored projects but had to settle for a portion that covered those indirect costs applicable to departmental budgets and burdens. Later, when the legislature demanded that recovered indirect costs be returned to the institutional general fund, their attractiveness, which had been based largely on their discretionary character, diminished. There was little advantage in pursuing difficult negotiations over indirect costs when the gain was illusionary. This legislative policy contributed to the decline in Michigan's relative support for higher education. Later (but well after the Hannah years) the legislature and other state officials began to recognize the relevance of research to the economy of the state as well as of the nation. A recent 1984 Commission on the Future of Higher Education in Michigan appointed by the governor has recommended state matching of institutional indirect cost revenue and appropriations for major research equipment through a Research Excellence Fund. The commission has also recommended that research be limited to four state universities, and there are indications that only four state universities approve of this recommendation.

## Effects of Federally Sponsored Research

Determination and allocation of indirect costs affected many universities adversely. Some researchers resented and resisted the imposition of indirect costs as an interposing step in grant and contract negotiations that slowed down and even endangered the success of negotiations. Researchers tended to develop a rapport with and loyalty to the individual granting agencies and developed an adversarial view toward institutional officers who insisted both on inclusion of indirect costs and on determining their allocation. Elaborate data collection forms required of the institution in accounting to granting agencies for fund expenditures were often resented by faculty members as unnecessary institutional impositions rather than as reasonable attempts to comply with accountability requirements.

On the whole, these problems were not as serious at Michigan State as at other universities. Good morale and good communication existed. During the Hannah years and for some years afterward faculty retained a sense of institutional problems and an institutional loyalty that fostered cooperation rather than competition within the university. There was no doubt in anyone's mind as to whom credit must be given for the development of the university and no doubt that administrative decisions were directed to improving the institution and maintaining a public service role for the state, the nation, and the world.

Inevitably there were some long-term undesirable effects of federally sponsored research. Many factors were involved in the tendency of researchers to transfer loyalty to fund-granting agencies.

1. Individuals receiving large grants expected recognition and reward. Subtraction of overhead seemed more like punishment.
2. Recipients of large research grants tended to view a research grant as a personal acquisition and, indeed, could carry it to another university, perhaps acquiring a better position (salary, title, university) thereby.

3. The close relationship that had once existed between the state and national economy and the needs of the people was disrupted. The mediating, disseminating role of the Experiment Station and of Continuing Education that had formerly operated was eliminated. Research reports were written to attain recognition among colleagues and continuing support from foundations or federal agencies rather than to help people.

4. The constant seeking for funds was complicated by the changing missions of federal granting agencies reflecting shifts in political priorities. At various times and from various agencies, the national priorities have included earthquake prediction, elementary particle structures of matter, eliminating poverty, energy resources, environmental systems and quality, excavation technology, highway traffic safety, international institute building, international institution building, improving the quality of urban life, long-range weather and climate prediction, origin and evolution of life, peaceful use of nuclear energy, solid state physics, structure and origin of the universe, transportation network, war on cancer, war on crime, and weather modification.

Many research possibilities dealt with pressing national needs. However, research was often separated from need by the federal granting agency and its interpretation of the need, which had been carefully adjusted to political pressures. Attention was often directed to the distinction, always baffling and irritating, among basic (pure) research, applied research, and development. Various attempts were made at Michigan State to deal with this distinction.

While applied research seeks practical applications, development goes a step further in seeking new and systematic use of scientific knowledge. New materials, devices, and processing methods are often necessary to make full use of research findings. Thus scientifically confirmed feasibility may prove during development to be economically impracticable. As problems and their solutions have become more complicated, development and dissemination may be incompatible with institutional values or may require more time and resources than are readily available in a university. Successful development may require new procedures and equipment that are themselves patentable. Hence industry and business may take over the development task and understandably seek to maintain secrecy and control over aspects of it. The university-based researcher may become a paid consultant, subject to any imposed secrecy requirements and to limitations on the use of the results of his or her own research. The university then suffers in two ways. The scholarly commitment to search for knowledge may become tinged by the search for increased personal financial benefits. Loyalty to the institution that encourages scholarship may be replaced by an opportunistic commitment to that institution and that research which provides the largest return. Commitment to an institutional mission to serve people is then easily replaced by a commitment to serve those who provide the largest return to the researcher. Classified research, whether federally or business supported, has been frowned upon as inhibitory to healthy interchange and is considered inappropriate to the university. But cooperation and collaboration involving university, government, and industry are possible provided each respect the requirements of the other.

Numerous other ethical issues arose out of the unprecedented increase in scientific research in the universities:

1. Conflicts of commitment on the basis of time spent in consulting, rewards received, and use of institutional resources and facilities
2. Rights and welfare of human research subjects
3. Humane treatment of experimental animals
4. Professorial or institutional use of work done by students or assistants
5. Names listed on publications
6. Endorsement of commercial products
7. Procedures in preparing and approving proposals
8. Recognition of assistance from colleagues in other colleges or departments
9. Conflicts of interest between research projects and other institutional policies or commitments
10. Safety of researcher's use of hazardous materials

In 1959 Milton Muelder foresaw the importance of many of these issues and prepared, with assistance from the Graduate Council, the first institutional statement of administrative policy regarding sponsored research and educational programs at MSU. First approved in May 1960 by the Graduate Council, after subsequent modifications it was approved later by the Board of Trustees. When, in 1965, the American Council of Education requested institutions to prepare and submit statements of policy regarding administration of sponsored research, Michigan State's policy statement received the highest rating (along with those of some thirty other institutions). Under Muelder's successor, John Cantlon, university policies on these matters were continued and expanded as necessary to meet new contingencies. In general, these policies assert that sponsored programs must be consistent with the policies, academic programs, and mission of the university. Despite the rapid increase in sponsored programs, these policies, supported jointly by the activities of the Office of Grant and Contract Administration and the vice president for research, have prevented many of the difficulties and excesses that occurred on some campuses where the extent of the research and development funds attracted to some units weakened the authority of administrators whose decisions then had little impact on these units. At Michigan State, the sums acquired did not promote such autonomy. Furthermore, the long tradition under Hannah of a total university commitment to public service, instruction, and research, and the frequent reiteration of this tradition in various contexts, discouraged fragmentation of the unity of effort required by that commitment.

Yet in retrospect, it is evident that the vast increase in largely federally sponsored research, coupled with a failure on the state's part to recognize the value of an expanded research capability, weakened the role that state funds (Experiment Station and state agencies) had long played in encouraging and supporting research related to the public service commitment. Funds available from the state seemed negligible compared with the funds that became available from federal and other sources for departments, centers, and institutes engaging in inter- or supradisciplinary research.

The sheer volume of research and its demands have in some cases also strained the close relationship among courses, academic degree programs, and organizational arrangements and structures. Yet graduate courses, programs, and dissertations have emerged from or been modified by research. The cumulative impact of research might (and did in biology, chemistry, and physics) require a new synthesis of knowledge and complete revision and reorganization of academic programs. Generally it was easier to set up new courses or add another department than to undertake the redefinition and restructuring of a discipline. Resources and techniques in interdisciplinary issues and problems became important and were accommodated in alternative structures such as centers, institutes, or subdisciplinary departments, which at times and for some people threatened to overwhelm or replace the traditional disciplinary departments.

The quality and volume of research and of faculty, graduate students, and postdoctoral fellows surely increased. The relation of research and researchers to people, and to the needs of people, became less clear. Some faculty members and administrators were (and are) no longer concerned about service as a general mission of the institution and as a responsibility of its faculty and staff. This view is perhaps most evident among those faculty members and administrators who confidently assert that what the institution has become is the natural and desirable elaboration of the land-grant mission. Others at Michigan State assert that the land-grant mission remains viable but largely limited to the primary land-grant units.

No president since Hannah has regularly and ably interpreted and emphasized the institution's service role, and public service as an institution-wide mission has become obscured. On the other hand, the general insistence that research be related to instructional programs has prevented the excesses in diversion of faculty time from the fundamental responsibilities and obligations of the university. The leadership provided by a new president arriving in July 1985 may be the critical factor in determining whether Michigan State restores service to society as one of its three major missions or turns to establishing a national and international reputation as a research institution.

# PART III
# *Applied Research and Service*

# 10
# Public Service:
# Extension and Applied Research

Many documents chronicle the valuable contributions of the Cooperative Agricultural Extension Service and the Experiment Station at Michigan State University. Rather than reappraise these units, this chapter will look at the change in and expansion of the land-grant mission over time and in its relation to the changing needs of the state, national, and world society and economy. The Extension Service and the Experiment Station were originally embedded in land-grant rurally oriented programs. The personnel involved recognized an obligation to improve the quality of living as well as to increase the efficiency of production, but they also recognized that production increases were regarded with greater favor and more likely to lead to increased funds. Although attempts to expand service and research functions to other fields, departments, and problems were inevitably suspected as attempts to disperse extension research funds more widely or to subtly alter the mission of the institution, President John Hannah was able to lead the institution from a relatively narrow state and rural focus to a service-oriented view and a commitment to improve the quality of life for everyone in the nation and the world.

For the past fifty years or so, any discussion of the nature of a land-grant college has included the three closely related activities of instruction (credit and noncredit), extension (Cooperative Extension Service), and research (Experiment Station). It was not always so. The federally subsidized Experiment Station did not appear until authorized by the Hatch Act of 1887. Extension services were quite limited until after the Smith-Lever Act of 1914. In its early years, the Agricultural College of Michigan struggled against almost overwhelming odds just to keep alive. Extension and research activities were fragmentary and essentially individual voluntary efforts. Transportation and communication facilities made extensive interaction with rural areas time consuming and difficult. At the date of the Morrill Act (1862) and for years thereafter, the majority of the state's people lived on farms that were not readily accessible for much of the year.

In this context, on-campus instruction, off-campus extension (or public service), and applied research could not be separate functions. They were, instead, different facets of the activities of professors committed to improving the quality of life of what was then the vast majority of the population. As these facets developed, expanded, and took on distinctive characters, many professors continued to teach students, direct work on the campus and farms, engage in investigation of problems, and personally communicate their insights and findings to rural communities and farms. In time, such tasks would require careful analysis and planning to identify resources, people, policies, and procedures for serving a nation increasing in size and complexity and changing from a rural agricultural society to an urban industrial one. Extension work, the Experiment Station, and instruction, in their expansion, gave rise to new structures, but their integrated development to serve society remained the heart and soul of the land-grant enterprise as seen by many land-grant supporters—including John Hannah.

## COOPERATIVE EXTENSION

President Robert Kedzie made the first systematic attempt, in 1875, to extend college services to farmers who could not or would not come to the campus, and the next year the college offered the first of many Farmer's Institutes. In 1885, the state legislature appropriated money to publish two bulletins a year from each of six departments focused on such matters as feeds, seeds, and farming processes. They were viewed as communicating information to farmers and constituted the first efforts of extension in disseminating systematically collected and organized information. The bulletins also encouraged research, for the persons writing them had to draw together relevant knowledge and occasionally engage in field experimentation to justify the recommendations made. But agricultural research on a continuing basis was hardly possible until Congress passed the Hatch Act of 1887. This act provided official sanction and continuing funding for the creation of experiment stations to perform agricultural research and disseminate findings.

Both extension and research programs reflected the conviction that the lives and work of the farmers and laborers could be greatly improved by applying science and technology. Applied research could assist people in defining problems, and existing scientific knowledge could provide the principles and concepts that might help to solve these problems. If existing knowledge was inadequate, problem-oriented scientific research was appropriate. The land-grant responsibility was to define these problems through interaction with people, research the problems to find solutions or mitigating practices, and disseminate the results through extension and on-campus instruction.

Presidents T. C. Abbot and Edwin Willitts, along with other land-grant college leaders, were influential in gaining support for the 1887 Hatch Act. When the $15,000 a year appropriated for experimental work in each state became available, the Michigan Experiment Station was authorized, and shortly thereafter substations were established at South Haven for fruit experimentation and at Grayling for studies of grasses that would grow on sandy soils and, ultimately, provide organic matter for grain production. Although the Engineering Experiment Station did not appear until 1924 (and then without direct federal support) its first efforts were directed to farm problems: waste disposal, rural roads, and the use of electrical power.

Extension services were broadly conceived. In 1892, the first off-campus credit extension courses, in history and economics, were offered in Charlotte and Lansing. Although these courses were based in the liberal arts rather than in agriculture, the request that they be taught was made by the Grange representing the agricultural community.

By 1893, sixteen Farmer's Institutes were offered in various communities of the state. In 1894, the first campus "short course," dealing with creamery operations, was provided. In 1895, the legislature appropriated $5,000 and authorized the appointment of a superintendent of institutes. The first superintendent was Kenyon L. Butterfield, who would return at a later date as president of the institution. Demonstration institutes were arranged in sixty-seven counties in that year and included involvement of a lecturer on home economics hired in 1894. The success of the Farmer's Institutes hinged on the fact that each institute presented two local speakers recognized for their experience in the topic and one speaker from the college. Such clearly cooperative early extension development recognized that expertise was not limited to college professors.

In 1902, when Levi R. Taft became superintendent of institutes, railroad specials designated as "Corn Gospel Trains"—a designation not original at Michigan State—carried information about selecting seed, planting corn, and fertilizing fields to all parts of the state. In 1905 winter short courses in general agriculture were available for the first time which consisted of two eight-week sessions offered in successive winters, with the intent that each person enrolling complete the two sessions.

In 1914 the Smith-Lever Act created the Cooperative Agricultural Extension Service supported by federal funds matched by state appropriations. The first agricultural agents in Michigan had already been appointed in 1909, but with assured funding, fifteen county agents, whose salaries came equally from state and federal funds and from county boards of supervisors, established the base for further development of Cooperative Extension. The work of the fifteen county agents was supported by nine specialists (employed within the regular subject matter departments of the college), whose responsibilities included assisting the agricultural agents and serving farmers in areas without an agent. Public service in the form of agricultural extension and the Agricultural Experiment Station was well established by the time of World War I. Extension courses for credit were also offered on topics other than agriculture, which represented—although perhaps not fully realized at the time—a shift from a focus on *things* to a focus on the development of *people*.

During World War I, there was necessarily some redirection of effort to support war-related activities, with much emphasis on the increase of production. The resulting farm surpluses of the postwar decade far exceeded demand and brought drastic decreases in prices. There was extensive pressure on the college to shift its attention to prices, profit, marketing, and distribution. The appointment in 1921 of David Friday as president was undoubtedly influenced by the fact that he was an economist. Although Friday supported such ideas as the development of farm cooperatives, storage of produce, and transportation, he also urged greater efficiency in production as well as reconsideration of the focus on agriculture in Michigan. Friday's views did not satisfy the farm groups. He resigned after only one year.

To revitalize rural society, President Kenyon Butterfield, appointed in 1924, introduced a program of continuing education designed to enlist every segment of the college in review of all facets of country living. To expedite this development, Butterfield hired (in 1926) as his director of continuing education, John D. Willard, who had served as director of extension with Butterfield in Massachusetts. Willard was to direct *all* off-campus education but, in fact, the college director of extension, R. J. Baldwin, continued to report to the dean of agriculture, as he had in the past. The issue of whether extension was a total institutional responsibility, and if so, how it should be coordinated, would be a concern for many years. In Butterfield's mind, Continuing Education was charged with responsibility to serve all of Michigan, thereby fulfilling the obligation of the Morrill Act to educate those who worked in machine shops as well as those who worked on farms.

If the teaching of agriculture entailed an off-campus duty, then the engineering faculty had an equivalent responsibility to industry and labor. In Butterfield's view, continuing education would include extension classes, correspondence courses, speaking engagements and conference planning, and evening courses offered over the college radio station, WKAR. The radio station, an arm of extension, had begun in 1922 with a transmitter constructed by the electrical engineering faculty and students.

Butterfield also planned to appoint a director of research who would control experimental activities and research of all departments and the Experiment Station. But Butterfield's vision and actions proved premature. Attempts to increase the functions of the institution extensively were watched with considerable concern by other state institutions of higher education. The development of a Division of Applied Science and a Division of Liberal Arts generated concern among many agriculturally oriented persons that the college was deviating from its primary mission and failing to deal effectively with the major problems of the rural communities. The Division of Agriculture was also alarmed by shifting power, influence, and funds. Butterfield's attempt to bring about rapid change was hampered by the fact that while the president was responsible to the Board of Agriculture in matters of policy, the secretary of the board was responsible for control of spending. Who then was responsible for deficits?

Although Butterfield's national prominence in affairs related to education no doubt had been influential in his selection as president, his continuing involvement in national and international affairs did not set well with many people (both on and off campus) who saw the role of the president as a full-time campus activity. Butterfield departed in 1928 and the concept of continuing education disappeared with him, although his ideas continued to have profound influence through the thinking and efforts of individuals who had been associated with him during his presidency. John Hannah, as a student in 1922–23 and subsequently as a poultry extension specialist, observed Butterfield's efforts and difficulties and learned thereby.

The events of the decade following the departure of Butterfield were not conducive to the development of the ideas that he planted. Depression years, beginning in 1929 with the stock market debacle, forced the college into a struggle to survive rather than to innovate and expand. Enrollment began to grow in the arts and sciences, in business and hotel management, and in other applied fields based upon the arts and sciences, although facilities for instruction and student residence were lacking. The addition of instructional programs in the arts and sciences gradually attracted faculty members oriented to the discipline and to research within the discipline rather than to public service and applied research activities. The concept of a liberal arts education as essential to the education of persons contemplating careers in the applied sciences and social sciences was no longer fully accepted in agriculture and engineering. Nor was it understood by some of the new arts and sciences faculty members who preferred to pursue their own interests. The issue of who made decisions about the mission of the institution and where and how they were made still had to be resolved. However faculty and administrators within the institution might regard that mission, others, both in the earlier constituency of the college and in other state-supported institutions, would view expansion or elaboration of that mission as a rejection or deviation from the primary mission and an infringement on their own.

## THE EXPANSION OF EXTENSION

Communication and transportation improvements opened the possibility for new approaches to extension. In addition, technological developments changed the nature of agriculture in Michigan and other states and profoundly affected the urban-rural balance in the state as well as having profound effects on the state's economy. By 1925, courses in agriculture and home economics were offered over WKAR Radio by the Farm Radio School. Examinations for credit (available since 1910) and certificates of accomplishment were made available. Market reports and information became an established part of the radio program activity. In 1927, the radio was used to communicate with agricultural agents, boys' and girls' clubs, and home economics demonstration agents. The dissemination of information was greatly expedited by the use of radio, but even more significant was the ready acceptance of radio as a means of continuing education in many fields.

In 1929, Mabel Miles began a Rural Music Extension Program reaching 818 teachers, 643 schools, and 20,500 children. By 1932, the program reached 1,116 schools and 44,000 children. In 1938, WKAR took over the Rural School Music Program, presenting a program of records and talks to students who were transported to campus by bus. Extension at that date clearly included the arts and addressed aesthetic as well as practical concerns.

By 1935, an extensive range of courses was offered in floriculture, gardening, rural electrification, farm building, poultry, dairying, farm crops, soils, feeding, and nutrition. Some of these programs were credit courses offered directly from the classroom. At that time the director of radio station WKAR was a professor and was involved in instruction of students, in public relations, and in extension program development and production. Likewise, the bulletin editor for extension was an assistant professor in public relations. An associate professor in institutional administration was manager of the women's residence halls. Composite titles involving academic status, on one hand, and operational administrative responsibilities, on the other, were still regarded as desirable and proper. Extension and campus operations would continue to be seen as appropriate aspects of academic responsibilities closely related to instruction as late as 1950, but academic degree credentials and disciplinary competency were beginning to be viewed as essential for faculty status and as distinctly different from the abilities required for institutional operations and cooperative extension services.

Despite the continuing acceptance of the land-grant trinity of resident instruction, extension, and Experiment Station, the nature and interrelationship of the three became an issue of recurrent concern. Resident instruction was originally regarded as instruction on campus where both students and faculty were in residence for prescribed periods of time (quarters or terms). Extension implied the offering of education services at a distance from the campus (perhaps in the student's *home*) by institutes, demonstrations, short courses, workshops, and free publications or bulletins. But all of these programs could be and were provided on campus to groups present but only *temporarily* resident, for one day or several weeks. Another distinction between resident and extension instruction was in degree credit as contrasted with certificate or other form of recognition for noncredit programs. Should a professor receive credit, extra pay, or simply a pat on the back for teaching a noncredit course? Extension services had long been provided free through the Cooperative Extension Service (because such service is a budgeted item) side by side with extension services (credit extension or otherwise) for which charges were assessed and collected by the institution or by professors who asserted that they provided the services personally (and beyond their obligation to the institution) rather than as institutional extension agents.

Although resident instruction was and has continued to be one of the three basic functions of the land-grant institution, the rudimentary stage of nineteenth-century scientific agriculture, based almost entirely on empiricism, made "demonstrate and imitate" or "show and tell" approaches essential both in the classroom and in the field. Hence, in terms of content and method, no great distinction could be made at that time between resident and extension instruction. Experimentation in some crude empirical sense was possible, thereby improving practice without advancing scientific understanding. As scientifically controlled environmental circumstances replaced empiricism, the laboratory replaced the barnyard. The researcher, at home in the former, could not always function well in the latter.

Increases in knowledge and in the complexity of knowledge, supported by technological demands and advances, forced recurrent if not continuous reconsideration of the structure, process, content, and methods of every educational dissemination and development effort. How was the three-part obligation of the land-grant institution to be most effectively discharged? What solution or services would the public support and accept? How much would the public be willing to invest in elimination of poverty, urban problems, and environmental pollution?

Ultimately, the availability of funds was the crucial factor in determining the range of services, especially since, in a publicly supported institution, the availability of dollars reflects both the sense and the appraisal of its efforts and services. For agriculture and home economics, these expectations—and needs—extended from the most elementary empiricism to frontier research required to identify concepts, principles, and facts on which scientific agriculture and human growth and development could be based. Technological improvement requires development of skills as well as advance in knowledge. An institution must indeed *extend* itself to identify needs, acquire and organize relevant knowledge, and find means of disseminating and encouraging the use of the results. As needs change, the services required and the personnel involved must also change. Flexibility and adaptation are essential but not easy to maintain, for staff and organizational structure tend to support and modify established views and practices rather than reject and replace them.

From 1930 to 1940, Michigan State faced these issues. Hannah, as secretary of the Board of Agriculture from 1935 to 1941 and then as president from 1941 to 1969, had earlier served in extension and was fully aware of the problems and the need to resolve them. Unlike some others more directly involved and entrenched in past practices, he had no personal commitment to existing patterns or traditions. He was rather committed to the improvement of services and to broadening their scope to include personal, social, and cultural benefits for all. He had observed former President Butterfield's efforts and their defects. He had similar concerns about the Experiment Station and had noted Butterfield's intent to appoint a director of research for the entire institution.

EXPERIMENT STATION — APPLIED RESEARCH

Although the Hatch Act of 1887 officially recognized and supported the experiment station concept, as many as two dozen such stations were in operation before that date.[1] As we have seen, the Michigan legislature had appropriated funds to publish two bulletins a year from each of six departments as early as 1885. Three of the first six bulletins reported on studies of seeds: success of sorghum seed distributed for trial to 400 farmers, germination rate of vegetable seeds, and vitality of weed seeds. The other three reported findings about a new damaging insect, feeding of livestock, and diseases of farm animals. The data collections and reporting reflected both the extension and the research components of the land-grant college commitment. Similar contributions, reflected in directions for construction of a haymower, statements of principles of stock-breeding, and reports on controlled agricultural experimentation, date back to the early 1860s. But until the 1885 appropriation, findings had been reported either in speeches or in cumbersome and not readily available board reports. The printed bulletins quickly communicated the studies of current problems and results to farmers and were also readily available for later requests. Thus, bulletins supplemented and expanded the Farmer's Institutes initiated in 1876. There was a cumulative quality to these early investigations, since questions generated by studies encouraged further study. For example, the first experiment in a chain leading to hybrid corn was carried out by Professor William Beal in the mid 1870s. The next and decisive step was executed by Perry G. Holden who, in the late 1890s, inbred corn varieties until they were pure.

The first long-range research programs were initiated in 1888 with the organization of an Agricultural Experiment Station financed with federal funds. The real expansion of extension work came later after passage of the Smith-Lever Act in 1914, which established the Agricultural Extension Service and permitted the appointment of fifteen county agents. A Farm Bureau, organized by groups in each county, advised the agent. Extension specialists, departmentally based in the college, assisted the agent by providing current scientific information.

The extension program provided direct contact with farmers and provided a channel for bringing problems either to the specialist who might be able to respond with current information or to the Experiment

---

1. David Madsen, "The Land-Grant University: Myth and Reality," in *Land-Grant Universities and Their Continuing Challenge*, edited by G. Lester Anderson (East Lansing, Mich.: Michigan State University Press, 1976), p. 38.

Station if experimentation or research were required. Responses could proceed in reverse to the original questioners and also become part of the current knowledge through bulletins and research reports.

Experiment Station projects were not necessarily dependent upon specific questions posed through extension contacts. Increased yields by use of superior parents stocks, by soil treatments, or by elimination of disease were always desired and the results could be readily disseminated through the extension channels to an appropriate audience. Pest control measures and improvements in harvesting, processing, and storing were and always would be of interest. Early research projects tended to be narrowly conceived and specifically focused. Only gradually did the recognition dawn that expansion of successful small-scale measures might have unanticipated and undesirable effects. Moreover, remedial or improvement processes must always meet criteria regarding cost, quality, and quantity, on one hand, and absence of obvious undesirable features such as crop damage, destruction, or other desirable or neutral conditions or organisms, on the other. To use a recent example, the application of DDT to isolated fields was a highly successful treatment for certain pests, but the cumulative detrimental effects of using DDT over many square miles for several consecutive years was not at first known. Most agricultural problems turned out to be more complex than they first appeared to be. Indeed, one of the contributions of research has been to show that all problems are more difficult and more complex than they first appear. Today's solutions to yesterday's problems often become tomorrow's crises.

Up to 1900, most research bulletins were written to interpret science for farmers. The Adams Act of that year provided $15,000 per year to support *fundamental* research reported in such a way as to serve the needs of fellow scientists rather than farmers. Whereas schedules of spraying of the insecticides to be used were directly addressed to the needs of farmers, a report on how contact insecticides kill was more appropriately addressed to other scientists seeking better means of insect eradication. The costs and side effects of complete pest eradication in contrast with maintenance of balance were also more likely to interest the scientist than the farmer, although a bulletin written or rewritten with care might have been addressed to both. Development and dissemination of statistical and mathematical models for analysis, interpretation, and display of data were evidently of interest only to other researchers. Applied research and contributions to research methodology became distinguishable. Practice can lead to theory, and sound theory will affect practice, but only when continued effort is made to that end.

In a large state like Michigan, with its diversity in soils and climate, a number of experimental sites were required for applied research. In 1929, the following existed:

Graham Horticultural Experiment Station near Grand Rapids
Kellogg Demonstration Farm near Battle Creek
Lake City Potato Experiment Station
South Haven Horticultural Experiment Station
Upper Peninsula Experiment Station at Chatham

The latter station dates from 1899. Other areas had, in effect, served as temporary experiment stations for study of a particular problem— for example, the sandy soils around Grayling had served for finding grasses that would grow on sand and, ultimately, restore some stability and utility. By 1969, there would be nine Experiment Station substations and three more by 1980.

### TRENDS AND PROBLEMS

Regional experiment stations tended to reinforce the rather flexible interactions of extension and Experiment Station personnel since experimental activity often involved close cooperation with nearby farmers or fruit growers. Before the formalization of Extension Service and Experiment Station, the functions of extension work, on-campus instruction, and experimentation were often, in fact usually, performed by the same individual, although the growth of the institution and, specifically, of the extension and Experiment Station staff and operations gradually forced specialization and a specification of the nature of an appointment. These changes were more an evolution than a revolution.

For years, from its initiation to the late 1940s, the Experiment Station listed among its increasing staff (100 individuals by 1935) research professors, research associates, and research assistants. Some of these were also jointly listed or appointed in a disciplinary department. By 1950, almost everyone of academic rank on the Experiment Station faculty also held a departmental post. A list of all faculty members associated with the Extension Service and the Experiment Station issued the following year showed each was also appointed to and assigned rank in a department. Rather than providing a list of faculty, the 1951 Experiment Station catalog stated that its staff includes "230 persons in 27 subject matter departments." That number would rise by 1969 to 280 persons. Departmental membership had become essential to attain academic status within the Experiment Station.

A parallel but later development is found in extension. Whereas in the early years of the Extension Service academic rank in *extension* was readily granted, the long-time trend was to grant academic rank only to those approved by a disciplinary department. This development reflects the move from experimentation, only a little removed from trial and error coupled with careful observation and record keeping, to research grounded in scientific knowledge and carried on according to rigorous modes of scientific investigation. The Ph.D. as the degree preparing for such research came to be a requirement. The extension specialist, in becoming departmentally based, was also required to have a Ph.D. to obtain tenure. Other extension staff members required competencies other than disciplinary depth and research skills and would gradually come to view their task as serving as resources or linkages rather than as problem solving. On one hand, the role of extension staff members became that of assisting people to form groups or organizations by which they pooled and developed their own abilities to define and resolve problems. On the other hand, as resource persons, extension workers had access to specialists, scholars, and researchers on the campus and in the Experiment Station who could bring additional insights and knowledge to bear on a problem. Extension could be viewed as a mediating role between those having knowledge—professors and researchers—and those needing to use it—farmers, homemakers, engineers, and such. Such a mediating role is clearly one of instruction oriented to what to do and how to do it rather than to why or how something works.

As more attention was given to attaining a more satisfying family life, to the development of Michigan youth, to the development and conservation of community and natural resources, and to increasing general prosperity, several problems and principles became evident. The various facets of extension represented by county agents, home economics, 4-H Club leaders and specialists had operated independently, but that was no longer appropriate. Rather, direction and overall planning should emerge from a single university-based source providing for regional and local coordination and flexibility. Independent actions and even occasional competition could then be replaced by collaboration of the extension personnel without concern for defining the prerogatives and responsibilities of individuals implied by title or funding source. The need for central coordination of the several facets of activity was made evident by the need for a shift in orientation and emphasis caused by national and international events.

Agricultural surpluses in one year can be followed by deficiencies in the next. Hence, agricultural extension and Experiment Station activities must be continually integrated with the real world, which makes the organization and staffing of such units difficult. As the attention of extension staff shifted from seeds, fertilizer, and other things to individuals and their personal development, and then to groups facilitating the development of individuals, the nature of extension activities changed and the status relations and responsibilities among the Experiment Station, extension, and departmental staffs became less clear.

As disciplinary departments became the basic units for selecting and rewarding faculty after 1945, the prestige of practical research and extension assignments diminished. Research was no longer a special assignment; every professor was expected to engage in it. Extension specialists (other than subject matter specialists) no longer held academic assignments in the eyes of the on-campus faculty, since extension personnel ordinarily did not do research and were not qualified to (or rarely did) teach advanced on-campus credit courses. Participation of off-campus extension personnel in on-campus academic decisions was resented and gradually eliminated by restricting academic designations to those selected or approved by departments. By the early 1950s, the appointment of a Ph.D. in sociology as a staff member in Continuing Education with an academic title of assistant professor was strongly resented and resisted by the department. Structure was taking precedence over function.

The interrelations between the Experiment Station and Cooperative Extension have been such that no discussion can treat them separately. Dual appointments were and continued to be common. The requirement of a disciplinary departmental base for academic rank would somewhat change this relationship as well as lead gradually to complete separation of academic functions, institutional operations, and public service.

### HANNAH AND COOPERATIVE EXTENSION

When Hannah came to the presidency in 1941, he had already been extensively involved with Michigan State. He was fully aware of and concerned about the issues and trends in the Extension Service. He had received the baccalaureate degree in agriculture in 1923, served as a poultry extension worker, and took leave briefly to engage in national and international activities. He returned to campus in 1935 as secretary of the State Board of Agriculture. During these continuing interactions with Michigan State, Hannah had built up a bill of fare for action including a review and reconstruction of undergraduate education with specific attention to general education. His influence in this area has already been discussed.

Perhaps rather more than most extension workers, Hannah had become interested in people—their needs and aspirations. It seemed to him that the extension program as then constituted was focusing too narrowly on the rural areas and that even within this limited vision, there was overemphasis on divisional or functional lines rather than on cooperation among the various aspects of extension activity to meet the needs of individuals. In brief, Hannah was sensitive to the fact that the farm and the farm home were changing and that many rural needs were identical with those of urban areas. His review and personal interpretation of the Morrill Act and the succeeding legislation dealing with Extension Service and Experiment Station led him to believe that the original intent of the Morrill Act was to create an institution oriented to the needs and concerns of the common people and dedicated to the optimal development of every individual. Michigan State had temporarily lost this broad view because of its immediate focus, no matter how timely, on agriculture and immediately related activities. In effect, Hannah challenged Michigan State to develop and carry out an all-inclusive extension program adding cultural, economics, and social aspects to the then almost sole emphasis on agriculture and home economics. He aspired to make available to all residents in Michigan the kind of information and services then limited to particular groups. To him this implied that all departments and units of the institution should be involved in extension activities rather than one division taking responsibility for all extension and research. He was not satisfied that either the existing approach to extension activities or the Experiment Station research took adequate cognizance of the range of problems or of the assistance that could be provided through personal contacts and through publications, radio, and visual aids. In simple terms, John Hannah asked that the nature and mission of the land-grant institution be reconsidered and reconstructed in reference to the needs and resources of the day. But immediate action had to be deferred. Six months after Hannah became president, the United States was at war.

By 1944, the college had adjusted to its wartime role and could begin to anticipate the future and the role of Michigan State in it. Hannah expressed his concern that the whole land-grant system had become extremely conservative and complacent. A review of the college extension program indicated that county agricultural agents, 4-H Club workers, and home demonstration personnel operated essentially independently. Some observers had already indicated the obvious need for unified control and direction at top administrative levels as well as the need for increased responsibility, authority, and flexibility at the local level. Concern was also voiced that extension was reaching only 50 percent of the rural population, that cultural and artistic themes were not being adequately treated, and that urban segments of the state were virtually untouched by extension activities. Although a large number of urban extension projects had been conducted by land-grant colleges even before 1900, they were of short duration and not notably successful. The potential urban clientele had been (and would be) elusive (possibly even illusory), controversial, and reluctant (even resistant), and urban problems were monumental.

At issue in 1944 was the level at which central functional planning and coordination of extension programs would give way to the necesary adaptations and flexibility required in particular geographical areas. Program needs and procedures might be essentially the same for adjacent counties but markedly different in scattered sections of the state, with some intermediate coordination between counties and the state required. Internal adjustments were obviously required to deal with these problems. Hannah felt that the individuals on the working front would be more objective and realistic about such issues than busy administrators, whose procedures, prerogatives, and authority might be endangered by change. He selected a committee that did not include administrators, to their surprise and irritation. He turned to Dr. Floyd Reeves as a resource and consultant. Dr. Reeves, a person of stature, widely known and experienced, and impressive and influential in action, had given much thought to and written about the problems of rural areas. Finding in Reeves a man whose ideas corresponded closely to his own, and fully realizing that his own wider range of concerns and specific desires with regard to extension would be jeopardized by extensive personal involvement, Hannah was happy to involve Reeves in this effort as he had in the earlier efforts with regard to the undergraduate program. Reeves's interests and experience in administration were particularly helpful. He emphasized the need to distinguish between line and staff relationships in order to develop a coordinated program of activity while maintaining a definite and single administrative line from the regional level to the college.

It became evident immediately that any major reorganization of the Extension Service to include all people and all parts of the institution would require a complete restructuring of the program. There were, indeed, vested interests not easily overcome. The University of Michigan already had an extension service for adult education and was unlikely to look favorably on the broad concept of extension that Hannah had in mind. A broadened concept of mission could also be regarded as a reduction of the commitment to serve agriculture and rural areas.

One of the early proposals of the committee was that an Extension Service Board be established comprising the deans of those schools making major contributions to the extension program. With the dean of agriculture serving as chairman, this board would formulate the policies for extension action. In effect, the extension program would become an all-institutional program reporting through the Extension Service Board to the president. Thereby, extension would be promoted but the role of agriculture somewhat demoted.

The concept of extension that emerged had moved well beyond the rural orientation, the practical emphasis, and domination by agriculture and home economics. This was indeed a threat to those who had successfully developed the more restricted view, but the new program could become fully effective only when accepted by the total staff. It would also require additional funding and staff. Moreover, it soon became apparent that coordination through a committee of busy administrators, most of whom were inevitably involved in their own on-campus problems, was not going to be effective. A new direction had been indicated, but the means of implementation were still uncertain.

Hannah, as usual, had foreseen a second problem that hampered and, ultimately, defeated some aspects of his determination to develop a unified institutional extension program. In the fall of 1944, Hannah requested from the legislature for the next biennium ending June 30, 1947, funds to reorganize and expand the Extension Service to include twenty-six new 4-H Club county workers, twelve assistant county agents, twenty-five county home demonstration persons, and more specialists. Reasonably explicit in this request was the intent to expand the range of services offered by the college to a larger clientele (urban as well as rural), and to include a larger range of institutional resources and disciplinary departments. An added resource was to be a department of audiovisual aids, particularly directed to enhancing extension programs.

Hannah was hoping to convince the legislature and the public that the service range of Michigan State should be much more extensive and to create a willingness to support such an expanded program. The legislature, however, proved unwilling to support an enlarged concept of extension. Its view was that, although the existing and relatively narrow rural service concept was a unique institutional mission, the larger concept would bring requests to fund such services from all other state-assisted colleges and universities.

Hannah's interest in the expansion of extension caused him to be alert to many new horizons. At the State Board of Agriculture meeting on April 21, 1944, he reported on a conference between college representatives and the Michigan Council of the Congress of Industrial Organizations (CIO) regarding courses in adult education and worker education. In that year, the legislature established a fund of $250,000 under the direction of the State Superintendent of Public Instruction for study and development of a statewide program in adult education. From this fund, $5,000 was obtained to study the existing activities in adult education and develop a statement of needs and possible programs. Orion Ulrey of the Department of Agricultural Economics carried out this study, reporting to a committee composed of the deans of agriculture, home economics, and liberal arts divisions with the board secretary, Karl McDonel, as chairman. The makeup of this committee reflected something of the past experience of the institution in extension: agriculture and home economics, of course, had been the primary sources of activity; McDonel had been assistant director of Cooperative Extension; L. C. Emmons, dean of liberal arts, had for some years coordinated all off-campus study offerings.

At the same board meeting, Hannah discussed a proposed Kellogg Institute of Rural Life and gave a further report on it at the next meeting of May 18. By October 19 he could report receipt of a grant of $6,550 from the Kellogg Foundation to continue study of the project. By the following July, a proposal was prepared and sent to the Kellogg Foundation requesting funds for a building to house continuing education activities and provide practical experiences for students in hotel and institutional administration. On September 20, 1945, the board passed a resolution accepting $1 million from the foundation for a continuing education facility.

Earlier, the Michigan Hotel and Restaurant Association had given the college $100,000 "to erect an inn which would serve as a hotel management laboratory and would admit campus visitors." On February 17, 1944, H. W. Klare, representing hotel interests, had appeared before the board and urged construction of an inn that would provide housing and meals for visitors and instructional and research facilities for the hotel and institutional administration programs. Some local businesses opposed the proposal as "unfair competition," but this was based on doubts and fears more than on actuality. In fact, local businesses actually benefited from the presence of the conference participants that the new inn attracted.

Meanwhile, the Ulrey study had been completed and indicated an extensive range of activity and projected significant expansion. Hence, in 1946, J. Donald Phillips was appointed as assistant director of extension in charge of special services—a term that had come to be used to describe services beyond those typically offered through Cooperative Agricultural Extension. Phillips's assignment was to develop and coordinate off-campus activities (other than the traditional extension program) through cooperation with county agents. A decision to broaden the extension concept by adding an individual in the extension office working through county agents suited Hannah's general conception that there should be a single, unified extension program that included conferences, discussion, noncredit course offerings, and similar programs. Dean Emmons remained responsible for off-campus credit courses, but individuals desiring to arrange for such courses were advised to contact Dean Emmons *or their county agents*.

Extensive planning of the nature of the program and staff for a building devoted to continuing education was required. The existing unit in extension headed by Phillips had developed conferences and discussion programs both on and off campus, but the location and the nature of the efforts made it difficult to enlist the efforts of most college departments. Moreover the amount of such activity in relationship to the size of the available extension staff kept the staff so busy that long-term plans were not developed. On March 18, 1948, Carl Horn, who had joined the staff of the Institute of Counseling, Testing and Guidance in 1947, was appointed director of continuing education and associate professor. He was to be in charge of all off-campus programs, except agricultural extension, and all on-campus noncredit courses, except short courses. He was given no direction about his relationship to existing extension programs. The weeks following his appointment were filled with intense and, at times, heated discussions. The result was that, at the board meeting of June 10th, 1948, the director of continuing education was made responsible to the director of extension and through him to the president, a change that did not resolve the underlying problems.

Horn was an able, strong-minded, and imaginative individual. He became devoted to the development of a program, the Flying Classroom, in which business and educational leaders were taken on an educational air tour of various parts of the world. It required extensive absence from the campus and thereby delayed resolution of the problems faced in defining continuing education, in developing programs, and in planning the use of the soon-to-be completed Kellogg Facility for Continuing Education. Furthermore, the Flying Classroom, though an intriguing venture on educational grounds, was a financial disaster.

The new continuing education facility was due to open on July 1,

1950 (because of various construction delays, it opened a year later), with most of the questions about staff and program as yet unanswered. In early June, Hannah felt compelled to move quickly. He called Edgar Harden, a personable, vibrant individual with extensive experience in the public schools in Michigan. Like Horn, Harden had been brought to Michigan State as a staff member of the Institute of Counseling, Testing and Guidance. At the moment of Hannah's phone call, Harden and his family were packed and ready to depart on a trip to California, where he was scheduled to teach summer school. After a few minutes' conversation with Hannah, Harden accepted the appointment as director of continuing education directly responsible to the president. A vacation was traded for a new vocation.

The relationship between Cooperative Extension and Continuing Education was momentarily clarified but by no means finally resolved. Hannah was still committed to a unified program. At the same time, the difficulties of the immediate past situation were evident. Moreover, Hannah was always inclined, when asking an individual to take on a new assignment, to give that individual autonomy in its development although assuring assistance when needed. Harden recalled in later years that although he was given complete freedom to develop continuing education programs, Hannah did indicate several ventures and groups (including labor) that he hoped would receive attention. Harden complied with these suggestions and continuing education thrived under him.

During the year 1950–51, continuing education programs reached more than 129,000 persons on campus and in local communities through conferences, workshops, and courses. Resident extension centers for coordinating continuing education and for credit courses were quickly established at Midland, Flint, Grand Rapids, and at Chatham in the Upper Peninsula. Plans had also been developed for a year-round program of adult evening credit extension courses in the several centers. While the role of the continuing education program in offering credit courses was that of coordination, the result was that of encouraging and assisting all colleges and departments to participate in off-campus credit work.

The program of evening adult credit courses that had existed for some years was extended in scope and content to include the concept of a resident center with at least one full-time college staff member. "Resident" was readily interpreted as implying "residence credit" to be included in the total number of campus enrollees used in justifying requests for state funds. The state legislature had traditionally supported on-campus credit instruction but had prescribed that off-campus credit should be self-supporting. Although other state institutions immediately recognized the implications of the resident center concept and, by using it, quickly made it an issue for the legislature and the state budget planners, the long-time policy that extension activity, other than Cooperative Extension, must be self-supporting remained unaltered.

Edgar Harden was instrumental in the rapid development of continuing education activities. His cooperative approach calmed some of the attacks by hotels and restaurants and eased, though it did not resolve, the concerns of the Cooperative Extension staff. Close cooperation rather than competition with colleges and departments likewise gained acceptance and support by involving faculty members. Harden was designated as dean in 1952, thereby recognizing continuing education as an activity on a par with the colleges. Continuing Education had grown at an astounding rate. When Harden resigned in 1955, leaving behind him a well-organized and thriving operation, Durwood Varner became vice-president of off-campus education and also temporarily assumed the task of directing Continuing Education.

In 1952, Durwood Varner had become director of extension, and in that same year the Committee on College Extension Organization and Policy reiterated points made in the earlier study: (1) there should be only one unified extension service; (2) the expansion of this service to include the cultural arts, social sciences, and professions was essential and would require more subject-matter specialists; (3) extension activities should be carried into urban areas but without sacrificing existing values and programs. The last point recognized that one of the difficulties in expanding extension activities was the difficulty in finding funds. Support of the Cooperative Extension and Experiment Station activities had become accepted by virtue of annual grants from federal, state, and local sources. The prevailing view was that these allocations were justified and their uses limited by national needs and economic benefits. If expansion of extension activity was at the expense of the existing funding for Cooperative Extension, then values and programs would be lost and criticism of the institution for moving away from what many persons regarded as its primary commitments would be forthcoming. Clearly, the relationship between Continuing Education and Cooperative Extension would have to be further examined.

At a staff meeting on October 9, 1952 Hannah recognized a developing faculty distaste for extension. "It disturbs me to learn that, with increasing frequency, faculty members will render no out-of-classroom service without added compensations." At the same time, he commented upon the faculty disposition to reduce out-of-classroom assistance to students. He might have remarked (though he did not) that the faculty now expected public service to yield private gain.

It was Hannah's hope that the Varner appointment would establish a firm, unified extension program. Moreover, Varner was given the responsibility of representing institutional interests to the legislature and might therefore tactfully present the broader concept of extension to that group. At that time Hannah was in Washington serving as Assistant Secretary of Defense, and thus Varner was also given responsiblity for dealing with the legislature regarding the 100th anniversary of Michigan State (1955) and the desire to redesignate the institution as a university—an interrelated but heavy burden. In addition, a succession of major events made it difficult to achieve the unity and integration of public service desired at the operational level. In 1953, the Kellogg Foundation granted funds to develop the Gull Lake Biological Station. The initiation of activity there, including conferences, workshops, and summer-school credit courses in science and education, called for speedy action and cooperation among Cooperative Extension, Continuing Education, several science departments, and the School of Education. Varner was overloaded. Cooperative Extension and Continuing Education continued to pursue their separate ways.

Another form of off-campus development occurred when Mr. and Mrs. Alfred G. Wilson in 1956 gave Meadow Brook Farms and $2 million to underwrite the establishment of a branch of MSU in Oakland County near Rochester. This gift obviously called for fine tuning with the legislature. Varner was also called upon to coordinate the planning of the new campus. Howard R. Neville became acting director of continuing education in 1957 and director in 1958. Meantime, Paul Miller, an agricultural sociologist, replaced Varner as director of extension and continued in that position until 1959 when he became provost.

Individuals changed positions and titles as if in a game of musical chairs. Varner was appointed chancellor of the new MSU campus at Oakland. Academic (on-campus) Vice President Hamilton had departed to become head of the New York system of higher education. The appointment of Miller, an individual well based in the extension concept, as provost was seen as another opportunity to bring together in one office the coordination of both on- and off-campus activities. But Miller, in turn, departed to become president of West Virginia University and was succeeded by Clifford Erickson in 1962. Erickson had developed the Institute of Counseling, Testing and Guidance that had engaged in extensive service activity with the schools of the state. He had been the second dean of the Basic College and had served as dean of the College of Education, which in itself carried on extensive activities with the schools and other educational agencies of the state. Howard Neville was brought from continuing education to the provost's office in 1964 to handle the academic budget. When Erickson died suddenly and prematurely, Neville succeeded him in that post (1965).

Armand Hunter, who had been director of broadcasting services for some years, become director of continuing education and brought radio and television, which had started in Cooperative Extension and later became an independent division, back to an extension role. Broadcasting services and programs had, like continuing education, moved to new audiences well beyond those reached by earlier extension services. The Kellogg Center now provided an on-campus site for conferences and special programs and the headquarters for out-state programs coordinated by the seven extension centers. Credit and noncredit courses and even complete degree programs were made available. A new Evening College also provided extensive offerings on the campus. Programs such as labor and industrial relations, community services, and highway traffic safety that were initiated within the center eventually developed into significant, self-supporting, continuing services backed up by related degree programs. An assistant dean for coordination with and supported by Continuing Education was now located in each college. Moreover, the Kellogg Center, as of 1961 and for some years thereafter, was the largest known university laboratory for hotel, restaurant, and institutional management students. The services assigned to Continuing Education continued to change with people and circumstances. In 1969, the Abrams Planetarium and the Lecture-Concert Series were reassigned from the provost's office to Continuing Education. The rationale for these moves was unclear, but both involved off-campus stars.

The essential identity of the land-grant philosophy as interpreted by Hannah and the aim of W. K. Kellogg and his foundation to "help people help themselves" had resulted in a new concept of and approach to public service. The center became the prototype for similar Kellogg-supported centers at numerous other universities. Indeed, at Michigan State the center became more widely known than Cooperative Extension as an integral part of the institution. The original Kellogg gift was augmented by the State Board of Agriculture to enlarge the original plans to make the center practically self-supporting on the basis of fees charged for rooms, meals, and conferences. Subsequent gifts from the Kellogg Foundation provided for air conditioning and for additional conference and office space. Other specific grants helped to define the programs and services of the center.

The success of the Kellogg Center destroyed the concept of a single, unified extension service. A review of Hannah's selection of key administrators underlines his commitment to unity, but rapid turnover of administrative personnel, combined with the many other issues that required attention in the rapidly growing university resulted in almost independent development of two public-service programs. Disciplinary departments showed less and less interest in extension or applied research unless added funds were made available. Service as an obligation was replaced by service as an opportunity for overload pay except in agriculture and home economics.

Both Cooperative Extension and Continuing Education, in response to critical needs, sought new and flexible relations with departments and colleges and cooperated in creating new interdisciplinary or problem-solving units. Thus, the field representatives and the campus administration for both extension and continuing education had become, as reported in a 1958 report of progress on cooperative extension, coordinators and resource-linkers rather than the possessors of the specialized knowledge and skills required to provide needed or requested service. Both Cooperative Extension and Continuing Education found it necessary to establish linkages to the several colleges and departments. Cooperative Extension has accomplished this primarily by dual appointments, the Experiment Station by dual appointments and departmental commitments, and Continuing Education by assistant deans located in the various colleges but paid for by Continuing Education. Rather than employing its own research staff, the Experiment Station funds research projects within departments.

As of 1969–70 the range of Continuing Education activities was reflected in its organization:

- University extension including the regional centers, the Evening College, and the University of the Air providing broadcasts of credit courses and noncredit cultural programs
- University public services including international extension, and cultural programs, then designated as Cap and Gown
- Television and radio broadcasting
- Community-college cooperation
- Highway Traffic Safety Center

Cooperative Extension, now definitely separate from Continuing Education, continued many aspects of its earlier programs but also made adjustments and additions as needs changed and funds were available. In the decade from 1950 to 1959, Michigan lost some 40,000 farms (from more than 150,000 in 1949), and farms were also becoming larger. Mechanization, automation, and energy requirements became matters of concern. There was an increasing tendency to view the farm as a business unit. Hence, marketing education and marketing information became major programs until reduced funding forced cutbacks in the 1960s.

Resource utilization, conservation, and land-use planning became important and involved some attention to urban developments and problems. Home economics rechristened and reshaped its extension activities to highlight family-living education and, particularly, nutrition. These themes were at least as important for urban populations as for rural ones. However, complexity of the problems and lack of continuing funding severely restricted urban extension.

### The Research-Service Dilemma

After several attempts at a single, unified extension program for the entire institution, Hannah established Continuing Education as a separate, independent unit reporting first directly to the president, then for a time to the vice-president for off-campus education, and finally to the provost, where it has since continued. Thereby, the continuing education program was placed at an administrative level corresponding to that of college deans, although the title of dean originally granted Harden was not again used until after restudy and redesignation of Continuing Education as "Lifelong Education."

The failure to establish Cooperative Extension as a single coordinating agency for public service can be traced to several factors:

1. From its creation, Cooperative Extension was an integral part of agriculture, and its staff was primarily oriented to working with rural areas of the state. Cooperative Extension was continuously funded from year to year and wished to avoid any dilution of funding that would result from an expanded program.

2. Relations of both Cooperative Extension and Experiment Station to departments were rapidly undergoing change as the departments expanded and took an increasingly narrow and disciplinary view of teaching and research.

3. Departmental and professorial focus was increasingly on advancement of the department, discipline, or individual scholar rather than on serving society.

4. Service, whether as consultation or applied research, offered limited opportunity for publication and little or no recognition

locally or nationally. Moreover, consultation frequently involves specificity of circumstances and confidentiality. Since the academic is, in effect, foregoing scholarly work to engage in service, compensation is expected. Institutionally tendered service becomes replaced by personally arranged, frequently lucrative, and often unreported consultation. There is little motivation for engaging in gratuitous public service when that same activity can yield private gain.

Cooperative Extension and the Experiment Station were originally authorized, in great part, because of economic implications, although personal development and enhancement of community were not ignored. As the attention of Cooperative Extension turned to personal and community development and a comprehensive concept of the people and areas to be served, the close interaction originally projected between Cooperative Extension and Experiment Station became less apparent. The latter continued to depend primarily on the natural sciences, while the former gave more attention to human dynamics and, hence, to the social sciences. With continuing support related to specific projects, it was not easy to shift persons from one task to another or to terminate some projects so as to divert funds and manpower to others. Line-item appropriations, when externally determined, can be vulnerable to external intervention and termination. They provide a degree of security for programs at the cost of flexibility in changing emphases.

In the years after Hannah's departure, the Cooperative Extension Service, the Agricultural Experiment Station, and Continuing Education have received less attention from central administration and from the faculty than formerly. Central administration has tended to emphasize the role and the success of the university as one of the top twenty or so universities in the nation. Research funds from other sources have made Experiment Station funding relatively unattractive. A president might speak and write glowingly of lifelong education, but departments and their faculties have been simply uninterested— unless of course, adequate funds can be found to research the problems. As the following chapter indicates, extension and applied research still attract able academics if funds are provided and if recognition and reward can follow.

As of 1980, the Agricultural Experiment Station academic staff numbered 280 persons, and the station was supporting research in eight colleges. It also had major responsibility for the Pesticide Research Center and shared responsibility for the Institute of Water Research. And it could report, quite factually, that "much of the teaching of the resident instructional staff and the work of the cooperative extension service is based upon the findings of the Agricultural Experiment Station."

As of 1980, the Cooperative Extension Service reported programs administered by resource specialists in eight MSU colleges and a staff of 275 extension agents directing local educational programs in agricultural production, management, and marketing; family living education, 4-H Youth Programs; and natural resources—public policy.

Perhaps only John Hannah, with Kellogg Foundation resources, could have succeeded in developing a new public-service unit. His own background in cooperative extension, his continuing close relations with faculty and staff in agriculture, and his success with the legislature and others generally brought enthusiastic acceptance of an idea rejected by some faculty members and of no great interest to others.

# 11
# Selected Public Service Projects in Departments, Centers, and Institutes

President John Hannah's attempt to provide institutional-wide extension and public service through a single agency, the Cooperative Extension Service, was not successful. Two agencies, the Cooperative Extension Service and the Kellogg Center for Continuing Education, emerged. In addition, MSU's size and range of disciplines and services resulted in the creation of a variety of institutes, centers, bureaus, offices, laboratories, programs, committees, and divisions, with purposes and specific objectives as diverse as the designations used. Many of them included the public service mission, but the sincerity and extent of that mission depended greatly on the availability and source of funds and on the orientation of the director or administrator of the moment. Specific service projects might be related to the Cooperative Extension Service, to the Continuing Education Center, or to both. Some projects became essentially autonomous.

These new service units arose out of many differing and contrasting concerns. Some units (even some colleges and academic departments) arose out of external demands or of administrative recognition of the desirability of grouping together an unusual array of talents not readily accommodated in existing structures. Others arose out of a need to foster interdisciplinary or problem-focused instruction, research, or service. Some units were created to prove institutional concern about an issue and provide a basis for seeking funds from public or private sources. A few units were politically inspired and represented little more originally than a reluctant acquiescence to pressure.

Existing departments and colleges sometimes viewed these new units as unnecessary and divisive competitors to disciplinary departmental structures. But the instigators of the units might justify their existence as a means to bypass departmental and college indifference or even antagonism to public service. Departmental insistence on control of academic rank, and hence of such new units, was of no concern to Hannah, who regarded rank as a university action and assignment as an administrative one. To Hannah, structures, though essential, were primarily a means to focus upon and accomplish institutional missions.

Since the various units came into being in diverse ways and sometimes changed purposes and character over time, a simple, consistent classification is not possible. However, if those units that were organized primarily to conduct research are omitted, there were five types of units that emphasized the service function. Some of them arose out of institutional concerns, some out of Cooperative Extension, and some from Continuing Education. Funding came from diverse sources: institutional general fund, special legislative allocations, foundation grants, and sponsored projects.

The first type of service unit is represented by the Offices of High School Cooperation and of Junior College Cooperation. Hannah was interested in recruiting more students, but he was also concerned with assisting high schools and colleges in developing programs and training personnel. Thus, these offices, which were both administrative and service in nature, recruited graduate and undergraduate students while (or by) extending services.

The second type of unit is exemplified by departments serving instruction, research, and service functions. Agricultural engineering and the resource development departments are notable examples.

The third type arose out of creation of an institute or center to provide public service to a particular group or in a defined area. The Centers for Labor and Industrial Relations, Highway Traffic Safety, and Science and Mathematics Teaching represent this type of unit.

The fourth type of unit arose out of interest in and attempts to expand public service into urban communities. The Institute for Community Development, the Charles Stewart Mott Institute for Community Improvement, and the project called Community Service in the Community College were of this sort.

A fifth type of temporary service unit focused on special projects supported by external grants to study and develop new programs meeting identified needs.

Examples of each of these five groups, which include outstanding successes and near failures, will be discussed in sufficient detail to indicate purposes, problems encountered, and results. In addition, the experiences with these units and the problem of terminating or institutionalizing them will be considered.

ADMINISTRATIVE AND SERVICE UNITS:
OFFICES OF HIGH SCHOOL AND
JUNIOR-COMMUNITY COLLEGE COOPERATION

On October 27, 1947, Hannah spoke to the Michigan Association of Junior Colleges at its annual meeting. His topic, "The Role of the Junior College in Higher Education," enabled him to emphasize his interest in adult education. Hannah asserted that existing colleges and universities could not meet already identified needs. As a former student of Grand Rapids Junior College, he expressed his hope that the public junior college system would expand to relieve pressure on other universities and colleges and provide preprofessional education in a relatively inexpensive manner. He called for regional colleges with sufficient size and basis for support that they would be autonomous from high schools. He also expressed the view that these colleges should be locally or regionally controlled and thereby provide programs adapted to local needs. He insisted also that general education should be the foundation for all curricula. His views were well received and formed a firm basis for continuing interaction with the community colleges.

Michigan State's general education program, the possibility of deferring career choice, and the new emphasis on high-quality career counseling and academic advising were attractive to high school and community college students as well as to teachers, counselors, and administrators. In suggesting that Michigan State cooperate with the high schools and colleges, Hannah wanted to portray the institution as one that provided quality programs in or based upon the liberal arts and sciences. He wanted to attract more and *better* students from all areas of the state. The Basic College faculty had found many poorly prepared students and had decided to provide remedial programs in writing, speaking, reading, and arithmetic, but they also hoped to foster changes in the secondary school programs themselves. In an era in which the service role was still highly regarded by most of the faculty and regularly reiterated by Hannah, the faculty and deans could and did emphasize in their contacts their desire and willingness to be of service. To assist in the development of this extension activity, the Office of High School Cooperation was created in 1949 with Professor Guy Hill from education as director. Hill was widely and favorably known by educators throughout the state as well as on the campus. Very soon faculty members from many segments of the campus were working with high school personnel, either in their schools or with groups coming to the campus. Similar relations developed with community colleges.

Erickson's Institute of Counseling, Testing, and Guidance also worked with teachers and counselors in the schools and attracted many of them to campus as candidates for advanced degrees. The evaluation unit (initially called Board of Examiners, later Evaluation Services) set up to assist in test development and in program evaluation on campus became involved with numerous secondary schools in which teachers desired to test "critical thinking and other thought processes" rather than simple recall. The impetus was that several Basic College courses attempted to emphasize thinking. Students had reported their anxieties about such courses and their approbation or disgust back to their high school teachers and principals at the annual conference of principals, teachers, and recent graduates who had enrolled at Michigan State.

In a few years, the Highway Traffic Safety Center and the Science Mathematics Teaching Center were also working with secondary school administrators and teachers in the development of science, mathematics, and driver training courses and the preparation of teachers to offer them. The conjunction of service and recruiting was effective, and it both acquainted Michigan State faculty with the problems of articulation and provided them with some insight into student needs and hence into the institution's personnel administration concerns and problems.

Increasing enrollments at Michigan State in the years after World War II as well as the mix of students might be offset by increasing junior college enrollments. The acceptability of community college course credits and grades was also questioned. Thus, by 1956, Hannah appointed a subcommittee of the Administrative Group to study MSU's relations with community colleges.

Many of the community colleges had duplicated and retained the traditional departmental courses they found in most four-year colleges. Acceptance of these traditional disciplinary offerings as equivalents of the Michigan State general education requirements was, in effect, a waiver of general education for community college graduates admitted to Michigan State. Evidence that some transfers withdrew or failed by the end of the first quarter suggested a hiatus in rigor or in environment between community college and Michigan State programs. There were conflicting views within Michigan State and between Michigan State and the community colleges as to the nature and resolution of such problems.

Community colleges viewed Michigan State's two-year certificate programs in agriculture, business, home economics, engineering, and general education as competitive with their programs. The intent in adding the certificate programs had never been to attract large numbers of avowed two-year students but rather to provide a meaningful experience for those who remained but two years. In fact, requests for two-year certificates were so rare that records of them were never kept, and eventually the programs disappeared from lack of demand.

The Administrative Group subcommittee recommended: first, that community college transfers should not lose time or credit other than that imposed by making up specific major course requirements; second, that a general education examination might be required for all transfer students; and, third, that a consultant be made available to provide information and assistance to all interested junior colleges with the purpose of developing understanding and closer bonds. The requirement that transfer students take a general education examination proved impractical because the general education faculty could not agree on a definition of such an exam other than that it represent content explicit in existing courses, which changed from year to year.

In 1956 Max Smith, a well-known, widely respected former community college administrator, was appointed director of the Office of Community-Junior College Cooperation. The program developed by Smith included the following points:

1. Provision of assistance in such matters as curriculum development, administrative organization, registration procedures, financing, formulating objectives, and program evaluation
2. Assistance to any community in planning for and developing a community college, by making available the resources of Michigan State University to work with people in the community
3. Interpretation of MSU entrance requirements and transfer credit policies to community colleges, and of their problems and concerns back to the university

In addition, Smith, as a professor in the College of Education as well as a staff member in Continuing Education, was able to develop several off- and on-campus programs (including graduate degree programs) for community college faculty and administrators. Perhaps even more significant was the decision of President Hannah to invite community college administrators to an annual dinner for informal discussion of common concerns. The personal interactions of university administrators with secondary school and community college personnel and the channels provided for communication and service with all parts of the university led to extensive cooperation and mutual understanding. This brought more students—both graduate and undergraduate. As expected, other colleges and universities took note and developed similar programs. Students, of course, benefited thereby—and that is what service and extension activities are about.

Unfortunately, Smith tended to emphasize financial and administrative matters rather than curricular ones. He was well known among community college administrators but not well known by MSU faculty. His office, therefore, was not as effective in encouraging faculty involvement as had been that of the Office High School Cooperation.

## ACADEMIC UNITS

### The Department of Agricultural Engineering

Since departmentalization had already taken hold in Michigan State by the early part of the twentieth century, much of the action on the research and service fronts was localized within departments and attributable to particular individuals within them. The Department of Agricultural Engineering (AE) is a prime example of a unit contributing to teaching, research, and service. Mechanization was a key aspect of developments in agriculture and in industry. Into the early years of the twentieth century, students were receiving extensive practical experience. Students in farm mechanics constructed buildings and furnishings. They worked with and repaired engines and other machinery. They made cement blocks, tile, and poured sidewalks. Extension activities provided demonstrations on improving rural farm and home conditions by solving the mechanical problems of building farm structures. Country home conveniences and operation of farm equipment were primary foci of attention. Extension work and the resident instruction program were extremely closely related. The first graduate courses offered by the farm mechanics department in 1922 dealt with farm structures, power and machinery, and farm conveniences.

By the 1920s the AE department was demonstrating farm building construction, and by 1929 its extension program included a total of 171 demonstrations. One of the difficulties with demonstrations was transportation. In 1924 a truck equipped with lighting, water, and sewage systems covered twenty-two counties. At each demonstration site, the necessary concrete forms were constructed and left for further use. One professorial demonstrator remarked that there was no more *fundamental* way to get close to individuals than to become involved in their sewage problems.

Land clearance played a major role in developing agriculture, as it had earlier in creating a college campus. The availability and use of war salvage explosives for land clearance resulted, in 1926, in a course in the use of explosives. Three years later a second course was added. These same on-campus courses were given at various points around the state.

In 1927 a rural electrification program in extension, teaching, and research was initiated. In cooperation with Detroit Edison and Consumers Power Companies, research in rural electrification was started using appliances loaned to twelve farmers by manufacturers. Wiring was designed by the agricultural engineering department. The research sought to determine the usefulness of electricity and the savings in time, money, and labor. The positive results were disseminated across the state. Michigan became the leading state in the percentage of farms using electricity. Members of the department worked to develop electrical devices and equipment especially adapted to farm use.

During the World War II years, the department developed and proposed a program in agricultural engineering jointly administered by engineering and agriculture. An innovative short-course program entitled "Farm Equipment Service and Sales," planned for returning veterans interested in acquiring jobs, was so successful that it was shortly developed into a two-year program and renamed "Power Equipment Technology."

The Rural Progress Caravan, another innovative postwar program, was an educational traveling exhibit of recent developments in farm mechanization. More than 150,000 people saw the models and displays during 1946 and 1947. The exhibit brought nationwide recognition and aroused interest in advanced study. Master's and Ph.D. programs had been approved in 1946. The first Ph.D. in Agricultural Engineering was awarded in 1948.

A new Agricultural Engineering Building was started in 1946 and was dedicated two years later. Its dedication was an event of both local and national significance and added greatly to the prestige of the department.

During the years 1945 through 1950, the three major research projects in the department had to do with sugar beet mechanization, frost prevention, and dairy structures. The sugar beet project was carried out in cooperation with the Sugar Beet Manufacturers Association, thereby shortcutting some of the processes usually involved in dissemination and development. By 1950 most of the sugar beets in Michigan were harvested mechanically.

In great part because of the efforts of this department, agricultural engineering was becoming accepted as a specialty. The department sought to obtain professional registration for agricultural engineers in Michigan. In 1949 the professional engineers of the state voted to accept agricultural engineering as a specialty.

The AE department planned a farm mechanization exhibit to celebrate the college centennial year 1955. It was the largest single public affair ever held on the campus and was estimated to have attracted 330,000 visitors. The event drew representation from leading companies in agriculture and machinery fields. A pageant showing the historical progress of farm machinery over the past 100 years drew international visitors. The event contributed to the growth of the graduate and research programs of the department. Among the forty to fifty students working on master's and Ph.D. degrees in the 1960s there were usually fourteen or fifteen different countries represented. Out of a total of 235 graduates through 1964, 115 went into educational positions. Many moved into administrative or research directorship roles.

Research and extension programs of the department attracted financial aid from many sources including dollars supplied by the U.S. Department of Agriculture. One of the notable trends in research was emphasis upon the processing and handling of agricultural products, especially in the mechanization of the harvesting operation for tomatoes, cherries, apples, cabbage, and cucumbers. The impact of these research and extension activities was reflected in the curriculum by the mid 1960s. Attention was given to the characteristics or properties of agricultural products and their environment in designing equipment. In the late 1960s and 1970s, extension and research began to emphasize the handling, processing, packaging, and storing of agricultural products.

As a result, new courses were introduced in food engineering, electrical technology, human factors engineering, systems analysis, agricultural pollution control, and family housing. Some of these were very practical and applications oriented while others were becoming highly theoretical. Mechanization, originally called "mechanic arts" in the land-grant act, now appeared as a new Ph.D. program in agricultural mechanization science, designed to improve agricultural production and processing by systematic planning and application of machines, power units, structures, environmental control methods, and water management. Energy shortages generated research programs to make use of waste heat from electric generating plants and to attain greater efficiency in food processing and in the home. Extension activities expanded to include work related to fuel requirements and energy conservation.

N.F. Meador, who wrote a history of the agricultural engineering department covering the years 1906 to 1964, commented:

> The greatest accomplishment of the department has been the training of 966 young men.
>
> Second, is the effect of our graduate training program.This program has been particularly effective in training more than 115 young men who have gone into education. Twenty-four of them are department chairmen, and many others are leaders of important educational groups. From this group also has come four directors of research for important equipment manufacturing companies.
>
> Third, is the service to agriculture in the field of research and extension. Many new ideas, including improved tillage, frost control, forage handling and storage, improved housing, and irrigation, have come from this department.
>
> Fourth, Michigan was the first state in the union to obtain 99.9 percent high line rural electrification. Much of this was due to the very effective research and extension program carried on by this department.
>
> Fifth, this department was one of the pioneers in the development and research in small tractors. While the trend now is toward the larger tractors, yet it was the small family farm tractor which really revolutionized American agriculture.
>
> Sixth, the department, through its research and extension programs materially changed the farm building program in Michigan.
>
> Seventh, this department developed close association with industry, and through the Farm Equipment Service and Sales course, contributed greatly to the solution of personnel problems for implement dealers.
>
> Eighth, the impact of this department on foreign agriculture has been great. Our students are presently employed in many countries in the world in key positions.
>
> Ninth, the department has been a leader in the development of the agricultural engineering profession and of the American Society of Agricultural Engineers.[1]

Meador's summary effectively demonstrates the pursuit of Michigan State's tripartite mission of instruction, research, and service. It is quite understandable that Hannah gave enthusiastic support to the department and to obtaining a new engineering facility.

Speaking to the Land-Grant College Association in 1944 Hannah remarked: "The greatest asset possessed by our land-grant colleges is the great confidence of common people in them. Public confidence is a fickle thing. To maintain it, it must always be cultivated and fer-

---

1. N.F. Meador, "History of Agricultural Engineering Department, Michigan State University, 1906–1964," unpublished, undated document in the MSU Archives and Historical Collections.

tilized—cultivated through continuing useful services and fertilized with new ideas, new programs, and new developments to meet the ever changing public need." The Department of Agricultural Engineering exemplified his views.

*The Department of Resource Development*

The Conservation Institute, authorized by the State Board of Agriculture on May 20, 1937, resulted from the termination of the Land Economic Survey, a division of the state Department of Conservation. The survey, which had provided an inventory of soil, slope, forest, land use, geology, potential power sources, and other economic facts, was terminated because of lack of legislative appropriation.

County agents and various groups asked Michigan State to continue this inventory, because public interest in land use, rural zoning, and natural resources management was growing. President Robert Shaw appointed a committee of deans and the director of the Experiment Station to look into the request. The committee recommended that the college create an institute supporting a balanced program of teaching, research, and extension concerned with conservation. Courses and instruction were to remain in the departments, and the institute staff was likewise to be based in departments. The institute, a planning and coordinating unit, was given a full-time professor-director and assigned to the Division of Agriculture. The unit was to engage in research and provide some teaching, but its primary obligation was service. The Conservation Institute continued for thirteen years but never had more than five full-time employees. For half of its life only the director was a full-time employee.

In the institute's first year, the director taught an introductory course in conservation to eighty-four students. Within a few years, the curriculum included:

Introduction to conservation
Soil geography and land use
Land utilization
Special conservation problems
Conservation administration
Conservation seminars
Conservation laws
Conservation of natural resources
Rural land use planning
Research problems in conservation

Obviously there was increasing conversation about conservation. A number of short courses were also offered. By 1950, the enrollment in conservation courses rose to 240 undergraduates, 18 short-course students, and several graduate students.

Major research projects included methods of land classification, development of land use plans, land type mapping, rodent damage to orchards, farmers' share crops of fur and game, relative utility of different land types, wildlife grazing investigation, swampland investigation, a state map showing land drainage on a physical geopolitical basis, and study of urban-rural fringe problems.

Extension activities included publications (some in the tens of thousands), guidance, and counsel for committees, commissions, teachers, county agents, and students. Radio programs were presented on a weekly basis. Zoning problems and appropriate legislation, recreation, resource inventories and studies, and planning of local resources and land were studied. Farm game management and soil conservation led to cooperative game management organizations and soil conservation districts.

In 1945 the institute received $25,000 to develop and support a new Tourist and Resort Industry Program which sought and received assistance on site selection, construction specifications, sewage disposal, and utility needs. The economic benefits of this Michigan State effort have never been determined but were estimated as being in the millions of dollars.

In 1950 the Conservation Institute was dissolved, and a Division of Conservation with four principal departments—land and water conservation, forestry, fisheries and wildlife, and wood utilization—was organized. The new Department of Land and Water Conservation expanded its courses and instructional program including off-campus courses for public school teachers. Bachelor of Science degree programs in land and water conservation, park management, and municipal and public utility foresty became effective in fall 1952. Extension provided services to various councils, associations, county and regional planning commissions, and local chambers of commerce. But instruction was, by far, the most rapidly growing aspect of the departmental activities. By 1956 instruction was provided to 811 students in regularly scheduled graduate, undergraduate, evening, and off-campus courses.

In 1955 questions were being raised about the range and heterogeneity of departmental functions included in the Department of Land and Water Conservation. In the fall of that year, a group of consultants reviewing division programs noted the lack of cohesion in the division that recommended against separate college status. That recommendation was indicative of an underlying conflict between production agriculture and natural resource management. Hannah insisted that the two must work together and resolve their differences rather than emerge as adversaries—typical Hannah philosophy.

Subsequent to this report Dean T. K. Cowden recommended to the State Board of Agriculture that the Division of Conservation be discontinued and that the four department heads report directly to the dean. In addition, by various transfers of courses and programs (tourist and resort management to the College of Business), the Department of Land and Water Conservation became the Department of Resource Development with three emphases: land and water use, soil conservation administration, and park management. The changes became effective July 1, 1956.

On April 3, 1958, the department head, Dr. Frank Suggitt, once again raised questions about the lack of cohesiveness in the department and the justification for its existence. He pointed out that a changing America required university attention to the basic and complicated problems of recreation, regional planning and development, water resources management, and new concepts of extension education. He emphasized that these four needs were all-university in scope and required central direction. In general, he deplored the tendency to expand and engulf new specific problem areas as "an awful lot of motion and commotion with little notice as to direction, depth, or velocity or consequences." The remarks were a sensitive reaction to institutional dynamics but hardly took into account that the university itself was rapidly growing on many fronts and seeking to redefine and establish its identity and missions.

In 1955 the School of Agriculture became the College of Agriculture; and in November 1966 the phrase "and Natural Resources" was added to its title in recognition of the expansion in teaching, research, and extension in the four departments concerned with natural resources. Yet in 1969 another effort was made by the four departments to sever ties with agriculture and establish a new College of Natural Resources. Their central concern was a feeling that natural resource units did not receive a fair share of the budget. The College of Agriculture and Natural Resources, having already been relegated to a less secure role by the expansion of other programs in the university, was resistant to loss of another popular and timely group of programs. By then Hannah had departed, but his philosophy prevailed.

No review of departments or other units at Michigan State would be complete without reporting housing moves from one facility to another on an expanding campus. The Department of Resource Development, originally located on the fourth floor of Agricultural Hall, moved to Wells Hall, the former men's dormitory, in 1959. Later the department moved to the Natural Science Building and on September 6, 1966, to the then new Natural Resources Building. At the time, this structure provided some of the finest teaching and research facilities in the nation.

In that same year, the department received permission to offer a doctoral program. In 1966, too, a director of natural resources was named, presumably to provide leadership and coordination of the departments oriented to natural resources. However, the divisional organization was not reactivated.

Tourism, earlier transferred to the College of Business, was announced in 1970 as a separate major "appropriate for travel agents, tour operators, tourism development specialists, travel sales positions, tourist associations, tourist councils and chambers of commerce."

Research activities of the staff in the early years tended to be limited by burdensome teaching and extension loads and service on various commissions and boards dealing with soil and water conservation and land planning and community development. By the middle 1960s the department and individuals in it began to receive significant grants and contracts for specific study projects.

By 1970 there were four major types of activities in resource development extension programs: resource organization, community resource development, soil and water conservation, and natural resources policy. These emphases, later condensed to two areas, corresponded to the teaching program emphases. An institute, created to meet a specific set of needs related to conservation, led gradually from service programs to research and instruction. The institute gradually achieved departmental status and continues to provide instruction, research, and service. It also led to the creation of a major in another college. The department early found it necessary to cooperate with other departments across college lines in its extension, research, and service activities. Perhaps this department exhibits, more clearly than any other, increasing attention to resource conservation. The history of the department demonstrates the interrelationship of service, instruction, and research. It also demonstrates the readiness and adaptability of Michigan State under Hannah to recognize and meet a significant educational need even when no funds were immediately forthcoming for it.

## SPECIFIC PUBLIC SERVICE UNITS

### *The School of Labor and Industrial Relations*

Although the Morrill Act assigned to the land-grant college a responsibility for providing education appropriate to the needs and development of the mechanic arts, early programs were limited to agriculture and only later extended to engineering. Education for factory workers, for skilled and unskilled mechanics, and for tradesmen remained an unknown quantity, whereas the economic benefits of improving technology through engineering were evident. So, too, were benefits of improving management. Education directly aimed at the improvement of the laboring classes was regarded with some skepticism, especially since there was no ready source of funding for it.

Study of labor practices and problems was acceptable, but advocacy of measures designed to improve the lot of organized labor was to be avoided. Such seems to have been the controlling view until after World War II. By 1929–30 Professor William Haber, an economist, offered a series of courses on labor including labor economics, labor problems (required for engineering students), industrial relations problems, and a graduate course in industrial relations. In 1933–34 a course in personnel management and one entitled "The State in Relation to Labor" were added. Haber's courses attracted such favorable attention that he was courted and hired by the University of Michigan in 1936. Haber's attention to labor problems had not been received with complete approval by everyone. Although Hannah, secretary of the State Board of Agriculture at that time, expressed some concerns about Haber's departure from Michigan State, Haber was not replaced. The courses were continued, but they were taught by junior nontenured faculty members who aroused neither apprehension nor approbation.

In the early years of Hannah's presidency during World War II, new course developments were suspended. Nevertheless, Hannah remained alert to what he regarded as both an obligation and an opportunity. At the board meeting on April 21, 1944, Hannah reported a conference between college representatives and the Michigan CIO Council regarding courses in adult education and worker education.

After some study by a committee, J. Donald Phillips was appointed in 1946 as assistant director of extension in charge of special services. Phillips was to develop and coordinate off-campus activities rather than the traditional extension program through cooperation with county agents. The decision to work through county agents fitted Hannah's general conception of a single, unified extension program. The list of topics treated in various types of sessions and the recollections of various people indicate that some successful sessions on labor problems were carried out without attracting unfavorable publicity. The brief tenure of Carl Horn as director of continuing education was oriented to school, business, and industry rather than to labor.

In July 1950 Edgar Harden accepted the appointment as director of continuing education directly responsible to the president. Harden (at Hannah's suggestion) early entered into some discussions with labor leaders in Michigan regarding their interests in educational programs. A labor education program was inaugurated in Continuing Education in 1953. Although this new program could be regarded as an expansion of the earlier activities, it was now clearly directed to labor.

In 1955, after two years of exploratory development of the Labor Education Program, the Labor and Industrial Relations Center was established with Professor C.C. Killingsworth as director, on January 1, 1956. In June 1956 Professor Jack Stieber was appointed as associate professor and succeeded Killingsworth as director in 1959. The action setting up the center indicated that its efforts would be directed to both workers and management as well as to related academic research. Although the center was essentially autonomous in its operation, it retained a working relationship with Continuing Education.

The 1956–57 report of the center notes that three branches were established: Labor Program Service, Personnel Management Program Service, and a Research and Planning Service. Program topics mentioned in the report included union management relationships, union organization and administration, economics and public affairs, and preretirement programs. The topics included cultural as well as functional, job-related programs. The cooperative nature of the effort was indicated by the appointment of an advisory committee made up of labor members that regularly met to talk about program needs. The summary of activity for the year 1956–57 indicated that more than 2,000 members of organized labor had attended classes and that the center had met with trade unionists from other countries in six-week programs. The latter was the first stage in the development of a special foreign team project programed by the U.S. Department of Labor and by the U.S. Department of State.

The objectives of the center as spelled out in its 1956–57 annual report are reminiscent of the commitment to the mechanic arts mandated by the Morrill Act and the state legislation assigning the land-grant role to Michigan State. They included: providing an education contributing to good citizenship, making union members more effective in their unions and in their communities, and developing pamphlets and research materials useful to labor groups and their educational programs.

First-year activities included nineteen conferences and institutes with numbers of attendees varying from 10 to 135. Twenty-eight noncredit courses were offered and nine special projects were reported.

Specific topics dealt with the job of the union steward, basic economics, effective speaking, communication skills, and the worker's family and finances. Subsequent annual reports indicate activities carried on with the United Automobile Workers (UAW); retail, wholesale, and department store unions; various organizations involving machinists, stoneworkers, electrical workers, railroad trainmen, and local labor councils; and the American Federation of State, County, and Municipal Employees. Particular topics were expanded to include Social Security, ethical practices, unemployment insurance, and the United States and Middle East.

By 1957–58 the topics were further broadened to include legislative issues, parliamentary procedures, and the development of the American labor movement. The center, by this time, was dealing frequently with state or local councils of labor, of teachers, and of the state, county, and municipal employees.

The annual report for 1959–60 reported forty-eight classes and institutes and thirty-one special projects with more than 3,600 members of organized labor in attendance at various programs. Of the participants, 40 percent were affiliated with the UAW, and 60 percent or more of the participants were officers in the local or international union. The average age of participants was thirty-nine. One new project was the development of consumer education sessions for spouses of union members.

By 1960–61 the program for union spouses had been enlarged to include nutrition and home decoration. Survival and disarmament had become topics of interest for discussion. In 1962, activities were further expanded, as a result of U.S. President John Kennedy's Executive Order on collective bargaining, to involve postal workers and federal employee union members. A program of lunches with labor leaders, which had been started earlier, became regular events.

In making the word *labor* prominent in the center's designation, the center became externally visible. When a former staff member of the center reported to a state senator that the center was strongly prolabor, a threatening investigation was launched in 1962. To the legislative investigation committee, Hannah, explaining academic freedom, commented, "This freedom from harassment is a hard won right, not to be surrendered lightly, and no university worth the name has any choice but to defend it." In retrospect, the nature of the program of the center did not seem to justify either the accusation or the resulting action, which was a joint resolution of the Michigan House and Senate indicating that if the center were to be continued, an equivalent amount of money would be deducted from the allocation to the institution. The resolution was never implemented even though the attorney general ruled that the center was unlawful.

Obviously, a freestanding center was vulnerable to attack. It also faced other serious problems. Academic personnel attached to the center were dependent upon departments for faculty rank, which meant that the center must operate with individuals, either temporarily assigned or holding dual appointments in a department that did not place high value upon center service activity. Furthermore, any credit courses that the center staff might propose had to be approved and offered by disciplinary departments.

By 1961 rank could be assigned in the center or maintained in a department. On July 19, 1962, the Labor and Industrial Relations Center was replaced by the School of Labor and Industrial Relations, an academic unit in the College of Social Science. Thereafter, the rank and tenure of a staff member would usually be in the school.

The academic nature of the school was further emphasized by the approval of a Master of Labor and Industrial Relations (MLIR) in 1965. Thus, the unit took on an instructional, research, and public service role very much in the land-grant tradition. Recognizing the fact that the service activities and the related practical research would seldom require the disciplinary-oriented research status of the Ph.D., it was specified that the doctoral degree not be required for tenure or professorial appointment in the school for those dealing directly with labor and management. The Ph.D. was required for those appointed in the academic program.

The MLIR degree was, and is, viewed primarily as a terminal degree for individuals preparing for positions in private companies, unions, government, and nonprofit organizations. Two different specialties are provided, one dealing with collective bargaining and employee relations and the other with manpower policies and programs. About two-thirds of the graduate students are full time, but courses have also been offered in the evening or late afternoon so that an individual can complete the master's degree in three years.

In 1968–69, the last year of Hannah's presidency, the total credit course enrollment was 348. By 1982–83 it had gradually increased to nearly 1,200. The number of majors in 1969 was 35 or 40, and this had increased to roughly 130 by 1982–83. Master's degrees granted gradually increased from 21 to 70 during the same period. Although the school has emphasized public service activities with the master's degree as a professional degree, the academic staff has gradually broadened its publications to include books, monographs, and articles or book chapters, of a scholarly nature related to its field activities.

As a result of the introduction of the academic program and its status as a school in the College of Social Science, the School of Labor and Industrial Relations became one of four or five leading programs nationally. The Labor Program Service and the Management Program Service conduct courses and conferences in Michigan and throughout the United States attended by 3,000 to 5,000 people per year. Since the Labor Program Service works through the various labor unions in developing programs, the school does not need to advertise or otherwise publicly promote its role and functions. In effect, it has its own state liaison persons who serve a role similar to that of cooperative extension workers or continuing education branch offices. Hannah's early efforts have borne attractive fruit, although not all worms have been eliminated. As of 1984–85 labor officials have taken exception to a professor's statement of views contrary to union policy and to his driving a foreign-made car to class sessions. Academic freedom is a fragile protection against special and biased interests.

*The Highway Traffic Safety Center*

In 1951 the Automotive Safety Foundation provided a grant to the Association of Land Grant Colleges and State Universities to undertake a study to determine whether a land-grant college or university could be of substantial assistance to highway traffic administrators. The study was also to judge the appropriateness of an educational institution assigning resources to such a service and to indicate the specific nature of the contribution. The study was undertaken at Michigan State University under the auspices of the association and began that same year. President Hannah appointed a fifteen-member faculty advisory committee with the dean of continuing education and the head of police administration as co-chairpersons. In 1952 a second grant was provided by the Automotive Safety Foundation to continue and conclude the study. The 1953 report, entitled "What Can the Colleges Do About the Traffic Problem?," had significant impact.

A special session of the Michigan Legislature was convened in 1955 to deal with the mounting traffic problem. One of its principal actions was the authorization of the State Board of Agriculture to establish a Highway Traffic Safety Center at Michigan State with a special six-month appropriation for the remainder of the fiscal year 1955–56. The legislation, in authorizing the center, charged it with three major functions—research, instruction, and extension services—and it was to study all facets of highway traffic safety.

The director of the center initially reported to the vice-president for off-campus education and later (1959) to the office of the provost. This reporting line reflected the interdisciplinary nature of the center and the fact that it was initially serving as a pilot model for the Association of Land Grant Colleges and State Universities.

The mission statement of the center can be readily paraphrased. The center was to focus the entire resources of the university upon traffic problems and its program was to include five major types of activities: (1) education of young people through undergraduate and graduate courses for career work in the many fields of highway traffic administration; (2) conferences and short courses for people already active in highway traffic administration and safety; (3) research and experimentation to evaluate methods and programs, develop new equipment, analyze problems, and develop standards for improved traffic administration and safety; (4) field services in study of local needs requested by town and counties; (5) information and materials services from a central clearing house.

The center immediately became engaged in extensive programs of research and special study, some supported directly from the center's budget and others using outside funds. For example, in 1958 the State Highway Department made a grant of $411,265 for a three-year center research program. These studies included a wide range of topics, as illustrated by the following:

- Prosecution of fatal accident cases
- Study and analysis of causal factor combinations from accident records
- Defensiveness and changes in driving behavior
- Personality characteristics of effective driver improvement interviewers
- Land use in the vicinity of selected interchanges on certain interstate highways before construction
- Computer procedure for evaluation of common traffic court records
- Decrement of driving skill in continuous driving
- Effect of small cars on traffic flow and safety
- Economic and social effects of highways

Anticipating numerous requests for its services, the Highway Traffic Safety Center developed three searching questions to be asked and answered before undertaking to provide the service:

1. Would the program benefit a large proportion of the people? The answer appeared obvious. The hazards of the highway and the cost in dollars and lives in Michigan and the United States were such that even a small improvement would be both economically and socially desirable.

2. Is there strong demand for such services? Here it was possible to point to many conferences and agencies which had called upon colleges for assistance. The availability of grants for a variety of studies provided another evidence of demand.
3. Would such services be appropriate to Michigan State? It was immediately evident that the various services suggested were much like those already provided in other fields. Hence, the research, the education programs, and the field and information services, which would be established in connection with the traffic problem, were viewed as consistent with the land-grant service function.

The remaining and possibly unanswerable question of whether the program would make sufficient contribution to justify its costs could be determined only after the program had been in operation for some time. But what is the worth of a human life?

The traffic problem is a changing one, with new types of vehicles, new drivers, and constant change in the personnel involved in management of highways. An effective approach to study the problems was seen immediately to involve such campus units and departments as physical education, health and recreation, urban planning, transportation and traffic administration, insurance, finance, taxation, social attitudes, government, legislation, budgeting, and others. As with all complex social problems, substantial advance would be made only if the activities of the center proceeded simultaneously on a number of fronts. Not only must instruction, research, and extension services be developed simultaneously, but means must also be explored to change attitudes and arouse concern of individuals and groups about the problems.

Clearly, the efforts of the center were valued by many agencies and individuals. Over a period of years, the center was able to accumulate statistics showing some alleviation of traffic problems. In 1955 the death rate was 7.0 deaths per 100 million vehicle miles of travel. By 1957 it was reduced to 4.7 deaths per 100 million vehicle miles of travel. The center did not claim full credit for this, but there was widespread acceptance of the view that center activities had suggested directions and had fostered attitudes that contributed to improvement.

In 1956 and 1957 the legislature, which had requested the State Board of Agriculture to establish the Highway Traffic Center, made specific line item appropriations for its operation. In 1958 support of the center was incorporated into the total budget allocation. In the spring of 1961, the university took a severe cut in appropriations and, in adjusting to this reduction, several units (including the center) were marked for elimination. Generally the view taken then and since by the faculty and administration has been that the departments and colleges constitute the central core and the basic strength of the university and hence that peripheral units should be sacrificed before making major cuts in departments. This view is, of course, supported by the fact that a large proportion of the budget in academic departments and colleges is committed to the salaries of departmental faculty.

There was also a tendency, evident in all state-assisted institutions, to regard any reduction in appropriations as temporary and certainly unjustified in the case of any one institution or unit thereof. On this basis, an institution naturally reacted on the grounds of expediency rather than of fundamental reduction in operations. In the particular case of dropping the Highway Traffic Safety Center, there is little doubt that the decision was based upon the assumption that the legislature, which had called the unit into being, would find additional funds to reinstate it. Indeed, the Highway Traffic Safety Center was reinstated in the following year, but through pressure and the legislature's sense of responsibility and this time not as a line item specification.

Since the center staff held rank in the College of Education, both undergraduate courses and graduate programs in driver training and highway traffic safety were developed. The center's extension activities with police and sheriff's departments have received national recognition, and its staff has produced numerous bulletins and research articles. Recently the designation as *center* has been withdrawn, that now being restricted to colleges. The Highway Traffic Safety Programs remain among the most significant units operating in the tripartite role of instruction, research, and service out of the Lifelong Education Programs Office. But there is more than a hint in these developments that, whereas credit instruction and research are academic and must be vested in departments, noncredit instruction and service are not. And the fact remains that the center deals with life-and-death matters in ways that most departments do not.

### The Science and Mathematics Teaching Center

The Science and Mathematics Teaching Center (SMTC) at Michigan State grew out of a program on science teaching held in Ann Arbor on March 1 and 2, 1956. Dr. T. Wayne Taylor of the University of Texas described the activities of the Mathematics Science Teaching Center at that university. The central problem of concern was that high school mathematics and science teachers were isolated from their disciplines.

Professional education courses offered in summer schools and in extension centers were essentially irrelevant to the need for keeping up with the developments in the basic discipline. The individual science or mathematics teachers who sought help from a college or university were unlikely to get it because most professors were not interested in assisting high school teachers. The university faculty emphasized graduate education and research.

Professor Frederic Dutton (MSU chemistry department), who attended the session, talked with Taylor at some length thereafter. Dutton proposed establishment at Michigan State of a center to deal with these problems. By December 28, 1956, only months after the Ann Arbor meeting, the SMTC was approved by the State Board of Agriculture with Dutton as head, a title changed in 1962 to director. Because of crowded campus conditions and little opportunity to design a space appropriate to its activities, the center was moved around in its early years. By 1963, however, it was provided facilities—teaching laboratories, preparation space, and five classrooms—in the academic area of McDonel Residence Hall. The center had already assumed the responsibility for the biological and physical science instruction for elementary teaching candidates. When it also took on the responsibilities for a new introductory biology sequence for the College of Natural Science, it was decided that the SMTC should be moved to a new residence building, Holmes Hall, to be built just east of McDonel Hall. A representative of the center, Professor Julian Brandou, was called upon to join the architects in designing appropriate classroom and laboratory facilities. In 1965 the offices for the center administration, some faculty members, and the teaching program in the physical sciences were moved to Holmes Hall. The biological sciences instructional program expanded into the released space.

In 1966 a new residential college, with a science emphasis, was to be housed in Holmes Hall. The SMTC returned to McDonel Hall, and Dr. Julian R. Brandou became acting director and later director. Dr. Dutton became dean of the new Lyman Briggs College.

The creation of the center had corresponded with the development by the National Science Foundation (NSF) of a program of support for science teacher institutes in 1956–57. The center carried out a series of fifty-two high school teacher summer institutes in the various sciences and mathematics with NSF grants totaling $2,924,490 serving 2,293 participants through the summer of 1976.

In the summer of 1958, an institute supported by an NSF grant of $47,000 was held for junior college teachers of physical science. In 1958–59, the first MSU in-service institute was operated for teachers of physical science and mathematics. After two years, the program was discontinued but later was reinstated for mathematics teachers. A total of twelve institutes attracted 407 mathematics teachers. Professor John Wagner, who was responsible for the mathematics aspect of center operations, later commented on the indifference of the mathematics department to the primary center emphasis.

The first of a series of academic year institutes for general science teachers in junior high school was held in 1960–61. This program was continued until 1969, with a total of ten institutes serving 416 teachers. In addition, many conferences and in-service workshops were held to alert teachers and administrators of new developments in curricula, teaching techniques, and content areas.

The SMTC also sought and received funds from the National Science Foundation for a Traveling Science Teacher Program. This program involved high school teachers who obtained a year's leave of absence. They prepared materials, equipment, and lectures and by the end of the year had visited 572 schools, served 2,125 teachers, and spoken to 306,000 students. Another project of the center was the development of an NSF-supported Summer Enrichment Program in Science for high school students. From 1959 to 1976, seventeen sessions were held involving 1,327 high school juniors; 20 percent of these appeared in MSU freshman classes a year later, and the names of many of them have appeared on the Honors College roster and among the winners of Alumni Distinguished Scholarships, the Rhodes Scholarship competition, and other competitions at MSU and elsewhere. This program has been continued.

One concern of the center was the lack of an appropriate master's degree for secondary school science teachers. Graduate courses in the sciences were very limited in the summer. The typical undergraduate education degree requirements severely limited the amount of science that a student could take. The result was that many science and mathematics teachers seeking a master's degree had inadequate backgrounds in their disciplines and therefore sought an education degree that did little to strengthen their science knowledge and instructional skills. The science departments were generally not interested in these individuals. A Master of Arts in Teaching was approved by the board in 1957. National Science Foundation grants helped to support and thereby attract teachers to a summer program. Although this degree still exists in some departments, it has not been extensively used because neither the science nor the education faculties are enthusiastic about it.

Other institute programs, particularly the Year Long Experienced

Teacher Fellowship Project, sponsored by the U.S. Office of Education, contributed to new developments in elementary science teaching. In 1960 the SMTC established a doctoral program in cooperation with the College of Education. Students in this program completed a degree in science education and assisted the center by their involvement in various aspects of the SMTC teaching and research programs. The center also developed an extensive collection of science resource materials and offered assistance to teachers wishing to use them.

The SMTC attained national visibility and became involved in several national projects including the Biological Science Curriculum Study, History of Science Cases Instruction Project, Chemical Education Material Study, Science Curriculum Improvement Study, and Intermediate Science Curriculum Study, as well as hosting many workshops and conferences for the American Association for the Advancement of Science (AAAS). Cooperation with industry groups and associations and individual companies interested in aspects of science education became a significant part of center operations. The center's activities also won it international recognition, with the result that many of its staff members were invited to teach in Central Africa, Mexico, the Far East, Africa, the Middle East, and the United Kingdom. One person served a full year with the UNESCO Project in Thailand.

This overview of the center's activities and contributions demonstrates its involvement in instruction, in course and curriculum development, in research, and in extension of its findings and experience to secondary and elementary school teachers and to other institutions and persons in the United States and elsewhere in the world. From 1956 to 1969, the SMTC received over $10 million. Despite this, the center was eliminated by 1982. Departments had always seen the center as somewhat competitive and perhaps duplicative of their efforts, but since it had extensive outside funds, it did not threaten them. When funds from external sources diminished and the on-campus instructional role of the center was seen by many as its major activity, support of the SMTC came to be viewed as depriving the departments of funds and staff. It was easy to argue that the departments would take over the functions of the center despite the fact that the center had arisen out of departmental indifference to the problems which it attacked. Continuing cooperation between the Colleges of Natural Science and of Education, the maintenance of teacher improvement programs, and the development of research directed to the improvement of teaching and curriculum were surely valued activities appropriate to any university, but they were not of much interest to the disciplinary-oriented professor and his or her disciplinary-based department.

### COMMUNITY SERVICE PROJECTS

The initial efforts of extension activities concentrated on the dissemination of knowledge about seeds, equipment, and procedures directed to increasing agricultural production. Over time, more attention became directed to individuals and the improvement of the quality of rural living. But as extension leaders turned their attention to other areas and groups, it became apparent that, while the individual must still be a primary concern, more attention needed to be focused upon groups and communities and on the development of services that would improve community living and operation.

Thus, in the colleges' and the president's reports of progress there are repeated references to the need for emphasis on community service. Indeed, the designation of a School of Business and Public Service made explicit that need. So long as most people lived on farms relatively isolated from each other, it was appropriate to focus on individuals and families. As urban population increased and as means of transportation and communication improved, the development of the individuals took place in some community. And the events of World War II and the following years perhaps focused attention on two or three different communities—the immediate and the remote—including the state, the nation, and the world. As a response to these concerns, a number of programs were developed, many of them evolving toward community needs analyses.

### *The Liberal Arts Program for Adults*

The Liberal Arts Program for Adults, financed by a grant of $335,000 by the Fund for Adult Education, began in 1957. This project aimed to demonstrate what land-grant universities might do to foster liberal arts education among adults. The program was conducted in cooperation with other Michigan-supported colleges and universities and included Albion College as a representative of a strong undergraduate liberal arts program. The focus of attention was on design of noncredit courses which were subsequently offered in selected communities. As with many projects carried out under a specific grant for a period of time, the abiding impact of that venture is difficult to determine. Some individuals regarded it as a significant personal educational experience that had continued effect on the thinking of those involved in it. A group of people, over a span of several years, interacted with persons in other institutions and in various communities to assess adult interests and consider how these might be developed into course experiences. A need was demonstrated and the meeting of it made respectable, but the major efforts in development of adult education were still ahead.

## Institute for Community Development

The Institute for Community Development (ICD) was established at Michigan State University in 1958, although community development activities had been carried on earlier by the sociology department. The institute was an outcome of a study completed by the Commission on Community Relations appointed by Vice-President D.B. Varner in December 1955.

Correspondence about the ideas considered by the committee was initiated by Vice-President Varner with Emory Morris, president and general director of the W.K. Kellogg Foundation. In 1958 the Kellogg Foundation funded the establishment and continuance of the institute for five years at $756,950. It was anticipated that the communities served would contribute in some way to the support of the institute and that, by the end of the five-year period, it would become self-sufficient.

The goals and project areas initially established by the Commission on Community Relations were altered during the life of the ICD. Generally, its original mission was to focus on the decision-making processes of social systems in modern settings. These processes were thought to be affected by the complexity of society, the rate of societal change, the need for specialized information, increasing interdependence of the individual and the group, and the need to involve a broad spectrum of interests in group decision-making processes. The first director (1958–63), Charles Adrian, shifted the emphasis of the institute from service to research. He favored dual appointments with urban planning, Cooperative Extension, and various other departments. In effect, the research appointment provided time for departmental research not clearly related to the institutes' mission.

The ICD had been housed in Kellogg Center and was related to both Continuing Education and Cooperative Extension. In 1966, after another failure to merge Continuing Education and Cooperative Extension, Cooperative Extension moved to eliminate the dual appointments.

When Duane L. Gibson became director (1963–76), he immediately shifted the emphasis of the ICD back toward its original goals. The early concentration on research had not developed a supporting clientele and had ended hope of further support from Kellogg. Thus, further activity had to be supported by the community requesting service or by some special grant. A problem earlier identified and a continuing difficulty was that no demonstrated solution to many community problems existed and that lack of funds coupled with the fact that many community issues were decided on the basis of emotion rather than on carefully established factual evidence often rendered the institute's efforts both frustrating and ineffectual.

While the projects of the ICD reflected current events, the project areas included (1) land use problems, (2) government organization and capital outlay, (3) economic analysis, (4) urban renewal, (5) human relations, and (6) community service needs. The institute helped communities to identify their own problems, mobilize human resources, develop solutions through programs of leadership and conduct, and apply results of research. Initial conferences at the Kellogg Center were followed up by staff participation in the community, only if the issues were clearly identified and funds found to support the activity.

In a brochure entitled "What It Is, What It Does, How It Can Serve Your Community" (ca. 1960), the anticipated relationship between the ICD and the client community was clearly outlined. First, content areas in which the ICD might provide assistance were identified. These included the assurance of volunteer help, commitment to a democratic process, assumption of some of the project cost, and the requirement that the proposed project have some educational significance. The steps that the institute anticipated the interested community would undertake included the following:

1. The community identifies a problem and contacts the institute.
2. Representative(s) of the institute review the problem with a community representative.
3. If deemed appropriate, agreement on the project is reached between the institute and the community.
4. Subcommittees are established and specialists assigned.
5. A course of action is selected and generated.
6. Progress and plans for a continuing community-coordinating group are evaluated.

Projects undertaken by the ICD were extensive and involved a wide range of activities and publications. Some of them were Michigan law enforcement, consumer surveys, race relations, Michigan's Constitution, anticipated population growth and impact, feasibility studies of various U.S. Department of Interior projects in Michigan, national lake shore proposals, local income tax studies, township studies, and annexation and incorporation practices. In staffing these various studies, the institute utilized faculty members from political science, sociology, urban planning, economics, geography, and police administration. Publications resulting from the project were extensive.

It has already been remarked that in hiring individuals in the Institute for Community Development and Services, as it came to be called later, the attempt was made to have joint appointments between instructional departments and the institute. The observations of various persons, based upon this and similar experiences, suggest that, when individuals long involved in a department move to a service institute housed some distance away, it is quite possible that they will continue a vital role in the department. In contrast, individuals imported into an institute and given joint appointments in departments may find difficulty in becoming involved in affairs of both units. The demands of a new job, the lack of knowledge and interest in departmental affairs, the time and inconvenience involved in moving about the campus—all contribute to making joint appointments ineffective. Department heads, lacking the service orientation, could also be sources of difficulty in rewarding dual appointees.

One department chair, commenting on his experience with dual appointments, noted that the constant travel required in project development and the fund raising for new projects kept full-time appointments in service institutes so busy that the department learned not to count on them as participants. The question was then raised as to why a department should accept joint appointments and support promotions for individuals whose departmental contributions are unknown and probably irrelevant. The alternative—making such an institute part of a department—according to this department chair, would impede an interdisciplinary approach and, in the long run, place additional burdens on a department already excessively burdened. Somewhat in contrast, another department chair argued that a department was the ultimate repository of expertise in a given discipline and that hence, as a matter of courtesy and maintenance of quality, an individual with a doctorate in any discipline should be appointed to any position in the institution only when the appropriate disciplinary department had reviewed and approved the individual and his or her credentials. On the whole, this latter view seems more suited to a strong graduate-research-oriented university than to a land-grant, public service institution in which the practical orientation in extension or research is an essential responsibility of the institution even though not always so regarded in some departments. Indeed, the early years of the institute suggest that strong departmental involvement tends to emphasize research rather than service.

Despite recurring discussions of such staffing problems, the ICD apparently met real needs. It carried out projects in many communities and attained funds from a variety of sources. It has continued as a vital part of the Continuing Education Services (now called Lifelong Education Programs).

The ICD is not an instructional unit, but it surely provides research and service in the original land-grant tradition. In recent years, the development of the view that institutes and centers should be college or departmentally based has posed something of a threat to the existence of this and similar units. The specific title of the unit is now Community Development Programs. The change in designation is less important in defining its role and mission than in reflecting the attitudes and commitments of central administration, deans, and department chairs. Land-grant traditions and commitments have notably weakened since 1969.

## The Charles Stewart Mott Institute for Community Improvement

The establishment of the Mott Institute for Community Improvement represents another aspect of the attempt to focus extension activities on community problems. The Mott Foundation had, for several years, directed much attention to community improvement in the Flint area. The community school concept that evolved included provision of information, partial financing, consultation, and support to a school district to implement community educational programs. At some point in early 1965, apparently by a handshake of John Hannah and Charles Stewart Mott, the Mott Foundation agreed to provide up to $3 million over a ten-year period further to explore and develop the community school concept. No formal proposal was ever acted upon although several were developed. As a result, there was little preliminary planning and a great deal of uncertainty about the nature of the program, both on campus and at the Mott Foundation offices. At one extreme, there was an impression that the institute would focus on the Flint situation.

The prevalent impression on the campus was that the project would explore the role of Michigan State in pre- and in-service teacher training for community education. This task would involve examining organizational patterns and developing and testing classroom materials and methods. In other words, the institute would identify ways in which a university could favorably affect such community problem areas as poverty, disadvantaged individuals, and underachieving persons.

The Mott Foundation grant was assigned to the College of Education, and after a year of confusion as to what should be done, Professor Clyde Campbell became director of the institute. He was already involved in a Mott internship program and, hence, the new program tended to focus on preparation of teachers for the disadvantaged, using the Mott internship program as part of the training experience. Reading, it was agreed, was one of the greatest weaknesses of the disadvantaged and, therefore, attention would be focused on development of a reading program. The objectives of the project included an increase in the aspiration level of the disadvantaged; the development of skills for eliminating deficiencies that hampered growth of occupational interests and skills; and the development of materials, teaching methods, and staff qualifications that would promote attainment of these objectives and improve the quality of community living.

One of the ideas developed was the use of differential staffing involving not only professionals but students, volunteers, and others who could contribute to removing the identified deficiencies. Of the twenty people who worked on the project, thirteen were present for one year only as interns, a turnover that tended to weaken the continuity of the staff's activities.

Although it had been readily assumed that the experiences and findings from this institute would markedly affect the teacher training program of the College of Education, the faculty was little aware of the activities of the institute. The constant turnover of staff in the college and in the institute, combined with limited dissemination of results, reduced the unit's impact on the college. At that time also the faculty of the College of Education was moving toward basic research and theory development rather than maintaining the practical people-centered, process-oriented activities implied by community education.

Howard Hickey became director of the staff in its sixth year, 1971, and attempted to promote writing, oral reports, and other means of dissemination of the results of the institute's research. An evaluation of the activity was made toward the end of the project. Because of the slow start and the vacillation in emphasis, slightly less than $2.5 million out of the proffered $3 million was actually expended. The major impact of the Mott institute program was on individuals, particularly the students, working on advanced degrees, who were exposed to the concepts of community education and community improvement. The project created sensitivity to community problems although it did little directly to resolve them.

*Community Service in Community Colleges*

One of the major objectives of community colleges is to develop and strengthen programs of community service and of continuing education. To Hannah and others concerned with the development of community colleges, a project designed to facilitate that goal would accord with the original land-grant theme. A proposal, "Community Services in Community Colleges," was made to the Kellogg Foundation, and a total of $266,369.63 was granted for the period May 1968 to October 1973. Obviously, most of the work of this project was undertaken after Hannah retired from Michigan State, but his interest was certainly a major factor in obtaining the grant.

The project operated through workshops, some devoted to particular types of service and others to developmental or philosophical aspects of service. There were also numerous conferences and demonstration activities, frequently carried out in community colleges. Among the various themes around which community services were developed were driver training for minorities, fire schools, pollution, consumer education, homemaking for disadvantaged mothers, and training centers for the handicapped. What was originally proposed to develop service agents and coordinators in the college diffused into a wide range of services involving many persons rather than a few coordinators. The project lacked clear objectives and aroused no great enthusiasm in the faculty.

In retrospect, the overall success of community services is questionable. But because of the program, many new projects were started among community colleges and many individuals in community colleges became acquainted with and committed to service activities.

*Undergraduate Education in Health Administration*

The Kellogg Foundation grant entitled "Undergraduate Education in Health Administration" was an example of Kellogg support of a Michigan State program aimed at fulfilling goals that corresponded to those of the foundation. The aim of the 1964 project was "to aid the development of baccalaureate and continuing education programs for the training of middle management personnel in the hospital field." Frank Borsenik, professor of hotel, restaurant, and institutional management in the School of Business, identified a national need for mid-level hospital administrators and concluded that a degree program for hospital administrators would meet that need as well as a university goal.

This program was designed to prepare baccalaureate-trained, upwardly mobile hospital administrators. Graduates, it was anticipated, would have careers in hospital and health facilities, and/or college housing and feeding. Borsenik hoped to attract 75 to 100 underclassmen (freshmen and sophomores) and junior college students. An award for $99,480 was made to initiate a four-year project.

From the beginning, the program faced continual challenges. Undergraduate students did not seem to find it attractive; thus, the anticipated numbers of students did not materialize. Lack of exposure and publicity, difficulty with placing students for externships, lack of adequate faculty, lack of integration within the health professional programs, and insufficient teaching and curricular materials were other problems.

In 1968 a two-year extension grant of $36,510 was provided by Kellogg Foundation, but the difficulties continued. Moreover, some male students were called to military service. After the first four years of the program, only forty students were enrolled. Of those, thirty-four graduated and found employment. Both the foundation and the program director questioned the wisdom of continuing a program characterized by a lack of students, insufficient funds, a high cost ratio per student, and an inability to arouse and retain student interest. The existence of a widely known health facilities management curriculum at the nearby University of Michigan also raised doubts about need.

*Training Administrators for Community Colleges*

An outgrowth of the Office of Community College Cooperation, one community service project responded to the need for administrators in the rapidly developing community colleges. The proposal was developed in the College of Education by the faculty in administration, research, student personnel, counseling, and other aspects of higher education. The proposal recognized that, as a relatively new movement, community colleges required individuals with a distinctive orientation and philosophy.

The initial emphasis on a preservice program to identify and educate potential administrators was shortly shifted to an in-service training program for administrators. The obvious reason was that most of the top administrators hired in community colleges were promoted from the ranks but lacked formal training for administration. The program extended from 1960 to 1967 with an initial grant from the Kellogg Foundation of $125,000, supplemented in 1964 by another $115,000. Most of the grant was spent on stipends of $3,000 to individuals completing doctoral programs. Some forty to fifty students obtained a doctoral degree in community college administration. An interesting by-product of this project was that, during the period 1961 to 1971, there was a 300 percent increase in the students enrolling at Michigan State by transfer from community colleges. The community college counselors and administrators with Michigan State degrees may have influenced this development.

*Intensive Extension Service*

The Intensive Extension Service Project was proposed by Director Durward B. Varner to the Kellogg Foundation to develop improved techniques for disseminating scientific information to farmers and to encourage the application of the information in five townships or areas distributed geographically about the state of Michigan. The Kellogg Foundation, in 1954, granted $275,000 to support this project. Designated agents worked with individual farm families using on-the-farm demonstrations, tours, meetings, and other educational activities. Each agent was to reduce his or her contacts to not more than 200 families with the expectation that the contacts would result in adoption of profit-making organizational changes on the farms, the use of profit-making technologies for farm and business operations, and on-the-farm and off-the-farm family adjustments yielding more satisfying lives. Another expectation was that, as a result of this project, continuing support would be found for expansion of the Extension Service. In 1954, also, federal legislation funded a Farm and Home Development Program supplying 1,000 new county and home agents to furnish counseling nationwide. Whether or how the federal program and the Kellogg-supported project were related is unknown.

At the close of the project, the comparison of groups involved in intensive extension service with groups not involved indicated the following: increased agricultural output—$5,600 compared to $3,400, increased farm earnings—$1,646 compared to $938, a marked acceleration in application of improved agricultural practices, higher levels of living for farm families, improvements in the economic base of communities, more vigorous and effective farm leadership, increased community spirit, and improved understanding between farm and townspeople. The benefit cost ratio of the program was reported as two to one. The program was apparently effective and quite well reported. To have continued it would have required from the various townships the amount of $6,000 to $7,000 per year. It was not forthcoming. Intensive work with small groups and individuals has often proved effective, but continued financial support has always been difficult to acquire.

*National Project in Agricultural Communications*

The National Project in Agricultural Communications was funded for a total of nearly $800,000 by the Kellogg Foundation for a period of nine years, beginning in 1953. Originally proposed as a five-year project involving a number of land-grant institutions and several related national organizations, the project apparently got under way slowly. It was extended for two years, and then for two years more, to bring it to satisfactory conclusion. The purpose of the project was to improve educational services through more effective communication. Sustained attention was given to training people to use the various means of communication currently available and to organize accumulated knowledge so as to facilitate dissemination. Training programs were provided on written communication, visual communication, research, and films. A major in agricultural communications was approved in 1957. In the original proposal, hope was expressed for increased cooperative research on communications problems, but the information available suggests that research was perhaps the least significant result in terms of the actual benefits. The greatest impact (and, undoubtedly, the primary one desired) was to make extension services nationally more aware of mass communication media and to train some of the extension staff to use them. The introduction of a major in agricultural communications at Michigan State was an unanticipated result.

### Summary

The sample of departments, centers, institutes, and projects that started with or developed a strong public service emphasis reveals, even in this somewhat abbreviated review, a number of the issues confronting the maintenance or expansion of the extension and applied research missions of the land-grant institutions.

The Offices of High School and of Junior-Community College Cooperation originated out of a desire to attract more students and a more representative group of students from all sections of state. There was also concern about publicizing and interpreting the Basic College general education program as well as the expanding curricular offerings in a variety of fields. By developing a multiple-pronged program, taking faculty members into the schools and community colleges, and bringing students and faculty from the schools and colleges to the campus, the two offices promoted exchanges that were mutually beneficial. Michigan State also received many more students.

Projects such as the Science and Mathematics Teaching Center, Community Service in Community Colleges, and Training Administrators for Community Colleges also engendered respect and collaboration that resulted in more students. The services and degree programs developed by the Institute for Counseling and Testing and Guidance were effective, too, again in an indirect rather than direct manner. But in a few years pressures on faculty and the reward system no longer permitted much faculty involvement or interaction with school and community college faculty members. Admissions became a professional task separate from the colleges and departments.

The Departments of Agricultural Engineering and Resource Development, despite providing strong undergraduate and graduate programs on campus, have maintained very active extension programs. The chairs or heads of departments were apparently selected because of commitment to the service function. The commitment reflects the continuing emphasis of the College of Agriculture and its deans. Funds for extension were regularly made available. Faculty activities in extension were budgeted, encouraged, and rewarded.

The Labor and Industrial Relations Center was initiated with a service emphasis but ultimately became an academic unit with a distinction made between the extension faculty and the academic faculty. The Ph.D. is not required of the extension or service faculty for promotion to tenure ranks.

The efforts of the Highway Traffic Safety Center, initiated for research, led to majors and graduate degrees, but administrative placement in Lifelong Education has caused it to be regarded as nonacademic. Fortunately for its continued existence, highway traffic is now widely accepted to be a life-or-death matter.

The Science and Mathematics Teaching Center arose from the recognition of problems of content and instructional methods in mathematics and the sciences *and* the availability of federal funds to attack the problems. Departments remained uninterested and were gratified at the demise of the center when outside funding was no longer available. Apparently neither service needs nor undergraduate teaching has high priority in most department missions.

Among other temporary projects funded by external grants, several distinctive factors seem to have been involved.

The Mott project appeared to have no enthusiastic proponents on campus and the College of Education emphases at that time were, if not contradictory, at least not supportive. Moreover, the purposes and expectations were never clear and seemed to shift with the personnel involved.

The Institute for Community Development suffered from lack of a consistent focus. Departmental participants redirected the program's emphasis from service to research. The ICD eventually returned to its origins as a service program, but inadequate funding and institutional commitment have continued to hamper the development of this unit.

The project in undergraduate education in health administration was not adequately explored before being initiated. It was isolated within the institution and apparently had no great outside support.

Had it been placed in the broader context of composite institutional commitment to health programs and given more publicity, the project might well have led to a sound and viable program.

Intensive extension services and the National Project in Agricultural Communications were both addressed to national problems as well as local ones. Each was apparently successful in the demonstration stage, but the first required massive additional funding which never became available. The second successfully completed operational development, which made continuance possible.

Of these eight temporary or exploratory projects, perhaps three might be regarded as failures and three as successes. Yet, in each case, numerous people were beneficially affected and something was learned. Investments in human potential can seldom be labeled as complete failures.

It is evident from viewing these projects that many colleges and departments assign relatively low priority to public service programs and related applied research unless special funds or grants are available. And even when there is financial support, it may be subtly diverted to matters deemed more important.

# 12
# International Studies and Programs

During the 1940s Michigan State took the first steps toward making an international commitment a part of its philosophic and programatic orientation. The introduction of the World Adventure Film Series on Saturday nights in winter 1942 was one small step in puncturing provincialism. Much of the credit for developing an international focus must be attributed to John Hannah. In his annual report of 1944–45, he described the challenge that faced Michigan State, then and in the future:

> Universities and colleges are built to serve the nation and the nation's needs. A living college or university must rise or fall upon its ability to serve. Today the service is war. So long as the war lasts, the responsibility of Michigan State College is to train young people for war, and we are dedicating ourselves to the earliest possible victory.
>
> ...After the war the devastated areas will have to be restored, great resources developed everywhere and there will be challenges to our young men and women on a scale never before equaled. But the greater challenge will not be material. The American democracy, the fundamental ideology for which we are fighting, must be made a beacon of fairness and opportunity to common people everywhere, a pattern that the world will want to copy and make work for all the peoples of the world, to their own immense advantage. That will be the greatest challenge, and the education of men and women who can meet it will be the new task of our universities.

### Beginnings of the International Dimension at Michigan State

The minutes of administrative group meetings in 1943 describe early efforts of deans and other administrators at Michigan State to anticipate needed postwar changes. One very practical concern was providing accommodations for returning veterans. Another interest was to adjust the programs for veterans with overseas experience, who might have

---

NOTE: The initial version of this chapter was written by Dr. David Heenan, who was himself extensively involved in international studies programs.

become more internationally minded. One idea discussed was the need for "general education" courses that dealt directly with the issues and problems of an interdependent world. The Basic College was a planned effort to move from preoccupation with Western civilization to an expanded interest in Latin America and non-Western studies.

The accommodation of an expanded international dimension required the recruiting of scholars with appropriate background and competence. On September 10, 1943, the Associated Press and the United Press publicized an announcement by President Hannah of the creation of a new Institute of Foreign Studies. The emphasis was to be on South America and Asia because, as Hannah explained, it was reasonable to assume that American involvement with these areas would increase. Two scholars appointed to launch the program were Professor Chao Chang Lee from the University of Hawaii and Professor Luis-Alberto Sanchez, a Peruvian lawyer, professor, and author from the University of Chile. Hannah expressed his hope for the institute in these words:

> "I regard the Institute of Foreign Studies as a real opportunity for Michigan State College to contribute in a small way to a great work that must be done. Its field is not limited to the making available of educational opportunities to the few foreign students from around the world who come to our campus. Its great possibilities lie in the direction of creating a consciousness in the minds of our students of the interdependence of the nations and the peoples of the world. Unless this objective is attained on a great, international scale, there is not likely to be an enduring peace."[1]

Dr. Lee, first director of the institute, taught classes, served as student adviser, organized international events and festivals, and provided counsel to Hannah and the deans. In addition to these campus activities, many of which were later assumed by the Office of International Extension, Professor Lee extended his mission to clubs, fraternal organizations, and schools. The institute attracted foreign students and scholars, who helped American students to gain knowledge of other countries.

The International Center, an outgrowth of the Institute of Foreign Studies, was an important contribution to campus life. Opened in summer 1944 in a refurbished faculty house designated as "International House," it became a favorite meeting place for student groups. Professor and Mrs. Lee lived on the upper floor and were responsible for its operation and control. The lower part was converted into social

---

1. Chao Chang Lee, quoting John Hannah, in "My Contributions to Michigan State's International Program," unpublished, undated paper in the MSU Archives and Historical Collections.

and reading rooms for foreign students. An International Club, composed of thirty-three foreign students and thirty-two American students, sponsored talks and discussions on social, political, and economic issues in other countries. The center became a visible symbol of the increasing importance of the international dimension.

## THE POSTWAR YEARS

When the war ended, a new concern for international involvement and cooperation emerged. No longer could the United States isolate itself from foreign entanglements; it was now part of an interdependent world. World problems could not be solved simply by exporting technology and values as other nations had previously attempted to do.

The years 1945 to 1948 were a period of resettlement and adjustment for war veterans, of reassessment of national goals and policies, and of optimistic belief that we were entering a new era of peace and prosperity. Michigan State demonstrated its commitment to a new world view in a number of ways. It welcomed foreign and American scholars, who lectured and met with students. New faculty members with extensive international and intercultural experiences came to East Lansing. Courses emphasizing the international dimension were added. Foreign educators and government officials seeking to learn from MSU's activities and programs frequently visited the campus. In 1947, 181 foreign students enrolled at Michigan State, making it sixth among land-grant institutions in international student enrollment.

Hannah was acknowledged as a national leader in higher education, especially among the land-grant institutions. In 1948–49 he was elected president of the National Association of State Universities and Land-Grant Colleges (NASULGC). He led the association and its member institutions to respond favorably and vigorously to the Point IV Program announced by President Harry S Truman in his 1949 Inaugural Address. Truman called on American colleges and universities to help developing nations attack their overwhelming social and economic problems. Hannah saw the service-oriented, land-grant universities as the best equipped institutions to meet this challenge; and, as president of NASULGC, he pledged the support of the organization. At Truman's request, he agreed to serve as an adviser to the Technical Assistance Administration of the Department of State, created to administer the new program.

Obviously, Hannah also envisioned an extensive role for Michigan State in this work and an opportunity to transform the institution. He believed it to be important to recruit Michigan State faculty members who would return to share their experiences with their students and colleagues, thereby helping to make the university more experienced in and oriented to the international dimension.

## THE OFFICE OF THE DEAN
## OF INTERNATIONAL PROGRAMS

By the late 1940s and early 1950s, Michigan State was deeply involved in international activities. The institution committed itself to a number of large-scale technical assistance programs and projects in Colombia, Brazil, Okinawa, and Vietnam. While technical assistance projects attracted much attention, there were many less obvious, but equally significant, activities taking place. As by-products of technical assistance projects and of direct funding by the federal government and various foundations, especially the Ford Foundation, numerous internationally oriented research projects became available for faculty and graduate students.

Faculty members were encouraged to use sabbatical leaves for overseas teaching and research. Many staff members went abroad to help foreign nations to reorganize their educational programs and, on campus, new curricular offerings emphasizing international aspects were constantly appearing. If these diverse activities were to be carried out with maximum benefit to the institution, coordination was necessary.

Thus, the Office of International Programs was established by MSU's State Board of Agriculture in 1956 and is involved primarily in the initiation, coordination, and support of internationally related activities. It has never offered courses and degrees, although most of its academic staff members have held academic appointments and teaching assignments in the various departments. The office provides liaison among the departments and organizations involved in international studies. It allocates funds made available by the university and outside sources for assisting the work of the centers, institutes, and other subunits in international studies and programs. It assists in the planning, coordinating, and monitoring of overseas projects and reports directly to the president and to the appropriate college deans about involvement in international activities. The dean also reports to the vice-president for student affairs and to the dean of graduate studies in matters related to foreign students.

The work of the office has been determined, at least in part, by the advice of various faculty, student, and administrative groups. Shortly after the office was established, Glen L. Taggart, the first dean, convened a faculty group to recommend the appropriate role of Michigan State in international activities. The Ford Foundation provided $135,000 for the released time of participating faculty members and for the support of faculty deliberations on five themes: (1) education and social change, (2) international communication, (3) international politics, (4) international economics and business, and (5) scientific and cultural exchange and technical assistance.

These study groups enabled faculty members to become better acquainted with the international component as part of the university's goals and objectives and with the vast array of possibilities, problems, and obstacles involved. Many of their suggestions helped to establish guidelines as international activities became more widespread. While the groups' recommendations covered many areas, most emphasized the teaching, research, and service functions consistent with the land-grant traditions of Michigan State. Hence, operations of the international program should not be highly centralized and independent but, rather, should serve to motivate and coordinate international activities in the departments and colleges.

The study groups concluded that (1) international dimension introduced early in the students' academic programs would stimulate interest and ensure that most of them acquire some knowledge of other countries and cultures; (2) students' acquaintance with another culture could serve as a base for understanding still other cultures later; (3) emphasis should be placed on expanding current offerings by using a comparative approach; (4) the study of languages should be promoted to facilitate the understanding of and communications with other people and to provide an additional avenue for obtaining new knowledge and ideas; and (5) students should be encouraged to participate in both academic and nonacademic programs to provide them better understanding and appreciation of our interdependent world.

The faculty committee was also greatly concerned with research opportunities for faculty members and graduate students. Opportunity for research would stimulate more faculty participation; faculty competence would increase by extending their knowledge through research; the new knowledge would be shared with other segments of the university clientele; and the image of the university would be enhanced, gaining it recognition and attracting new students and faculty. In retrospect, it appears that *the possible conflict* envisaged between the immediate practical assistance desired by developing countries and the research interests of the faculty did not fully materialize. The Ford Foundation granted $1.5 million to further faculty and graduate assistant research.

The faculty advisory function introduced by Dean Taggart through the faculty seminars has continued. The Academic Council created an International Program and Steering Committee in 1960, charged with advising the dean, provost, and the Academic Council on matters related to overseas projects and their coordination with the university's academic program. The committee was also to evaluate such projects as to their contributions to the university's research, service, and educational goals and to consider the academic propriety of current and proposed overseas projects. This committee was later replaced by the Advisory and Consultative Committee, comprised of faculty and student representatives, with a primary function to advise the dean on the feasibility of projects that might be politically sensitive or be construed as illegal or unethical.

## AREA STUDY CENTERS

In supporting the university's move into international activities, Hannah repeatedly emphasized that students and faculty needed to be better informed about the people and cultures in areas other than those associated with Western or European civilization—namely, Africa, Latin America, and Asia. The several area study centers established in the early 1960s were a direct attempt to respond to this concern.

The first such unit was the African Studies Center, created in 1960. It originally emphasized teaching, especially that of African languages, as stipulated under the terms of the National Defense Act, which provided matching funds for founding the center. Later the African Studies Center developed a broader program of instruction and research on African institutions, culture, and economics and on other societal institutions and practices—one that has served as a model for other centers at MSU and throughout the country. Other functions of the center include serving as a home base for African students at Michigan State, awarding an African studies certificate to students who complete at least thirty hours of study in African-related courses, also organizing and sponsoring annual exhibitions and festivals to reach other students, and providing students with study-abroad and Peace Corps opportunities in Africa.

The Asian Studies Center appeared in 1962, followed by the Latin American Studies Center in 1963 and the Middle East Studies Committee in 1972. Each of the centers supports teaching and research to promote a better understanding of the areas indicated. New courses (based always in departments), publications, lectures, discussions, and exchanges of students and scholars are typical of the varied activities of these centers. The Middle East Studies Committee was a post-Hannah development and exemplifies the longer-term impacts of the Hannah-stimulated international involvements.

The Canadian-American Studies Committee was formed in 1956 to further the understanding and knowledge of our Canadian neighbors and Canadian-American affairs. In the ensuing years the committee sponsored and encouraged faculty and student exchange programs between the two countries, organized seminars for the discussion of issues and problems of mutual concern, and helped to develop courses and programs in the appropriate departments and colleges at Michigan State and in Canadian institutions.

In 1964 a Russian and East European Studies Program was initiated. Its primary purpose was to provide a means for faculty and students to gain a better understanding of that portion of the world and its peoples through courses, lectures, films, and speakers.

### INTERNATIONAL INSTITUTES AND OFFICES

Somewhat similar to the area study centers, the international institutes trace their beginnings to small groups of faculty members with common interests meeting with the dean of international programs and the college deans of relevant areas. A common pattern for financing salaries and other operating costs has been a sharing arrangement between the dean of international programs and the college involved. Funds came from foundation grants, especially the Ford Foundation; from contracts with sponsoring agencies for technical assistance projects; and occasionally from the general fund of the university.

A primary purpose of these institutes is to foster international research and the instructional and service interests of the units they represent. The institutes evaluate research proposals, assist in obtaining funds, and facilitate the publication of research findings. They also participate in developing new courses to enrich the international dimension in their colleges and are involved in the development and administration of overseas projects. Each of the institutes has a director based in a college and department and operates under the guidelines of the Office of International Programs.

*The Institute for International Studies in Education*

A primary purpose of the Institute for International Studies in Education (1963) is to contribute fundamental knowledge about the role of education in development and to reinforce the work of graduate students and faculty in this topic. Its mission is based on the premise that people must be so educated that societies gain a better understanding of each other and achieve goals that will bring out the greatest potential of their members.

The College of Agriculture and Natural Resources was involved in overseas activities for more than a decade before this institute was established. In the years 1951 to 1962, the college participated in technical assistance projects in Colombia, Okinawa, Pakistan, and Nigeria. A coordinator of the Foreign Agricultural Programs Office was appointed to the staff early in the 1950s, but the institute was not created until 1964. Since its inception, it has coordinated many technical assistance/institution-building projects overseas. In addition, it has carried on important campus functions—initiating, formulating, and funding research projects; assisting with the selection and orientation of faculty assigned to overseas projects; administering foreign student and scholar programs; conducting a number of training programs in agriculture for foreign participants; and hosting many visitors from abroad.

The chief concern of the International Communication Institute (1963) is to identify and support faculty members with interest and competency in curriculum development and research related to international communication. A major undertaking of this institute was a U.S. Agency for International Development/MSU-sponsored study of the diffusion of innovations in rural areas in Brazil, Nigeria, and India. Other research interests of the institute include cross-cultural communication, communication with illiterates and recent literates, studies of the various means of communication used throughout the world, and instructional programs in international communication.

*The Office of International Extension (OIE)*

Thousands of Michigan residents have participated in both on-campus seminars and meetings on world affairs sponsored by the MSU Office of International Extension. The OIE operates as an organizational unit of the Continuing Education Service, the Cooperative Extension Service, and the dean of international programs and works closely with other units of the university. Its functions include providing overseas study opportunities, adult education activities, and student and faculty exchange programs. The office also has offered summer and other special sessions designed to inform teachers on world affairs and has made available films and filmstrips on international topics.

International extension includes a variety of programs. For example, the Office of Overseas Study has developed extensive academic offerings and has a large student enrollment in overseas study programs. This office was established early in the 1960s, when Hannah suggested that the program of the American Language and Education Center (AMLEC) be made available through the Continuing Education Service. It has cooperated with a nonprofit Swiss foundation to offer inexpensive opportunities to study Spanish, French, German, and

Italian languages and experience the culture and daily life of the countries in which these languages are spoken. By the mid 1960s the program was expanded to include political science and, later, courses from other departments.

### The International Library

The International Library was established in 1964 as a separate component of the main Michigan State University Library. The international librarian and staff work closely with other units on library acquisitions required to serve teaching and research needs of faculty and students.

### The English Language Center

Many foreign students who came to the campus after the war lacked adequate language competency. Since 1961 the English Language Center has provided courses in English as a second language to give intensive training to these students. Only after they achieve sufficient proficiency are they admitted to regular academic programs. This center is part of the Department of English, and the staff comprises faculty members who have had extensive educational experience in the teaching of English, linguistics, and English as a second language.

### The Office of International Students and Scholars

The Office of International Students and Scholars, originally known as the Foreign Student Office, was established to enable increasing numbers of international students and scholars (in 1941, 40, and in 1969, 1,237) to pursue academic programs at Michigan State. The office provides advice on legal, logistical, financial, and service matters. It also offers orientation programs, assists in locating host families, and develops informal activities to make the foreign visitors' environment and experience more pleasant. The office represents the university in matters relating to U.S. and foreign governmental agencies and to sponsoring organizations interested in foreign students and scholars.

## TECHNICAL ASSISTANCE PROJECTS

### Overview

A new term, *technical assistance*, became widely used following World War II. Technical assistance pertains to transferring knowledge and developing capacities rather than providing economic and financial aid. Colleges and universities had previously been requested by the government, industry, and other agencies and institutions to consult, conduct research, or otherwise furnish expertise and counsel in fields such as agriculture, education, technology, economics, public and business administration, health, home economics—areas in which, through research and teaching, institutions of higher education had become reservoirs of knowledge. Perhaps what was "new" was the level of aid that universities were now asked to supply. Much of the manpower for technical assistance came from colleges and universities, but the initiative and the funding stemmed from national goals and legislative actions.

In 1946 the Fulbright Act made it possible for foreign currencies owed to, or owned by, the United States to be used, by mutual agreement, to support international exchanges between this and other countries for teaching, research, and similar educational activities. Surplus from the sale of agricultural commodities provided fellowships for American scholars and travel expenses for non-American participants. The United States Information and Educational Exchange Act of 1948, better known as the Smith-Mundt Act, became the means for establishing information and cultural relations programs through congressional appropriations.

The Marshall Plan of 1948 and President Truman's announcement of the Point IV Plan in 1949 moved the technical-assistance-abroad program into high gear through three agencies: the Institute of Inter-American Affairs (IIAA) for Latin America; the Economic Cooperation Administration (ECA) for Europe and the Far East; and the Technical Cooperation Administration (TCA) for Africa, the Middle East, and South Asia. In 1953 these groups were combined within the Foreign Operations Administration (FOA), and in 1961 their programs were incorporated into the Agency for International Development (AID). In 1961, also, the Fulbright-Hays Act consolidated the earlier Fulbright and Smith-Mundt Acts and other legislation that dealt with the support of international programs.

The spark that fired Michigan State's involvement in extensive overseas technical assistance was President Truman's 1949 Inaugural Address. He called on Americans to assist in restoring order around the world and in providing for the well-being of less fortunate people. Truman's decision to ask universities to play a major role in technical assistance projects was based on several factors: (1) these institutions had the knowledge and talent required, (2) university educators were readily accepted by their counterparts in recipient nations, (3) professors were less likely to become involved in internal and political affairs.

Truman's desire to involve universities in overseas projects met with something less than wholesale enthusiasm in the institutions. Despite the fact that such programs were to be self-supporting, many viewed this extension of university activities as an irrelevant and even conflicting diversion from their central missions.

University administrators already confronted complex problems. Expanded enrollments and instructional programs required recruitment and training of new faculty, in itself a difficult enough task without seeking additional personnel for positions abroad. Even locating persons with both the relevant experience and the willingness to undertake overseas projects was a dilemma. Some institutions hired "outside experts" who had little or no connection with the university involved. At MSU Hannah avoided this approach, arguing that the only way the campus program could benefit from the overseas experience was by the faculty returning and sharing their insights with colleagues and students. In the long run, Hannah's decision proved to be wise.

Another unanticipated problem arose. Many people, including President Truman, were optimistic that, with the war over, all efforts could be directed toward building a peaceful world. It was in this spirit that the idea of international technical assistance was conceived and that universities pledged their support. But total peace did not come; it was quickly superseded by the "cold war." Many of the touted beneficial postwar intentions, both at home and abroad, became regarded instead as the means to further national goals and security.

Despite the difficulties, programs in technical assistance persisted. There were some setbacks, but there were many successes. For years, universities continued to send faculty and staff members to serve as resource people in other countries. As time passed, there was greater demand for short-term rather than long-term consultants to assist indigenous experts with their immediate problems. Universities learned to concentrate on the institution-building efforts and human resources development required to provide direction, continuity, and permanence to the whole development process.

Michigan State and other land-grant institutions were a step ahead of some of their sister institutions in that they adhered to the view that a university should serve the practical needs of the people. This could be done by simultaneous and integrated emphasis on instruction, research, and *service*. The central theme of the service emphasis— helping people to help themselves—was precisely that needed in offering technical assistance to underdeveloped nations.

In Hannah's view, the provision of service to a new and distinctive clientele was also a means to develop further the public service philosophy and potential of the university. Thus, the stance of Michigan State involved much more than an offer to help. It meant a commitment to encourage the active participation of the faculty and staff in conducting research and in providing on-site technical assistance projects and programs. It meant development of the research and service potential of the university. It meant also the creation within the faculty of an awareness of and a degree of sophistication about the global needs of mankind. It meant creation of on-campus instructional programs and off-campus extension programs that would alert its students and service clientele to the nature of these global needs and foster in them a sense of responsibility for resolving them. The effort was ambitious and even idealistic but, in greater measure than many cynics predicted, it succeeded.

The United States provided a large share of the funds and personnel for overseas development programs, but many other countries were involved. Inevitably, the surge of humanitarianism and desire to reconstruct the world were blunted by those—in both the free world and the Communist bloc—who wished to exploit the developing nations for strategic military bases or markets for exports. Some "donor" nations tried to persuade Third World countries to accept a particular political ideology or economic philosophy. In the recipient countries themselves, individuals, political parties, and pressure groups used their contacts with donors to gain political or financial advantage, destroy existing political authority, or attain other ulterior goals. In an evaluation of the impact of technical assistance, such self-serving episodes must not be ignored. Unfortunately, they were sometimes blown out of proportion by persons who opposed the technical programs or sought to cast aspersions on those who supported or directed them. Most of the assistance was provided by university personnel who gained little, if anything, from the economic, political, or diplomatic considerations. Participants generally believed that much good came out of these efforts and that faculty members of the participating institutions were enriched by their efforts.

*Selected Technical Assistance Projects*

*Colombia.* The first technical assistance project of Michigan State was in Colombia. Early in 1951 the government of Colombia requested that the U.S. Technical Cooperation Administration (TCA) assist in expanding and strengthening its two agricultural colleges, one in Medellin and the other in Palmira. A contract was signed by Michigan State, the TCA, and the government of Colombia. Four faculty members were sent to Medellin and three to Palmira. These professors and some special consultants were asked to help with curriculum development both in the colleges and in field training. They also assisted in developing research farm demonstrations and extension work for farmers. There was a further significance in this and other projects in that, although the U.S. government maintained that it had a "good neighbor policy," many Latin American people thought otherwise. The constructive and positive work done by the universities helped improve the nation's image.

*Ryukyus.* Another project in 1951 was the development of a new institution, the University of Ryukyus. During World War II, some of the fiercest fighting took place in the Ryukyuan Islands, part of the Japanese Empire. When the war ended, Okinawa, the largest of the Ryukyuan Islands, became an important military outpost in eastern Asia. While the peace treaty signed with Japan recognized the "residual sovereignty" of Japan over the islands, it specified that the United States would occupy them indefinitely.

Okinawa had never had a university. Most Ryukyuans who sought higher education attended Japanese institutions. The U.S. Civil Administration in 1950 established the University of the Ryukyus, sponsored jointly by the U.S. Department of the Army and the American Council on Education. The decision was made to create a land-grant-type university with Michigan State as the mentor institution. Eventually, the land-grant philosophy was combined with the traditional approaches of Japanese education since the islands were to be returned to Japan. Many faculty members from Michigan State worked with the Okinawans in developing programs in agriculture, home economics, education, political science, natural science, business administration, and English language training. In addition, the advisers assisted in designing buildings, acquiring equipment, developing a library, and training staff. When the Ryukyus reverted to Japan, the university became a national university of Japan.

*Brazil.* During the 1950s, a number of requests were received for the assistance and support of Michigan State in technical assistance/ institution-building projects. One that received considerable attention was a long-term project undertaken by the School of Business and Public Service to help with the development of the first School of Business Administration in São Paulo. The original student body consisted of businessmen ranging in age from twenty-five to fifty. Basic instruction was provided in management, marketing, production, accounting, finance, public relations, personnel, and labor relations. Many Brazilian faculty members came to Michigan State University to earn advanced degrees. In its first decade the school proved so successful that similar programs were introduced in the University of Rio Grande Do Sul and the University of Bahia. Schools of business administration now exist in most universities in Brazil.

*Vietnam.* The largest technical assistance program, as well as the most publicized and controversial, was in Vietnam. This project demonstrates how problems can arise in sensitive areas and how well-intentioned activities can go awry. Most of the negative criticism of the project did not appear until years after it had ended, and many suggestions that Michigan State's role was somehow sinister were inaccurate and ill-founded. Adverse reactions to a losing war, doubts as to the justification of our involvement in it, and one especially emotional magazine article raised questions about the university's motives in this and other overseas projects. Admittedly, there were some personnel and organizational problems in Vietnam, but there was no evidence of malicious intent either on the part of the university or the project leaders.

The facts of the case may be stated briefly. When World War II ended, much of old French Indochina (Vietnam, Laos, and Cambodia) had been ravaged by the Japanese. The French attempted to reestablish dominance, but at the same time the Communists were trying to gain control. A third movement towards national independence added to the turmoil. The French attempt to regain control failed. A treaty was finally drawn up in Geneva that divided the country at the seventeenth parallel, the north going to the Communists and the south to the Nationalists.

The new government in the south asked John Foster Dulles, then the U.S. Secretary of State, to nominate an American to attend the Geneva conference and assist the new government in the negotiations. Dulles contacted Dr. Hannah, who, after careful consideration, suggested the name of a Michigan State professor. Some time later, the Department of State asked if MSU would apply for a contract to aid the new government of South Vietnam. Michigan State sent four faculty members to review the situation; and when they returned, they recommended that the university extend assistance. A contract, approved by the Board of Agriculture and signed in the mid 1950s, involved help in four areas. Public administration received top priority since the Vietnamese people needed training for government positions that had been held by French officials for many years. The people also needed training in economic matters, particularly budgets and taxation. Public relations was another necessity; the Vietnamese had to be taught how to deal with the media and present a positive image to the rest of the world. Finally, a civilian police force was required to maintain law and order. But South Vietnam was threatened by more fundamental problems, which destroyed the new republic and in the process cast doubts on all measures taken to assist it. When Hannah was queried some years later about the project, he responded,

> We never felt any need for the University to apologize for its participation in the project [or] for what we tried to do in Vietnam. We learned a great deal from that experience and became much more careful that we did not allow ourselves again to be put in a position where an outside agency might compromise us.
>
> I think that if Michigan State were to face the same choice again in the same context, it might well agree to assist the U.S. Government as we did then.[2]

*Examples of Other Technical Assistance Projects*

Every college at Michigan State has been involved in overseas technical assistance. The policy in funding overseas projects was the same for the entire institution. State appropriations were restricted to service to the state and educational programs for Michigan residents—no Michigan tax dollars were used for overseas projects. Outside funding was sought and received before such projects were initiated. However, new instructional or service programs on campus that resulted from overseas projects might be supported from the university's general fund.

The College of Agriculture was more heavily involved in overseas projects than any other unit at Michigan State. The early projects in Colombia and Okinawa have already been mentioned, and the institution-building project at Nsukka, Nigeria, will be examined in some detail later in this chapter. The following illustrate other overseas activities of the College of Agriculture:

- A consortium for the study of Nigerian rural development (1965–1971)
- The development of the Colleges of Agriculture at the National Taiwan and Chung Hsing Universities (1960–1964)
- A research project (1964–1966) on Food for Peace which included India, Korea, Egypt, Brazil, Pakistan, and Tunisia
- An institution-building project to improve the Faculty of Agriculture in Balcarce, Argentina (1965–1971)
- An agricultural education survey (1963)
- A research project evaluating the effect of PL-480 surplus commodities on agricultural prices and production in Colombia (1960–1965)

---

2. *A Memoir* (East Lansing, Mich.: Michigan State University Press, 1980), pp. 131–32.

- Communication research—diffusion of agricultural innovations in India, Brazil, and Nigeria (1964–1968)
- Agricultural sector simulation research in Nigeria (1967–1971)
- Food marketing research in Puerto Rico (1965–1966)
- Research in marketing in Brazil and Bolivia (1966–1968)
- Research on market coordination in Colombia (1968–1970)
- Research on agricultural mechanization in Ethiopia, Kenya, Uganda, Ghana, Gambia, Nigeria, Senegal, and the Ivory Coast (1967–1970)
- A higher education project in agriculture in Indonesia (1969–present) in conjunction with the Midwest Universities Consortium for International Activities (MUCIA)

All of these projects, amounting to a cost of more than $15 million, were sponsored by the United States Agency for International Development (USAID). In addition, there were sixteen other projects in as many countries, involving more than sixty contract years and sponsored by other government organizations and agencies, foundations, consortia, and other institutions.

The College of Education was also actively involved in overseas projects. Many a Third World country had adopted—or had had imposed upon it—a colonial educational system having little relevance to its needs. One of the contributions to the College of Education was to help improve such an educational system and another was to arouse consciousness and concern about the performance of that system. Internal and external evaluations made it possible to appraise the quality and quantity of the educational offerings. MSU faculty members thus gained a more cosmopolitan point of view for further development of their own programs.

In 1962 College of Education faculty members were asked to conduct research on the secondary and higher educational systems of Central American countries. The outcome was the establishment of a new Institute for Educational Research and Improvement, which became universally accepted and highly regarded as the regional educational center for research and coordination of education in all of Central America.

Another major project undertaken by the college in the early 1960s was a series of surveys, studies, and conferences culminating in the publication *Preliminary Assessment of Education and Manpower in Thailand*. This report laid the groundwork for an Educational Planning Office in the Ministry of Education and for self-study in depth of secondary education in Thailand. The program continued for five years. Many Thai officials were trained on-site. More than forty were sent to Michigan State (and more to other U.S. universities) to earn graduate degrees before returning to fill important positions in educational administration and teaching.

In 1968 a similar five-year project was begun in Turkey, where faculty members from Michigan State worked with the Ministry of Education to develop an Office of Research, Planning, and Coordination, which would provide the leadership and direction for dealing with the nation's educational problems and issues. Nineteen officials received specialized training for specific jobs at Michigan State.

Other projects in which the College of Education was involved included a cooperative program with The Netherlands Ministry of Education and Sciences to assist the University of Utrecht in developing a graduate school counseling program; studies and surveys in Taiwan to provide for better qualified agricultural workers in the skilled, technical, supervisory, and semiprofessional levels; opportunity for students to student teach abroad; graduate education courses in England and Japan; studies on financing education in The Netherlands; and programs to improve elementary and secondary education.

The College of Business's involvement in institution building, which established schools of business administration in three Brazilian universities, has been mentioned. The college has also worked on projects in other Latin American countries, especially with marketing problems and procedures, since expenditures for food take up a major share of the income in developing countries. Other activities included assisting business academies in four centers in Turkey—Ankara, Istanbul, Izmir, and Eskiseher—in cooperation with the Turkish Academies of Economic and Commercial Sciences. Additional projects dealt with electric power in Israel and economic development in Argentina.

The College of Communication Arts and Sciences has concerned itself with a variety of research, institution-building, and training activities abroad. One of its major activities was the development of a graduate program in communications at the Agrarian University at LaMolina, Peru. Research projects focused on Asian theater and Asian drama, national and international systems of broadcasting, communication patterns in five nations, and the East European press. A major undertaking—the "Diffusion of Innovations" project in Brazil, Nigeria, and India—gained national and international attention and resulted in a number of fine reports and publications.

*Consortia*

Another way of extending the international activities of Michigan State has been through its participation in a number of multiuniversity consortia. One of these has been the Midwest Universities Consortium for International Activities, Incorporated (MUCIA). This consortium includes Michigan State, the University of Illinois, Indiana University, Ohio State University, and the University of Wisconsin. Originally funded by a grant of $2.5 million from the Ford Foundation and aided by overhead on contracts, MUCIA has been a major source of funding faculty and graduate student research and a collaborative interuniversity staffing for international projects.

## INSTITUTION BUILDING

One type of technical assistance in which Michigan State was involved has been called "institution building." The concept of institution building is based on the premise that universities and other institutions can be vital components in attaining greater productivity and an improved life for people in developing countries. The institutions, once established, continue to help people help themselves. The concept of institution building also implies a systematic and organized process by which institutions can be built. Michigan State made a number of significant contributions in such development activities.

What are the essential components of institution building? Many years after Michigan State first became involved in this process, systematic studies showed that a number of factors are important. One study conducted by Michigan State faculty members, sponsored by the Pittsburgh Consortium under a grant from the Ford Foundation in the early 1960s, sought to determine how and why institutions or organizations involving new ideas, values, or processes became accepted, valued, or retained in low-income countries. Researchers concluded that *leadership, linkages, doctrine,* and *rules and processes* for getting things done were the major factors.

The new institution must evolve a *leadership* structure appropriate to the developing country. The quality of leadership is probably the most important component because it helps the institution gain acceptance and fosters the continuance of innovations. In the two case studies of institution building that follow, the significance of leadership is vividly demonstrated by the interaction between the cooperative leadership in the recipient country and the leadership at Michigan State.

The institution must also have certain *linkages* or supportive connections, with other units, organizations, and agencies within the developing country. Such linkages take different forms. Some are necessary to provide a continuous flow of financial support (for example, the Ministry of Finance), and some are required to encourage or assist in the hiring of graduates of the institution (industry, government, schools).

Essential, too, in the institution-building effort is a distinctive *doctrine*, mission, or philosophy stating the underlying reason or purpose guiding the institution's operations. For example, the "land-grant philosophy" of Michigan State University emphasizes the three-part mission of teaching, research, and service. This guideline has been used for all overseas institution-building activities. The inclusion of the service function as a vital part of the university's role perhaps explains why land-grant institutions had particular success in working overseas.

An institution must then establish *processes* and *rules* through which decisions can be made. It must have an *organizational structure* that functions efficiently in day-to-day operations. And it must have a program that conforms to its doctrine and charter. In the early stages, leadership plays a vital role in establishing rules, processes, and structures. Two examples of institution building that were greatly influenced by the land-grant philosophy and tradition will be described in some detail: the University of Nigeria at Nsukka and the Rural Development Program at the Comilla Academy in Bangladesh (formerly Pakistan).

## The University of Nigeria, Nsukka

The story of the University of Nigeria at Nsukka must begin with Dr. Nnamdi Azikiwe, upon whose initiative this venture in higher education was launched, nurtured, and developed. Dr. Azikiwe was an uncommon person with uncommon experiences that forged his life values, his commitments, and his work. He was born and spent his early years in an area administered by British colonial rule. He received much of his early education in missionary schools that were predominantly British in orientation and subject matter.

Unlike most of his Nigerian contemporaries, a few of whom pursued further studies in England, Azikiwe came to the United States. From 1925 until 1934, despite limited resources and experiences with discrimination, he completed graduate studies at Columbia and the University of Pennsylvania while also teaching at Lincoln University.

He returned to West Africa in 1934 and was refused a teaching position in Lagos—presumably because his graduate degrees from the United States were regarded as substandard. He turned to journalism and, as an editor and writer, hammered on the related themes of racial equality and the need for positive action against prevailing injustices. He gained widespread attention as a political activist and, eventually, as a political authority. In the period 1934 to 1949, he became the acknowledged nationalist leader in his country. After World War II he headed the strongest political party in eastern Nigeria, and in 1954 he became premier of the Eastern Province.

Largely through the influence of Azikiwe and a few of his colleagues, legislation was enacted in Nigeria in 1955 authorizing the establishment of a university in eastern Nigeria. The government allocated funds for buildings, staffing, and other facilities. Azikiwe and the Minister of Education, I. U. Akpabio, traveled through Europe and the United States seeking help and counsel for this endeavor. They met with officials in the U.S. International Cooperation Administration (ICA) and requested support. The head of the educational division of ICA wrote to John Hannah in 1957 asking if Michigan State would be interested in participating in establishing a university in eastern Nigeria. Hannah responded positively but insisted that any feasibility study should include a British contingent.

In the spring of 1958 a three-man team—Dr. J. W. Cook, vice-chancellor of Exeter University in England; Dr. Glen Taggart, Dean of the MSU Office of International Programs; and President Hannah—went to Nigeria under the joint sponsorship of the ICA and the Inter-University Council for Higher Education in Overseas Territories of Great Britain. There they held discussions with government and educational leaders, visited the proposed Nsukka site, and considered the problems in establishing and organizing the proposed university. The team agreed that the project was desirable and should be supported and in their report also asserted that the new university should be committed to meeting the needs of the Nigerian people. Azikiwe was pleased with the report; some officials and educators expressed the view that, to be prestigious, the new institution must follow the model of traditional British universities.

The contract between the ICA, Michigan State University, and the Nigerian government, signed in March 1960, called for advisory services from MSU in planning, administration, and organization of a university at Nsukka, Nigeria. Work started on the first building in April, and classes were under way in October 1960. The insistence on fast action, motivated by the desire to open the university at the same time that national independence was established, led at times to near chaos. One of the administrators at Nsukka wrote in April 1960,

> He [Azikiwe] was planning to offer practically everything in the legislative act setting up the university. It was the plan to recruit staff from European countries, England and the United States. I could go on ad infinitum detailing his aspirations and plans for this autumn almost all

of which were fairly unrealistic and unaccomplishable...[the] staff has had difficulty in getting him to modify his approach.[3]

Nearly 5,000 applications for admission were received for approximately 200 places in the new university. Neither the academic buildings nor the residence halls were ready for occupancy. Equipment and other facilities were lacking. There were many problems with the administrative organization. The hectic pace and difficulties with faculty recruitment created morale problems that were heightened by hardship and inconvenience. Both faculty qualifications and academic program specifications were questioned by interested and critical observers. The library was less than adequately staffed and equipped. Textbooks were not available in sufficient quantities. Those students who were admitted were not ready for the demands of a new and somewhat primitive environment in which electrical power might be unavailable for hours, water had to be hauled, and many problems were handled by makeshift solutions.

The curriculum problem was resolved by offering only courses that the original staff was competent to teach. Nevertheless, the basic goals and objectives were retained, and they provided guidelines for a better academic program in the ensuing years. The white paper of the Cook-Hannah-Taggart committee recognized that the traditional educational institutions brought to Africa by the colonial powers and missionaries were not appropriate for Nigeria. They envisioned an institution that could deal with and provide for the economic, political, social, and cultural needs of Nigeria and its people. There were special technical requirements for educating Nigerians as individuals and citizens. There was an urgent demand for elementary and secondary school teachers. The importance of technical training and education for teachers was accepted, but there was some question as to how many of these needs—for example, in areas such as home economics, agriculture, and engineering—should be met by the university. There was also still a strong feeling among those educated in or oriented to the British university that the Nigerian institution must fit that mold. For these traditionalists, being proper was more important than being appropriate.

The requirement of general education—education for personal, social, and national development—met with considerably more skepticism, if not outright opposition. The students and many faculty members regarded general education as a distraction from a student's major field. The negative attitude was so strong that, at one point, students

---

3. GT to John Hannah, April 10, 1960.

actually called for a boycott of registration. Yet the idea of general education prevailed through the insistence and support of Azikiwe and others and because more faculty members and administrators recognized the students' misunderstanding, and even denigration, of their own culture and heritage.

Underlying the problem of general education was the issue of differing traditions, cultures, content, and values. Colonial boundary lines bore no relation to tribal memberships, mores, and customs. Nigeria existed as a political and economic unit, but not as a nation; identification of an individual as a Nigerian was meaningless. Was general education to perpetuate a culture or to develop one? Proposed courses in history, language, geography, geology, and biology had little to do with Nigeria or even with Africa. University education in the traditional mold was not directed to educating a Nigerian to live and serve in Nigeria but rather to establish a cultural status equivalent to that of an educated Englishman, a European, or perhaps even an American if general education were to be offered Michigan State style. It is noteworthy that general education did not become a significant issue in American higher education until after 1930, and in the 1980s the argument regarding educational balance still continues.

Despite its critics, general education carried the day at Nsukka. To graduate, a student had to pass five courses: language and literature, language and society, natural science, social science, and the humanities. All were to be taken in the first three years of the degree program. The fact that the degree program was set at the U.S. four years, rather than the British three years, reflected the American concept and somewhat eased the argument between general and specialized education.

After surmounting the handicaps of the first two or three years, students, faculty, and visitors generally accepted the Nsukka project as successful. That early victory can be attributed to many factors and people. The personal involvement of Dr. Azikiwe was of paramount importance, and his leadership exemplified many of the components of a successful institution-building project. A number of innovations were accepted, or at least tolerated, because of his support. Without him, there would have been no university at Nsukka.

The continuing interest and support of President Hannah and of the British, the Dutch, and many others were also important. Many of the strengths of Michigan State and its colleges were drawn upon to aid the project. Faculty members, administrators, and supervisory personnel who went to Nigeria during the course of the project numbered 148, and seventy-nine of them were on multi-year assignments. If early efforts seemed calculated to develop a branch campus of Michigan State at Nsukka, these very shortly were modified toward building a university indigenous to eastern Nigeria. The commitment of the university at Nsukka to service to the country and its promise to bring about economic and social betterment made the institution highly supportable. A total of $12.5 million was contributed by non-Nigerian sources, more than $1 million of it donated by the Ford Foundation. The Nigerian contribution was $33.5 million, bringing the total amount to about $47 million.

In October 1960 the university had thirteen Nigerian staff members; by 1966, it had 448 senior staff members, of whom 80 percent were Nigerians. In 1960 there were two classroom buildings, one dormitory, a health center, a student services building, thirty-six senior staff houses; by 1967 the physical plant represented an investment of about $20 million, most of which came from Nigerian financing. The Azikiwe Library started almost from scratch; but by 1967, 80,000 volumes were on the shelves, and it was receiving more than 1,100 journals and other periodicals. Nine colleges were established by 1966, including agriculture, business administration, education, engineering science, social studies, arts, law, and human medicine.

Michigan State University's participation ended in the summer of 1967 with the Biafran Revolution. Much of the university was destroyed. Michigan State was not invited to assist when it was later reestablished, but the MSU influence remained alive in those who had experienced it.

*The Academies in Pakistan*

In the 1950s Michigan State became involved in the Comilla experiment in rural development in east Pakistan. Like many other developing countries, east Pakistan was beset with poverty, inadequate health care, illiteracy, hunger, unsanitary conditions, malnutrition, and disorder. The focal point of the project was in Comilla. The Comilla region then consisted of a land area of approximately 100 square miles, and its primary center was the city of Comilla.

There had been previous attempts to foster rural development in Pakistan, most noticeably the Village Agricultural and Industrial Development Training Institutes (VAID), established in 1953 and sponsored by the government of Pakistan, the government of the United States, and the Ford Foundation. Training programs were offered to assist middle- and lower-level administrators to become more effective participants and leaders in development projects. The VAID program did not effect the changes that had been sought, and the Ford Foundation then attempted to create a more effective change agent.

In 1956 Dr. George Gant of the Ford Foundation invited Dr. Floyd Reeves and some of his colleagues to come to Pakistan to study the situation and make recommendations for establishing a new program. The team made its visit and came up with several suggestions, among them the creation of a new institution with a modified land-grant approach to provide the means for government leaders and villagers to gain the knowledge and capabilities to further rural development.

The recommendations of Dr. Reeves and his colleagues were discussed and accepted officially by Pakistan in July 1957. A letter of agreement was signed by the Pakistan government, the Ford Foundation, and Michigan State and provided for the latter to supply technical assistance to two academies, one at Comilla in east Pakistan and another at Peshawar in west Pakistan. The first director of what came to be called the Academy for Rural Development was Dr. Akter Hameed Khan.

The Comilla academy began very modestly. The first instructors hired included thirteen with master's degrees and four with doctorates. More important was that these instructors, who were to be the teachers of the public officials, had firsthand knowledge of the conditions, needs, and attitudes in the villages included in the program. The seventeen trainers and two directors (from Comilla and Peshawar) spent six weeks in predeparture orientation in Pakistan, the next nine months studying at Michigan State, and a final six weeks on observation tours in other Asian countries. During the orientation period, they met with representatives of the Pakistani government, the ICA, and the Ford Foundation. The participants were prepared for experiences they might encounter and for what they were expected to achieve during their study tour.

Upon their arrival in East Lansing in the summer of 1958, the Pakistanis as well as their Michigan State counterparts received further orientation. The tentative training program had to be changed as the needs and capabilities of the group became more apparent. Teaching techniques and learning materials effective with American students were alien to this group. An early decision to include cooperatives, family planning, home industries, and youth and women's groups as parts of the program presented some problems since the participants had expected a program devoted exclusively to technical matters such as agricultural production, fertilizers, pesticides, and irrigation. Yet the idea of social change as a part of rural development eventually became an important part of the work of the academy.

As the MSU staff gained knowledge of the Pakistanis, other changes were made. Formal seminars were replaced in part by field trips to study and observe development projects. The participants were encouraged to enroll in regular courses. Some individuals attended regional and national conferences to gain exposure to a wider range of ideas and projects. The university library organized special collections related to Pakistan and other countries. The Pakistanis witnessed firsthand the operation and philosophy of the land-grant approach. Akter Khan proved to be a natural and dynamic leader. He had been acquainted with the land-grant philosophy and tradition and was convinced that it was appropriate for the new academy.

In August 1959 three months after the participant training program was completed, the first training program was begun at the academy. The program had two major objectives: to increase agricultural production through training, research, and demonstration and to improve the quality of rural living through community and social development. Training, the central thrust of the program, was to be based on facts and goals but made explicit through demonstrations and pilot programs. A primary concern was to provide government officials and village leaders with the skills and knowledge needed to deal with practical problems and issues at the local level.

Village leaders, the communications links between the academy and the people, had to convince their constituents that changes were needed and desirable. These leaders, selected by the villagers (one per village), attended the academy each week, then returned to their villages to share what they had learned. The people listened to their leader's presentation, and their reactions were taken up at the next week's training session. As the word spread about these activities, other villages began to send representatives. There were only ten in the first group, but by seven years later about 6,000 people had participated in the program at the academy.

Early in 1960 the government of Pakistan granted the academy permission to use the entire Comilla region, an area of over 100 square miles, as a demonstration laboratory to conduct agricultural experiments and exhibit to farmers and villagers new methods of improving agricultural production. The demonstrations had a great impact throughout the country. Government officials, aware of the implications for other parts of the nation, came to the academy to observe its operation and participate in training programs. The academy became recognized as the center to which people could turn for advice on rural development.

*Cooperatives.* As the program grew, it became obvious that immediate and direct contact with villages was necessary to gain their support for changes and innovations. Village cooperatives appeared to be the logical economic organization and communication links. They provided a means of obtaining consensus and community support for larger-scale action, including such new activities as improved water supply, a centralized machine shop, a cold storage plant, and establishment of a capital fund created by the savings of the members. These funds were then used to extend credit to the membership, permit bulk purchasing, obtain farm implements for the common use of cooperative members, and set up accounting procedures.

The cooperatives were not limited to programs related to agriculture. During the 1960s, cooperatives were formed for butchers, rickshaw pullers, and other groups. They were also used for organizing projects in literacy, public works, and family planning.

Public works attracted much attention. Between 1961 and 1966 there was marked improvement in road construction, in the building of bridges and culverts, and in water control. Other projects were also initiated, such as the building of schools and community centers, as part of the public works program.

One of Akter Hameed's major concerns was the plight of women, as expressed in 1963:

> One cause of our misery and poverty is that we keep our womenfolk at home, guarded over constantly. We keep them indoors. We have almost imprisoned them. We do not educate them, and because they are confined they cannot educate themselves; so they are nearly all illiterate, they are timid. And so long as women are uneducated, development can hardly be expected in our country.
>
> If the mother is illiterate, if she has no courage, how can one expect courage in her children? The mother is the teacher. . . .
>
> I think that our country can never progress until we emancipate the women.[4]

The academy undertook a project to improve the status of women. It was first necessary to convince women that they could and should participate in the program. It was also essential that it be operated through the village cooperatives because it was easier to gain a consensus by group action than by gaining the support of individual males. A few women, with permission from their husbands, agreed to participate in this new and radical activity.

In March 1962 the first classes were offered—in child care, maternity diseases, and family planning. But it was soon discovered that the program would be more acceptable if instruction were provided in less intimate subjects, such as sewing, spinning, sanitation, nutrition, first aid, poultry raising, gardening, and handicrafts. With these skills,

---

4. Arthur Raper, et al., *Rural Development in Action: Comprehensive Experiment in Action* (Ithaca, N.Y.: Cornell University Press, 1970), p. 157.

women could earn a small cash income without leaving their homes. Much of the credit for later economic and social changes affecting women can be attributed to the corps of women who were trained at the academy and who returned to their villages to serve as teachers and models for other women.

The academy also offered a rather intensive course for midwives. Initially it consisted of a three-day program for practicing and novice midwives. From the original group, the most promising trainees were selected for an internship program at the Comilla Maternity and Health Center. In 1965 a year-long program was introduced to give extensive training to midwives. As was the case with most other innovative programs, family planning discussions took place in the village societies. Contraceptives were made available by the government through local retail outlets.

*Rural Education.* A new approach to education in the rural areas was instituted in Comilla in 1959. One priority was to orient the curriculum more towards agriculture. Youth organizations, which emphasized farm and home projects, were established in schools. The adult literacy program was expanded. School-building projects became an important part of the public works effort. After seven years, the estimated number of literate persons doubled. Men were most affected since about 95 percent of the women in the villages remained illiterate.

The academy at Comilla provided, through its pilot projects, the basic structure for instituting desired changes by promoting research and initiating programs in rural development. It also established the linkages and contacts necessary to implement these changes. During the ten-year period from its inception in 1947, many people contributed to the undertaking. Michigan State was represented by ten long-term resident advisers who stayed for two years or more and an additional six educators on short-term assignments. Four advisers came from Denmark, six from Great Britain, twelve from Japan, and eleven from other U.S. universities and from national and international organizations and agencies.

### THE IMPACT OF INTERNATIONAL PROJECTS ON MICHIGAN STATE

Michigan State's involvement in international activities enhanced the university's reputation both nationally and internationally. Although such activities were a radical departure from the traditional role and responsibility of institutions of higher education, Hannah and other administrators felt that the nation and its institutions could not do otherwise. But in the late 1940s and early 1950s, Michigan State and most other universities were ill-equipped and ill-prepared to take a major part in reconstructing a war-torn world. Too few faculty members were available to allow for many to be spared for off-campus activities. Even fewer had the needed expertise for assisting developing countries or for training prospective advisers for overseas field assignments. Many professors were neither sufficiently concerned nor willing to give long service for an apparently ill-defined and uncertain cause.

There was also a problem of public support. Many taxpayers felt that too much money was directed to programs about which they had little knowledge or concern. They believed that universities received public support to provide benefits to a particular geographical area or domestic clientele. The idea of extending university programs far beyond the immediate interests of the state or the nation was less than enthusiastically received.

Despite these doubts, Hannah remained a staunch advocate of using the knowledge and expertise of American universities to improve the conditions and well-being of less fortunate people. His convictions and perseverance were instrumental in helping to reeducate and reorient the people who, fiscally, made the university's operations possible. In a speech given November 9, 1960, Hannah described the changed status of the universities and the progress that had been made to help improve the standards and hopes of the people throughout the world.

> The long-term results are yet to be observed, but I am sure that the world today is a better world than it would have been had there been no programs of university assistance in the developing areas.
> One of our great strengths . . . is that much of the missionary zeal with which these programs were inaugurated . . . still remains. The American spirit of helpfulness, the desire to give everyone a decent chance is far from dead within us.
> Next, we can say with conviction that it has been proved again that higher education can be put to use for mankind's benefit, that professors can be practical, that they can make contributions in a variety of fields in the developing countries.

A conservative appraisal of the involvement of universities in international assistance indicates that, despite many difficulties, the experience has had a payoff for all parties concerned. Through a variety of training programs, institution-building projects, and opportunities for thousands of people to study in universities such as Michigan State, the developing countries obtained a large contingent of trained human resources (human capital), trained manpower, and institutional capabilities. These resources have enabled these countries to deal more effectively with problems in social, economic, and educational development.

Perhaps the most obvious and general payoff to the universities was creating a new international perspective on the campuses and bringing a global understanding to many of its people. Projects in technical assistance made possible contacts and communications between scholars and supplied access, facilities, and funds for conducting research. Many foreign students were able to use project funds to pursue graduate studies in the United States. The universities also gained by providing rich experiences to many of their faculty members and some of their graduate students and by bringing new excitement and new horizons to their teaching. Professors have had the opportunity to apply theoretical learning to practical situations and thereby make their knowledge more utilitarian and pragmatic. They have also furnished the incentive for developing special resource collections on numerous geographical areas in the libraries of their home campuses. Indeed, through teaching and research, they have helped establish a community of global scholarship.

At Michigan State, one example that points up the impact of overseas technical assistance was the institution-building project at the University of Nigeria at Nsukka. This project created a core of faculty who, because their Nsukka experience generated interests and commitment, have played a significant role in the subsequent growth and development of a broad array of international studies and programs at the university:

1. Thirteen of the present core faculty at MSU's African Studies Center served on the University of Nigeria program.
2. The project was responsible for the establishment and early growth of the African Studies Center.
3. Michigan State's recognition and reputation as a leading institution of African education and research had its origins in the Nigerian program.
4. The experience with the University of Nigeria was the beginning of involvement in and commitment to a dozen or more other projects in Africa in research and training related to rural development, the rural economy, agricultural mechanization, marketing, food production and marketing, and small-scale industries.

In the period from 1951 to 1971, some 350 Michigan State faculty members participated in thirty-five overseas technical assistance projects on either long- or short-term bases. This represents about 10 percent of the entire MSU faculty. A study made in 1971 by Rose

Hayden and sponsored by the Office of International Studies and Programs showed that 218 faculty members in this group were still on campus. The following table indicates the number of faculty and their affiliation in the university.

| College or Program | Number of Faculty | Percentage |
|---|---|---|
| Agriculture and Natural Resources | 67 | 30.7 |
| Education | 48 | 22.0 |
| Social Science | 22 | 10.1 |
| Business | 22 | 10.1 |
| Arts and Letters | 10 | 4.6 |
| University College | 10 | 4.6 |
| Engineering | 7 | 3.2 |
| Communication Arts | 6 | 2.9 |
| Human Ecology | 6 | 2.9 |
| Natural Science | 6 | 2.9 |
| Veterinary Medicine | 2 | 0.9 |
| Human Medicine | 1 | 0.5 |
| Miscellaneous (International Programs, Registrar, Library, etc.) | 10 | 4.6 |
| | 217 | 100.0% |

The figures show that, while there was widespread involvement in these activities, the distribution by college was very uneven. More than two-thirds of the faculty members who participated were from the Colleges of Agriculture, Education, Social Science, and Business. Despite less involvement in technical assistance programs overseas, the College of Arts and Letters and the University College developed a strong international dimension in campus programs, later encouraged and augmented by a Ford Foundation grant of $250,000.

*The Impact on Curriculum*

Before World War II the principal general educational goal of Michigan State and of most institutions in higher education was to acquaint students with American thought and traditions and to prepare them to become useful citizens. The primary focus was on the Western world with little more than a nod given to Africa, Asia, or even Latin America.

The 1941–42 catalog of MSU shows that only twelve departments were then offering courses that went beyond parochial attention to the United States: agricultural economics, art, economics, English, foreign languages, forestry, geography, history, political science, sociology, soils, and speech. Altogether they offered 128 courses, many taught only in alternate years. Of these courses 101 were in foreign languages with primary emphasis on learning the language: 29 in French, 21 in German, 6 in Greek, 6 in Italian, 15 in Latin, and 24 in Spanish. Only 27 courses were in other academic areas; and of these 16 dealt with Western civilization, three concerned the non-Western world (two on Latin America and one on Asia), and eight could be classified as general conceptual/comparative courses, including a course offered by the Department of Speech, "Foreign Dialects." All these courses were related to the Western tradition.

By 1951–52, twenty-one departments were offering internationally oriented courses. One significant addition was the Department of Foreign Studies (see page 266), which offered courses in Far Eastern studies, Latin American studies, and west European studies. A breakdown by department is as follows:

| Department | Western Civilization | Non-Western World | International General |
|---|---|---|---|
| Agricultural Economics | ... | ... | 1 |
| Art | 9 | 3 | 1 |
| Economics | 1 | 2 | 6 |
| English | 29 | ... | ... |
| Foreign Studies | ... | 26 | ... |
| Geology-Geography | 1 | 3 | 4 |
| History | 8 | 7 | 2 |
| History of Civilization | 3 | ... | ... |
| Literature and Fine Arts | 3 | ... | ... |
| Music | 6 | ... | ... |
| Philosophy | 8 | ... | ... |
| Police Administration | ... | ... | 1 |
| Political Science | 3 | 3 | 5 |
| Public Administration | ... | ... | 1 |
| Psychology | 2 | ... | ... |
| Religion | 5 | ... | ... |
| Social Science | 1 | ... | ... |
| Sociology-Anthropology | 2 | 3 | 3 |
| Speech, Drama, and Radio Ed. | ... | ... | 1 |
| Textiles, Clothing, and Related Arts | 1 | ... | 2 |
| | 82 | 47 | 27 |

There were a number of additions in the language department, too. The 1951–52 MSU catalog listed 34 courses in French (plus 2 graduate courses), 31 in German (plus 2 graduate courses), 10 in Italian, 7 in Greek, 16 in Latin, 1 in Hindu, 6 in Arabic, 6 in Chinese, 3 in Japanese, and 6 in Russian.

By 1969 forty-four departments were offering courses dealing with world regions, international developments, and cross-cultural areas. A significant change was noticeable in the number of undergraduate offerings (285). This compares with a total of 128 courses in 1941 and 279 in 1951–52. One of the most striking innovations was the increased emphasis on non-Western countries and cultures. The 1969 catalog lists thirty-five courses dealing with Africa and African languages offered by ten departments. Ten of these courses were concerned with the teaching of African languages, and the remaining twenty-five with African societies and cultures. Asian studies also showed a marked increase, with thirty-two courses in Asian languages. A total of forty nonlanguage foreign studies courses were offered in the university. Twenty-eight graduate and undergraduate courses dealing with Latin America and twenty-seven courses in Spanish and Portuguese were listed. Seventeen nonlanguage courses focused on the Soviet Union and sixty-eight (graduate and undergraduate) on the Russian language. In addition, students could take courses with an emphasis on Canada and on Australia. From Hayden's study, one can deduce that approximately 20 percent of all courses offered at the university in 1969 contained some comparative or international area content.

The effect of overseas experiences on classroom activities is difficult to assess. Hayden asked thirty-four faculty members what impact their experiences in international projects had on their teaching. Eight of them, or 24 percent, indicated that they had completely revised their course content and introduced new material as a result of their work overseas. The remainder stated that they had used their experiences at least indirectly to provide examples or case studies to illustrate certain points.

### The Impact on Research

One of the three major facets of the land-grant philosophy is research. In overseas projects, many problems were initially encountered when attempts were made directly to transfer our society's technology and knowledge to the less developed nations of the world. Too often, the needs of a given country were determined on the basis of economic or political considerations rather than careful and well-planned research. The determination to get on quickly with the job outlined in the Point IV Program and the inexperience of those assigned to do the work caused many of the early participants to think that we had only to export and explain our answers to the world's ills. The demands for immediate action made this a tempting approach. But it was soon apparent that successful projects had to be based on realistic assessments of the needs and circumstances of the recipient country. The lack of research—and hence the lack of basic and necessary information concerning the needs and possible and acceptable steps to meet these needs—produced some of the obvious shortcomings of the early projects in technical assistance.

There are many reasons for conducting research. Scholarly research focuses on the discovery of new knowledge. Some search and re-search increases the knowledge of those who teach in both formal and nonformal educational settings. Applied research provides immediately relevant information to social, economic, political, and educational decision makers. All these types of research were utilized in technical assistance activities, yet there is another kind of research that is vital in such activities, namely, research in social dynamics. A function of this type of research is to help determine the appropriate steps, methodology, and techniques that will lead to acceptance of changes that will be both beneficial and lasting. Customs, traditions, taboos, suspicions, and insecurity can destroy development efforts or slow progress to the point where benefits are not apparent.

Research efforts in overseas projects were hampered by lack of finances and lack of willing and able patrons. If universities did not have the resources, private foundations often helped, but they tended to support action rather than research. Finances for research were forthcoming from the federal government, but unfortunately not for the kind of research required to enhance the work in international projects.

Nevertheless, overseas activities did provide many faculty members and some graduate students with the base and support to conduct important research. A number of faculty members undertook research projects on their own time. Some students were able to carry on field work because the university and project organizers insisted upon including in contracts provisions for project-related research that not only contributed to the project itself but also helped advanced students meet the requirements for graduate degrees.

Yet some faculty complained that insufficient funds were earmarked for research. Perhaps so. But even if more financial support had been made available, a realistic review of the circumstances makes it evident that major pressures would have been for research that led to decisions and action. The problems of serving in a foreign country and the risks of overt or covert involvement or intervention by various politicians and government officials made objective and conclusive research nearly impossible.

## SUMMARY

During the years when John Hannah served as president of Michigan State, it became an internationalized institution. There were great changes in the objectives and mission of the university: an increased emphasis on non-Western cultures, the development of many new, internationally oriented courses; the establishment of area studies centers, institutes, and programs; and the development of a strong international library, to name a few.

There was an influx of foreign students and scholars who came to study at Michigan State, and American students had corresponding opportunities to study abroad. New horizons were made possible for faculty members who participated in international technical assistance and research projects. The university became more knowledgeable and recognized its role and responsibility as a part of an interdependent world.

Certainly one of the important elements in maintaining communications and cooperation among the diverse units on campus dealing with the international dimension was the establishment of the Office of the Dean of International Studies and Programs. This office has kept international interests alive on the campus and provided for their liaison and continuity.

In the mid 1970s, a survey of the colleges of agriculture in American universities was conducted. Data were collected from fifty-eight institutions including the fifty first-Morrill-Act land-grant colleges and universities, the seven second-Morrill-Act land-grant colleges, and Southern Illinois University. The results of the survey were compiled by Professor John Blackmore, director of International Agricultural Programs at the University of Minnesota; his report was included in the *Congressional Record*. A committee of the Land-Grant Association gathered statistics on prior and current levels of involvement in international agricultural work. What was discovered was that, at that time, these institutions were providing instruction to more than 5,000 foreign students, that more than 1,000 of their faculty members were engaged in significant international research, and that more than 2,800 had gained foreign experience from service abroad in the preceding decade. During the previous twenty years, these universities had had cooperative ventures with more than 1,000 foreign institutions.

One thousand faculty members had Asian experience, 1,400 had Latin American experience, and more than 700 had worked professionally in Africa. In the year the survey was taken, U.S. colleges of agriculture offered special training programs to more than 500 *groups* of foreign visitors who came to the U.S. campuses. In the same year, there were 410 foreign professors and postdoctoral students in residence in these colleges.

The survey identified colleges of agriculture that had had (1) 200 or more foreign students and visiting professors, (2) 50 or more foreign undergraduate students, (3) 100 or more foreign graduate students, (4) 15 or more foreign postdoctoral students and visiting professors, (5) 200 or more AID- and FAO-supported students, (6) 10 or more faculty currently serving abroad on assignments, (7) 15 or more faculty members with experience in Asia and/or the Middle East, (8) 15 or more with work experience in Africa, (9) 15 or more faculty with work experience in Latin America, (10) 10 or more engaged in international research, (11) 20 or more special training programs for groups of foreign trainees, and (12) cooperative programs with 15 or more foreign institutions in the past twenty years. The leading five universities listed by rank were (1) Michigan State University, (2) University of California at Davis, (3) University of Wisconsin, (4) University of Florida, and (5) Cornell University.

In 1965 another report was released, based on a study of the involvement of six major universities in the United States: Cornell, Indiana, Michigan State, Stanford, Tulane, and Wisconsin. It was produced by Education and World Affairs and entitled "The University Looks Abroad: Approaches to World Affairs in Six Universities." In the summary of the section dealing with Michigan State, the report has this to say:

> More than any other of the universities included in this survey, Michigan State appears to have deliberately built upon its international activities as a means of moving the institution up to a major university status. In a few short years it has lifted itself from a provincial college with an agricultural orientation to a university of national stature and worldwide recognition.
>
> Looking back over this Operation Bootstrap, three forces can be seen to have combined to provide the leverage. One is the personality of the president and the insisting role he has performed in the university's internationalization. The second is the fact that President Hannah has had the support of a small but committed group of international-minded members of his faculty and administration. And the third source of strength has been the fact that the president, his administrators, and a portion of this faculty have held to a deliberate strategy—a long-range plan to internationalize the institution.
>
> The course chosen—a succession of technical assistance contracts overseas, involving many of the university's professional schools—has not been without cost. Within the academic community the image projected by MSU, as an institution over-eager for overseas involvements and often

overextended in its areas of competence—has become almost a cliche. MSU faculty members are understandably sensitive on this point.

The image is unjustified; if it ever applied, it is now well out-of-date. It may take some time to blur away at the edges, but it should fade more rapidly as the academic community comes to realize that Michigan State in the past year or so has accomplished more than perhaps any other American university—certainly more than any of those included in this survey—in building a continuing relationship, a feedback to its campus, between its activities abroad and its teaching and research functions at home. In contrast to those where the international program development consists of an isolated center of international facility, Michigan State has moved in the direction of achieving a real international dimension throughout the institution.

As MSU provided a model in its early creation of a centralized administrative apparatus to coordinate its international activities, a functional step that has been followed and adapted by several other universities, so too, its pioneering efforts in internationalizing its curriculum and providing linkages between its field projects and its campus learning and research could serve as models for its sister institutions in the United States.

# PART IV
*People, Policies, and Politics*

# 13
# Student Involvement

John Hannah liked students, individually and collectively, and they reciprocated in their regard for him. The resulting interaction was attended by changes in campus mores, in institutional operations, and in governance. Some changes were certainly a result of program alterations and the attraction of a more cosmopolitan student body. Some reflected changing social values and mores. But mutual regard played a major role. To capture and reveal that relationship, its background and development over time must be considered.

The involvement of students in governance and decision making in the early years of the agricultural college, like that in other nineteenth-century colleges, was more notable by its absence than its presence. The institution was new. It was small. Its very existence was in doubt for many years, and its location, only three miles from the seat of government in Lansing, brought it immediately under critical scrutiny whenever the behavior or comment of any student or faculty member provided the opportunity. The hazing of freshmen or the occasional rowdy behavior of a few students could be taken as an excuse for severe criticism which might affect the next appropriation and the student enrollment. Students came primarily from a rural background, and their morals and behavioral standards reflected that background. Parents expected the institution, in the fullest sense of the phrase *in loco parentis,* to define and maintain morals and standards. Students attending the college were obviously preparing for careers in agriculture or domestic science, and the combined program of courses and field work left them little time for errant or aberrant behavior. Indeed, it was seldom that they were not under observation by the faculty. President Willitts, in the late 1880s, reported that he never retired at the end of the day without making the rounds of dormitories. College attendance was a privilege and an opportunity and was so regarded by the general public, by the legislature, and by faculty and students.

In 1858 President Williams reported to the legislature, "The use of tobacco is almost entirely abandoned. No spirituous liquors are ever found upon the place. No games of hazard are tolerated." In 1885 President Willitts confidently assured the legislature that there was no smoking and no drinking on the campus. He apparently enforced this by his evening rounds of the dormitories. Whatever the truth, the legislature was gratified.

The continuing concern about student behavior and morals on campus was reinforced by public reactions to campus events. Thus, in the 1890s an episode of student rowdiness provided opportunities for critics to question institutional standards, and even the need for the college's existence. Perhaps even more serious was the fact that such incidents were reported widely by newspapers throughout the state, which undoubtedly had some impact on enrollment. Since formal education in agriculture was virtually an unknown, student and faculty morals and decorum may have been more critical for survival than scholarship and the quality of the program.

Colleges in the nineteenth and early twentieth centuries generally assumed responsibility for student morality and conduct. Religious overtones reverberated. One means utilized by the colleges to cultivate moral and ethical behavior was through required daily chapel services. When Michigan State began operation in the spring of 1857, a chapel program was scheduled each morning. It was expected that hymns, homilies, prayers, and preachments would prompt students to seek and act the good life. Athletics was a dubious endeavor hardly to be encouraged. Farmers had no time to waste. When the college proposed to hire its first athletic coach in 1900, the board agreed largely because the person proposed was the Reverend Charles O. Bemies, who would have joint responsibility for coaching and conducting chapel services. Prayer might accomplish what limited practice and talent could not. The chapel requirement was abandoned in 1911, when the chemistry lecture room which had served as chapel could no longer accommodate the students. Multiple chapel sessions were apparently not proposed, suggesting that neither faculty nor students were perturbed.

In the late nineteenth century, a students' organization briefly acquired a role in disciplining students, but when President Snyder arrived at the turn of the century, he immediately revoked its disciplinary power. By tradition, student offenders of rules and policies (stated or unstated) had been brought before the total faculty, but Snyder handled these matters himself. He also appointed proctors to report unacceptable behavior in the residence halls. The faculty did not object.

When Morrill Hall for women opened in 1900, the dean of women had an apartment on the first floor. Home economics instructors were housed on upper floors—whether for maintaining their own decorum or that of the students is not known. Behavior in the hall was under continual observation and out-of-hall evening hours were virtually nonexistent. Recreational activities were generally confined to lectures given by local ministers or faculty members and to weekly debates. These were augmented at times by a musical recital or a literary reading. Students were invited occasionally to the homes of faculty members. On rare occasions, student gatherings included young women from the Michigan Female College in Lansing (more often referred to as the Female Seminary). Picnics, husking bees, and the like were other forms of planned recreation; but organized sports were virtually nonexistent. The Red Cedar River provided boating and swimming in the summer, ice skating in the winter, and fishing any time. The rural influence was evident.

The rules and views implicit in the preceding remarks continued unaltered for years, although from time to time, they were reenforced or expanded as a result of changing campus conditions. Such student governance as existed remained well under the domination of the administration. This is reflected in college records of the early 1900s, which show that student organizations confirmed rather than initiated rules and regulations, such as those pertaining to walking only on sidewalks, dormitory hours, and so forth. Despite the traditional practice of near-autocratic control by the administration, there was a gradual trend toward liberalizing certain regulations. For example, female students were permitted extra hours out of the residence halls if they maintained a B average or better. Later, in 1932, this privilege was extended to all undergraduate students with a B average. Apparently it was assumed that good grades assured decorum and good sense.

As with most colleges, the educational programs were decreed and approved by the Board of Agriculture after development by the faculty. Although the precollege preparation (or lack of it) of the students to a great extent molded the course requirements and levels, the courses were determined by the faculty. The curriculum was not the cafeteria it became in later years, but a prescribed meal, presumably nutritious if not always attractive. The combination of course work and practice by students under the supervision of teachers, themselves engaging in study and dissemination of knowledge, gave the classroom, laboratory, and field work a more relevant tinge than became evident in later years when knowledge and theory tended to overshadow practical experience.

The college was a conservative institution, as reflected in its student body, its board, and its faculty. Except when the Civil War and World War I drew students and faculty away and forced emergency procedures and programs upon the college, the students tended to ignore much of the world beyond the campus. In April 1935 there was a national movement among college students to stage a peace strike, but at Michigan State there was little or no enthusiasm—except that potential speakers from Ann Arbor were escorted to a dunking in the Red Cedar (an experience not yet as life threatening as pollution would later make it). But in 1937 a labor union's attempt to extend Lansing sit-down strikes and picketing to the closing of East Lansing stores and restaurants aroused the student body to meet and forcibly turn back the union members and their cars. There was a flurry of excitement on the campus and a sense of exultation and power, fed for several days by favorable reactions (not including those of unions) from around the state. But it is more noteworthy that it was not until 1939 that the student paper, the *State News*, expanded its coverage to include events outside the college community.

In 1934 faculty reaction to student absences on the Wednesday before and the Monday after the Thanksgiving recess resulted in elimination of the holiday. Double absences for days preceding and following holidays, as well as the long-existing rule of cancellation of one credit for six to twelve absences in all classes combined, had proved inadequate to deal with the problem. The scheduling of Friday and Saturday examinations to control Thanksgiving absences, while effective, was generally regarded as inhuman by students and faculty alike. The elimination of the holiday made the double-absence rule inoperative and so had less impact than anticipated. Moreover, many faculty members were irritated by the new policy, which negated their own holiday plans.

In 1934 an *expected* football victory over the University of Michigan became the basis for declaration of a half-holiday on the following Monday. The *unexpected* victory in the previous year had effectively resulted in a half-holiday. But the pep meeting and dance planned for the anticipated 1935 victory was a dismal failure, and that for 1936 was little better. When a fourth victory seemed likely in 1937, the student paper opportunistically suggested that students renounce the Monday half-holiday and request restoration of the Thanksgiving vacation Thursday through Sunday. So it was. On the whole, the faculty and staff were as pleased as the students.

By 1936 the absence policy was further altered as much because of faculty dislike of checking and reporting class attendance as because of student antipathy and the retirement of the attendance officer.

Absences were still to be reported to deans, but no penalty would be applied until more than one-fourth of the scheduled class meetings had been missed. Some faculty members—tongue in cheek—asserted that students were now serious seekers after knowledge and stopped reporting absences. Those who recorded them might find some individuals walking out of large lecture sections immediately afterward. Faced with these brief "sit-ins" and "walkouts," some professors deferred taking attendance to the latter part of the class period, delegated it to a student, or forgot it. Other professors used unannounced examinations to force attendance.

The years from 1941 to 1969 markedly affected student attitudes, concerns, and involvement in institutional policies. Experiences during the war years, with military units and officers and with self-reliant female students during the absence of most males, resulted in recognition of the capability and responsibility of young men and women and some adverse reaction to the regimentation (however necessary) observed with military units. The Basic College program, combined with counseling services, emphasized the possibility and wisdom of individual choice and the freedom to change majors or programs. Returning veterans—male and female, including many former officers—did not accept the restrictions on drinking liquor, smoking, and other personal and social behavior. Traditional regulations also had to be discarded for faculty and married students in university housing. The right to privacy superseded traditions and regulations. College attendance became regarded as a right rather than a privilege, and professors found that they might have to earn respect rather than simply expecting it and justify rules rather than simply enforcing them.

With the marked expansion in courses and programs, the once relatively direct relation between programs and jobs was clouded. Even so, college was viewed by returning veterans as a means to an end, rather than as a period of maturation. Student activities, "busy-work" courses, and general education courses were experiences that could be readily foregone and forgotten—and often were by waiver, by examination, or by policy changes permitting substitutions. An expectant father—and there were many of them in what was known as Fertile Valley—involved in a second battle of the bulge was not to be bothered with trivia.

## THE STUDENT PERSONNEL PROGRAM

In 1935 the Office of Dean of Men was instituted, balancing the Office of Dean of Women, which had existed for many years. There was some cooperation between the two, but their basic views were rather different.

The first attempt to develop a unified student personnel program at Michigan State was signaled in 1944 with the appointment of Stanley E. Crowe as dean of students. The former deans of men and women were rechristened as counselors for men and for women, much to the dismay of the incumbents. The intent in creating this new office and title was to develop a closer cooperative relationship between the student personnel program and the academic program. Some functions—such as advising, career counseling, placement, admissions, recruiting, credit by examination, grade reporting, and student records that had long been regarded as academic functions based partly or entirely on divisions and departments—had been neither well nor uniformly performed. Departmental or faculty indifference or convenience seemed frequently to supersede recognition of these functions as essential student services. A dean of students presumably could improve these services by taking over some of the functions and coordinating others.

Dean Crowe had been a long-time member of the mathematics department and had directed the summer session and the Lecture-Concert Series. He also acted as dean of the general college, a program he initiated for students with deficient high school backgrounds or unsatisfactory college grades. Crowe had worked with Hannah on many matters. He had excellent rapport with students, faculty, and other administrative officers. His appointment was well calculated to ease any suspicion generated by creation of a new unit impinging on territories long controlled by others.

The Counseling Center, charged originally with advising and counseling all Basic College students (although not limited to this), was placed in the new office. The Board of Examiners, assigned the task of developing comprehensive examinations for the Basic College and also committed to other examination functions such as credit by examination, admission by examination, research, and evaluation of educational programs (especially the Basic College) and with assisting faculty members in improvement of testing and grading, was also placed with the dean of students. These functions, combined with the logistics of registration, placement, scholarships, and financial aids, would give the Office of the Dean of Students a definite academic role while tending to assure that all these activities would be conducted with student benefits in mind. The advice of Floyd Reeves, based on the University of Chicago structure, was the controlling factor.

The unified student personnel office was a relatively new concept, especially at Michigan State. It was intended to be coordinate with, rather than separate from, academic programs. It did not work out quite as anticipated. In the rapidly growing institution, residence halls, food services, automobiles, disciplinary problems, social and other nonacademic activities demanded urgent and constant attention. Some of these matters involved heavy financial obligations and had to be dealt with in conformance with business requirements and legal procedures. Some involved violations of law and, hence, the police and courts. When student misbehavior attracted public notice, attention focused immediately on the president or the dean of students and his staff. Backgrounds in law, athletics, or public relations seemed to be more appropriate for administration of student personnel work than education, experience, and recognized stature in the field of student personnel work.

The emphasis on nonacademic matters, which became evident under student deans following Crowe, caused some academic deans and faculty members to regret that academic responsibilities had been placed in the student personnel office. The Counseling Center moved in the direction of personal, clinical counseling. Academic and vocational counseling were somewhat deemphasized. By demand of the Basic College faculty and dean, the Board of Examiners was shifted to the Basic College, where more direct Basic College control could be exercised over examinations and grading. In time, the registrar's office, the admissions office, and the placement office were also separated from student personnel. Responsibility for student organizations related to colleges or departments were returned to those units.

Like many other student personnel organizations across the country, the office became distinctly disciplinary and was even viewed by most students and professors as something of a policing operation. Reporting inappropriate student behavior was encouraged, as a way to identify those who should be eliminated from the institution for the protection of others. The fact that for years a major portion of the students came from rural areas, characterized by a strong religious influence and complete rejection of homosexuality, drinking, and premarital sexual activity, gave credence to the idea that prompt and stern action with regard to violations was necessary to protect students and the reputation of the institution. Criticism and investigation of the college was an easy means of publicity for ambitious politicians. Successive deans of students were quickly caught up in these traditions and pressures.

Knowing well the history of the institution and the recurring threats to its growth and even its existence, John Hannah found it difficult to accept publicity that tended to exaggerate student disorder or misbehavior and that often included false statements and invalid criticisms. Further, he was frustrated at the distractions involved—the time and resources that had to be devoted to refutation of unfavorable publicity lest enemies of the institution enlarge upon them and friends assume that unrefuted criticisms were justified. For a man with high hopes for the future of the institution in serving the state, nation, and the world, relatively petty matters could become deeply irritating. Hannah's concerns undoubtedly affected the operative student personnel philosophy. How much is difficult to say since similar situations existed in other universities. The student personnel function never quite achieved the respect or fulfilled the purposes originally anticipated at Michigan State or elsewhere. In many universities, the student personnel program has been markedly reduced because of a combination of financial exigency and doubts of its efficacy. Furthermore in the 1970s and 1980s, it became recognized that enrollment of an individual in a college or university does not give that institution a right to observe, direct, or control all aspects of his or her behavior.

Nevertheless, there were facets of the Michigan State student personnel program that deserved and received wide recognition. The graduate program in student personnel work, in cooperation with the residence halls and student personnel services, attained national prestige and international recognition. Emory Foster, who long directed the residence hall operations, was always alert to and cooperative with any venture pertaining to student education or welfare. For many years, under the leadership of Dr. Walter Johnson and others, Michigan State Ph.D.s in student personnel appeared as deans and presidents at other colleges and universities. Many of them had served in subsidiary roles in the Michigan State residence halls and student personnel office although only one attained the top student personnel post at Michigan State. Many Michigan State Ph.D.s in counseling served internships in the Counseling Center. The most successful aspects of the student personnel program are those that have continued to be closely related with the academic program.

Having become aware, during and after World War II, of the extent to which the institution could and would adapt to changing demands and mores, students of traditional college age became less reticent about making demands. The faculty and administration found institutional concerns and energies shifting toward new undergraduate programs, new organizational structures, a developing graduate program, and faculty growth and development. The student body was also changing in character with far more students coming from out of state and from urban areas. Fear of unfavorable attention being attracted to the campus by undesirable student behavior was no longer accorded top ranking on the list of administrative priorities. With student personnel matters effectively separated from academic, *in loco parentis* no longer had strong support by faculty members, who tended increasingly to favor more freedom for students. Indeed, the faculty was no longer willing to accept the work loads, restrictions (no smoking, office hours when not in class), and lack of benefits once characteristic of the institution. Degree completion, promotion, salary increases, research grants, and adequacy of office and research facilities along with attainment of visibility on the national and international scene tended to displace commitment to public service and instruction. Faculty members became less available to students, and administrators less available to both. Lack of communication became a matter of concern causing both faculty and students to seek channels for two-way discourse with administrators and involvement in decision making. International events and projects of the institution (Korea, Sputnik, Vietnam) and national issues (civil rights, tenure, Communist sympathizers, minority students, and faculty recruitment) shifted the loyalty of some students and some faculty from the institution to personal concerns and aspirations and to social action or political protest.

In the face of these many concerns, pressures, changes, and an influx of new faculty, the support formerly given by faculty to the long time paternalistic policies of the institution gradually shifted to support of student demands for liberalization. Moreover, viewing students as adults helped to alleviate any concern the faculty had about its responsibility for the welfare of the individual student beyond providing academic and career development experiences.

### CHANGING ATTITUDES TOWARD NONACADEMIC FACETS OF STUDENT LIFE

Generally, the attitude of the institution toward the nonacademic aspects of student life, such as living arrangements and the keeping of student records, continued to be paternalistic into the late 1950s and early 1960s. In the early years, except for married students, students living with their parents or close relatives, or those living in supervised men's cooperative houses (co-ops), all other students were required to live in campus dormitories for at least a year. Dress regulations for female students were enforced, and rules governing conduct were quite strict. Smoking was not allowed in academic buildings or on the grounds and only in designated rooms in dormitories. Even in 1945, bed checks were not uncommon in women's dormitories. Freshman women had weekday curfews of 9:00 p.m. and upperclass-women of 10:00 p.m. Possession or use of liquor was grounds for immediate dismissal. Women's dormitories had housemothers who might reprimand a student about her behavior while saying good night to a date or counsel with her about the hours she was or was not studying. As late as in 1964, several women students who had attended an "illegal" mixer in an adjacent county returned late. In addition, they had been drinking. Even in 1964 this was considered scandalous behavior, at least since they were caught. They received campuswide censure but were not automatically dismissed. And, again, there was concern that such behavior might affect legislative responsiveness toward the university.

The following list of traditions, rules, and events—extracted from various documents and usually reworded—indicates the gradual change over time of MSU's attitude toward the nonacademic life of its students. The mores of the day dictated special attention to the dress and conduct of women students. There were many more.

### 1928–1933

- Walking was permitted only on the sidewalks—shortcuts weren't allowed across the grass.
- Many rules applied specifically to freshmen, although sophomores were also expected to give precedence to upperclassmen.
- Women students were required to live in approved college houses and their residence could not be changed during the term without permission from the Office of the Dean of Women.
- Women had curfews: 7:45 p.m. on Mondays, Tuesdays, and Thursdays; 9:00 p.m. on Wednesdays; 12:15 a.m. on Fridays and Saturdays.
- Women with a B average or better could stay out until 10:00 p.m. without penalty.
- All women students were required to have gymnasium suits: bloomers (extending below the knee), gym shoes, tank suit and cap, dancing costume, and ballet slippers.
- In 1932 the "cut system" was relaxed to grant *all* last-term seniors, as well as sophomores, juniors, and seniors with a B average, the right to skip class at will.
- Long-standing customs were further relaxed in 1933 when the Student Council approved a reduced list of traditions limited to prohibiting smoking on campus, cutting across the lawns, and defacing college property.

- It was "approved tradition" that all students greet each passerby.
- The dean of women issued an edict that girls selling the yearbook at registration must *sit behind a table*. (No one was quite sure what she had in mind.)
- All pictures of female students to appear in *Wolverine* were to be approved by the dean of women. (Anyone who had seen a recent *Wolverine* was quite sure what she had in mind.)

1933–1938

- Students in off-campus houses who wished to change their residence during the term were required to obtain a permit from the housing inspector.
- Houses listed as approved for men were thereby excluded from approval for women students, as men and women students could not rent rooms in the same house.
- Angered by student misconduct on Homecoming Day, the Faculty Board passed a series of reform measures including a ban on drinking and the abolishment of the homecoming dance.
- Gymnasium suits for women now consisted of knickers with fullness confined at the knee rather than bloomers draping to the ankles. (Could this have been part of the general attempt to raise standards?)

1940–1943

- Regulations regarding student driving on campus included the following:
  1. Any student receiving a traffic violation ticket was required to respond within forty-eight hours, otherwise the driving permit was revoked.
  2. Three or more traffic violation tickets resulted in a report to the student's dean.
  3. Drinking (liquid unspecified) in a car (whether on or off campus) was subject to disciplinary action.
  4. Male students responsible for the late return of a female student dependent on his transportation and thereby causing her to be subject to disciplinary action could also be subjected to disciplinary action.
  5. Student driving permits might be revoked for a minimum of three months.
  6. Students driving *in East Lansing* after their permits had been revoked were subject to expulsion (my emphasis).
- Gymnasium suits for women were now short bloomers rather than knickers.

- Each instructor at midterm was required to report absences for any student reported deficient in scholarship. (Some ignored the rule.)
- Each instructor, at the end of the term, was required to report the total number of absences incurred by each student during the term. The random reporting of absences to avoid censure (by instructors who kept no records) could be embarrassing to the faculty if students protested.
- The registrar included the number of absences from each class with grades reported to parents or guardians. (This did not last long.)

1943–1948

- Winter 1943 was the first time female students were permitted to wear slacks to class, but only if covered by a full-length coat and only during winter term.
- Freshman women had to be in their residence halls by 9 p.m. during the week and upperclasswomen in by 10:00 p.m. The deadlines were extended to 12:30 a.m. on Friday and Saturday and until 1:00 a.m. during winter term.
- There were bed checks and mandatory lights-out at 11:30 p.m. Monday through Thursday for females unless they received special permission to study late. This mandate precluded evening mandates.
- Ration stamp books, modeled after gasoline ration books, included two A stamps, which allowed one night each away from the residence hall during the week if arrangements were made in advance with the housemother. There were two C stamps, each good for one complete trip of any duration away from MSC with advanced arrangements. (Where and why were to be specified but were not verified.)
- In 1944 men could call on women in residence halls after 12:00 noon. Previously this was not permitted before 4:00 p.m.

1948–1953

- Drinking was still prohibited on campus, and any person caught in the act was immediately suspended. This warning was displayed on the front page of every *Michigan State News* "Welcome Week" issue.
- Students were reminded that it was illegal to play in East Lansing streets. (Source of ruling and punishment was unspecified.)

1958–1963

- Students and the *State News* exulted that ROTC training had become voluntary by a four-to-two board vote.
- In the *State News* a front-page picture showed a student in uniform surrounded by a group of children. "No son, you won't have to take ROTC," the student tells the relieved tots.

1963–1968

- The *State News* editorials promoted fair-housing codes, rights of female students, and the creation of a "Hyde Park," where students could express their opinions freely.

1968–1969

- The *State News* documented student unrest and protests.
- The first major protest at MSU was in April 1968, when thirty-five black athletes called a boycott of all spring sports and practices. They charged the MSU athletic department with discriminatory practices toward blacks. They claimed the department discouraged blacks from participating in some sports and that they didn't have enough black coaches, trainers, or even one black cheerleader. MSU took immediate action to resolve the complaints, and the boycott ended after two days.

Student governance had little to do with these events or changes in rules. Only a few students were interested in student governance; it had no funds and no power. Whether discouraged by the unwillingness of the college's administration to loosen the reins of control or uninterested in becoming involved in making political changes, some students preferred to direct their attention and efforts to such extracurricular activities as panty raids. In the 1950s, this was the thing to do on many campuses across the nation, and Michigan State was no exception. Here, a group of approximately 1,000 male students raided the all-female Mason Hall. The women turned the fire hoses on them, the police were called, arrests were made, and some students were suspended. Hannah, as an absentee administrator, appropriately expressed his embarrassment and displeasure from Washington, D.C. Most administrators and faculty members were simply amused, crediting the behavior to spring fever.

In 1961 the shortage of off-campus housing which had existed since the end of World War II began to ease. Soon there was even an excess, often cheaper and certainly more permissive than on-campus housing. Students began to ask for the option of living off campus and were recurrently refused. Meanwhile, they suggested many adjustments that might make on-campus living more flexible and suitable to their needs—for example, later hours for women, keys for senior women, living in dorms without hours, dormitories based on thematic ideas (such as premedical studies)—all of which were denied at the time but may have paved the way for later changes. As students found ways to move off campus, some university officials considered trying to apply the same standards used for on-campus behavior, such as no alcohol and no visits from the opposite sex. It was quickly established that the university had no legal jurisdiction, that college students were simultaneously students and citizens of the state and nation, and that the university could not in any way compromise their rights and privileges. What the university could not ban, it had to ignore. It also had to weigh campus policy in the light of changing social values and standards and the necessity of keeping residence halls occupied. What students would no longer tolerate it could not enforce.

In 1963 John F. Kennedy was assassinated. Following the assassination, the student editorials in the *State News* increasingly were directed to national issues and the freedom of speech. Students were shocked into becoming concerned citizens as well as students.

The keeping of student records is another example of the institution's paternalistic attitude toward students. In the 1930s and 1940s, hearsay and personal judgments, recorded as matters of fact, influenced those who had later contact with students and their records. Students were not permitted access to their records, nor were the records systematically destroyed at some later date. Students had neither recourse nor appeal to staff judgments about personal values, disciplinary actions, or academic performance. It was assumed that students placed on report were in the wrong and required discipline or discharge. Yet the intent was not so much to punish the individual as to prevent a proliferation of offenses and retaliation from the legislature. It was not until the late 1960s that students were given token representation on committees making decisions that affected them. Driving and parking policies and discipline are examples. Furthermore, student groups were curbed by being under the continual supervision of a staff member from the Student Personnel Office. In effect, student committees were advisory and used to support rather than formulate policy. Appropriate institutional procedures for a student questioning a decision or policy were not established until the "Academic Freedom Report" of 1967.

In many respects, the student personnel staff had continued to reflect a policing approach which was, at least in part, a heritage from an early dean of students, former coach, lawyer, and director of the program in police administration. In 1937 the program in police administration introduced a laboratory course that permitted its students to police the campus as a way of providing practical experience. However, it was certainly not a typical internship for police training, and it raised some doubt about putting undergraduate students in a disciplinary role over other students. Some questions were inevitably asked as to whether the major concern was with the internship or with control of student behavior. The policy was soon rescinded. In retrospect, this use of police administration students was as ill advised as would be the staffing of the student health center with medical students. It was, however, symptomatic of the tendency of student personnel administrators, reinforced by administrative concerns, to associate policy and policing. The history of student personnel programs demonstrates that Michigan State was not unique in this regard.

There were other factors contributing to the problems of student committees and student representation on institutional committees. Schedules, discontinuous attendance, interest or indifference, and lack of understanding all operated to make students somewhat ineffective contributors or even nonparticipants. Typical committee procedures, such as delays for further deliberations, may have contributed to student frustration and a resulting lack of effectiveness. Students were concerned with the immediate; the faculty could take a longer view.

In 1947 Hannah established the Spartan Round Table. Its creation expressed his concern over his diminishing contact with students, a desire to reemphasize overtly his interest in the problems of students, and a conviction that students were frequently frustrated because some of their questions were ignored and others were given inadequate answers. Irritating institutional policies and practices were maintained, and students perceived neither progress in resolving them nor admission of any need to do so. Gradual, quiet change there was, but it was not always made evident to students. Students of the 1950s were generally unaware that the traditional regulation against smoking on campus had been dropped in 1946. In that year, women were permitted to smoke in residence halls. Restrictions on student driving were also eased, although the dean of students argued that cars were involved in approximately 75 percent of the cases of student disciplinary action. But policies predicated on statistics did not alleviate student concerns about their rights.

The Spartan Round Table was a representative rather than a membership group. A selected group of key organizations was requested to send representatives to bring issues of concern to the round table at twice-a-term meetings. Major administrators in an announced area of general interest were present, and others—indeed anyone—could be invited to discuss a topic or respond to questions. The practice was to address questions to the administrator or individual most knowledgeable and responsive in regard to the issue. No question was too touchy to handle in some manner. Hannah in his calm, measured way was adept and frank in explaining why some issues could not be discussed in detail or resolved immediately. Students usually understood and respected the sensitivity of such issues. At the same time, Hannah and others became aware of the depth of student concern about some issues and the reasons for it. Discussions initiated in these sessions over the years 1947 to 1969 included residence hall living and room assignment policies; dropping students for failing grades or unacceptable behavior; driving and parking restrictions on campus; possession, consumption, and transportation of liquor on campus; rebates when three or more students were assigned to a room; intervisitation among men and women in residence halls; cheating in all its forms; tenure and nonreappointment of faculty members; invitation of off-campus persons to speak on campus; permission for off-campus living; minority representation among students, faculty, and administration; discrimination in housing; campus bus tickets; and academic freedom for students.

Procedures for defining and enforcing such policies began to change in the early 1960s, but substantial change didn't take effect until late in the decade. The outside speaker policy, generated primarily out of concerns about Communism, is one positive example of change accomplished so as to satisfy both the internal and external institutional clientele. The unwillingness of the university in the 1940s and 1950s to eliminate women's hours, to allow women to sign out for men's apartments overnight, or to change policies relating to birth control and pregnancy out of wedlock suggests that some changes were more difficult than others to institute.

The university's attitude toward the official student newspaper, the *State News*, was often one of ambivalence and frustration. The newspaper was supposed to be "of the university," but it was not an official organ of the institution. Students used university facilities to produce the paper but wanted full responsibility for all facets of publication including editorials and censorship. The institution's hope was that those involved in producing the publication would be competent and would also cooperate to avoid embarrassing the university. But student and administrative ideas about appropriate material for publication differed widely on many occasions. In 1950, for instance, the *State News* was suspended from publication by the Board of Agriculture for a portion of a summer term following an offensive editorial. The suspension itself was offensive to many. Again in 1967, an offensive and critical article caused much controversy. Rather than suspension, methods for increasing appropriate supervision of students and a clearer definition of the relationship of the university to the *State News* resulted. Two complicating factors were that (1) some legislators and Michigan citizens read the *State News* as their primary source of information about the university and its activities, and (2) many students used the newspaper as their primary source of information about the university and the rationale of administrators and faculty. Thus, because the *State News* was not always reliable and at times exercised editorial prerogatives on what were intended to be official notices or statements, the clarification of communication from top level administrators became increasingly important. In 1971 the *State News* became an independent organization although it continued to use institutional facilities.

In the 1960s, when many issues relevant to student governance erupted, the draft was paramount. For a while, students were able to get a deferment from military service by being enrolled in college. In the late 1960s a national draft lottery was instituted, and the value and function of college attendance became further politicized. Attending college primarily to meet draft board standards for deferments and simultaneously working with faculty, clergy, and others regarding draft resistance became as important for some students as attending formal classes for career preparation was for most. The strongly career-oriented students in the sciences, technologies, and business were not prominent in draft resistance.

At the next-to-last meeting of the Spartan Round Table during Hannah's presidency, the issue of hours for first-term freshman women arose. Many students felt all restrictions should be dropped, and others were concerned that such freedom would constitute an abuse for other students in noise, loss of privacy, and even in ejection of embarrassed roommates. There was also discussion of continuing student protest against regulations on alcoholic beverages. Hannah noted that the Board of Trustees must consider policy in terms of the current climate, which includes the attitude of legislators, taxpayers, and parents. He remarked also that there was currently the possibility of a legislative investigation committee looking at the university. Hannah had recently raised some of these issues with the board, specifically residence hall hours for women, only to have them thrown back in his own lap.

Shortly—and for the first time since 1941—he could dump his problems into another person's lap.

At the February 24, 1969, meeting, the last attended by Hannah, students asked how the university justified the amount of money allocated to supportive and remedial work. Others had raised this question and would again, but it was somewhat surprising to hear students voice concern. There was also a discussion of outside agitators, ending with a comment by Hannah that dissent and discussion of differences should be encouraged but that disruption could not be tolerated. In fact, under Hannah's immediate successors disruptions did occur, and they were, in effect, tolerated because there was no satisfactory way to act otherwise. Fundamental revisions of academic governance, providing fuller participation of students, did not come until 1971 and then primarily through faculty channels of deliberation.

## THE 1965 REPORT OF THE
## FACULTY COMMITTEE ON STUDENT AFFAIRS

On December 16, 1965, Hannah addressed a letter to Professor Frederick B. Williams of the history department in which he indicated his growing concern about the relationships of students at Michigan State University with other members of the university community. Professor Williams was at that time chairman of the Academic Council Committee on Student Affairs and had already been requested by the Academic Council to undertake such a review. Hannah noted that many conditions under which the university was operating were much different from those of the past and that it seemed therefore appropriate to review all rules and regulations affecting students to see whether they were sound and practicable under the new circumstances.

Hannah spoke to the phraseology then in use, "academic freedom of students," and suggested that the phrase needed to be clearly defined lest it take on meanings destructive of the broader significance of academic freedom. Hannah also suggested that something more basic than the juggling of existing course offerings and the use of novel ways to expose more students to the same old patterns of teaching and evaluation were needed. He noted that there were new curricular developments at the secondary school level and that other post-high-school institutions had emerged. He commented on the nature of the education required to enable young people to adapt to a changing world and on the lack of relevance that many students reported in their courses. Although the student rebellion of the 1960s had not particularly affected Michigan State at that time, Hannah also indicated his sensitivity to student concerns and to their desire to voice their views about matters of policy.

The committee proceeded deliberately and thoughtfully and, drawing heavily upon a 1964 report of Committee S of the American Association of University Professors, developed a statement that after extensive revision was approved by the Academic Council on January 10, 1967, by the Academic Senate February 28, 1967, and by the MSU Board of Trustees March 16, 1967. Article one of this statement dealt with student rights and responsibilities at Michigan State and, regarding the university as a community of scholars including faculty, students, and administrators, emphasized the freedom of expression and communication as essential to the extension, dissemination, and application of knowledge. The point was made that students have a dual citizenship in that they are still part of society while they are at the university. The university may impose relevant rules and policies, but it may not deprive a student of civil and societal rights.

The report also emphasized the need to protect student rights but at the same time to identify student responsibilities and expect students to recognize and acquiesce in regard to these. In particular, the report called for minimizing regulations and making them public, brief, and specific. Channels for appeal and review should be provided for resolution of conflicts.

The document pointed out that the faculty is central to maintaining the integrity and the scholarly atmosphere of the institution. While students have the responsibility to meet standards established by the professor, they should also have freedom to disagree without reprisal. The committee asserted that students are entitled to a good-faith assessment of their performance and a clear, accurate statement of requirements for courses and for degrees. The statement also took the view that the faculty have certain professional rights. For example, while students may have channels for expressing their options for instruction, final judgment of the performance of faculty members rests with the faculty. The document dealt with many other matters that had formerly been handled by specific rules or by an administrator's or committee's interpretation of what was acceptable. By this document, students were given assurance of regard and equitable treatment but also informed that, on entering the university, they subjected themselves to many academic policies and rules derived from faculty expertise. The document also made clear that neither the faculty nor the administration should attempt to impose upon the "individual student as a member of society" rules or policies that might, for good and sufficient reasons, be enforced on campus.

The document sounded a new chord on faculty obligations to students as well as on student rights and responsibilites. But its impact on departmental teaching and advising was limited. Hannah's attention was elsewhere, and his successors apparently regarded faculty and departmental obligations as faculty and departmental responsibilities. Nevertheless, the report was a landmark.

### THE OMBUDSMAN

In 1967 Michigan State instituted the Office of the Ombudsman. It may have been the first university to do so under that title, although it was surely not the first to identify the need. The ombudsman was to listen to the student, determine the legitimacy of the complaint, and make a referral, clarify or review university procedure, intervene or direct the student to other offices as appropriate. Reporting directly to the president, the ombudsman had status and influence, but no personal authority.

The office was designed to operate with both formal procedures and personal charisma, the latter the more effective of the two. The first ombudsman, James Rust, referred to his several years on campus before being ombudsman as providing the basis for the smooth handling of many issues. He reported that the most used functions of the office had been sharing information and clarifying problems as well as giving students the opportunity to talk about their concerns. Student activists did not make use of the ombudsman. They demanded direct administrative attention and immediate action.

Rust further noted that on an individual basis most student problems were easily clarified, but solutions satisfactory to all could not always be found. Some students' requests were simply inappropriate. For others, useful channels for redress could be identified. A few faculty members who had apparently been insensitive or unfair in their dealings with students resisted any discussion and adjustment. For example, some departments that exploited graduate assistants would not admit it. The housing office was not always accurate in predicting vacancies and hence in promising apartment availabilities. When matters were brought to the attention of appropriate administrators, often Hannah himself, some resolution could usually be found. Often the complaint resulted less from what had or had not been done than from how it had been done.

In the only year for which detailed records were available, many complaints to the ombudsman were directed to grades or to instructors. These two occurred in two to ten times the numbers of various other complaints such as getting into required or desired courses, examinations, degree requirements and certification, fee reductions, financial need, desire for release from housing contracts, and personal or legal problems. Complaints were most frequently registered by juniors and seniors.

The continuing success of the office of the ombudsman is a tribute to the sensitivity, tact, and discretion of those who have held the office and the resulting respect for it on the part of all university personnel.

### STUDENT ACTIVITIES

The concern of an educational institution for its students is reflected in only a very limited way by student govvernment and student activities at a given moment in time. Only 60 to 70 percent of entering freshmen remain for four years. Students transferring into the institution further reduce that average stay. Many graduate students are enrolled on a part-time basis, and most of them are primarily attentive to their departments. Doctoral candidates, especially graduate assistants, may have an average residence time much longer than undergraduates, but they seek their own means of communication and policy formulation separate from undergraduates.

Since student government and student activities do not really represent all students, the best evidence of attention and fulfillment of students' needs is found in admissions and enrollment. Michigan State—in the Hannah years—was obviously doing some things right. Those things went far beyond listening and responding to the student voice.

The university has systematically promoted activities to give students recreational as well as educational experiences. The campus itself is a good example of how planning has made Michigan State a beautiful, functional, but student-oriented environment. In his memoirs, Hannah expressed the wish that keeping the campus beautiful would continue to be a high priority in future generations:

> If the management of M.S.U. in the years ahead will maintain the park that is the present campus, it will perform a great public service for those who will be here long after we are gone. If people born and raised in apartment houses in the cities find themselves on a university campus where they can walk leisurely among trees, shrubs, birds and flowers, they may be inspired to learn something about the facts and forces of nature that add significance to human life.[1]

To Hannah, beauty was a means of education as well as an end to be sought through it.

During the Hannah years, many programs and activities were or-

---

1. *A Memoir* (East Lansing, Mich: Michigan State University Press, 1980), p. 64.

ganized to augment the formal educational offerings with nonformal academic experiences. The Lecture-Concert Series brought outstanding professionals in music and theatre to the campus, enabling students, faculty, and residents of the community to gain cultural experiences at nominal prices. The World Travel Series provided films portraying countries and people around the world long before Michigan State entered the international arena. Abrams Planetarium with its panoramic space science theater has done much to popularize astronomy. While perhaps intended primarily for academic instruction, its attraction has been in special programs developed to provide educational entertainment for schoolchildren and the general public. The MSU Museum is concerned with education through exhibitions and with supportive research through the accumulation, preservation, and study of documented collections. International festivals presented by foreign students help to acquaint MSU students and the general public with the culture and society of many foreign lands. These are only a few examples of the kinds of educational opportunities available in extracurricular activities.

One of the most notable activities, of course, is athletics, with events scheduled in almost every sport in which there is intercollegiate competition. And, while intercollegiate athletics has received most of the publicity, there is another segment of athletics/recreation designed for the active participation of all students on the campus: the intramural program.

Physical education—physical conditioning and exercise—had been stressed in students' programs at Michigan State for some years, but a significant change came in the later 1930s based on the philosophy that physical well-being is a lifelong concern and that a college should be a place where students learn athletic and recreational skills that carry over into later life. One facility that helped to make this new program possible and feasible was the Jenison Field House and Gymnasium, constructed in 1940.

The field house contained many facilities important for intercollegiate athletics, but the structure also was designed to provide space and equipment for students who did not participate in intercollegiate sports. Hannah, along with Ralph Young, the athletic director, planned a facility that helped to change the whole approach to the physical education program. Together they developed a new emphasis that promoted the teaching of such recreational activities as tennis, golf, badminton, and even fly casting and tap dancing. Hannah emphasized his concern for the program in the first staff meeting over which he presided as the head of the college: "The intramural program is far short of reaching 100% of our students . . . . We should urge at every turn the development of strong bodies to house a well-trained mind through the use of our gymnasium, health service and proper living."

During the war years, especially in 1943, most intercollegiate activities were canceled, and on campus the military personnel had their own conditioning program. But after the war, physical education underwent massive changes as did most of the other programs in the college. The enrollment explosion and the need for many additional facilities to house and otherwise accommodate the students forced many changes. Jenison Field House was fine for the prewar years but was woefully inadequate to meet the requirements of the postwar students. While indoor facilities were desperately needed, Hannah and others thought that the immediate concern was to develop outdoor as well as indoor space and equipment. Two important issues were at hand: (1) other facilities were more urgently needed to provide for housing and academic needs, and (2) if more students were to be involved in the intramural program, it was necessary to provide facilities as close to the dormitories and married housing units as possible to avoid problems of time and transportation. Playing fields, courts, equipment, and organization of teams were furnished by the intramural department working with student services.

During the 1950s a proposal was submitted to construct the present intramural building for men and to reconstruct the women's gymnasium into a more adequate facility. The new building necessarily had to be multipurpose. The sports arena can seat 2,000 spectators for such events as wrestling, fencing, and gymnastics; but most of the time it is used for intramural activities, badminton, tennis, basketball, and volleyball. The building also has an indoor area that is used during the winter term by the baseball team for preseason practice but is available to other students throughout the rest of the year for a variety of sports. In addition, there are a space for indoor golf practice and an indoor swimming pool. Outside the building is an Olympic-size swimming pool. Continuing the multipurpose theme, the facility contains four classrooms and offices for coaches of various sports.

Attention to intramural athletics resulted from a student-oriented philosophy: providing opportunities for students and developing beneficial lifetime skills. Hannah recognized this goal as a more fundamental concern than intercollegiate athletics.

### INTERCOLLEGIATE ATHLETICS

The question has frequently been raised as to the significance of intercollegiate athletics in Michigan State's progress to national recognition. There is no easy answer because national recognition is a multifaceted concept. A listing as first or second in a nationwide football poll brings awareness of an institution to some persons who have never heard of it before and may never hear of it again unless it reappears on the poll. Effective performance in research or science yields a more permanent recognition by a more significant clientele. And good performance on many fronts reinforces the recognition and expands the audience. The first time Michigan State defeated the University of Michigan in a football game undoubtedly led more than one Michigan legislator to believe that the institution had emerged out of obscurity. And the recognition then and later may have affected more than one vote in favor of increasing the state's appropriation to MSU. After several years of success in football, veteran faculty members found, with pleasure, that even cab drivers and hotel clerks in faraway places were aware of the existence of a second major university in Michigan.

Certainly, successes in sports help to bring out more students, especially athletes, if the necessary funds are available. But successful intercollegiate athletics neither create nor augment the academic reputation of a college or university. One has only to look at the weekly football ratings each fall to verify that outstanding football performance does not necessarily coincide with academic excellence. On the other hand, the University of Chicago, which has no intercollegiate athletics, is known throughout the world as an excellent institution. Hannah was well aware of these points and was by no means the rabid football fan some took him to be. One of his characteristics was his concentration at any moment on the issue before him, whether it be a student complaining about unfair treatment, a faculty member with a novel idea, or a phone call from the President of the United States. An athlete or a coach could leave a discussion with Hannah "knowing" there was no more important matter at hand and that it would be kept in mind and acted upon next week, next month, or next year, as might be appropriate.

As with most other aspects of Michigan State, there was no tradition of excellence in athletics and no constant support for it before 1900. The college had begun with and had continued until 1896 a program in agriculture that operated during the spring, summer, and early fall, requiring three hours work in the field each day, three or more hours in the classroom, and three to six hours of study time. Students had little time or energy left over for sports, either intramural or intercollegiate. There was no need for physical education and, hence, no funds to hire athletically inclined and experienced individuals who might also have served as coaches. There was no money for equipment and no adequate indoor facilities for any kind of athletic activity. And, in addition, the governing board was against a venture into athletic competition.

Athletic activities before 1900 were largely confined to games or to individual or pair competitions such as boxing, wrestling, track, and cross country, arranged and carried out with little formality. The Red Cedar River provided for swimming in summer and for ice skating and hockey in the winter (after the calendar change in 1896 to fall, winter, and spring sessions).

By 1899 the board authorized intercollegiate competition. It was, however, easier to authorize competition than to schedule it and produce teams. Few students coming from rural areas had prior experience with competitive sports. The minimum of twenty-two bodies needed for football scrimmage was not available for some years. It is no wonder that agricultural extension agents became informal scouts for athletic talent or that their recruiting efforts were geared more to encouraging the development of capable young men than to attracting the best athletes available in the state. Financial aids were virtually limited to finding places for these students to work for room and board and perhaps to earn a few extra dollars for books, clothes, and fees. These later merged into a work program whereby athletes could earn funds to cover essential expenses. Fees for individuals could be waived under some circumstances, but that required board action. Such seemingly meritorius practices would in later years be abused by interpreting *work* as presence at practice and games.

By the 1920s, when Hannah came onto the scene at Michigan State as a poultry extension specialist, there was regular intercollegiate competition in wrestling, swimming, baseball, track, tennis, basketball, and football. Regular competition in fencing, soccer, gymnastics, hockey, and golf had not yet been inaugurated. No thought of intercollegiate competition for women had yet occurred to anyone, and the suggestion would have been rejected as indecorous and offensive.

The initial football competition came from nearby liberal arts colleges: Albion, Adrian, Alma, Olivet, Kalamazoo, and Hillsdale. There was no glory in winning and considerable indignity in losing. The excitement in one such game focused on reaching a score of 100 or more points before the final whistle. The University of Michigan and Notre Dame were first scheduled in 1898. After 1909 Marquette, Wisconsin, Lake Forest, Oregon, Nebraska, Purdue, Ohio State, and other major universities were on the roster. But scheduling was difficult because limited (15,000) seating capacity produced too little income to attract prestigious opponents.

The gradual increase in the stadium's seating capacity to 23,000, 55,000, and ultimately more than 76,000 and the hiring of a sequence of able coaches brought Michigan State to a point where membership in the Western Conference (the Big Ten) could be sought when the University of Chicago resigned. Not surprisingly, abandonment of the work program was required to enter the Big Ten.

Support for Michigan State membership in the Big Ten came from many of the members (especially the land-grant institutions). There was also strong opposition, and alternative names were suggested. But Hannah's continuing efforts prevailed. On May 20, 1949, Michigan State became a full member but continued to receive recurrent scrutiny to root out practices not acceptable under Western Conference rules. Hannah did not knowingly tolerate unacceptable practices or rule violations. Notes in the archives show that he attempted to monitor, correct, and reprimand coaches where unacceptable practices were reported. Like many other presidents in many other institutions before and since, he found that otherwise upright individuals did not hesitate to engage in subterfuge when a successful season was at stake. Distinguished conference membership and coaches with national reputations compounded rather than resolved the problem. There are those even in universities who really do believe that the end justifies the means.

Hannah sought to ease the continual pressure on the coaches to win, and thereby keep stadiums filled, by granting rank and tenure to coaches. This practice proved not to be a solution. It also degraded academic rank. Coaches marched to a different band than the faculty. They were not willing to accept a regular teaching load and professorial pay. As the field of health, physical education, and recreation matured and lost the heavy load of required freshman and sophomore courses, coaches were not generally qualified to teach or hold faculty rank.

Hannah seized the opportunity in 1951 to chair a national committee of presidents to look into the problems and abuses of intercollegiate athletics and to make recommendations to remedy the situation. The committee was sponsored by the American Council on Education. Its recommendations received widespread praise and publicity. Hannah demanded that his own institution abide by the spirit and letter of the rules of all national and regional groups with which Michigan State was associated.

That committee report did not solve the problem either. As with recommendations made before and since, it became quickly evident that the problem is not with the diagnosis of evils and the spelling out of rules and procedures to eliminate them. Rather it lies in the emphasis on winning at all costs. It is only a piece of what many believe to be the widespread deterioration of moral and ethical standards apparent in all walks of modern society. Whether in winning games, encouraging gambling by state lotteries, acquiring money, or achieving power, the desired ends justify the means for all too many persons in business, industry, government—and even in education.

In the universities, presidents generally either will not or cannot—because of lack of authority or integrity and the opposition of alumni—clean out the offenders and clear up those practices so widely used as to have become regarded as necessary and acceptable for success. The only serious lapse is in getting caught and, as of the mid 1980s, there is doubt that punitive measures can any longer be imposed and enforced on institutions or coaches because of television contracts and monies involved.

Hannah, in his early ventures into athletics, tended to view it as one of the student services, inseparable from programs for health, physical education, and recreation. Intramural sports, credit courses focusing on development of recreational skills, and coaching for intercollegiate competitions could thus be seen as interrelated. Athletic competition could then be viewed as

- An excellent example of democracy in action bridging color, creed, and class
- A natural and unrestrained outlet for energy and enthusiasm of the entire community
- A means of attracting, supporting, and developing individuals who might not otherwise have attended college
- A common interest providing a degree of unification among students, faculty, alumni, and community
- A means of attracting and entertaining visitors whose interests and activities might be beneficial to the institution
- A source of financial support for other programs

Hannah's views were reinforced by those of Ralph Young, long-time director of athletics. Had the president's views prevailed, the evils of intercollegiate competition on a grand scale might never have appeared. But just as disciplinary specialization and professional aspirations destroyed the early unity of instruction, research, and service, so coaching specialization and aspirations destroyed the unity of intramural activities, concerns for the health and physical well-being of all students, and the training of teachers and directors of health and recreational programs. Ultimately, it became necessary to relate intramural sports to the student personnel program and the residence halls. The Department of Health, Physical Education, and Recreation was freed to pursue excellence in its own domain.

The one factor that was never fully acknowledged by Hannah or by any other group studying the evils of college athletics has been the impact over time on students, faculty, and the athletes themselves of constantly confronting or involving themselves in activities—carried on under the auspices of an educational institution—that call for duplicity, dishonesty, and violation of all the values for which higher education supposedly stands. If the public has lost faith in the universities, it is simply because many universities no longer deserve it. As president, Hannah made more efforts than most to maintain integrity in athletics. It is not surprising that in his later years as president he came to remark frequently, if somewhat ruefully, that winning more than half the games should be considered a good football season. And he usually added that it would be nice if the wins included victories over Michigan and Notre Dame. But coaches, players, faculty, students, and alumni continue to expect a trip to the Rose Bowl.

### REVIEW AND REFLECTIONS

In the preceding discussion, student activities such as social organizations and governance structures such as the Student Council and the Associated Women Students, have been almost ignored. This omission reflects a judgment that these activities had little or no long-term cumulative impact on the development of the institution. Neither did they have much impact on the current rules and policies until the 1960s. Changing social mores, changes in sources of students and faculty, the impact of veterans, the introduction of graduate programs, the increasing size, and the modifications in attitudes of the administration were major factors in liberalizing and modernizing policies relating to students.

Thus, the preceding review of long-standing policies and rules regarding campus behavior reflects the changing scene into which John Hannah came—first as a student, then as a faculty member, and in 1935 as an administrator. In completing his degree in essentially one year, after spending two years in community college and one year at law school, Hannah was too busy to become very involved in student activities. To a large extent, he must have been unaware of them. Yet, even as a student, he recognized that the institution was emerging out of a long period of self-doubt, extremely limited program offerings, and small enrollments. It was also in the process of trying to determine what it should become. As noted elsewhere, Hannah as an extension specialist in poultry began almost immediately to make contacts with young people around the state and to interest prospective students. When he became secretary of the State Board of Agriculture in 1935, one of his initial activities was to stimulate visits to high schools to recruit students. While it would be inappropriate to credit the full impact to Hannah as secretary, the enrollment increased from 4,942 in 1935–36 to 8,457 in 1940–41, his last year as secretary. Among these enrollees were a number of athletes in whom he had taken a personal interest, including Arthur Brandstatter, who later returned as a faculty member largely because of continued contacts with Hannah. There were many similar cases.

As board secretary, Hannah devoted much of his attention to building residence halls and other facilities. He effectively used the increase in enrollment to impress upon the legislature the necessity for providing more funds. In 1937 he pointed out that the long-standing ratio between the University of Michigan's budgetary allocations and Michigan State's allocation of three to one should be markedly changed. It was shifted to two to one.

It has been pointed out elsewhere that many prospective changes in the educational programs of the college were foregone by the necessity of regirding for the war years. That period made administrators and faculty at Michigan State aware that some changes must be made. Social mores and standards were themselves changing and were rather different after the war than before. But, at the same time, the female students on campus during that period demonstrated levels of concern and responsibility that rendered archaic the many rules that had been applied in the past.

The solemnity of the young men in the military programs convinced many faculty members that the male students should be treated as adults. And the returning veterans, with their seriousness of purpose and their disinclination to heed what they considered to be petty rules or policies, forced a change. One veteran stood on the steps of the administration building for several days with an empty pipe in his mouth pointing out to every passerby that he was heeding a ridiculous tradition, because he could walk across Grand River Avenue and smoke in front of or in any public building. Whether or not he took his comment directly to Hannah as he indicated, he and others effectively made the point that, if students were to be regarded as adults, continuing attempts to enforce regulations of that sort were not defensible and could not long stand. The tradition against smoking was dropped in 1946. By 1984, that tradition—as a health measure—would appear more defensible than it did then.

As the college grew after he war, Hannah realized that communication was becoming a major problem. Students heard of most problems and decisions but had no opportunity to provide input or feedback. Informal reports through administrators, faculty members, and the student paper were not always reliable and frequently generated unrest. Furthermore, Hannah himself felt cut off from the student body. While always willing to see students, he found himself more likely to be confronted by an individual expressing a grievance rather than one concerned about the welfare of the institution and about general student concerns.

Out of this came the Spartan Round Table, which met for the first time on April 28, 1947. Although the group had no legislative power, the raising and discussing of issues and the reporting back to other individuals and groups by those participating generated confidence and had an unanticipated impact. For example, a discussion in 1960 of the rule requiring dismissal of any student for possession or use of liquor on campus apparently brought about a realization that this was a highly arbitrary rule and one that was not enforced uniformly or fairly. By 1961 students were no longer automatically dismissed for liquor in possession or imbibed. In other cases, the pressures under which the university operated were communicated to students and, in turn, apparently communicated by them to their organizations in such manner that understanding and acceptance or further negotiation rather than confrontation resulted. A great part of this effect, of course, was due to the serious and forthright way in which Hannah reacted to student questions. When the occasional question arose that at the moment could not be openly discussed, a statement to that effect with brief explanation, while perhaps not entirely satisfying, was always accepted. This open communication permitted an airing of complaints, achieved some common understanding of them, and ultimately if not immediately led to alterations or mitigation—if not elimination—of the circumstances or policies involved. Perhaps more important was the ever-present assurance in Hannah's words and actions that concern for student well-being was a major component of all decisions.

Indeed, from the beginning of his employment by Michigan State in 1923 as a poultry extension specialist until his retirement in 1969, Hannah's primary concern centered on the students. In his first staff meeting in September 1944, after he outlined the needs of the institution and the financing required, he said, "If the money is not provided, it is the students who are cheated. . . . Some of us forget the college revolves around the student. The college is maintained for them, we are paid to help them."

In his 1956–57 annual report, Hannah reported with dismay, "Another discouraging development was the insistence of the legislature that fees charged to students be raised substantially." He frequently cited the unfair burden placed on students: "the insistence of the legislature that the costs of water, lights, and other utilities be charged against the income from dormitories and married housing units . . . aggravates the financial situation confronting the students."

Students recognized and responded to Hannah's outspoken concern and support, and few college presidents enjoyed the respect and affection demonstrated by the student body. For instance, the July 5, 1951 issue of the *Michigan State News* was dedicated to Hannah on his tenth anniversary as president. After a review of his accomplishment and honors, the editorial closed with these words: "But to John A. Hannah these titles are superficial. One name we have a hunch he prefers over all his appositions is perhaps much more typical and representative of the esteem in which he is held by the students of Michigan State. That's plain and simple 'Uncle John'" (*Michigan State News*, July 5, 1951, Editor's Note).

Shortly after World War II, when students were overflowing the campus and dollars were scarce, it was suggested that an admission fee be charged students for the Lecture-Concert Series, as was customary at most schools. Hannah responded by saying, "As long as I am president, no student will be denied the privilege of hearing a symphony or seeing an opera or ballet because he lacks the money to buy his way in."

In 1962 students asked that pianos be provided in residence halls. The request raised questions as to the costs of instruments, maintenance, appropriate sound-proofed space, and possible duplication of facilities already available in the music building. In a letter to Emory Foster on April 16, 1962, Hannah asserted that "if students want to play pianos in Case Hall, we should provide pianos for them to play. Anything that encourages our students to carry on their appropriate recreational activities in the dormitories should be encouraged."

Hannah was quick to compliment others in the university community for their successes but seemed to be embarrassed by and therefore avoided compliments to himself. But students demonstrated their respect and gratitude. A *State News* article in the September 1964 Welcome Week issue reviewed the "Great Leap" of Hannah's twenty-three years and reflected on his continuing commitment to the institution and on his regret that he now lacked the time to visit with students as he once did. The Welcome Week issue three years later remarked on Hannah's accessibility to students, his insistence on personally signing each of the thousands of diplomas granted each year, and his attempt to visit each of the residence halls once a year.

In February 1969 the *State News* again reviewed Hannah's contribution to MSU and concluded, "And for the drive to upgrade the quality of the university, in the face of a mostly indifferent public, and a penurious and often actively hostile legislature, the credit is mostly his." For more than thirty years the focus of concerns for and with students had been in Hannah's office. Students had been well served by him—and they knew it.

# 14
# Faculty Development and Involvement

Before World War II, the role of the Michigan State faculty in governance at either the institutional or departmental level was limited. Even in course planning, instructional patterns, and load assignments, divisions rather than departments made many decisions. Departments, even in agriculture, were largely informal groupings of individuals with some common elements in their prior education and current assignments. The institution served certain social and economic needs and provided a number of degree programs. The divisions and departments carried out their instructional, research, and public service responsibilities in relation to degree programs, to needs of other departments, and to overall institutional objectives. Most of the faculty of the 1930s and early 1940s understood and accepted this. If faculty loads were heavy, so were those of the clientele served both by on-campus instruction and extension. Faculty members might be drawn to better paid instructional or administrative positions at other land-grant institutions, but few received offers from major prestigious universities. Most faculty members, despite the many problems and shortcomings, seemed satisfied to remain.

The size of the institution, the limited number of administrators, and the involvement of faculty members in student discipline, maintenance, and operation of the institution and in the extensive and intensive system of communication about current problems permitted faculty members to voice their opinions on institutional issues. They could accept the view that the faculty existed as a means whereby the institution, under the president and the board, could carry out the purposes for which the institution existed. The responsibilities, goals, and welfare of the institution superseded the aims and preferences of divisions, departments, faculty, and even administrators—as the frequent presidential change indicated.

The limited role of the faculty stemmed from the necessity to provide low-cost instruction. Most of the courses offered were introductory. Since extensive scholarship was not required for teaching, many faculty members were employed and remained as instructors. Before 1924 the rank of professor was limited to those who administered departments. As late as 1931, 39 percent of the faculty were of the instructor rank. Another 26 percent were assistant professors and were not regarded as "full" faculty members for many years. When in 1954 a voting faculty organization was established, membership included only those few assistant professors who had been granted tenure. The established pattern of governance until well after World War II was that professors ran the departments, deans ran the divisions or schools, and the president ran the college—so long as the board agreed with him. The extant committee structure supported this mode of governance.

During the years from 1929 through 1941, there existed from fifteen to nineteen standing committees of the faculty. These committees were largely advisory and chaired by administrators. In 1938–39, thirteen of eighteen committees were chaired by the president, deans, board secretary, or registrar. The others were headed by professors or department heads. Several committees were composed entirely of administrators although most also held faculty rank. In 1935 the Student Loans Committee had as its new chairman J. A. Hannah, who in that year had just become board secretary. In 1938 three new committees appeared: dormitories, retirement, and union. Hannah was the implementer of all three and chairman of the first and third. President Shaw chaired the Retirement Committee.

On October 6, 1941, in his first appearance before the faculty as president, Hannah emphasized in various ways the primary responsibility of the faculty to address the mission of the institution and the needs of its clientele. Before launching a discussion of aspirations and plans for the future, Hannah elaborated upon the point, "We should determine exactly what it is that we are trying to do." He called attention to the historic public service role of the land-grant institution while recognizing the pressures and possible demands of war. He then outlined the institutional needs required to fulfill MSU's role in the future, including an extensive building program.

Students were ever on Hannah's mind as the following remarks indicate:

> The tradition of friendliness has always been a great asset to Michigan State College. I wonder if some of us are not forgetting its importance. Last Friday morning I spent more than an hour watching the registration procedure. It was not an exemplification of friendliness. Freshmen were

bewildered by it, as all of us were, the first time we saw a similar function in operation. I saw freshmen stand in a long line to reach the desk and then be told: "sorry, section closed." There was little organized effort in evidence to help these new students work out their schedules.

The registrar's staff and the business office as well as the faculty were thereby notified that, henceforward, staff convenience would not be the major consideration in arranging student enrollment and collection of fees. It was a point to which attention would be directed again and again, but some functionaries neither heard nor heeded.

In subsequent faculty meetings, Hannah often mentioned a recent personal observation or concern and enlarged upon it. He regularly commended meritorious performance of individuals and departments and accepted comments favorable to himself with an embarrassed smile and/or brief self-deprecatory response. He was very likely to remark as he did in the September 28, 1944, faculty meeting: "Compliments are nice to receive but they don't really help us to improve. Constructive suggestions are never resented and even constructive criticism is more valuable than commendation. If we are alert and cooperative and don't make too many mistakes this can be not just a good college but an outstandingly useful one." He seemed also to be slightly embarrassed when addressed as Dr. Hannah—the honorary degree of Doctor of Agriculture having been conferred on him at the MSC commencement, June 14, 1941.

In Hannah's beginning year as president, 1941–42, the standing committees increased from 19 to 26; they further increased to 38 by 1944–45 and to 45 by 1958–59. At his initial meeting with the faculty in October 1941, Hannah appointed a committee to formulate the first tenure rules. Several associate professors and even two assistant professors were among his committee appointments. During the next several years, new standing committees were established, with such diverse charges as student traffic, foreign studies, out-of-state admissions and fees, adult education, international center, all-college educational research, and educational costs and other related matters.

Not only was the charge of these committees focused by their designation, but frequently specific requests were made. The All-College Educational Research Committee was asked on April 6, 1953, to conduct studies and recommend more effective means of communication that would (1) make faculty opinion directly available to the president rather than being relayed through unit administrators, (2) provide the faculty with the opportunity to deliberate on questions of educational policy before action, and (3) bring about increased involvement of teaching members of the faculty. The specifics indicated Hannah's preference for face-to-face contacts with teachers rather than with amateur faculty politicians or would-be administrators. Hannah was not, as some faculty members thought, averse to faculty involvement in decision making. His responses to faculty members who sought formal faculty organization and delegation of authority on academic matters repeatedly emphasized these points:

1. Many of the changes required at Michigan State would be resisted by many, perhaps a majority of, faculty members representing traditional emphases and practices.

2. Faculty meetings and faculty committees tended to deliberate at length, introduce irrelevancies, and quibble over words and phrases, thereby delaying expedient action.

3. The State Board of Agriculture was the final authority; and it was uncertain, judging from past experiences, how far that board would accept faculty recommendations or even tolerate faculty intervention in institutional policy.

In brief, Hannah was pragmatic and action oriented. He was also aware of and sensitive to past difficulties and confrontations between the board and the administration. Many faculty members, noting Hannah's moves with regard to retirement and tenure policies, sensed his commitment to institutional improvement and faculty welfare. They welcomed action rather than discussion. One staunch supporter of the general education program remarked, "It was always clear that the program would have been voted out overwhelmingly if ever subjected to the vote of the entire faculty." Another, favorably commenting on Hannah's leadership, noted, "If universities had developed by faculty votes, they would still be seminaries for training ministers."

Hannah's conception of Michigan State as a service institution also caused him to be somewhat skeptical about faculty desires. He was convinced that the institution as a whole must be responsive to the public, to its students, and to the changing needs of its service area. Hence, the growing desire of some faculty members to draw a tight distinction between academic (teachers and researchers) and other employees did not seem right to him. The 1959 Committee on the Future of the University asserted, "Academic rank, if it is to have any meaning, should be conferred only upon those who engage in instruction or research in one of the units of the university devoted to these purposes." Public service is conspicuous by it absence. Hannah found this distinction troublesome and continued to regard all appointments to academic rank as institutional rather than departmental designations. Indeed, as late as 1963, Hannah wrote to other administrators:

At the luncheon last week honoring retired personnel, it occurred to me that we were making a mistake in separating our employees into two categories with the labor and classified employees in one group and the faculty in another.

I would like to suggest that we think this one through again and see if it would not be better to treat them all alike, giving them all the same kind of a certificate and exactly equal treatment.

Of course, that did not happen, for faculty members had become concerned with degree standards and differences.

Hannah's views about faculty involvement in governance are clearly stated in his memoirs:

> I believed that the university needed the best possible internal communications systems, not only up and down but crosswise. We had to have a system in which everybody knew where the university was trying to go and one which provided them with ways to express their opinions. Their suggestions might not be followed, but the rule of the game was that everyone concerned should know all the facts and have a chance to discuss them before an administrative decision was made. In the end, if there was disagreement over important matters, the president would present all sides of the matter to the board of trustees who made the final judgment. Once it was made, we followed it out until we found a better way.
>
> ...I think administration by faculty committee is bad. I think it has slowed down change, and I think it will get worse before it gets better. It is a mistake to encourage employees of an institution to think that they have an inherent right to manage it. The board of trustees is elected by the people of Michigan and given by the state constitution the sole and exclusive responsibility to appoint a president for the university. The trustees are the final authority for the management of the university, and it is the responsibility of the board of trustees to project the public interest. The public interest and the selfish interest of the employees of the university are not always the same—in fact, I think in most instances they are not the same.
>
> If the administrative system of the university is to work successfully, it is necessary that the board of trustees recognize their role. Their role is to see to it that the university always remembers the purpose of *all* education, the purpose of *public* education, and particularly the educational purpose of Michigan State University.[1]

The difficulties of the university in the late and post-Hannah years indicated that an individual board member might not fulfill this role and might indeed have "selfish interests" of his or her own. The distinction between personal and public interests is not one upon which individuals are clear or on which unanimity exists.

---

1. *A Memoir* (East Lansing, Mich.: Michigan State University Press, 1980), p. 81 and pp. 104–5. Italics mine.

Consistent with his views and concerns, Hannah preferred open channels of communication and ready access of faculty and students to administrators. He preferred study groups or task forces with a specific set of charges rather than standing faculty committees. The study group approach—combined with a terminal reporting date, selection of group members from faculty nominations, allocation of staff and budgetary assistance, and an injunction to maintain two-way communication with the faculty while the group deliberated—proved to be an effective alternative to formal faculty structures for faculty participation in governance. It had worked well in revising the extension service and in the changes associated with the creation of the Basic College. It was an educational experience for the faculty as well as a means of crystallizing and unifying faculty preferences in operable terms. If, at times, there was more attention to structural changes in college and university organization than to educational policies, this was largely due to rapid growth in size which frequently seemed to render nonfunctional or even counter-functional a structural change made only a few years earlier.

Although the task force conception worked effectively for resolution of all-institutional policy issues, the division-school-college and departmental structure was directly responsible for most issues involving curriculum, instruction, and faculty selection and promotion. Hannah recognized the importance of exercising influence on this substructure and involved himself directly in selecting new faculty members and administrators. For some years, he insisted on interviews with all new faculty members being considered for the top two ranks. In these interviews, Hannah underlined the importance of all faculty members taking interest in liberal education and in promoting communication skills. In the selection of faculty members, Hannah noted the relevance of such criteria as awareness of the current scene—nationally and internationally, effective communication, effective teaching at all levels, concern about liberal and general education, awareness of the relevance of their disciplines to other areas, interest in the history and philosophy of their disciplines, as well as other criteria of concern to the departments and colleges. However, the increasing emphasis on research tended gradually to deemphasize many of these characteristics as a basis for selecting faculty members. For some years, Hannah also made the final decision in hiring new department heads and assured himself of their concerns about teaching and their commitments to both internal and external service.

The experience of Laurence L. Quill, appointed professor of chemistry in January 1945, is illustrative. Chemistry provided a basis for much of the work in the sciences and, in turn, was essential to certain programs in agriculture, home economics, and engineering. For some years, this department had been headed by a person of diverse talents who participated in many aspects of the life of the college, including directing the band. Like many other professors of that period, he had only a baccalaureate degree. When he retired in 1944, it was evident that an experienced person, possessing both a doctoral degree in chemistry and demonstrated research ability, was required. Quill, at that time at the University of Kentucky, was invited to Michigan State to be considered for the job. Dean Emmons took Quill to Hannah. After some questions and a discussion of teaching and the service role of the chemistry department, Hannah apparently satisfied himself as to the suitability of the appointment.

Quill had agreed that a chemistry department must be a service department and that good teaching must be the primary activity of the department. He added that good teaching requires a progressive teacher who engages in research and continues to grow in his under-standing of the discipline. Quill also insisted that no teacher could avoid the issues and obligations involved in student progress, grading, advising, and service on committees. He believed that, in a state supported school, it was important to conduct research on the natural resources of the state. A chemistry department should not become totally industrialized, but it should assist in programs developing the natural products of the region. Pragmatically, he argued that the de-partment would profit because the citizens of the state would recognize the institution's contributions and continue to support it. Hannah, of course, agreed heartily and suggested that Emmons make an offer immediately.

In interviews with candidates, Hannah emphasized, as he had with Quill, that public service had always been freely and gladly extended by the institution through personal contacts, conferences, bulletins, correspondence, and research, if necessary. But not all faculty mem-bers joining the expanding departments even during the late 1930s agreed with this view. They regarded such service as extra work and expected extra pay. Inevitably extension workers, who frequently put in a twelve- to sixteen-hour day including travel time, would observe and resent the tendency of their colleagues to expect recompense for extra activity.

On May 20, 1943, Hannah stated that there should be "no outside consulting without prior written approval." And, recurrently, he re-marked on the necessity for a clear policy on outside work for pay. Repeated attempts at resolution of this issue never yielded enforceable policies. Indeed, the reduced teaching load, increased faculty quality, emphasis on graduate study and research, combined with sabbaticals and other developments designed to attract and hold able scholars, increased the difficulty. Despite every policy or rule, there have always been professors who assert that, having met their classes, the rest of their time is their own. Hence lucrative consultation might not have been reported. Arguments against reporting were intriguing and self-serving: surely any consulting done on Saturday or Sunday or in the evening was done on one's own time, and if consulting done on Tuesday is made up by grading papers on Saturday or Sunday, one's conscience could be clear. Administrators, too, were not of one mind on the consulting issue. One provost commented that one should either trust faculty members or get rid of them, a pertinent remark that was soon invalidated by tenure rules and appeal procedures.

IMPROVEMENT OF INSTRUCTION

The quality of the faculty and of classroom teaching was of recurrent interest to Hannah. On June 4, 1942, a program of probationary appointments before granting tenure was instituted with the implication that the Ph.D. and documented performance in at least two of the three fields of research, teaching, and public service would be required for tenure in the future. In 1943, in recognition of the many instructors on the faculty who lacked the Ph.D., a system of leaves for study (with full pay) was instituted. Also in 1943, an improvement was made in the pension system first introduced in 1935. And on November 11, 1943, an All-College Committee on the Improvement of Teaching was appointed with an oral charge much like the written one given to another committee sixteen years later. Hannah's charge to the Committee on the Future of the University, appointed in 1959, was as follows:

> The university, whatever else it may be, is a teaching institution. The effectiveness of this teaching can in the last analysis be measured only by the extent to which student behavior, either covert or overt, is changed in a desirable direction. The university which has lost sight of its instructional mission broadly construed and at all levels will soon find itself less than a complete university.

That 1959 charge reflected an ever-present concern heightened by the recurrent efforts that had been made to focus faculty attention on the importance of teaching while, at the same time, insisting upon the upgrading of the quality of faculty by requiring the Ph.D. and continuing evidence of scholarly productivity.

In 1943 the first formal teacher-rating scale had been distributed, accompanied by a faculty handbook discussing its nature and use.

Professors could ignore it and many did. There was, especially on the part of the nontenured junior faculty, considerable grumbling and some fear about the use of the results by department heads and deans. In many respects, the January 18, 1945, final report of the Committee on Improvement of Teaching summarized faculty views when it suggested that the best way to improve teaching might be to hire good faculty members and leave them alone. However, the fact was that faculty teaching had been left alone. Yet there was a widespread recognition of poor teaching, which pointed up the need to upgrade teaching qualifications and practices of the entire faculty. Consistent with the policy of study leaves for completing a doctorate, opportunities were developed for faculty members to improve their teaching and enhance student learning. The too ready assumption that department heads or senior faculty could or would provide this assistance had proved false.

Meanwhile, several additional steps were taken in regard to teaching. A survey was undertaken by William Combs in 1945, in which he asked alumni for recollections and judgments about their best and worst teachers. In a separate effort, a rating scale was devised and circulated to the deans and departments with the request that the five best teachers in each school be identified. This request was stimulated by Hannah's observation that appraisal of teaching seemed to play a minor role in departmental and deans' recommendations for salary increases and promotions. The request did bring in additional names beyond those initially recommended for raises or promotions. More significantly, it alerted all concerned that in the future due regard should be given to competencies in undergraduate instruction when recommending faculty rewards.

The 1945 report of the Committee on Teaching and Teaching Methods led to the appointment of a continuing committee to administer a rating scale. Several student rating scales were developed and requirements for their use specified. Whether or not teaching was improved thereby remained unknown, but the use of the scale provided evidence, to students and to faculty, of concern about the quality of teaching and learning. The requirement could also be used with effect in responding to questions and criticisms from those outside the institution. Yet despite repeated changes in the questionnaire and in requirements for distribution and use of the results, the rating scale remained for years highly controversial. Poor ratings on the questionnaire were not accepted by recipients as evidence of poor teaching. Good ratings were not necessarily accepted by the administration as indices of good teaching.

At Michigan State, as elsewhere, many studies were launched in attempt to eliminate the various doubts about and criticisms of ratings. Researchers confirmed their own biases but convinced no one else. The central issue, often forgotten in this process, was that teaching is but a means to learning and must be appraised by its effects on student learning. Thus, everyone could agree that defining and assessing good teaching were rather more complex than implied by a scale rating student opinion. Nevertheless, the use of the rating scale continued to be specified through 1956–57. The costs were considerable, the impact on teaching was minimal, but the symbolic implications were great. Students, denied access to "official" ratings, from time to time launched and published their own, accompanied by great fanfare but ending in futility. The pressures of expansion in the immediate postwar period left little time for exploration and improvement of classroom teaching.

The appointment in 1959 of the Committee on the Future of the University led to a reexamination of teaching evaluation policies, of faculty reactions to them, and ultimately to a different approach to improvement of teaching in which content, learning objectives, learning experiences, and the resources of a developing educational technology were viewed as interrelated. The classroom performance of the professor came to be viewed as but one part of a sequence of student interactions with the environment, with course content, and with people, so planned as to foster student commitment and involvement in learning experiences as a means of personal development. This 1959 committee also had the advantage of reviewing the success or lack of it of various previous ventures in instructional innovation and renovation.

In 1950 an Audio-Visual Center, directed by Dr. Charles Schuller, was created to provide free assistance to the faculty. In the latter 1950s, Schuller proposed to President Hannah the addition of a film production unit to the center, and shortly thereafter $25,000 was granted to purchase material for the unit. Prominent among the services provided by the center at that time was a film distribution unit available to the public schools of the state. The center also supplied equipment and operators for on-campus classes and produced visual materials for classroom use on or off campus. In his 1959 annual report, Schuller reported a 31 percent increase in the use of services. By this date, also, the center's staff was engaged in research; training of students; and in cooperation with the College of Education, teaching graduate courses and offering graduate degrees in instructional development.

The land-grant trinity of instruction, research, and service was much in evidence.

By 1962–63 the center included a 7,000-print library of educational films, a wide range of projection and sound recording or reproduction services, portable closed-circuit television, and expert production capability in the graphic arts and motion pictures. In 1963–64 an educational media specialist graduate program at the master's, six-year, and doctoral levels became available for students in education and communication arts. The center received international recognition.

By 1969, twenty-one students had completed doctorates in instructional and learning areas, and ninety-six completed the doctoral program through the winter quarter of 1980. These degree recipients acquired positions at such institutions as Arizona State, Case Western Reserve, University of South Carolina, Univerity of Calgary, University of Colorado, Ohio State, University of Wisconsin, University of Maine, and University of Texas.

The Audio-Visual Center became one of the major resources in the Educational Development Program, which was announced in 1961 and which projected a seven-point program stated—and brashly interpreted—as follows:

1. Students should be expected and enabled to take increasing responsibility for their own education. [College students should have been weaned before admission.]
2. Educational objectives should be defined more concretely and so worded as to be understood by students and related to their own purposes or objectives. [Teaching must be directed to students rather than to content coverage.]
3. Faculty assignments and activities should be defined (without regard to rank) to determine the most productive use of faculty time. [Professorial rank or status provides no guarantee of superior performance.]
4. Instruction should make use of new knowledge and technology on teaching and learning. [Even ancient history must continually be rewritten and presented in more effective ways than lectures.]
5. Academic use of the residence halls should increase to ease some of the problems of travel on a large campus, to relate student residence to the academic purposes of the institution, and to make fuller use of space. [Large campuses can, without efforts to the contrary, maximize the inconvenience of everyone.]
6. Efforts should be made in every way to combine the advantages of a large university with the traditional advantages of smaller

institutions. [Learning is largely an individual experience facilitated by interpersonal communications and other learning resources.]

7. Financial support should be provided for those departments and colleges working toward redefining their objectives. [Units seeking to improve teaching should be assisted in so doing and rewarded for it.]

The report of the Committee on the Future of the University contained more than forty specific recommendations, including those above, for actions to be taken to strengthen the academic program and the general operations of Michigan State. One of the recommendations indicated that the degree requirements should be reduced from the existing minimum of 192 to 180 credits, inclusive of the 3 credits of required physical education. The committee agreed with data presented from Evaluation Services that the existing degree credit requirements were heavy, in part because the total class-hour load had always been heavy in the institution and also because there had long been a tendency to add new course requirements in fields like engineering without eliminating existing courses or reducing their credits. The committee also recommended that larger credit blocks be provided by combining and eliminating courses.

The recommendations tended to adjust excesses created by earlier actions. In 1930 Lloyd C. Emmons had recommended to President Shaw, and he to the faculty, that the four-credit pattern characteristic of that period should be replaced by courses carrying five, three, or two credits. This change, in effect, added a full day of usage to the then available classroom space. But in making the change, the faculty tended to make extensive use of three- and two-credit courses and occasionally even of one-credit courses. Over time, the result was that students might readily be enrolled in as many as seven courses, and successive class meetings of a course could be in different rooms. This circumstance caused one professor to irritate his colleagues by suggesting that anyone enrolled in as many as seven courses who regularly attended each for a ten-week period ought to pass them all automatically. The recommendations of the Committee on the Future of the University were accepted and acted upon, although few courses disappeared.

The committee also recommended that ROTC be made elective, which resulted in a good deal of both approbation and criticism. Approval was delayed but ultimately forthcoming.

In general, this committee attempted to provide better educational opportunities for more students by better use of the resources already at the faculty's disposal. Considerable evidence was presented indicating that, despite the large enrollment and the existence of many large classes, there were also many small classes at the junior and senior level and, especially, at the graduate level. While accepting the fact that some lower limit on class size must be introduced, there were many who felt also that there were advantages in small classes if professors took advantage of the size to do something other than lecture.

An array of services and technologies entitled the Educational Development Program was created as a means of pursuing these various issues. Faculty reaction to many of the points in the program caused it initially to be suspect, as infringing on professorial and departmental prerogatives. Undoubtedly, some of the projections made on the basis of the recommendations and assumptions were unrealistic. In time, however, the Educational Development Program under the leadership of John Dietrich, assistant provost, became a significant part of the provost's office and contributed greatly to alerting faculty to rethink all aspects of the educational programs in the light of knowledge about human learning, the educational technology available, and the mission of the institution.

Some years previously, a language laboratory, in which conversational skills were emphasized, had been constructed in Morrill Hall. But the experience with it demonstrated that provision of technical facilities to a faculty did not necessarily result in their effective use. The traditional emphasis in foreign language courses on literature resulted initially in vocabulary and grammar drills which had been dealt with in the past without technical facilities. But with time and emphasis on the oral aspects of language, the Language Laboratories, now housed in one of the newer buildings, Wells Hall, became very useful.

Later, when Akers Hall was built, a request was made to provide language laboratories in that facility, too, as a way of bringing academic activities into the residence hall. On April 8, 1964, the proposal cleared through to the provost's office, and the Office of Space Utilization was asked to remodel room 107 Akers Hall to accommodate a thirty-two station language laboratory. This required air conditioning, a control room, and thirty-two booths. A little later, it was found that the facility was not sufficiently used to justify its existence, and it was dismantled. About $35,000 had been expended for the remodeling originally and something less than that for the dismantling. The aborted effort had been based on an overly optimistic estimate of the extent to which interest in language could be generated among the students.

In the years after Hannah retired, the Educational Development

Program and its associated services continued to expand and become further restructured in the light of the services provided. In 1972 the Instructional Development Service and the Educational Development Program included a Learning Service, headed by L. T. Alexander, and an Instructional Media Center, headed by Charles F. Schuller. Under the Instructional Media Center, Closed Circuit Television, Production and Distribution, and the Instructional Development Service appeared. The list of services provided gradually changed and expanded to include the following:

1. Initiating or collaborating with other units in conducting empirical studies on university-wide programs related to learning and teaching
2. Initiating or responding to requests for consultation on programs involving organizational research, development, and evaluation
3. Providing information and consultative assistance on course and curriculum design and evaluation, test design, choosing and using instructional modes, developing effective classroom presentation techniques, and conducting field experience, such as internships and practicums
4. Maintaining a scoring office to provide test scoring and other computational services related to course management
5. Providing departments with consultative assistance in designing and developing training programs for teaching assistance
6. Maintaining and managing a teaching laboratory designated as the Experimental Classroom Facility, to be used to develop and test instructional materials and techniques, analyze teaching techniques, and provide video feedback to students
7. Consulting with faculty·on writing grant proposals, especially with regard to program evaluation
8. Assistance in utilizing computers for instruction, course management, and record keeping
9. Providing consultation and assistance in the general area of faculty, student, and program evaluation, through the Learning and Evaluation Services

Meanwhile, the study and research on university operations, which had been developed originally with a focus on the Basic College, had gradually expanded and been incorporated into the Office of Institutional Research. The continuing efforts of that office to develop a data base provided much of the rationale for conducting such specific studies as departmental analyses to determine load, service pattern, and budgetary needs, course and section size, elimination of courses infrequently taught, credit by examination, grading practices; studies of programmed learning materials, development of film material in physics, the university budget, the use of academic assistants, cocurricular involvement, large enrollment courses, and the use of various instructional techniques including closed circuit television in teaching these courses. Some of these studies provided the basis for educational development programs in particular areas and others were, in effect, on-going evaluation programs which provided for adjustments and alterations in direction of various projects. It became clear that the attitudes of administrators, departments, and individual faculty members were crucial to the success of any of these endeavors. With their support, innovation was becoming institutionalized.

John Hannah, addressing a national conference on Instructional Innovation in Large Universities in November 1966, commented that there must be administrative commitment to innovation, including commitment by the governing board of the university.

> Administrators must make a conscientious effort to interrupt their accustomed patterns of thought, they must be willing to look at new proposals, they must be determined to put the likely ones to the test of practice, and they must be courageous enough to risk occasional failure. Administrators must plan for constructive change and seek the best way to accomplish it. They must find a way to reward those who produce new ideas, and see to it that new ideas are given visibility and made subject to the give and take of free discussion and debate. There must also be a commitment to innovation on the part of the faculty and the administration when matters relating to curriculum and instruction are involved. The faculty must be persuaded of the need for innovation and of the necessity for faculty commissions and committees charged to examine critical problems and to propose new solutions. Student concerns and complaints should not be ignored, but neither should these dominate the deliberations. Students are dissatisfied with the way universities operate. Perhaps we can capitalize upon this discontent by challenging students to state their objection and objectives plainly and to offer their own suggestions for reform. Under such conditions they might even help. These efforts will take time and money, but it will be time and money well and profitably invested. Hence there must be catalytic agencies established to stimulate the development and evaluation of innovation.

A few additional observations beyond these of Hannah can be made in the light of experience. All humans—not solely professors—resist objective evaluation. Initial enthusiasm for an innovation will go far to make it successful, but when enthusiasts depart or lose their enthusiasm, that initial success may disappear. Hence, new teaching materials, the use of educational technology, and changes in curriculum, even though seemingly effective, may be of very short duration.

A great amount of time and effort is required both to initiate and maintain innovation. Acquiring a grant or a release of time for curricular or instructional improvement brings administrative regard and approval and is a heady experience, but it must be followed by hard work. Initiation of an effective program can also be satisfying, but the faculty members responsible for areas of change and the interests and efforts of those who remain with a particular program also shift. Too frequently, faculty members who spent much time in instructional innovation found that this effort, no matter how successful, was not highly regarded by the department as compared with the research and scholarly efforts of their colleagues. Hannah was very much aware of this and continually reviewed deans' and chairs' recommendations on faculty. He did not hesitate to reopen recommendations on salary and promotion when it seemed that efforts in the direction of teaching and learning had been ignored.

Hannah recognized that if administrators assume that curriculum and instructional matters are largely the domain of the department and colleges and refuse to engage in review or encourage innovation in these areas, dynamism in the educational process is likely to disappear. Not surprisingly, however, this omission is unlikely to stimulate widespread faculty criticism. There is no enthusiasm for spending funds on instruction and curriculum review. The Educational Development Program, while it succeeded in bringing in dollars from various sources, always constituted an extra charge against general funds. Some deans and faculty members would have preferred that the money be channeled to the departments and used as departmental needs indicated, but it is unlikely that they would have been used to improve teaching.

The committee reports of 1959 and 1967 clearly reflect the importance that Hannah attached to undergraduate education and also his success in using task forces to analyze and make reports on these matters, with the aim of awakening faculty members to their responsibilities. In appointing committees or task forces to study and formulate recommendations on a problem or problems, Hannah always emphasized the significance of intensive study in depth and extensive interchange with the entire faculty. The task of the committee was as much that of educating the faculty as of producing a report. Not infrequently, this process produced an accord on recommendations that otherwise might have been highly controversial.

For example, the Committee on the Future of the University[2] in its 1959 report stated:

---

2. "A Report to the President of Michigan State University." In the MSU Archives and Historical Collections.

All undergraduate curricula should provide a coherent, continuous educational experience specifically designed to equip an individual to cope with subsequent changes in the fields of knowledge. No curriculum resting on specific technique or narrow skills, or geared to mere assimilation of present knowledge, can ever achieve this.

After reviewing program requirements in several areas, the committee concluded:

No planned or ill-conceived accumulation of elective credits will achieve the purposes of this liberal arts education, but a carefully thought-out program of courses can do much to enrich the life of the student. Any departmental program which does not involve a strong series of liberal arts elective courses should be subjected to rigorous scrutiny in allocating resources.

The two preceding quotations together make a potent statement about liberal education. The committee noted also that several colleges had a significant number of elective enrollments from other colleges. For example, 30 percent of the enrollments in business and 25 percent of the enrollments in agriculture were by nonmajors. Whether selected on the grounds of career or personal interests, such courses provided for these cross-college enrollees a breadth of experience with something of a liberating nature. In effect, the committee recognized that liberal education should not be regarded as either restricted to or implicit in so-called liberal arts disciplines.

The Committee on Undergraduate Education in its 1967 report[3] gave serious attention to the order and coherence of undergraduate major fields. The following five questions were developed to aid faculty members in reviewing programs.

1. Does the applied field of study depend upon or bear relationship to one or more of the basic disciplines in such a way as to insure that students engaged in it will be required to weigh evidence and make judgments on matters of some substance and complexity?
2. Does the applied field of study promise to deal seriously with important social problems or needs?
3. Are other institutions within the state or region currently engaged in teaching programs similar to the proposed program, and, if so, will there be needless duplication?
4. What physical and human resources will be required to conduct the teaching program, not only in the applied field itself but in the ancillary fields it will hope to call upon?
5. How narrowly conceived is the proposed professional field? Is

---

3. "Improving Undergraduate Education." In the MSU Archives and Historical Collections.

it designed to equip the student mainly with those skills required at the entrance level of the profession, or does it attempt to equip him or her with the understanding of principles upon which future innovation will depend?

Another set of questions to be used in reviewing the total array of courses offered included the following:

1. Has the department introduced for its majors an inordinate number of unrelated single-term courses?
2. Have too many 400-level courses been introduced at the expense of courses at lower levels?
3. What has happened to the prerequisite system once systematically employed in the curriculum?
4. How many *tight* sequences (two- or three-term sequences of courses considered as a unit and employing specific prerequisites) does the department now offer?
5. How many *loose* sequences (two- or three-term sequences which deal with a similar subject but which may be entered at any point in the sequence) does the department offer?
6. What degree of choice is the student allowed in building his or her major? May the student elect to complete a program consisting entirely of single-term courses? Does the department offer options?
7. Are appropriate supportive courses from related disciplines utilized as part of the basic curriculum? How specific are the requirements for cognate fields?
8. What culminating experience (for example, senior proseminar) has been provided for the major?

The committee was also concerned with flexibility in courses, with the pressures of the ten-week quarter, and with grading problems.

The 10-week course confers other disadvantages upon our undergraduate program, disadvantages which are too rarely noticed. Clearly it contributes to the feeling of anonymity which students acknowledge after shifting every three months to still another set of classmates, still another instructor—who himself must confront still another strange-sounding list of names on still another new classlist. Clearly, too, it makes of some courses, chiefly those calling for extensive reading and reflection and writing, nothing so much as a rapid dash over quiz, mid-term, paper and final hurdles, each set but a few days or weeks from that which came before or will come after. And, less clearly though no less true, the year-long sequence consisting of three 10-week courses in succession works a viciously artificial process of elimination upon the average student. If at the close of each 10-week course in the sequence the bottom fifth leaves the class, it is more than likely that the student with an average grade in the first term will not survive through the third.

The Committee is mindful of the futility of speaking to these problems by proposing absolute calendar change. The 15-week semester, while obviously superior in some ways, can boast of an equally impressive list of disadvantages. A five-week extension beyond our present term is not likely to solve the problems to which the Committee's attention has so frequently been called.

The Committee recommends that departments and colleges give active and serious attention to any and all possibilities for improving the quality of instructional program by planning and conducting undergraduate courses which are conditioned by neither the usual credit weight nor the usual time span of our present offerings.

In many ways this 1967 report reemphasized and enlarged upon factors involved in the earlier injunction of the Committee on the Future of the University.

Strength or excellence should be sought in every area of knowledge that Michigan State University elects to enter or continue. Only in this way can the University be strong as a whole. It should be recognized, however, that there are at least four kinds of strengths or excellence: (1) excellence in an approach to an entire subject matter, or in the nature of the approach, (2) excellence in one or more aspects of a subject matter, (3) excellence in giving support to other disciplines, or (4) excellence in complementing other disciplines. It is unrealistic and indeed impossible to expect to obtain general strength in all aspects of all areas.

Several general criteria are relevant in choosing areas of future emphasis. First, emphasis should be given to those areas of significance for society as a whole and to Michigan and its region in particular.

Student activities of the 1960s and their demands for representation in governance, concerns about equity for women and minorities, unionization of nonacademic staff and increasing specificity in regard to job definition (including salaries, promotions, terminations, and interpersonal relations), expanding use of internal appeal mechanisms, and the gradual invasion of state and federal agencies into institutional policies and actions—all these combined to generate elaborate statements of policy and procedure. The resulting prescriptions suggest that colleges and universities had lost any claim to respect and trust either intra- or extramurally. The long-time concern for teaching quality at Michigan State was made evident during the Hannah years by recurrent attempts to assist professors in improving teaching and in evaluating it so as to identify and reward good teaching or eliminate poor teaching. These efforts certainly had beneficial effects, but they did not and could not eliminate ineffective or indifferent teaching. Student complaints tended to get nowhere even when carried through several appeal channels because there existed no generally acceptable statement of teaching responsibilities. The following statement on teaching responsibilities from the 1977–78 catalog is an attempt to demonstrate obligation and to provide both a substantive and procedural statement evaluating or appealing complaints.

Code of Teaching Responsibility

1977–78:

The teaching responsibilities of instructional staff members (herein referred to as instructors) are among those many areas of university life which have for generations been a part of the unwritten code of academicians. The provisions of such a code are so reasonable to learned and humane individuals that it may appear redundant or unnecessary to state them. However, the University conceives them to be so important that performance by instructors in meeting the provisions of this code shall be taken into consideration in determining salary increases, tenure, and promotion.

1. Instructors are responsible for ensuring that the content of the courses they teach is consistent with the course descriptions approved by the University Committees on Curriculum and the Academic Council. Instructors are also responsible for stating clearly to students in their classes the instructional objectives of each course at the beginning of each term. It is expected that the class activities will be directed toward the fulfillment of these objectives and that the bases upon which student performance is evaluated will be consistent with these objectives.

2. Instructors are responsible for informing students in their classes of the methods to be used in determining final course grades and of any special requirements of attendance which differ from the attendance policy of the University. Course grades will be determined by the instructor's assessment of each student's individual performance, judged by standards of academic achievement.

3. Examinations and other assignments submitted for grading during the term should be returned with sufficient promptness to enhance the learning experience. Unclaimed final examination answers will be retained by the instructor for at least one term so that they may be reviewed by students who desire to do so. Examination questions are an integral part of course materials, and the decision whether to allow their retention by students is the responsibility of the instructor. Term papers and other comparable projects are the property of students who prepare them. They should be returned to students who ask for them, and those which are not returned should be retained by the instructor for at least one term. Instructors who desire to retain a copy for their own files should state their intention to do so in order that students may prepare additional copies for themselves.

4. Instructors are expected to meet their classes regularly and at scheduled times. Instructors will notify their units if they are to be absent and if appropriate arrangements have not been made so that suitable action may be taken by the unit if necessary.

5. Instructors of courses in which assistants are authorized to perform teaching or grading functions shall be responsible for acquainting such individuals with the provisions of this Code and for monitoring their compliance.
6. Instructors are expected to schedule and keep a reasonable number of office hours for student conferences. Office hours should be scheduled at times convenient to both students and instructors with the additional option of prearranged appointments for students when there are schedule conflicts. The minimum number of office hours is to be agreed upon by the teaching unit, and specific times should be a matter of common knowledge.
7. Instructors who are responsible for academic advising are expected to be in their offices at appropriate hours during the preenrollment and enrollment periods. Arrangements shall also be made for advising during registration.

*Hearing Procedures*

1. Students may register complaints regarding an instructor's failure to comply with the provision of the *Code of Teaching Responsibility* directly with that instructor.
2. Students may also take complaints directly to teaching units' chief administrators or their designates.* If those persons are unable to receive matters to the student's satisfaction, they are obliged to transmit written complaints to unit committees charged with hearing such complaints. A copy of any complaint transmitted shall be sent to the instructor. A written report of the action or recommendation of such groups will be forwarded to the student and to the instructor, normally within ten working days of the receipt of the complaint.
3. Complaints coming to the University Ombudsman* will be reported, in writing, to chief administrators of the teaching units involved when in the Ombudsman's opinion a hearing appears necessary. It will be the responsibility of chief administrators or their designates to inform the instructor and to refer such unresolved complaints to the unit committees charged with hearing such complaints. A written report of the action or recommendation of such groups will be forwarded to the University Ombudsman, to the student, and to the instructor, normally within ten working days of the receipt of the complaint.
4. Students wishing to appeal a teaching unit action or recommendation may do so as outlined in Provision 2.2.8.1 of the *Academic Freedom Report*.

*Such complaints must normally be initiated no later than mid-term of the quarter following the one wherein alleged violations occurred. Exceptions shall be made in cases when the involved instructor or student is absent from the University during the quarter following the one wherein alleged violations occurred.

This statement is a refreshing departure from the long-time emphasis on academic freedom; here is an admission that such freedom entails responsibilities. It is long on *shoulds*, shalls, and *oughts* and short on means of assessment and procedures for enforcement. There is a slight bite to this statement in the phrase "shall be taken into account in determining salary increases, tenure, and promotion." On the other hand, many of these statements are ambiguous or meaningless. For example, note the phrases from item 1—"bases upon which student performance is evaluated will be consistent with these objectives", item 2—"judged by standards of academic achievement", item 6—"a reasonable number of office hours", and item 7—"responsible for academic advising". The first phrase poses the problem of meaningful objectives and relevant and adequate evaluation. The core problem in improving teaching lies in pushing objectives beyond mere recall of content and development of evaluation procedures to reinforce this demand. Almost any figure under 100 percent could be proposed as indicating the proportion of the instructional staff that fails to meet this responsibility. But who is to judge and on what evidence? The second phrase refers to standards of academic achievement. Objective standards do not exist for most courses and instructors. The third, "a reasonable number of office hours," lacks any basis for determining the meaning of *reasonable*. The fourth admits a responsibility of some instructors for academic advising but settles for simple availability. In effect, excellence is ignored.

The following statements pertain to student evaluation of instruction.

*1977–78*

This system provides an opportunity for students to evaluate the instruction they receive in relation to (1) the provisions of the Code of Teaching Responsibility, and (2) the various instructional models in operation in the University. The purpose of this system is to provide student input toward assessing and improving course design and teaching performance. The University and individual departments are responsible for designing and administering their respective survey forms to obtain such evaluations. The results of these surveys are made available to the instructor and to persons involved in personnel decisions, but are not made public. In addition, the Student Council may design and administer a third survey form. Individual instructors are encouraged, but not required, to authorize the use of this form in their courses. The results of this survey may be made public.

*1979–80*

Student Instructional Rating System (SIRS)

PREAMBLE

The *principal objective* of the student instructional rating policy is to *secure information which is indispensable to implementation of the University's policy of providing its students with instruction of the highest quality*. This information is put to two principal uses: (1) providing instructors and teaching units with an accurate account of student response to their instructional practices, to the end that classroom effectiveness be maintained at the highest level of excellence; and (2) providing teaching units with one kind of information to be considered in deciding on retention, promotion, salary, and tenure, to the end that effectiveness in instruction constitutes an important criterion in evaluating the service to the University of members of the teaching faculty. In order to accomplish these objectives more fully, the following procedures were established.

1. Every teaching unit shall approve *one or more common student rating instruments* through its own channels of participation, in accordance with unit bylaws and customs of collegial decision making. Regardless of the type of instrument adopted, it must prominently display the following notation:

   The Michigan State University CODE OF TEACHING RESPONSIBIL-ITY holds all instructors to certain obligations with respect to, e.g., course content consistent with approved descriptions, timely statement of course objectives and grading criteria, regular class attendance, published office hours, and timely return of examinations and term papers. This Code is printed in full in the SCHEDULE OF COURSES AN ACADEMIC HANDBOOK. It includes specifics about complaint procedures available to students who believe that their instructors have violated the Code.

2. Each teaching unit shall make regular and systematic use of student instructional ratings as part of the unit's evaluation of instructional performance. Each teaching unit shall formulate and promulgate a comprehensive policy covering all aspects of student instructional rating procedures, and shall be responsible for implementing that policy within the framework of the provisions contained in this document. Students shall not be required or requested by faculty members to identify themselves on the rating forms.

3. All instructors, regardless of rank, including graduate assistants, shall use unit-approved student instructional rating forms in all classes (every course, every section, every term). For team-teaching situations, units shall develop procedures consistent with the intent of these provisions.

4. Individual instructors may use other instruments to gather additional information.

5. Results of student instructional ratings shall be used in accordance with the following provisions:

   a. Results shall be returned promptly to the instructor for information and assistance in improving course design and instruction.

   b. Instructors shall have the opportunity to comment, orally and/or in writing, upon the ratings received. These comments shall be taken into account by persons or groups charged with making or advising on personnel decisions.

   c. Results of student instructional ratings shall be systematically consulted, with due regard for strict confidentiality, in conjunction with other means for assessing individual effectiveness, according to the review criteria promulgated within each unit. Other means might include, e.g., classroom visits or consideration of course syllabi, assignments, and examinations.

6. Procedures for implementing the rating process and for utilizing the results shall be promulgated by each teaching unit, subject to the following provisions:

a. Duly promulgated unit procedures shall be filed in the offices of the appropriate Dean and the Provost, where they will be matters of public record.

b. Unit administrators are responsible for implementing in their units SIRS procedures which follow fully the requirements of this document.

c. Teaching units may have the required SIRS instruments administered by a person other than the instructor. If the unit does not administer the instruments, instructors are obligated to do so, and to return all results to unit offices within the time period specified in the unit procedures.

d. At the time instruments are administered, students shall be informed who will have access to the results and how the results will be used.

This statement contains a series of specific requirements to be met by "teaching units" and instructors, and though it provides evidence of university commitment, it furnishes no definitive way of determining compliance and no penalties for noncompliance. Central administration has delegated enforcement to the colleges, departments, and faculty, to individuals and units that have for years demonstrated indifference. The heritage of Hannah's concern for the pragmatic aspect of the teaching process has been, in succeeding years, largely reduced to rhetoric without substantive support in assisting, monitoring, and rewarding successful efforts. This has resulted because departments and colleges encouraged decentralization of responsibility. Officers in central administration became hesitant about probing too far into faculty performance and were increasingly concerned with other matters. Financial exigencies forced elimination of individuals and units introduced to assist and study instructional problems. The additional demands and costs of equity, combined with financial exigencies, led to cutbacks, and these were most easily made in the academic services area.

### FORMAL FACULTY GOVERNANCE STRUCTURE

Before 1942 no formal structure for faculty governance existed at the divisional level. Faculty participation at the department level depended largely on the professor-head who had usually been appointed with little or no faculty involvement. In 1942 Hannah encouraged the formation of divisional faculties with the expectation that they would take an increasingly important role in establishing policies at the divisional, school, and college level. Not all deans were pleased. Some faculty members immediately proposed faculty committees to sit with the dean regularly for discussions and decisions on almost all issues. This demand was a challenge to the authority of department heads as well as of the dean. One dean resolved the matter after a stormy faculty committee meeting by announcing that he would not call another. Nevertheless, from 1942 on, the faculty voice was more clearly heard.

At the institutional level, the task force approach preferred by Hannah continued to provide much of the deliberation and policy formulation that faculty committees might have served. It did so more efficiently and rather more intrusively into matters that might have been left to departments and schools or colleges by standing committees in which members tended to represent unit interests rather than the broader all-institutional concerns that prevailed in task forces.

By 1957–58, the committee list of the university had become so extensive that it appeared under several headings: faculty affairs; student affairs; university services; instruction; curriculum; and research, administrative, and board established. Academic Vice-President Hamilton chaired several key committees. The dean of students chaired all but one of the committees on student affairs. Dean Combs chaired the university services group. Administrative committees (course scheduling, Hidden Lake Gardens, patents, summer school) were dominated by deans, assistants to deans, or department heads. Board-established committees were also dominated by deans, heads, and assistants. The combination of specific task assignments and administrative presence assured that the committees were advisory. A few students appeared on student affairs subcommittees and on the Student Publications Committee. Committees now could, and did, slow down decision making and even influence but seldom determine it. But the faculty voice was heard.

In addition, there existed an Academic Council Advisory to the President on Academic Affairs, made up of sixteen administrators, eighteen elected representatives, and five representatives from the Steering Committee of the Academic Senate. Even with this enlargement of the committee structure, the faculty voice was diluted by the presence of administrators, but it was by no means muted. By the latter years of the Hannah era, other factors were operating to make the faculty governance structure much less effective. The number of units (colleges, departments, institutions, and so on) resulted in large, almost unmanageable committees and other groups. Representatives from the various units expected to weigh the impact of any action on their department or college rather than on its relevance to the institution and its clientele. The increase in faculty and the emphasis on improvement of faculty stature and of departments in scholarship and research posed something of a threat to the long-time land-grant mission.

Two other aspects of the faculty governance structure were inimical to effective operation. Adding students to committees slowed down some deliberations but neither satisfied student expectations nor verified faculty fears. The proliferation of committees and their lines of responsibility ushered in a more serious problem because it became uncertain, in many cases, where an issue should be initiated and how many different groups must be given an opportunity for deliberation and rejection, modification, or approval.

The Academic Council, as it existed in 1956, included the president, two vice-presidents, registrar, secretary, twelve deans, two elected representatives from each college (eighteen in all) and five members of the Steering Committee of the Academic Senate—a total of thirty-nine individuals. In addition, there were forty-three standing committees and subcommittees. By 1969 the Academic Council included ninety-one persons. Standing committees and subcommittees also existed in profusion. A structure originally based on a much smaller institution had increased in size with the university and had simply gotten out of hand. Faculty members tended to criticize the growth in administration as costly and as interfering with faculty involvement in governance. Actually, the growth in the faculty governance structure would in itself have required an increase in administrative staff just to maintain contact with all the meetings. The faculty had increased from 343 in 1935 to 2,450 in 1969, more than a sevenfold increase. The administrative staff had increased from 66 to 260, a fourfold increase. The enrollment in 1969 (44,274) was about 13 times that in 1935 (3,323). Despite Hannah's expressed concern in the early 1940s about uncritical extension of tenure, the percentage of faculty on tenure had increased from 31 percent in 1935 to 58 percent in 1969 and would further increase in the next ten years to 70 percent. As he predicted, a high tenure rate unaccompanied by competitive salaries posed threats to the long trek towards quality.

In the years subsequent to 1967, several other factors began to interfere with decision making at all levels and in all phases of the university's operation. These included extensive detailed documents regarding experimentation on human subjects, access to and use of confidential information, student rights and responsibilities, faculty rights and responsibilities, academic freedom, detailed employment procedures, grievance procedures, and student appeal procedures. Promotions, salaries, nonreappointment, and tenure became issues for appeal through several levels within the institution and even to the courts or federal agencies. State and federal auditors of expenditures and of policies employed in making expenditures probed at times into issues that strongly affected educational policies. Appointment of an ombudsman (and secretary) and a faculty grievance official (and secretary) and an enlargement of legal staff have reflected a further expansion of central administration, a further stretching of ever-shrinking resources, and a diminution in the autonomy of the university—and hence in the authority of the faculty and the administration.

External pressures and demands have dictated many decisions. Procedural matters have drained resources and displaced much of the attention formerly directed to substantive ones. Management of decline is difficult when past expansions are entrenched and current demands force new expansions. The pursuit of quality and program improvement, so evident in the Hannah years, has been replaced by concern for survival and maintenance of employment. Faculty aspirations for fuller participation in governance have been thwarted by the necessity of giving students more voice, by the dire and worsening financial exigencies in Michigan, and by lack of leadership.

## REFLECTIONS ON HANNAH'S REACTIONS TO FACULTY INVOLVEMENT

Although Hannah was always interested in student and faculty views, he tended to be impatient with student and faculty desires for a structure of committees and councils with assigned areas of broad concern and delegated responsibilities and authority. Many faculty members who served under Hannah recall that he did not like to work with committees and avoided it whenever possible. He found them given to interminable discussion, support of impossible policies, and compromise and ambiguities of statement that complicated rather than resolved the issue at hand.

He was especially reluctant about faculty commitments in his earlier years as president, during which he had an agenda for action that required quick and clear decisions. He sought major changes in the character of the institution that were not cordially received by many long-time faculty members who might have resisted actively had faculty had a formal role in policy formulation. In view of the unrest created by various actions in the 1920s, the institution could ill afford lengthy and inane discussions in the 1930s and 1940s about institutional mission, role, and programs. As one long-time faculty member and administrator noted, a faculty senate was resisted by Hannah not because he ignored faculty concerns but because:

1. Action was required in directions and at a rate inconsistent with the slow, deliberative processes of faculty groups.
2. Most of the action required involved an institutional focus rather than a departmental, divisional one.
3. Most of Hannah's agenda was aimed at bringing into existence a very different institution from that which currently existed.
4. Faculty tendency toward elaborating issues and seeking agreement by compromise or by elimination of issues rather than by trial, evaluation, and modification contrasted markedly with Hannah's pragmatism.
5. Although deeply concerned with faculty quality, satisfaction, and enthusiasm, Hannah viewed the institution as serving the state and nation and the people and deplored the faculty tendency to place personal convenience and aspirations ahead of those of the students and the clientele served by the institution.

Hannah also found irritating, even if amusing, the recurrent demand from an elderly dean for the precedent for any proposal. Hannah cared little for precedent and academic tradition as such. There were other administrators who deliberately and stubbornly stood in the way of change. Said one registrar in response to a suggestion for a change of registration procedure: "It's been this way since I've been here, and it'll be this way until I leave."

Hannah concluded that the faculty as a group will rarely make significant changes in which individuals see no immediate personal or department benefits unless forced to do so by persuasion, leadership, or pressure—internal or external. Yet he believed that changes must come, or at least should seem to come, from within, or else resistance or indifference will destroy the desired effort. He preferred the ad hoc task force made up of presidentially selected individuals from nominations submitted by departments and colleges. Selected in this manner, the individuals were of broad orientation, open-minded on most issues, and of sufficient stature to carry weight individually and as part of a group on recommendations made in regard to any problem studied. The ad hoc task force could be dismissed with gratitude, its appropriate recommendations acted on immediately, and its dubious or impractical ones referred to standing faculty committees for lengthy discussion and ultimate emasculation or destruction. Especially able task force members could be moved into administration. Others had learned that faculty views were desired and could be influential if identified, brought into focus, communicated effectively, and implemented with reasonable speed.

The effectiveness of this approach depended on the presence of a dynamic, charismatic leader with a clear and clearly stated set of goals and objectives. It also depended upon a supportive board and the availability of resources. Most of these were no longer present in the post-Hannah period of 1969 to 1984. Nevertheless, the structures and the faculty participation developed during the later years of Hannah's presidency enabled the faculty to take constructive positions on issues of importance and to delay, modify, or derail some administrative proposals that seemed ill considered, inappropriate, or whimsical. Hannah's approach to decision making on the basis of mission and principle rather than on faculty discussion and compromise built a faculty approach to governance better than he or they recognized.

# 15
# Funds, Facilities, and Functions

Expediency and opportunism pay a greater role in obtaining funds and acquiring facilities than advocates of planning, based on specific objectives and goals, will readily admit. Functions and accomplishments depend on both funds and facilities. Thus, ultimately, the growth and development of an institution, especially a public one, depends upon leadership and politics. For example, when in 1916 fire destroyed the engineering facilities on the Michigan State campus, only the prompt and successful appeal of Frank S. Kedzie to R. E. Olds for funds ($100,000) for a new engineering facility averted a resurrection of the proposal to move engineering to Ann Arbor. Politicians who might have supported that action could not be parties to refusing $100,000.

When John Hannah became secretary of the college in 1935, the enrollment was 4,006. No major classroom buildings had been constructed since the Home Economics Building was erected in 1924, when the total fall-term enrollment was 1,873. There had been an addition to Giltner Hall in 1931, when the enrollment was 3,374. Mary Mayo was the only dormitory designed and used fully for student housing. In fact, in 1935 the college physical plant had already outgrown the needs of the university. The situation worsened despite Hannah's repeated warnings and pleas for assistance.

The college benefited during the Great Depression because the federal government embarked upon a building program designed to provide needed employment. One such program was the Public Works Authority (PWA), which supplied 55 percent of the cost of certain public construction, requiring the other 45 percent to be furnished by the recipient. John Hannah seized this opportunity to construct dormitories and other buildings, using borrowed funds to be repaid from building income as the 45 percent. Dormitories generated income and thus were ideal projects. Williams and Campbell Halls were built for women and Mason and Abbot Halls for men. Other self-financing buildings made possible by the PWA program were the MSU Audi-

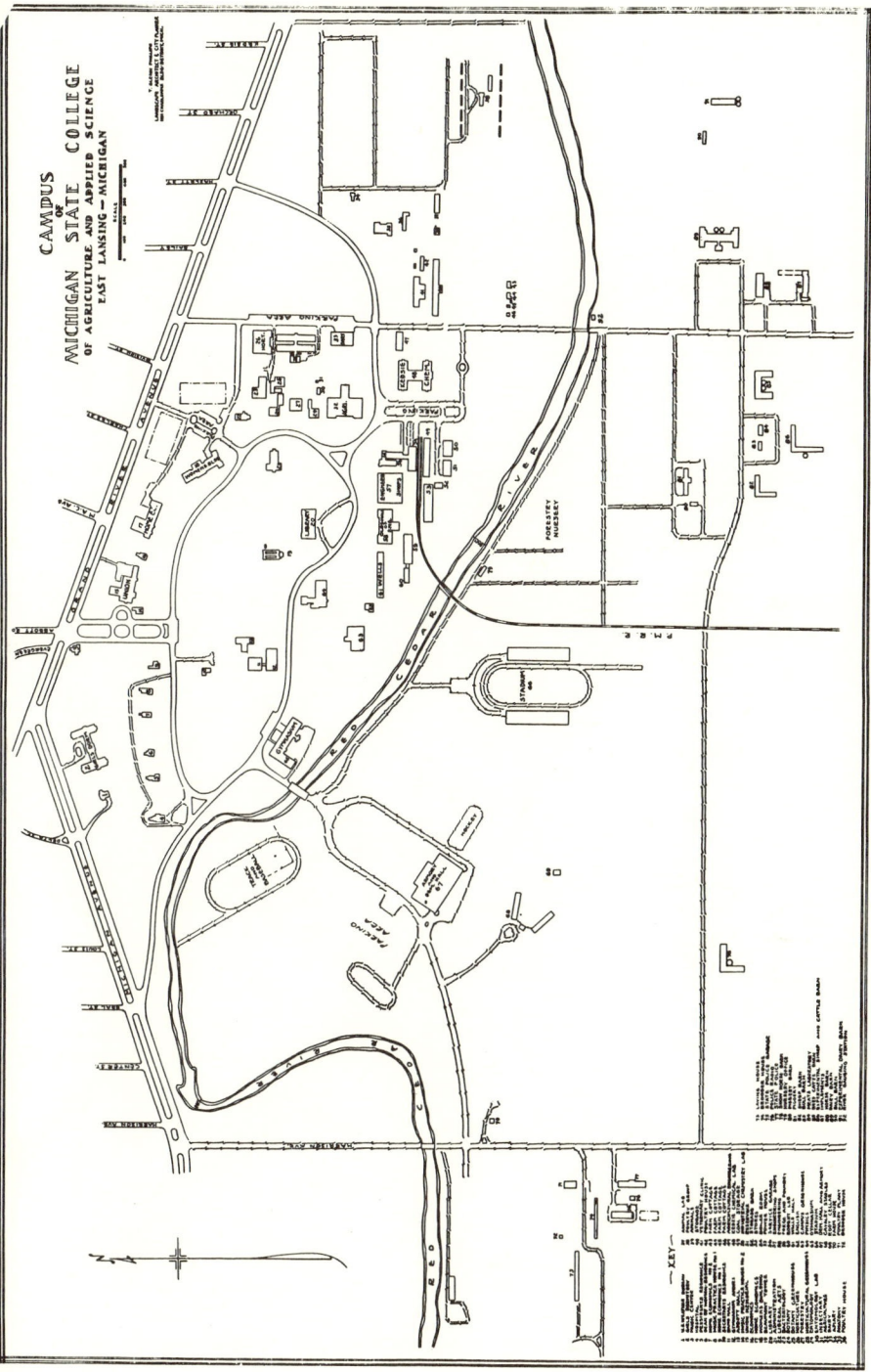

MICHIGAN STATE COLLEGE CAMPUS MAP, 1931 (*courtesy Michigan State University Archives and Historical Collections*)

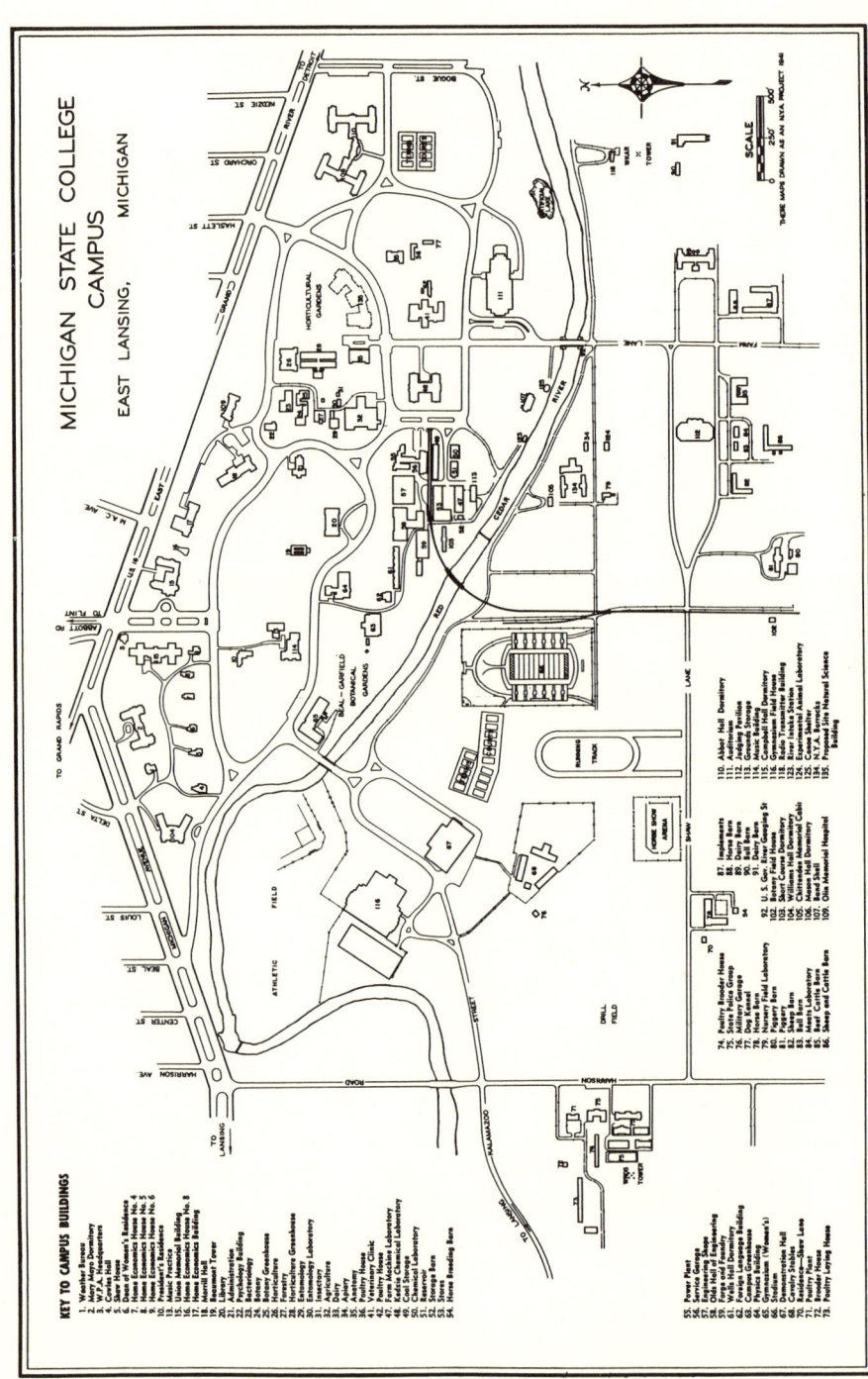

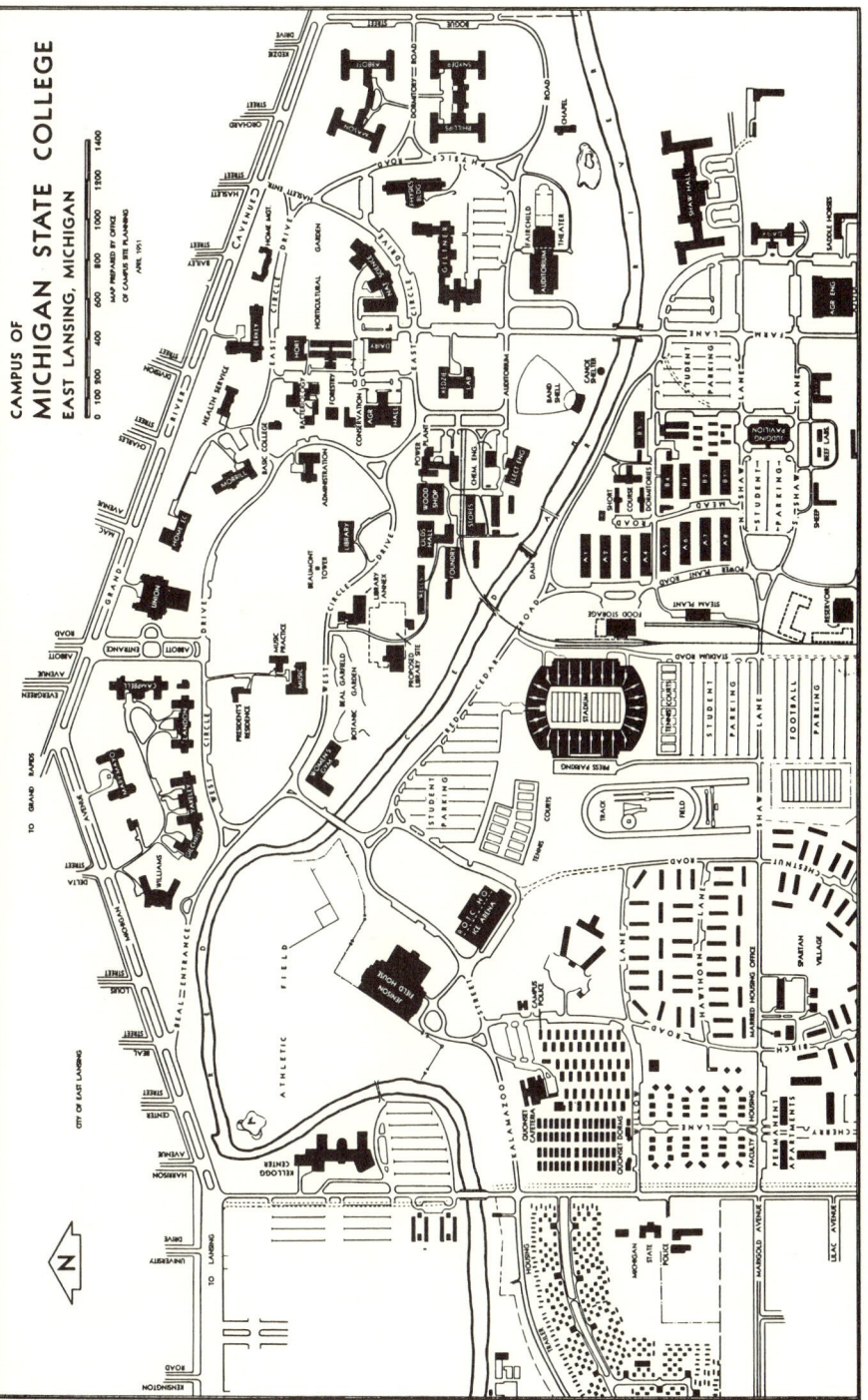

MICHIGAN STATE COLLEGE CAMPUS MAP, 1951 (*courtesy Michigan State University Archives and Historical Collections*)

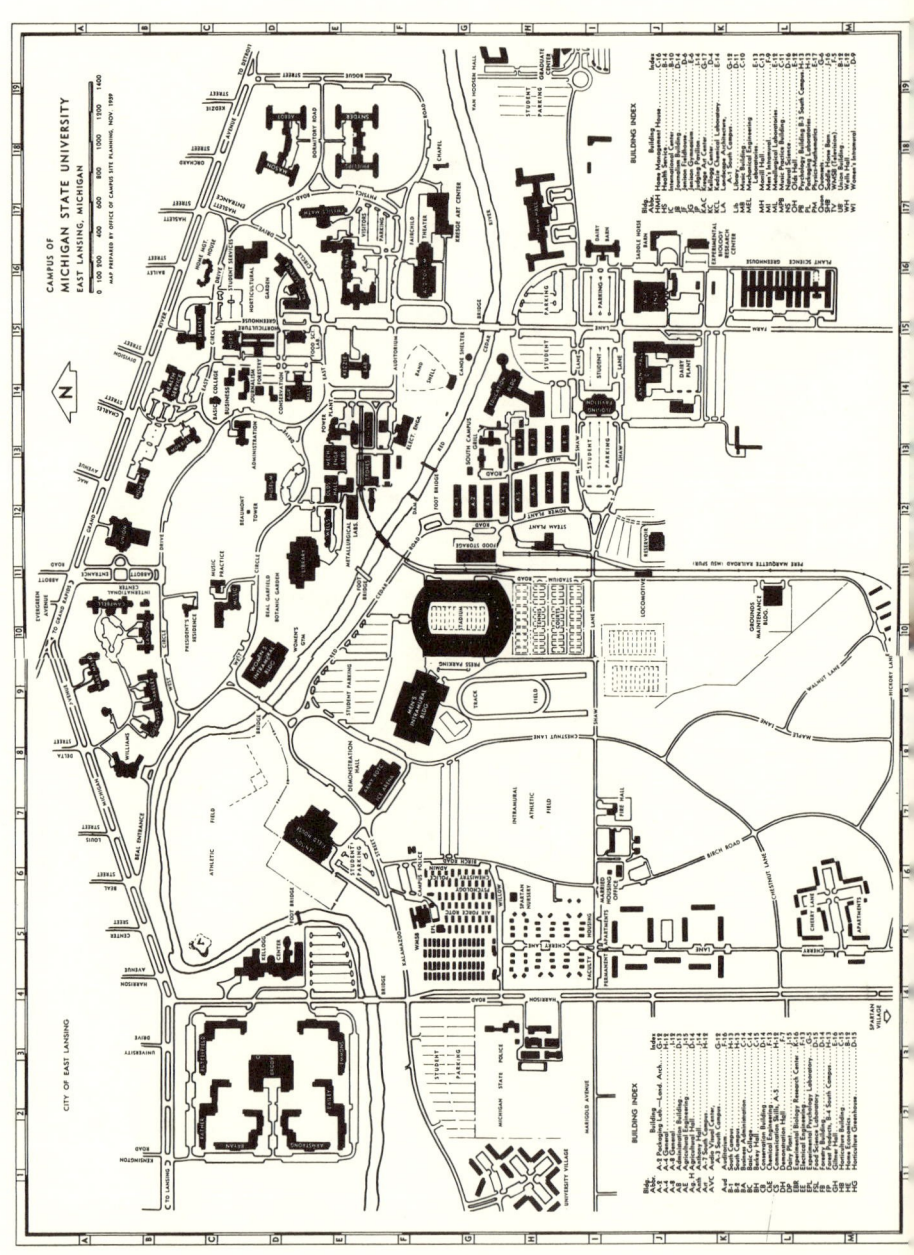

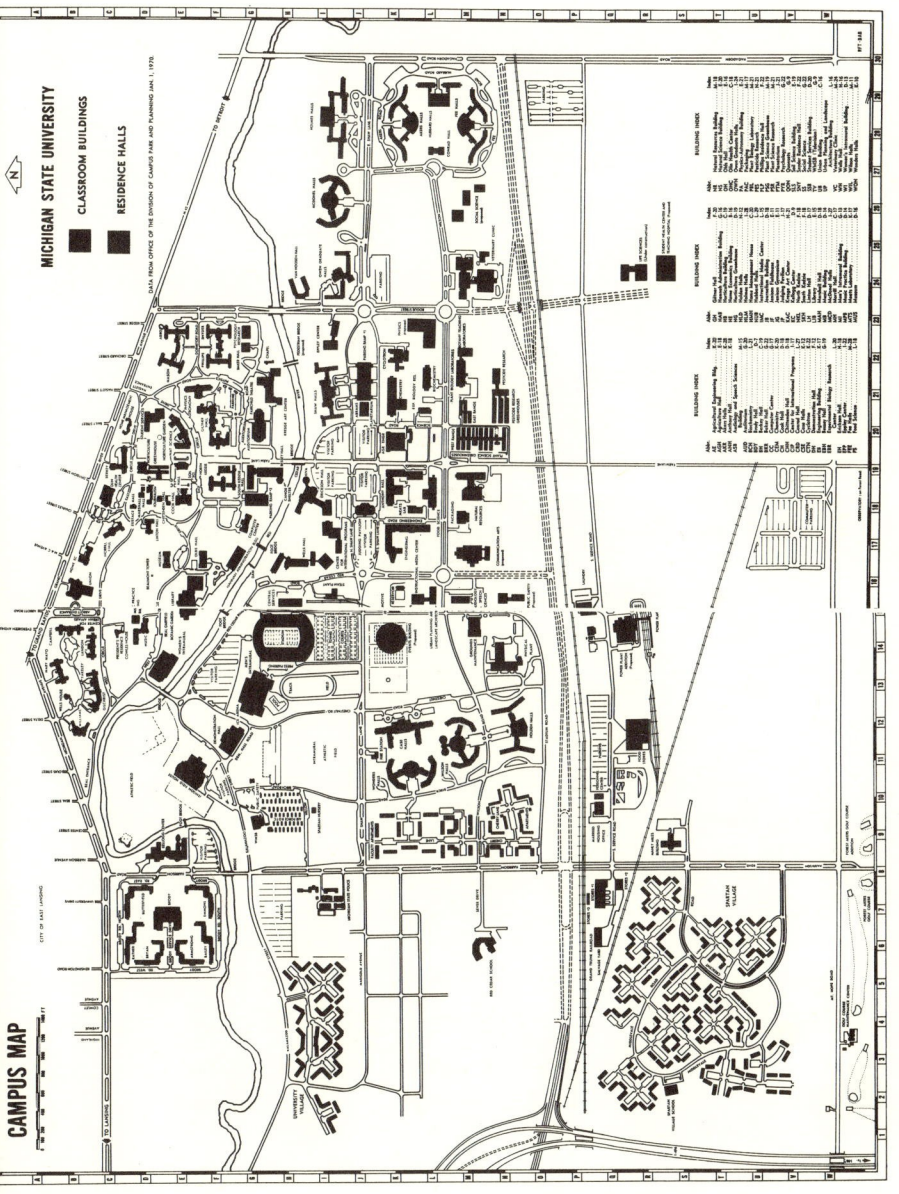

MICHIGAN STATE COLLEGE CAMPUS MAP, 1970 (courtesy Michigan State University Archives and Historical Collections)

torium, Jenison Field House, and the Music Building. These, plus the enlargement of the Union Building, more than doubled the space to be heated and lighted—from 14 million cubic feet to 31 million cubic feet—and so required the enlargement and modernization of the power plant. From 1935 to 1941, nearly $5 million in new facilities were added to the campus. The multipurpose concept, later pursued with more planning and greater vigor, was already evident. The auditorium, for example, provided extensive office space, a combined small theater and lecture hall, and an auditorium capable of seating nearly 5,000 persons, yet the building was so planned that its main floor served for such diverse activities as dances, Farmer's Week exhibits, and registration, and the basement housed the museum.

Construction funds were jealously guarded. In November 1940, when toilets were to be added to the agricultural engineering laboratory building, the board decided against adding them for women as too costly for the few women involved. There was an underlying implication that women really should not be in the building.

In 1941 the United States was plunged into World War II. The war required the services of many students, would-have-been students, and would-be students. Enrollment was 6,340 in the fall term of 1941, but by 1944 the civilian enrollment had decreased to 3,463, including only 1,153 men. Several contingents of trainees—army, air force, and some civilians assigned to the munitions plants in Lansing—were housed on campus with made-to-order educational programs.

The total physical plant, when Hannah became secretary, measured 1,055,519 square feet of floor space, of which 749,290 was primarily for academic use.[1] This included the library, offices, and teaching and experimental laboratories. With fall-term enrollment in 1935 at 4,006, there were 187 square feet of floor space per student. The 1941 fall-term enrollment of 6,390, when Hannah became president, resulted in a decrease of floor space per student to 133 square feet. Only three academic buildings were erected in those six Depression years.

By the end of the war, in 1946, with no new buildings of any kind and an enrollment increase to 13,282, the average amount of space per student was reduced to 64 square feet. To use every bit of space to the best advantage, classes started at seven o'clock in the morning, continued through the noon hour, and extended to ten o'clock at night. Even the unheated rooms in Beaumont Tower, housing the clock and carillon, were pressed into service for classes and offices.

---

1. Merrill Pierson prepared the original materials from which most of the next several pages is drawn.

Faculty members and students shivered in their overcoats during the winter. Because enrollment increased so rapidly, the space per student declined even further to 56 square feet before temporary army buildings could be procured for classroom use. To provide the physical facilities for MSU's expanding college population, the university in 1945 launched a postwar building program that would cost $50 million during the next ten years and more than $200 million in the next twenty years.

Governor Kelly and the legislators were well aware of the building needs of Michigan's publicly supported institutions and agreed on a "victory building program" that was carried out between 1949 and 1950. It was, by comparison with earlier years, a generous one, but at its close Michigan State had only 1,577,315 square feet of academic area for 16,243 students, or only 97 square feet per student. Considering new courses and programs, especially at the graduate level, space was still losing out in the race with rising enrollment and new programs.

Classroom space was only half the problem in accommodating the rapid influx of postwar students. They needed places in which to live and sleep, study and eat. One of the first emergency measures was an arrangement of cots and pallets on the gymnasium floor. Five hundred trailer houses were procured and installed on what was then the perimeter of the campus, to house married students and their families. Although uxorious, this housing was not luxurious.

Steel quonset huts obtained from the federal government were set up and divided into study-living space and bunk compartments, with each hut housing thirteen men. A "portable" army field hospital unit was obtained from the federal government and converted into a kitchen-dining unit for use by quonset hut residents.

Released barracks buildings were taken apart at their original sites, shipped in, and reassembled as family apartments. Fifty similar but individual prefab housing units, known as "flat-tops," were brought in and erected for use for new faculty people required by the growing enrollment. A common tale of that day was that this was "British Empire" housing, destined to provide homes for bombed-out Britishers, and that after being rejected by them, it was accepted by Michigan State. "Where there's a will, there's a way" represented the spirit at Michigan State College. Hannah's presence provided the will, and no one got in his way.

The first and quite early attempt to provide better accommodations for returning veterans was a dormitory planned for men. Steel was still available, but only by special rationing provisions and subject to the approval of local residents. Apparently fearful of losing the rental income from their back bedrooms and attics, residents of the college community voted against release of the steel. The project languished until structural steel became available on a nonrationed basis. Snyder-Phillips Hall emerged in 1947.

Encouraged by the success of borrowing for part of the cost of the prewar dormitories under the PWA program, plans were made for three new dormitories for women (Landon in 1947, Yakeley in 1948, and Gilchrist in 1948) and two for men, the larger of which would accommodate 1,000 at normal occupancy. Shaw Hall for men, at the time of its construction, was claimed to be the largest dormitory anywhere, then housing 1,500 men. Due to the great need, residents were requested to live three to a room instead of two. This crowding avoided rejection of applicants and yielded more fee income. It also expedited paying off the indebtedness. It did not then, as it would later with more critical students, generate complaints and demands for reduced charges.

Because of rapidly rising costs for materials and labor when price controls were removed, contractors were obliged to allow rather large margins of "profit" to protect themselves against costs they could not control or even accurately estimate. To deal with this situation, a cost-plus plan was used by the college. Instead of contracting for a certain cost figure, bids were based on estimates of cost plus fixed fee. The fee would not be increased in the event of cost overrun. This plan worked so successfully that postwar building was done on this basis for several years, until price stabilization occurred.

Bonds were issued and sold to provide the funds for construction of the dormitories. Net earnings of the dormitories were pledged for the bond interest and retirement installments. Since these bonds were tax free, the rate of interest was reasonable. There was never a default on any part of a debt that still amounted to $76.6 million at the close of the Hannah administration. Of that amount, $68.3 million was for dormitories and $8.3 million for other self-liquidating projects.

To allay public alarm over the cost of the many buildings being erected almost simultaneously, those financed by borrowed funds were so designated and marked by white signs lettered in green and placed in front of the several buildings with this inscription: "Constructed without expense to the public—financed by borrowed funds to be repaid by earnings from the building."

The signs made a point but also aroused criticism. Some people reacted against the obvious expectation that students and/or their parents would pay for the buildings. Others, including some legislators, resented the implication that the state had failed to provide facilities. A few grumbled about charging to state-appropriated funds the maintenance and operational costs of buildings that were earning money.

Legislatures in Michigan and elsewhere have been traditionally reluctant to finance dormitories. Many members of the legislature apparently believe that students can find places to live in adjacent residential areas or that they can enter other colleges and universities. Many local residents believed that they should. But back rooms and attics no longer met the need. Student admissions would obviously be severely limited by the lack of either classroom space or dormitory facilities. The successful financing of Mary Mayo Hall for women in 1931, by pledging revenue from the dormitory operation, inspired the similar financing plan for all the later ones as well as for other Michigan campuses. Students residing in residence halls ultimately would pay for them and also for their maintenance, as was demanded by the legislature. The legislature came to regard these as being college projects, while the financing of classroom buildings and libraries were accepted as legislative projects. The biggest surge in enrollments and new buildings was yet to come. The need for dormitories and the need for classrooms, library, and laboratories go hand in hand.

Legislators were awed by Hannah's November 1945 statement of a $10,843,200 building program. There arose in the legislature a feeling that the cost of utilities—heat and light generated by the university power plants—should be charged against the dormitories. This practice was initiated in the late 1940s and incorporated into each subsequent budget request. When residence halls containing classrooms were built in the 1960s, the legislature required that utility and maintenance charges be allocated on the basis of the ratio of classroom space to residence hall space. The multipurpose role of this space was ignored although a formal definition of dual-purpose building space as "academic space located in a building administered by Housing and Food Services" and the precise number of "academic square feet" came to be required. The fact that this creative and innovative approach reduced the requests for classroom and laboratory space was also ignored. Residence hall accounts were billed $1.2 million. And $300,000 was transferred to the general fund for cleaning halls and maintenance. When, much later, baghouse filters, at a cost of approximately $10 million, had to be installed on the main power plant to reduce air pollution, the residence halls were charged an appropriate share.

The years from 1949 to 1969 witnessed a phenomenal increase in enrollment, from 16,243 to 42,541, and a corresponding increase in the number of buildings, both academic and residential. It was something of an innovation to build apartments for married students, a new need required principally by three factors: (1) the older age of students because of military service, (2) a longer educational period due to the increase of graduate work and advanced degrees, and (3) an increase in individuals returning for advanced degrees.

The construction of the Kellogg Center for Continuing Education, to serve groups coming to the campus for special educational projects, was financed by grants from the Kellogg Foundation for its initial construction in 1951 and an expansion in 1955 and again in 1959. This represented a commitment to continuing education.

Success in football, plus the expanded student enrollment led to the enlargement of the stadium by 27,250 seats in 1948; 9,000 more seats in 1956; and 15,000 more in 1957, to a total capacity of about 76,000.

The dormitory capacity grew to 18,500 at normal occupancy rates. Actually, many more students were housed but crowded. Apartments for married students increased to 2,200. Some people smilingly referred to John Hannah's "edifice complex"—but no one laughed at his foresightedness. Despite all of the academic buildings added to the plant, the number of square feet per student at the end of President Hannah's tenure was 125, less than the 133 that existed immediately before World War II and substantially less than the 226 in 1932 at the beginning of the Great Depression, when laboratory facilities were much less complex.

The time lapse from planning for new facilities to obtaining funds and completing construction could be several years, especially when state capital fund appropriations were required. More than one department falling just one priority level short of funding in a particular year shook off its disappointment by anticipating deferred gratification in the subsequent year. But priorities frequently underwent changes from year to year because of pressures for enrollment, administrative reconsiderations, or, especially, the "saleability" of a facility to the current crop of legislators. The Communication Arts Building first appeared on the wish list when the architect for a new Communication Arts Building was named on July 19, 1957. The building, after recurrent replanning, was finally occupied in 1981.

Delays brought new chairs and sometimes new departmental organizations, requiring changes in plans. Many new facilities underwent modifications before or following occupancy because of shifting needs. Inflation also forced changes because the allocated funds were inadequate to meet the original plans. Wings might be clipped; a top floor might be lopped or left unfinished. In Berkey Hall in 1945, plastering over cement blocks was omitted in favor of direct applications of paint. The result was effective in appearance as well as in cost. The original plan was to have five floors in the Hannah Administration Building; the number was reduced to four. Since the plan had included offices for board members, many persons later felt that the loss of the fifth floor was actually an unanticipated benefit. Experience had suggested that board members should not be encouraged to be on campus except at board meetings.

In another building, inflation forced elimination of a wing. Departments had to adjust. When unexpectedly low bids came in, the wing was reinstated. Elation changed quickly to dejection when the previously prospective tenants found that the added space had been assigned to others.

When Erickson Hall was being completed in 1957, air conditioning was sacrificed to inflation and was not added until seventeen years later. In Michigan, air conditioning tended to be regarded as a luxury useful only a few days of the summer. It was much easier to sell air conditioning for the computer, for temperature-controlled research, or for animals than for people.

Each new facility involved occupants of offices in a series of moves, each of which usually required extensive refurbishing, and perhaps extensive remodeling. This could, over time, take an individual on an extensive tour of the campus. One retired professor, veteran of something more than fifty years, recalled having offices at various times in Olds Hall, Morrill Hall, the Union Building, Linton Hall, Berkey Hall, Demonstration Hall, Eustace Hall, Erickson Hall, Hannah Administration Building, Fee Hall—and several different offices in six of these buildings. These moves necessarily had a domino-like effect, with a delay anywhere in the sequence evoking frustration and causing further delays along the line. When one department—informed of an immediate short-term relocation before moving into a new, yet uncompleted building—rejected the intermediate move, the ire of numerous persons was aroused.

The moves did, however, encourage interdisciplinary exchange. The move of a department might need to be spread over several months, thereby bringing together individuals of different disciplines in a manner that would not otherwise occur. In a few cases of large departments, members were located in facilities literally miles apart. However, this circumstance was less alarming and surprising at Michigan State than it would have been in many universities. Extension, continuing education, living-learning facilities in residence halls, residential colleges, institutes, and centers at various times had encouraged commingling of individuals and disciplines. Some retirees with extensive moving experiences recalled them with pleasure. This was true even with some who had been housed in the temporary structures imported to the campus after World War II.

The last of the temporary housing for faculty and students was phased out in 1961. Despite all of the expansion and moving, some of the other facilities remained for years. As of the fall of 1984, there were two World War II quonsets still in use, although the relocation of the television station to the Communication Arts and Sciences Building in 1981 led to the removal of most of these structures by 1982.

### PROPERTY ACQUISITION

Land acquisition was an important item on Hannah's agenda. It was evident that increased enrollment and the consequent expansion of the campus and facilities would require many acres of land previously devoted to agriculture and Experiment Station research. Edward G. Hacker and a representative of the Michigan Real Estate Association approached Hannah early in 1944 to discuss the possibility of a course in real estate education. At the close of this discussion Hannah suggested that Hacker, head of the realty company by that name, might assist the college in acquiring properties adjacent to the campus. During the subsequent years of acquiring properties, the right to eminent domain was never exercised. Hannah was often impatient at the delay but insisted on persuasion and negotiations. From 1935 to 1969, MSU acquired 3,698 acres, including 181 separate parcels of land—a nearly continuous block of 5,000 acres, two miles wide and three and one-half miles long. In the early 1980s Hannah would view with regret and even some anguish the actions of another president and board in selling off segments of this heritage. They had not learned, as he had, that acquiring land is a long and difficult process and relinquishing it in a moment all too easy.

Building problems were not the sole outcome of the school's growing pains. The same sudden and substantial surge in enrollment required more staff, more supplies and equipment, more fuel for heat and light, and more money for all these as inflation began. Student fees furnished almost as much as two-thirds the amount appropriated by the legislature. In the 1947–48 budget, students' fees were projected at $4,729,769, whereas the legislative appropriation was only $6,112,221 for the general college fund operation, the Agricultural Experiment Station, and the Cooperative Extension Service. The year before, when fall-term enrollment jumped from 5,284 in 1945 to 13,282 in 1946, it had been impossible to construct a balanced budget, and the year began with an anticipated deficit of $680,625. The budget books had been bound in red by the chance decision of the binders. But Hannah pointed out to the finance committee of the legislature that the unprecedented rapid enrollment increase would unavoidably result in a deficit budget. The explanation was accepted by the legislature as an aftermath of the war, and a special appropriation was made to balance the budget.

The college/university never had a more able or convincing person representing the institution to the governor, the state comptroller, and the legislative committees than John Hannah. His intimate knowledge of even the smallest detail; his forthrightness; his integrity; his impressive, persuasive, and yet succinct presentations backed by evidence and sound judgment were extremely helpful in supporting requests for operating funds and construction appropriations. Nevertheless, it was a constant challenge to seek appropriations from the legislature to accomplish both "catch-up" and "keep-up" increases. This was compounded by the need for funding new programs, although many of these were financed by dollars received for enrollment increases. It was generally found easier to acquire money for specific purposes than some influential clientele found justified and attractive rather than to acquire an overall increase in a general appropriation. Labor and industrial relations, the Highway Traffic Safety Center, the Oakland branch of the university, elimination of fire hazards, and several war-related projects were examples of line items, each of which had to be "sold" to the legislature. Such special requests were made reluctantly for they encouraged accountability audits, thereby compromising constitutional autonomy. However, the special requests tested the prospects of continuing support and could usually be included in the total general fund a year or two later.

The Agricultural Experiment Station and the Extension Service had been traditionally budgeted as parts of the agricultural program. In 1941, when Hannah became president, they were parts of a total appropriation of $2.5 million. In 1948 Hannah requested that the funding for these two activities be made as line items, thereby differentiating between these applied research and service functions and the purely teaching activities. The dean of agriculture and the division directors were given greater influence and responsibility in promoting their respective activities. In addition, a more accurate figure was established for comparing the Michigan State appropriation with that of the University of Michigan. The now more obvious disparity called for more equitable treatment.

There were other benefits to the college in the establishment of separate appropriations for the Experiment Station and Cooperative

Extension. Those working within these two units could not accuse the college administration of discriminatory treatment if their respective programs were not financed at the desired level. Furthermore, line-item appropriations decreased the probability of administrative or board reductions by presidents or deans not strongly committed to the land-grant philosophy. Reduction or elimination of these particular line items seemed unlikely in view of the traditions and politics involved.

Salary levels of the college staff were low, as they had been for many years, when Hannah became president. He knew that they had to be raised in order to be competitive with other educational institutions and with industry, especially in science and engineering. Without adequate salaries, there would be little hope of increasing the effectiveness and stature of the college.

In making and justifying his budget request to the governor and the legislature, Hannah used tables of average salary statistics prepared to show how Michigan State compared with other similar regional schools. The unfavorable comparison suggested the need for more generous appropriations. So did the charts that showed that, in all four academic ranks, the effective take-home pay in 1952–53 was less than in 1939–40, because of income tax withholding and inflation. One of the greatest aids in getting additional funds for salary increases was the autonomy enjoyed by the State Civil Service Commission. Under law, the commission was authorized to set rates for compensation of civil service employees without regard to the availability of funds. If necessary, vacant positions were left unfilled to keep within the allocations. The result was that the legislature usually appropriated enough money for the state departments to cover most of the increases. Otherwise, the legislature would have been in the unpopular position of causing layoffs of civil service state employees or seriously understaffing governmental operations. By common consent, Michigan State was allotted about the same percentage of increase for academic salaries as those of civil service administrative and clerical employees. Yet this did not help to catch up.

Michigan State perennially argued for as much money per student as was appropriated for the University of Michigan. The argument, pressed by Michigan State in 1968, was that increases in enrollment in all twelve of Michigan's colleges and universities from 1960 to 1968 totaled 94,452, with Michigan State accounting for 24 percent of the increase, more than twice that of the University of Michigan. The gradual increase in graduate and professional school enrollments was also transforming Michigan State from a primarily undergraduate university to one much more comparable to the University of Michigan. But Michigan State found that these statistics were subject to many interpretations, not all of which supported its contention. The mysterious but prestigious concept of quality and reputation played an elusive role.

## NEW FACILITIES

Professor Laurence L. Quill, who succeeded Professor Arthur J. Clark as head of the chemistry department, commented that in the early expansion of the institution the central administration tended to think in terms of expanding existing facilities rather than planning new ones. When called into a discussion of planning for the expansion of the Kedzie Chemical Laboratory, he argued that neither the location nor the existing facilities and equipment were adequate for what the discipline of chemistry had become. He also pointed out that the expanding natural science program in the Basic College would soon require facilities that would use that building completely. He insisted that a new chemistry building and a new site were the only answers, and planning was immediately begun. With the growth and size of the institution and the change in its character came recognition of the necessity of placing more responsibility for facility planning on department heads. Both the new chemistry building and the new biochemistry building were completed and occupied by 1963.

The dependence on departmental chairs and faculty in planning facilities resulted in expensive, last-minute alterations because of changes in personnel or oversights in planning. Hannah's view generally was that the efforts of the faculty, department chairs, and deans were too important to be constrained or thwarted by dissatisfaction with inadequate facilities. But last-minute changes did become common.

Funds for new facilities came from many sources, as indicated in the accompanying table. Residence halls and other income-producing facilities have been sustained by self-liquidating borrowed funds. Instructional facilities have been financed by gifts and state capital appropriations. Administrative and library facilities have been supported by the state. The Kellogg Foundation has repeatedly and generously granted specific funds for continuing education and extension facilities and programs, including those at Gull Lake.

Kellogg—including W. K. Kellogg himself, the Kellogg Company, and the Kellogg Foundation—has also assisted the university as a whole over many years. Major grants for extension, continuing education, and health programs have been previously mentioned. But there were also many smaller gifts or grants from the Kellogg complex that

Revenues for New Plant Construction
at Michigan State University

|         | Borrowed Funds | Gifts and Other Funds | State Appropriation |
|---------|----------------|-----------------------|---------------------|
| 1954–55 | $   3,500,000  | . . .                 | . . .               |
| 1955–56 | 15,125,784     | . . .                 | $ 8,120,000         |
| 1956–57 | 2,420,000      | $     80,000          | . . .               |
| 1957–58 | 10,220,000     | 150,000               | 400,000             |
| 1958–59 | 13,325,000     | 2,170,000             | 5,900,000           |
| 1959–60 | 900,000        | 600,000               | . . .               |
| 1960–61 | 3,200,000      | 1,270,000             | . . .               |
| 1961–62 | 12,400,000     | 2,311,500             | 6,600,000           |
| 1962–63 | 11,800,000     | 1,572,000             | . . .               |
| 1963–64 | 2,825,000      | 2,880,000             | 195,000             |
| 1964–65 | 18,850,000     | 13,925,000            | 6,000,000           |
| 1965–66 | 15,075,000     | 2,995,000             | 14,140,000          |
| 1966–67 | 12,416,667     | 4,398,733             | 12,016,600          |
| 1967–68 | . . .          | 4,500,000             | . . .               |
| 1968–69 | 1,425,000      | 1,525,000             | 5,600,000           |
| 1969–70 | 1,509,300      | 4,413,400             | . . .               |
| 1970–71 | 125,000        | 1,107,600             | . . .               |
| 1971–72 | . . .          | 7,850,000             | 6,400,000           |
| Totals  | $125,116,751   | $54,748,233           | $65,371,600         |

were highly significant in the development of the total program. Examples follow:

1941  $200 from W. K. Kellogg for Dr. Pirnie to study wild turkeys

1941  $1,000 from W. K. Kellogg toward the cost of $3,000 for the log cabin at the Kellogg Forestry Tract

1941  $5,500 from the Kellogg Company to support dog ration research

1942  $4,000 from W. K. Kellogg for a poultry brooder house at Kellogg Farm

1943  $3,500 from Kellogg to remodel the calf and dairy barn

1945  $4,500 from W. K. Kellogg for the Group Service Building at the bird sanctuary

1945  $7,500 from W. K. Kellogg for a facility at the Kellogg Forestry Tract

Recovered overhead or indirect cost funds financed numerous facilities, including the International Center. Grants from agencies of the federal government have supported new research facilities. Student fees have been applied in building such facilities as the Student Union and the Health Center. Several of the large items in the budget's "gifts and other funds" reflect the indirect costs deposited initially in MSU accounts.

### BUILDING NAMES AND DESIGNATIONS

On a rapidly growing campus, the naming and renaming of buildings is a way to honor individuals and attract potential donors. From MSU's origins until relatively recent years, there was no definitive policy in the naming of buildings. During most of the Hannah years, Hannah himself was central in selecting names although he regularly consulted others, including board members and the institutional historian. Board members of long standing and influence constituted one ready source. Forest H. Akers, Clark L. Brody, W. G. Armstrong, William Berkey, Stephen S. Nisbet, Matilda R. Wilson, and Sarah VanHoosen Jones were recognized because of their significant contributions to the development of the university, including in some cases extensive financial gifts. Previous presidents Theophilus C. Abbot, Jonathan L. Snyder, Robert C. Kedzie, Kenyon L. Butterfield, Robert S. Shaw, and John Hannah himself have been honored. Hannah felt somewhat embarrassed in moving as president into a building named in his honor, and perhaps because of his comments the board has since decided that names of living individuals should not be used in christening facilities.

Although unverified, it may well be that more deans have been honored at Michigan State by having buildings named after them than on any other university campus. Deans who were thus distinguished included Ernest L. Anthony (Agriculture), Ernst A. Bessey (Graduate Dean), Claude S. Bryan (Veterinary Medicine), and Howard C. Rather (Basic College). Other administrators similarly honored included Karl H. McDonel, long-time secretary under Hannah; Registrars Elida Yakeley and Robert S. Linton; and the first full-time physician, Richard M. Olin. Linda E. Landon, librarian and the first woman instructor, was also honored as was Mary Mayo, an early extension worker. Other faculty members recognized included Albert J. Cook, Alfred J. Chittenden, Louise H. Campbell, Harry J. Eustace, George T. Fairchild, Maude Gilchrist, Charles Edward Marshall, and Manly Miles (first professor of scientific agriculture in the United States).

Several of these names appear on buildings that had existed for many years before being named. In one case, it turned out, to the surprise of the president and faculty, that the individual was still alive. Some of his students proposed that there be a rededication of the building at spring commencement. For a building some eighty years old, this seemed inappropriate to Hannah, and the ceremony was averted.

Founding fathers Bela Hubbard, Hezekiah G. Wells, and John C. Holmes have buildings named after them. Other buildings and facilities are named after major donors: John W. Beaumont, Forest H. Akers, Albert H. and Sarah A. Case, Talbert and Leota Abrams, Eugene C. Eppley, Harry A. and Jessie T. Fee, Frederick Cowles Jenison, W. K. Kellogg, Floyd W. Owen, R. E. Olds, Matilda R. and Alfred C. Wilson, Wallace K. and Grace Wonders. Former coaches thus honored include Hugh "Duffy" Daugherty (football building), John Kobs (baseball field), Ralph Young (track), and Clarence L. Munn (ice skating arena). Politicians and statesmen have received relatively little attention in the naming of facilities at Michigan State. Stephens T. Mason, the first governor of Michigan, and Justin S. Morrill, the progenitor of the Morrill Act, are the prominent exceptions.

The naming and renaming of buildings has been a source of amusement at times. The designation of buildings by function has many advantages but in a growing institution can result in numerous changes and some confusion. A building initially constructed to house horticulture was, as its functions changed, successively designated as Liberal Arts, Philosophy and Psychology, Basic College, and finally Eustace Hall after an early horticulturist, Harry J. Eustace. Each shift in function also resulted in considerable remodeling, and it took years before the residual odor of early work on pickles was finally eliminated. Despite MSU expertise with hatcheries, there was also a case of premature counting of chickens. A facility was named after a former staff member who had prospered in the world of business. The expectation was obvious but in vain. After some years and extensive additions, the name was changed.

A football stadium, seating approximately 25,000 people, was built in 1923. In the list of facilities, the number of square feet and cubic feet supplied thereby were both zero: there was no *enclosed* space. Likewise, the cost per square foot is not reported. Later additions brought the available enclosed square feet to more than 200,000, including press box and storage space under the stadium. Data on space utilization in the stadium have not been widely circulated. However, utilization on five or six Saturdays in the fall has been widely reported and has provided both an index of football excellence and the basis for continuing or terminating the appointment of the football coach. For years, the use of the stadium for spring commencement, unless it rained heavily, yielded several hours of distinctly academic usage. That use so impressed some guests that a new African university included a stadium as one of its early buildings.

When facilities are designated by function, names can also be descriptive and sometimes humorously provocative. This is especially true on the campus of a land-grant university, which differs in some respects from other private or public universities. The following list is indicative: Judging Pavilion (1938), Swine Research Center (1951), Dairy Loose-Housing Group (1951), Pure Bred Beef Cattle Teaching Center (1953), Meats Laboratory (1955), Grain Dryer (1955), Plant Science Head House (1956), Dairy Loose-Housing Group Milk Parlor (1961), Swine Research Gestation Building (1961), and Animal Waste Dehydration Shed (1965). One might readily guess that the Judging Pavilion relates to judging cattle rather than to courts, although the intervention of judges into university matters is becoming more common. Loose-housing was and is perfectly clear to those concerned with dairy cattle, but to others might conjure up activist student demands concerning residence hall assignments in the 1960s. A head house might suggest a museum exhibiting head-hunter trophies but actually refers to the workroom or preparation room attached to greenhouses.

Other facilities not apparently having profound academic implications might exist on many campuses and elsewhere as well. These are exemplified at Michigan State by the River Intake Station (1940), River Water Research Laboratory (1946), Memorial Chapel (1952), Parking Ramps (1963), Baseball Toilet and Storage Building (1966), Salvage Building (1966), Laundry Building (1968), Radioactive Waste Facility (1972), Driver Training Range Garage (1974), Pathological Incineration (1975), and Coal Car Thawing Shed (1976). These buildings reflect in their names the increasing range of functions and thus facilities required in the modern university. Pathological Incineration is not a crematory although it serves somewhat the same purpose. The Coal Car Thawing Shed applies heat to thaw coal to generate heat to thaw people. In addition, the Lifelong Education Center, the existence of two nursery schools, and the Willed Body Program demonstrate the acceptance by the university of cradle-to-the-grave responsibilities.

Another quick perusal of the list of university facilities yields the following: pole barn; box barn (house, garage, corn crib); round roof barn; seven bus stop shelters; Bush Dwelling; Clever Dwelling; Hall Dwelling; Hicks Dwelling; Intramural Recreative Sports; Parson's

Dwelling; Wells Hall (third of successive buildings by that name); and Well House (Nos. 1–28).

As Michigan State grew, it took on many of the characteristics of a large business or municipality. The self-supporting dormitories and food services and a number of other divisions had to "make" their payrolls. Pledges of millions of dollars, due on residence halls notes and bonds, had to be met on time. The nonacademic phase of running a large university became big business.

The City of East Lansing furnished fire protection for many years without charge. Then came a time when East Lansing was no longer primarily a living area for faculty people, and a plan of shared cost was instituted. A fire station was erected on the campus at college expense but was staffed, equipped, and managed by the East Lansing Fire Department on a shared-cost basis. Fire equipment and personnel from both stations are available at any location when needed. For a long time police protection for the campus was also provided by the City of East Lansing on a shared-cost basis. But as traffic control problems increased and police duties became somewhat different in the two areas, the institution set up its own department. The two separate units work together amicably and effectively as needed.

Although Michigan State had always had its own water supply and storage system, it maintains a connection with East Lansing for emergencies. There have been occasions of assistance in both directions. Likewise, the institution generates its own electricity but has interconnection with the local system for emergencies.

As more students have come to reside in the community, acquire voting rights and use them, a rather different relationship has developed between "town and gown." The university no longer exerts the control over behavior that characterized an earlier era. Block parties and "Cedarfests" get out of hand, much to the dismay of mature members of the East Lansing community. Older homes near the campus, many owned by faculty members seeking extra income, are inhabited by an excessive number of students and surrounded by erratically parked cars. Many of these houses are poorly maintained, unattractive, and destructive of property values in the immediate area. The student campus and the faculty town and the easy cooperative interaction of the Hannah years no longer exist. The year 1969 marked the end of an era in many ways.

SPECIAL ADMISSIONS, SERVICES,
AND PROBLEMS

No one knows when the first handicapped students were admitted to Michigan State. Part of the uncertainty rests with the definition.

Special services were provided in the late 1930s to blind students through a contract with the State Services for the Blind. Some wheelchair users, including nonveterans, were admitted in the 1940s. Assistance was also available to students with speech and hearing difficulties through the speech department.

In addition, students with low high school grades, inadequate reading ability, deprived social backgrounds, or below-average intelligence were regarded as handicapped. In a sense, the land-grant college was created to offer them a more appropriate education than they would otherwise receive. Michigan State accepted some such students from the beginning and attempted to provide remedial experiences. Hannah repeatedly urged faculty, administrators, and admissions officers to make special efforts to attract and serve such individuals.

Race, educational opportunities, and social background are interrelated. Hannah recognized this and directed that special efforts be made to attract disadvantaged students from the Detroit area. An Office of Supportive Services was created, and a Development Program was launched. Fifty-five students were accepted in an Upward Bound Program in 1966.

The number of severely handicapped students seeking a college education had been small, and hence each could be individually accommodated. But by the late 1960s, facility accessibility and program adaptations were becoming serious problems. Barrier-free access on the campus required long-time planning and extensive funding. It also required a rationale and a value commitment.

Faced with a particular case—be it accessibility to the facilities and programs in the arts, in science, or in medicine—it is difficult to deny an individual admission or access on grounds of cost, competency, or need. Need includes personal dignity and autonomy. It is clear, however, that resources are limited and that allocation to one program or person's need denies resources to others. Just as admission of poorly prepared or marginally competent individuals requires extensive remedial or developmental services and ultimately some reduction in other resources, so admission of and adaptation to unusual physical conditions and characteristics or unusual talents bring responsibilities, costs, and opportunities.

A college or university is often in an especially exposed and ambiguous position because it seeks rare talents. Seven-foot basketball players are sought, admitted, supplied with eight-foot beds, first-class airline seats, training tables, and faculty or Honors College student tutors. Students of diverse talent in music, art, athletics, and other areas are contacted, contracted, and counted. In some of these cases the institution benefits more than the students. But most educational institutions do not exist for self-glorification by accumulating talent. They justify the search for talent as a means of enhancing service and quality, anticipating that that service and talent will attract funds.

There is a still larger problem. A democratic society encourages and even enforces a wide range of services in its institutions, but is generally unwilling and unable to foot the bill. The long-range result is twofold: (1) institutional performances are always strained and reduced toward mediocrity, and (2) an accumulating debt is passed on to future generations, thereby handicapping them and their potential for development. The answer to this dilemma cannot rest with an individual institution. Yet it takes the brunt of criticism for doing too much or too little. So it has been at MSU.

## PROJECT ACCESS

Although Project Access, as it has been called, did not appear until 1975, well after Hannah had departed, the first efforts at planning new construction or altering existing facilities for access by the handicapped dated from 1967. The use of year-end balances for such projects was an effective and defensible means of financing much of this activity. From 1967 to 1973 or 1974, most projects were remedial, amounting simply to constructing concrete ramps of grade-level access to some of the busier campus buildings. These early alterations were generally made in response to requests from individual students, faculty, staff, or members of the public. The total cost has been estimated at $100,000. Either the operating units or the secretary's office funded the work. In addition to these efforts, Michigan State had also been complying with early state regulations governing new facility design for handicappers. Through 1974, at least ten buildings with at least some degree of accessibility were erected.

A largely remedial series of alterations was initiated by the MSU Board of Trustees in April 1974 with an allocation of $65,000, but the funds almost immediately expanded to about $300,000 when the federal government provided matching funds. Project Access addressed several aspects of university activity in many buildings as follows:

Resident Halls—eliminated barriers in living accommodations for eight persons in Case Hall and four persons in Owen Graduate Hall and modified two public restrooms in each building

Married Housing—eliminated barriers in five Cherry Lane student apartments

Kellogg Center—eliminated barriers in four guest rooms

Interior Ramps—constructed new interior ramps at both Morrill Hall and Kellogg Center

Restrooms—eliminated barriers in two public restrooms each in Kellogg Center, the Library, Bessey Hall, and Intramural West (including one shower/locker area in the latter)

Transportation—purchased one small bus adapted for the handicapper transportation program

Outdoors—constructed concrete path-ramps and grade-level entrances at approximately fifty-five locations, facilitating building entry and cross-campus mobility

Subsequent to the expiration of the matching grant, the university—at an additional cost of about $68,000—completed "Phase I" of Project Access with reconstruction of the broad, brick-paved main entrance to the Natural Sciences Building at grade level, several grade-level entries to the Engineering Building, Bessey Hall, Owen Hall and several other residence halls, and the Biochemistry Building.

In subsequent years additional expenditures have been made for building approaches, path-ramps, parking and signs, elevators and doors, restrooms, crossing signals, translators, and special equipment. The extensive construction of the Hannah era required and still requires expensive remodeling if complete access is to be attained. Hannah's foresight generally was brilliant, but this development was unforeseen. The efforts to comply surely accord with his view that "only people are important." But recognition of that requires facilities related to the functions in which those people want and need to engage, and this all comes back to the question of who pays.

# PART V
*Perceptions and Prospects*

# 16
# Michigan State and
# Hannah in Retrospect

This and the following chapter are very different from preceding ones. This chapter reviews the successes and the problems of the Hannah years and attempts to reach some specific insights about the land-grant mission and how it has been maintained. Michigan State is the land-grant institution in a state that also has a widely renowned state university, the University of Michigan. This situation poses a somewhat different problem than when the state university and land-grant mission are combined in a single university. The subsequent chapter considers the future of the land-grant university, the subject of many papers, discussions, and seminars in recent years and not only significant for these institutions but also for the nation and the world. Some insights can be provided by reviewing the Michigan State experience.

The land-grant institutions originated out of the conviction that the lot of the common people could be improved by seeking and applying knowledge to the immediate and essential aspects of living. The classics and religion that had previously dominated in the founding of colleges in the United States offered little of relevance or of immediate benefit to this group.

The clientele that was to be served by the new institutions did not demand colleges dedicated to their needs; many resisted the idea that the efforts of an educational institution could be beneficial to farmers and the rural population. In fact, the land-grant college experiment station and extension activities could immediately benefit only those who accepted and used them. And that group was but a fraction of the total. Not infrequently, however, the changes made by the progressive farmer were later adopted by others. Successful examples of new practices attract attention and emulation.

The services of the early land-grant college were by no means focused entirely on increased production, although this certainly provided personal satisfaction and more money while simultaneously serving the needs of the expanding nation. But increased production could lead to overproduction and to problems of preservation, distribution, and consumption. Problems and, hence, the services needed changed with time and with the increasing complexities of society. Indeed, maintaining an institutional flexibility to adapt to changing needs became one of the timely and timeless problems of the land-grant institution. Structures, organizations, programs, and even people successful in a timely mission may resist or complicate further change. Ends and means to achieve those ends are seldom completely separable.

Other timely and timeless problems relate to improving the quality of life. Clothing can be attractive as well as warm, can be uniform or individual. Food can be nutritious, tasteful, attractive, and reasonably priced. Art and beauty need not be limited to the museums and the well-to-do. Music can be more than hymns in church and symphonies or operas in the concert hall. Living can be more than mere existence. Tastes can be cultivated, but some will still prefer beer to ambrosia. These views and the practicality and immediacy of the implied goals were also essential parts of the land-grant philosophy and mission. They are just as valid today as they were in 1862, although technological developments have markedly changed the means and the agencies for improving life's quality.

Viewed in this broader sense, the land-grant institution emerges as a means of applying knowledge to reality, alleviating some of its distresses and rigors and bringing to it something of the pleasures and satisfactions heretofore restricted to those of some wealth. This public service mission was revolutionary in the mid 1800s. Today it is a mission that is surely not ignored but is interpreted by too many colleges and universities in relationship to institutional advantage rather than regarded as an institutional responsibility and obligation.

The latter interpretation of the land-grant mission came easily in Michigan State's earlier years. But as the school grew, many changes took place that made it increasingly difficult to maintain public service as a major commitment for the entire university.

Perhaps the chief characteristic of the Hannah years was the existence of the long-term vision of what the institution could and should become. Many of the thoughts involved in these plans must have developed during Hannah's years as a student, extension worker, and secretary to the State Board of Agriculture. In the few months before Pearl Harbor, Hannah had already laid before the faculty many of his ideas for the development of the institution. The quick replacement of these ideas by others more immediately relevant to the war effort demonstrated that with Hannah any planning for the future had to be relevant to the needs of the nation and people in a rapidly changing scene.

In the 1960s and 1970s a great deal of the literature on higher education emphasized planning. As the actual experiences of institutions show, planning *for* decline is simply not done and planning *in* decline tends to be a matter of expediency. Thus, in a sense, the planning involved in much of the Hannah period at Michigan State was rather simple and straightforward for the goals were clear and widely acceptable. Relative to some of the later developments, the conditions of that period, while by no means ideal, were at least reasonably predictable, and funds (while not available in the quantity desired) were sufficient if wisely used to accommodate expansion and innovation. New programs, new facilities, and new faculty were being added so quickly, immediately after the war, that the institution seldom faced the problem of explicitly denying plans or ambitions or of reducing or eliminating an existing program. In a few circumstances where this did happen, the individuals could be readily shifted to some other aspect of the growing institution without suffering great disappointment or setback in their career development. Hannah was especially sensitive to an individual's feelings and, while encouraging innovation and experimentation, he recognized that occasional failure was inevitable unless changes and adaptations at appropriate points were made to avoid abject failure. Flexibility and adaptation were the earmarks of the period rather than elimination and replacement of programs. Planning during this period called for review and evaluation of existing programs and contemplation of new ones. The general pattern was renovation and innovation in expanding into new programs and developing new ideas.

Planning has sometimes been contrasted with a combination of opportunism, expediency, and competition. Opportunism is taking action when there is opportunity to do so but especially when there is a chance of success. Expediency involves taking the path of least resistance, doing what one can or must at a moment in time without much concern for long-term consequences. Competition, referring to countering the moves of others or improving upon them, arises out of a concern for quality based upon comparison with others. In the extreme these three aspects of institutional development can lead to unplanned acquisition of programs and resources with little regard for long-term implications. It can even lead to deception and to the presentation of selective information and devious interpretation carefully contrived to attain unfairly something perhaps for no other reason but because it is there.

Michigan State was unfairly accused of expediency, opportunism, and competition. The scope of the plans at Michigan State during its years of growth was such that it was simply not possible to move on all of them at once. Hannah was a master of keeping ideas before the faculty, the legislature, and the people of the state. He was able from year to year to highlight those aspects of the long-term plan that seemed likely to gain the greatest support. In the sense of becoming a university in its own right, there was clearly competition with other institutions within the state. In the sense of carefully assessing the circumstances at a particular moment, expediency and opportunism did play a role in developments but always within a larger framework which maintained the same ultimate ends in view. Priorities in terms of actual needs within the institution and priorities in terms of the opportunities to gain the resources needed from outside the institution had to be shrewdly adjusted from year to year. They were and with great success.

The statistics of growth at Michigan State in the Hannah years from 1935 to 1969 were not only impressive quantitatively, but they reflected a marked change in the character of the institution. This is evident in the following selected items.

1. The enrollment increased from 4,401 in 1935 to 40,820 in 1969, nearly a tenfold increase.
2. The percentage of in-state students decreased from 92 in 1935 to 78 in 1966 and rose to 83 in 1970. The change from 1966 to 1970 resulted in great part from expressed legislative concerns. Michigan State responded by imposing greater selectivity and higher tuition on out-of-state applicants.
3. The percentage of out-of-state students increased from 8 in 1935 to 20 in 1959 and decreased to 14 in 1970. Obviously this change is related to the preceding and immediately following one.
4. The percentage of foreign students increased from .34 in 1935 to 3.00 in 1970. This increase brought an international orientation to the campus.
5. The percentage of students enrolled in the original land-grant units (agriculture, engineering, home economics, veterinary medicine) decreased from 44 in 1935 to 16 in 1970. In the 1850s, about 90 percent of the population lived in rural areas. By 1900 this had decreased to 60 percent, by 1947 to 14 percent, and by 1964 to about 6.3 percent. It was no longer expected that most graduates would return to the farm or that most students would

be from rural communities. The institution had broadened its interpretation of the clientele and areas served.

6. The percentage of students enrolled in the liberal arts with no specific career implications during the same period, while difficult to determine exactly, has varied somewhat but never moved far from 20 percent. Career concerns remained dominant but did not become exclusive.

7. The graduate student enrollment increased from 4 percent in 1935 to 24 percent in 1970. In numbers, this is a change from less than 200 to about 10,000. The change reflects and contributes to increasing faculty commitment to research and scholarship.

8. The faculty increased from 343 in 1935 to 2,590 in 1969 and to 3,528 by 1983. In 1935 there were about 13 students per faculty member; by 1969 there were 16. Freshman and sophomore classes inevitably increased in size as the number of advanced courses greatly increased.

9. The number of divisions/colleges increased from 6 in 1935 to 15 in 1969. The four "land-grant" colleges of agriculture, home economics, engineering, and veterinary medicine were now outnumbered.

10. The number of departments increased from 44 in 1935 to 104 in 1969. This change reflects increasing specialization in faculty research, in graduate programs, and in undergraduate student majors.

11. The total budget increased from $9,038,133 in 1935 to $85,195,792 in 1969. It is not entirely accidental that, despite inflation and change in character, the budget increased at approximately the same rate as the enrollment.

12. The percentage of the faculty holding the rank of professor or associate professor increased from 31 in 1935 to 54 in 1969. This data reflects a liberal promotion policy and the developing expectation of every young Ph.D. that tenure and professoriate would be forthcoming.

13. The number of persons holding administrative titles increased from 66 in 1935 to 260 in 1969 and to 455 by 1983.

The preceding selected statistics reflect an institution that has increased its enrollment nearly tenfold. At the same time, this student body is changing in character. The percentage of in-state students decreased, while that of out-of-state increased. Likewise, the percentage of foreign students increased. The result was a more heterogeneous student body, especially since the percentage of in-state students from urban areas had markedly increased. Legislative concerns resulted in more careful screening of out-of-state applicants and a marked differential between in-state and out-of-state fees.

Graduate student enrollment increased from 4 percent of the total in 1935 to 24 percent in 1970. Requests for increased funding from the legislature generated suggestions that fees be related to costs, but increasing use of graduate assistants with out-of-state fees waived cushioned the impact.

Perhaps the statistic indicating the greatest change in institutional character is found in the decrease from 44 to 16 percent of the enrollments in agriculture, home economics, engineering, and veterinary medicine—the original programs of the land-grant college. With the disappearance of arts and sciences courses especially devised for these groups, many faculty members had no contact with these original programs.

The increased number of colleges and departments, on the whole, reflected an increase in career programs rather than an increase in liberal education majors. The latter group, because of the career implications of many departmental programs (such as psychology), became more and more difficult to estimate. Greater faculty involvement in graduate programs tended also to introduce a graduate-degree career orientation, rather than a liberal education, to undergraduate majors. The liberal arts division in 1935 enrolled about 22 percent of the students, but these included career programs in art, music, hotel administration, business administration, and secondary school teaching. Though some of these programs were later shifted elsewhere, others (nursing, for example) replaced them. For 80 to 90 percent of the undergraduates, traditional courses in the liberal arts and sciences continued to be subsidiary or contributive to career development. In this respect, the early land-grant emphasis on career preparation remained constant although some liberal arts and service faculty members interpreted the new strength in the arts and sciences as a growing institutional commitment to liberal education.

The increase in faculty from 343 in 1935 to 2,590 (7.5 times the earlier figure) in 1969 was somewhat less than the nearly tenfold increase in enrollment. Recalling the expanded size of the graduate program, this discrepancy becomes even more significant. Faculty credit hour instructional loads had also decreased. Large classes had become the rule in many courses, although small classes at the advanced undergraduate level remained more common than many administrators thought to be really necessary.

Although the budget had apparently increased ninefold, the 1969 budget, corrected for inflation, was actually less than four times the 1935 budget. Moreover, the increased costs of the newer graduate and professional programs suggested that financial difficulties might lie ahead. Residential colleges, Honors College, and services directed to improvement of instruction, however desirable and beneficial, required dollars that might otherwise have been distributed to colleges and departments. Only by increasing class size, by reducing the excessive degree credit requirements from 200 and more to 180, and by providing relatively inexpensive general education for all students, was it possible both to expand programs and maintain an innovative spirit.

The swelling percentage of faculty in the upper ranks also meant higher salary demands and increased educational costs. Yet in terms of expertise in discipline and emphasis on research, newer and younger faculty frequently stood out above their seniors. Salary differentials reflected this, somewhat to the dismay of long-time faculty members.

The faculty hardly realized that from 1935 to 1969 the administrative staff had increased fourfold, although there was some grumbling that there were too many administrators, too much red tape, and consequent unnecessary expense. The further increase to 455 administrators by 1983 was still far ahead. Nonetheless, consideration of that continuing growth of administrative personnel reveals that

1. Hannah tended toward a lean administrative hierarchy and preferred direct interpersonal interaction with individual students and faculty members. He cautioned a successor to avoid allowing deans to come between the faculty and the administration, in part because he had found many deans unwilling to shoulder responsibility for communicating or enforcing necessary but unpopular policies.
2. Nevertheless, increasing faculty involvement in an ever more complex committee and governance structure required more and more committee time by administrators. Hannah would delegate much of this to assistants and later to vice-presidents, as his own calendar filled up and his absences from campus became more frequent.
3. Formalization of procedures for selection and evaluation of personnel including appointment, promotion, salary recommendations, and tenure actions increased the reports, records, and staff required for collecting and organizing them.
4. Equity considerations required more staff, more special programs, more detailed procedures, and increases in decision-making time to assure equity and fairness.
5. External accountability demands from state and federal govern-

ment agencies were beginning to force more elaborate procedures in allocating and accounting for the use of resources. Discrepancies between state and campus allocation procedures caused difficulties and occasional misunderstandings.

Everything considered, the size of the administrative structure of the late 1960s was fully justifiable and even modest by comparison with many other institutions at that time.

In an earlier period, certainly before the appointment of the first academic vice-president, Tom Hamilton, most administrative decisions of any significance were made by Hannah. Complexities and distinctive details generated by increasing size and by Hannah's off-campus involvements forced more delegation to others. On the whole, Hannah favored such decentralization. Yet as inevitable and desirable increasing autonomy might be for departments and colleges, it also deprived the institution of a sense of coherence and direction. Variation in faculty load assignments among departments was an example.

The Hannah era was one of continuing growth, in which facilities and faculty seemed always to be less than what was required. Temporary facilities and temporary underpaid faculty bridged the gap; both were used for longer than intended. Yet, despite inadequacies, those temporary facilities created an informality and an accessibility that encouraged productive faculty and student interaction. Living-learning facilities in the residence halls also encouraged such interaction. The spread of departmental faculties over the campus was inconvenient, but it too created interdisciplinary exchange and rapport and kept departments for a time from becoming the isolated, self-sufficient, and externally oriented units that they would later tend to become. Dependence upon the university's general fund or on extension or Experiment Station allocations was also a powerful force in generating and maintaining an institutional commitment and loyalty which would be weakened as departments and faculty members sought and acquired funds from sources external to the university.

But the single most significant factor in generating morale and institutional commitment during the Hannah years was Hannah himself and the sense of progress he conveyed in identifying and meeting the educational needs of students and of the state and nation. Hannah's repeated rejections of generous board increases in his own salary or retirement contributions were not widely reported, but it was evident that he served for love rather than money. So long as Hannah personally participated in selecting department chairs and senior faculty, every new faculty member understood the obligation to contribute to the land-grant mission. As departments and colleges attained more autonomy, decisions on hiring and rewards tended to be based on the needs and priorities of the departmental discipline rather than on those of the university and its clientele. Ambition to attain excellence on an interinstitutional and international basis superseded concern for good teaching and for public service, a characterization many departments would find objectionable.

The word *excellence* was largely unused in the Hannah years. The prevailing view was that the quest for excellence implied smugness and hauteur based upon past accomplishments rather than humility and continuing effort. Both modesty and a desire for continuing improvement required that the judgment of excellence be made by others rather than by those directly involved. Even so, an accent on excellence was likely to be discounted or dismissed by Hannah, since his attention was on other innovations and needed improvements.

As Hannah expressed it many times, "we should do our very best in everything we do." In fact, excellence was regarded by Hannah as a comparative, and therefore a restrictive, concept. Since resources are always limited, especially in publicly supported universities, claims to excellence are invitations to reduction or reallocation of resources. Attainment of quality—ignoring professions of or pretension to excellence—in some programs in a university might seem to require avoidance of some programs and acceptance of mediocrity in others. But what is mediocrity? Does it lie in the instructor's degrees, in the courses, in the quality of students enrolled, or in the purposes served? A two-year sequence in statistics required in a business program will never qualify for *excellence* as the term is usually used. Yet such a sequence in mathematics and statistics, effectively integrated into a degree program, may contribute significantly to the performance of graduates.

Excellence is not a permanent state of grace, but rather an end toward which all parts of the university should cooperatively aspire for the benefit of the institution as a whole. The true excellence of Michigan State in the Hannah era was in its commitment to serve the state and the nation. *Excellence* was not a word to be used loosely and uselessly but stood for an obligation and responsibility made evident in both long-term goals and day-to-day decisions. Hannah's goal was simply that of doing, as well as possible, everything that one undertook to do. A corollary was that one should be selective about one's undertakings.

Nevertheless, the concept of excellence on a comparative and competitive basis was operative at college and departmental levels and was reflected in their ambitions to emphasize research and the acquisition of a research faculty with little attention to the possible impact on undergraduate programs or on the public service mission of the university.

Size was never an end in itself although at times it seemed to be. Before World War II, the increasing size of the university provided evidence of a broader set of programs and a wider appeal. After many difficult years, the continuance of the institution was assured. Growth was widely viewed as a sign of vitality and was of prime importance in convincing the legislature of the need for increased appropriations. As MSU enrollment approached that of the University of Michigan, the two institutions sought either to expedite (Michigan State) or delay (University of Michigan) the inevitable. Again, size was not in itself regarded as meritorious, but growth and comparative size were obviously influential in attaining public recognition and financial support. Moreover, as tuition and student fees were raised, increased enrollment, especially when numbered in the hundreds and thousands, brought immediate dollars, most of which were discretionary—that is, uncommited by previous budget allocations.

Legislators criticized the continuing increases at Michigan State and even proposed that an enrollment ceiling be imposed. This suggestion was reinforced by the implication that enrollments above such a ceiling (40,000 was suggested) would not be counted in determining the institution's annual allocation.

By systematically eliminating all small classes, and thereby increasing average class size, Hannah found ways to accept more students without seriously affecting the student-faculty ratio. For 1,000 additional students (only a 2.5 percent increase over 40,000) fee income could be nearly $1 million dollars against the possible alternative of vacant residence hall space and less tuition.

Limitations in enrollments were discussed on several occasions. But Hannah could not agree to turning away qualified students, and he did not believe that the institution should become elitest. Furthermore, as one of Hannah's successors found, significant reduction in enrollment by restriction of admissions had a continuing impact for at least three subsequent years.

Many administrators, faculty members, and friends of Michigan State looked at the post-Hannah university and described it as overexpanded. Such criticism comes easily from the vantage point of a later era in which funds became inadequate for support of existing programs. A similar statement could be and has been made about the totality of state-assisted colleges and universities in Michigan and in many other states. The judgment of overexpansion of higher education at the state level is often made as though it were a criticism of the institution when, in fact, the institution was created to meet identified needs, often over the objections of existing institutions that would have preferred to expand their own operations rather than share limited resources with another institution. Moreover, the severest critics commonly displayed no willingness to eliminate educational institutions in their own immediate area.

Overexpansion within an institution is a somewhat different problem. With faculties tenured and with facilities already on hand, abandonment of programs is not a certain way to reduce expenditures and will surely incur criticism and resistance from without as well as from within the university. Even the elimination of a course not offered for a year or two almost surely arouses opposition. In state-assisted higher education, any move to cut back on programs within an institution or to eliminate institutions incurs widespread opposition and budgetary threats.

There is little incentive in any university, and especially not in publicly assisted ones, to reduce expenditures below the funds allocated in a particular year. Unexpended balances may be withdrawn or transferred to other units. The carry-over of allocated funds from one year to another is likely to be regarded as evidence of overfunding. Hence the carry-over may become a double deduction from next year's appropriation. The result is an attempt—often an end-of-year rush effort—to expend all available dollars. Planning beyond one year is thus hampered, and adaptive flexibility from year to year is destroyed. Enrollment and tuition increases become especially important as sources of new funds.

Growth in size at MSU required continued and extensive hiring of new personnel, a time-consuming and often unrewarding task for a department chair and faculty committee. Replacement in some departments can be and was minimized by quick promotions and generous salary increases. Chairs or deans seemed to ignore the fact that easy and quick promotion would in some future day lead to an overtenured faculty when an enrollment plateau or decline would terminate faculty expansion. Though Hannah reportedly issued cautions, it was difficult to reject promotions recommended by departments and seconded by deans. Almost automatic promotions and quick attainment of tenure (with few exceptions) became the norm. This trend was further supported by pressures to hire and retain women and representatives of minority groups. Denial of tenure for these persons took on the overtones of firing and consequent appeals.

The rush in the 1930s and 1940s to launch graduate programs led to some weaknesses and abuse of policies and standards in certain departments. The attempts of a graduate dean to correct this situation resulted in changes that produced a graduate office restricted to program review. Though most departments exercised care in appointments, controls on admissions, and enforcement of program standards, there developed cases of recurrent concern. This was inevitable, for professors tended to be autonomous on these matters. Colleagues might take note and exchange remarks with close friends but carefully avoided public criticism of fellow professors who, because of personal deficiencies as scholars, laziness, or undue concern for graduate-student egos, permitted advisees to complete graduate degree programs with minimal requirements. Michigan State was, of course, not alone in the tendency to turn over to departments and professors the determination and enforcement of standards. The argument that only scholars in a discipline can judge quality of performance in a discipline is not valid for all disciplines or all performances.

Faculty members objected to imposition of specific standards, to limitations on promotion and tenure, and to restrictions on course and program additions. They regarded these as an invasion of their competence and prerogatives. Yet when such principles or rules were lacking, they displayed neither the willingness nor ability to enunciate and enforce them.

Although the transformation of MAC—a small, relatively unknown agricultural college—to MSU—a university recognized worldwide—was surely a success story of almost unparalleled magnitude, it is evident that, if judged from the viewpoint of later developments, some problems can be identified. Hindsight yields perspectives and judgments not possible at the moment of decision. It is not even possible to determine to what extent a particular decision or policy influenced the subsequent stream of events upon which retrospective analysis and evaluation are based. Some events—such as, in this case, the concerns for equity—were certainly not foreseen but markedly affected institutional operations in the 1970s and 1980s and were complicated by the earlier quick attainment of tenure.

In review and discussion of some events of the Hannah years and their aftermath, Hannah himself remarked that, even had he been somewhat aware of later developments, he probably would have made the same decision. Why? In his often expressed philosophy of "only people matter," decisions inflicting hardship or anguish on others were seldom made. In response to concern and restraint, many individuals performed beyond what might reasonably have been expected. Such is the impact of leadership and charisma.

The preceding discussion points up some of the problems of the Hannah years as viewed in retrospect. The following statements express the insights of the author and some of his collaborators and colleagues that resulted from this retrospection. Hannah read and generally concurred with these points but insisted, as always, that in applying them concern for the individual as well as for the institution and its constituency must be present.

1.  The mission of a state-assisted college or university may change over time, but its reformulation is not the prerogative of the faculty or even of the president at any point in time. The university serves the people and must—within limits to be determined by weighing many considerations—be responsive to the public's expectations. Verbal statements of mission, however, are not effective unless reiterated and applied in decisions about organizational structure, budgeting, and hiring and rewarding faculty members, chairs, and deans. Over time, the actual mission supported by an institution and its units can differ greatly from the formal statement of mission. The land-grant mission is especially vulnerable because it differs from that of most of the highly prestigious American universities.

2.  The function of an institutional board is neither that of routinely approving details of a prepared agenda nor of probing into every aspect of an institution's operation. Rather, the function is that of determining the mission of the institution and selecting as president an individual committed to that mission both in words and past deeds. The president must also be capable of exercising leadership over a diverse faculty and constituency by arousing enthusiasm and support while providing a sense of direction. The board is responsible for recurrent evaluation of the president's performance.

3.  In the selection of a president, the board should avoid individuals who would use the office for advancement of personal ambitions. The board should also avoid use of the office to reward political performance and party loyalty. It should seek an individual who will identify with the institution, its mission, and its clientele and provide leadership over a span of at least ten years.

4.  The Michigan State experience suggests that gubernatorial appointments of governing board members would be preferable to election. Party nominations brought to the MSU Board of Trustees a number of individuals so deficient in stature and understanding of higher education that they were liabilities to

the institution. The open-meeting law encouraged comments and speeches demonstrating party loyalties rather than responsibility to the public for fulfillment of the institutional mission.

5. The president should be available to faculty and students and have such presence and experience that he or she merits and receives respect and support for his or her interpretation of the institutional mission and policies and decisions in supporting that mission.

6. Faculty views should contribute to decisions including selection of chairs, deans, and vice-presidents; but final choice should be that of the president and board. No university can long maintain a distinctive mission and character if faculty members can select deans and chairs who support faculty aspirations regardless of consistency with the mission.

7. Departments, colleges, and other units should have considerable autonomy in formulating plans but only within the framework of an overall institutional plan consistent with the institutional mission and the role (which may change over time) of each subdivision in contributing to that mission.

8. No matter how tight the budget, the president should retain or find discretionary funds to encourage and support innovative ideas and efforts.

9. Extensive and uniform data should be collected and analyzed continuously to insure that department and college operations are consistent with institutional mission statements and with operational rules and policies. This essential practice is amply justified by the fact that departments are greatly influenced by other departments in the immediate institution and by corresponding departments in other institutions. Scholarly egos easily rationalize a desired practice or policy as a reasonable extension of a stated one or as reasonable violation of one no longer justified. On university campuses, as elsewhere, things may not be either as they seem to be or as they are reported.

10. Publicly assisted universities, especially the land-grant institutions, are supported to meet public needs rather than those of the faculty. This requires the existence of policies and procedures for interpreting and enforcing those policies that preserve a flexibility of response in dealing with unanticipated contingencies such as enrollments, courses and program disciplines, financial exigency, technological advances, or social needs.

11. Departments, colleges, and other units are convenient for grouping faculty and for providing coordination and direction

to programs, but their nature and continued existence should depend upon their performance of missions and functions. Personalities and people are more important than organization in determining effectiveness and efficiency in operation. Reorganizations may be effective mostly because of the introduction of new personalities, but they may also pose new problems because of unforeseen factors, interactions, aspirations, ambiguities, and personalities. Organizational changes that look good on paper may not function at all because of the people, not solely faculty, involved and the covert but effective understandings and interactions that are disrupted. Difficulties in adjusting to a new structure may direct attention to matters unrelated to the reasons given for the change.

12. The most immediate and obvious response of an institution to the public served by it is found in the students enrolled at any given moment. Students are part of the public and will continue to be part of the public for many years. The student voice, like that of the faculty, should always be heard although it, like that of the faculty, cannot always be heeded. Nevertheless, the quality of programs and services for students should not be crippled or destroyed for the convenience of faculty, deans, or business offices. Forthright and continuous communication about problems and the rationale for changes made to resolve them are essential. Maximizing faculty and administrative convenience may maximize inconvenience for students.

13. People are important; each and every person must be treated fairly and humanely. But the larger obligation of the publicly assisted university to its total student body and to the public requires that some students be dropped and that some faculty members, tenured or otherwise, must be terminated. The responsibilities and obligations of the faculty members and students generally and of the expectations for individuals specifically should be determined, disseminated, and continuously applied and enforced. Laxity in review, evaluation, and action can only lead to confrontations, confusion, and accusations inconsistent with the essential characteristics of a learning environment.

14. Realistic planning requires denial of some aspirations as well as clarifications and confirmation of others. Plans are not promises; they are but indications of desired directions subject always to modifications because of changes in faulty vision or altered circumstances. Effective planning must also allow for alternative

and for unforeseen and even cataclysmic contingencies. The maintenance of flexibility for adjustment noted earlier is essential. Flexibility is difficult to maintain because the tendency of any enterprise dependent on annual appropriations is to expend or obligate every cent not only for the immediate year but for the future. Some programs and services are more important than others, but opinions often differ depending upon personal advantage. Failure to recognize this tends to result in equal percentage reductions in the face of financial exigency rather than applications of priorities related to institutional mission. Departments, programs, and professors are not of equal importance, but the distinctions are difficult to make and hence are often avoided.

Most of the preceding statements actually reflect or describe considerations of policies operative in the Hannah years, but they by no means explain the unparalleled growth of Michigan State. The years 1935 to 1969 provided unusual opportunities for institutional advancement. Hannah was the right man in the right place at the right time—but more important, he made the right decisions for sound, long-term development of a land-grant, people-oriented institution.

# 17
# Prospects for the
# Land-Grant University

In *The Land-Grant Universities and Their Continuing Challenge*, G. Lester Anderson remarks that

> . . .the concept and function of the land-grant university have not significantly changed in this century. The diminishing of their uniqueness is due to the adoption by other institutions of the basic concepts of the land-grant idea: democratization of education, applied or mission-oriented research conducted to benefit the people of the states; and service rendered directly to these people through extension agents, short courses, and continuing education. At the same time, the land-grant universities were developing and expanding even in those states where there was another public university. This created land-grant universities which were coequal with other public and private institutions.
>
> Clearly the land-grant universities and the non-land-grant public universities no longer constitute, in any major sense, two distinctive categories. But the idea of the land-grant university does and should persist. The values that have infused these institutions for over a century continue to be emphasized and constitute a system that merits consideration as the future of higher education in this nation is planned.[1]

In subsequent pages, Anderson characterizes the land-grant idea as embracing these commitments or values: a political ideal, a democratization of higher education, utilitarian goals, and research findings taken to the people. But as he notes above, the land-grant institution is no longer distinctive. Furthermore, land-grant institutions are not and never were homogeneous, which becomes evident when they are considered in more detail.

Both land-grant universities (seventy-two in number) and non-land-grant universities (fifty-eight) are members of the National Association of State Universities and Land-Grant Colleges. However, inclusion of the free-standing Connecticut Experiment Station and a university

---

1. (East Lansing, Mich.: Michigan State University Press, 1976), p. 1.

system office within this total reduces the number of non-land-grant state universities in the membership to fifty-six.

The seventy-two land-grant colleges or universities received their designations and federal grants in diverse ways: fifty-four by the 1862 land grants or scrip, four by cash grants (University of Hawaii, University of Guam [1952], University of the Virgin Islands [1972], and Federal City College [1966]), and eleven by nothing initially other than the designation. Two private universities, Cornell and Massachusetts Institute of Technology, are also land-grant institutions.

The original land grant itself was a significant but not determining factor in gaining acceptance of the land-grant idea. The ultimate value of the land-grant endowments (originally 34,000 acres for each senator and representative in Congress) varied widely, depending heavily, of course, on the wisdom exercised in disposing of land or scrip. Anderson (in an appendix) reported the 1862 Land-Grant Endowment Fund for the University of Minnesota as $45,701,377 and that for Michigan State as $1,059,379. However, as earlier reported, the MSU endowment had been appropriated by the state legislature for other purposes, although the presumed income at 7 percent interest continued to be paid from other sources. Furthermore, the decision reached in some states to deduct the land-grant income from requested state funds destroyed the practical value of the land-grant endowment. The grant for Kentucky State College amounted to only $20,925. For Massachusetts Institute of Technology, it was $73,000. According to Anderson, only three institutions of the fifty-four sharing in the 1862 Land-Grant Endowment Fund were, as of 1974, receiving an annual income therefrom of more than $1 million. Obviously the income from the Land-Grant Endowment Fund could not be regarded, in most cases, as the most significant factor in maintenance of the land-grant mission.

The formerly black colleges created as land-grant institutions were not furnished the resources and they did not have the clientele or staff to exploit the land-grant mission. They tended to emphasize teacher training, a relatively inexpensive program and one providing many jobs in the segregated schools of the South.

The land-grant colleges and universities not only differ in origins but in other respects that depend partly on origins. There has long been a widespread consensus that every university should be strong in the arts, social sciences, and sciences. When the land-grant designation was assigned to an already existing institution, the sciences, social sciences, and humanities disciplines neither owed their existence to nor depended for their development on their contribution to the land-grant mission. In contrast, the sciences and the arts in those institutions created or designated as land-grant colleges, but separate from one or more other state universities, were reasonably expected to develop and maintain a more practical orientation to the sciences and social sciences and refrain from undue expansion of the humanities. For the state university, which also became the land-grant unit, duplication of graduate programs posed no problem. For the land-grant college coexisting with the state university but desiring to become a university in its own right, there has been a problem. Must doctoral programs in English, foreign languages, and the humanities be added for the land-grant college to become a university? Professors in these disciplines assert that a superior program in a department or discipline of a university is unattainable unless the Ph.D. is offered. Obviously they thereby deny quality to any program below the doctoral level. Some land-grant institutions have refused to offer the Ph.D. in disciplines not directly related to the land-grant mission and have recognized that permitting all departments and colleges to offer a Ph.D. means that each may pursue its own ends without regard for the overall land-grant mission. Since the Ph.D. is oriented to disciplinary research and graduate instruction, rather than to applied research and service, the tendency is for the land-grant institution to become a combined state university and land-grant college rather than to remain primarily a land-grant university committed to serving the current needs of people and the nation. To avoid this, Purdue and Indiana have long avoided unneeded duplications, insisting that, between them, the people are better served and with less expense.

Much of the early success of the land-grant colleges was due to enthusiasm and commitment of faculties. The Hatch Act of 1887, providing funds for experimental stations, was preceded and encouraged by the efforts and accomplishments of the land-grant college faculties. Similarly the Smith-Lever Act of 1914, supporting the development of extension activities, recognized the existence and success of previous extension activities rather than creating a new idea. In requiring the matching of federal funds by local funds, that act successfully brought support for extension to the local level, where its efforts and successes were also most visible.

The 1862 land-grant act (Morrill Act) created an ideal, the pursuit of which depended upon the efforts of persons whose commitments to the land-grant mission included almost as much volunteerism as compensated service. Supportive of that dedication was the long work day characteristic of the rural population and of land-grant college faculty members and students. They believed in Ben Franklin's adage that "early to bed, and early to rise makes a man healthy, wealthy, and wise," although they may have doubted the "wealthy."

Since the land-grant colleges or universities are so diverse, they are not easily characterized as a group. Private universities with land-grant colleges, state universities, *and* land-grant colleges are significantly different in origin and possibly different in mission from the separate land-grant institutions. As Michigan State moved from college to university status, John Hannah invariably spoke of the institution as a land-grant university. Later presidents spoke of Michigan State as being both a state university and a land-grant college, emphasizing its membership in both the American Association of Universities and the National Association of State Universities and Land-Grant Colleges. This dual designation, in effect, implies the restriction of the land-grant role to agriculture and human ecology and tends to free the arts and science departments from the land-grant obligation of public service or research related to concerns of the state and its people.

The early success of the public service mission—embracing both extension and problem-oriented research—of the land-grant college and the clientele to which that mission was directed made the land-grant college a distinctive institution. Its effectiveness was not to be measured by the scholarly characteristics of its faculty or by their research and writing. More important was the impact of its programs developed to meet specific needs of its designated clientele. These needs underwent continued change in a rapidly expanding nation. In addition, the land-grant college continually expanded its clientele as its early public service ventures confirmed that national well-being and development depended ultimately and directly on individuals and their collective actions and values in a democratic society.

The utilitarian mission of the land-grant college initially required involvement in the same activities as those to whom its services were directed. If the college was to assist the farm family to increase production; improve product quality; increase ease, efficiency, and safety of farm and industrial operations; increase income; improve the quality of rural living; and conserve resources, the faculty must not only be able to offer realistic advice but also demonstrate that the advice was based upon experience and validated by it. Faculty members had to model in college facilities and on college grounds what they undertook to demonstrate to others.

Thus, the service mission required a distinctive type of faculty member. Pragmatism, practicality, and technological competency were at least as important as scholarship. To secure confidence and maintain rapport with those served, a cooperative rather than directive approach was essential. Focus on specific problems and on immediate solutions was also necessary if extension efforts were to be successful. Costs in time and dollars of any new practices had to be small relative to prospective benefits. Cost-benefit concepts were therefore operative, if not always recognized as such.

The extension and Experiment Station staff were necessarily involved in determining problems and in research and development of practical ideas, followed by demonstration and dissemination. These ideas frequently provided content for credit and noncredit courses on campus as well as for extension programs. Extension, research, and instruction were interrelated into a cooperative public service program—with *service* implying humility and acceptance of the obligation to collaborate with and assist others.

Such service is without price because the chores involved are often dirty, routine, and menial. Much of the service supplied in public endeavors, hospitals, and churches has been (and to some extent still is) voluntary service freely given either as a felt obligation as a citizen, as a means of personal pleasure and satisfaction, or even perhaps to accumulate credits for admission to heaven. So it was in the early land-grant college, in which faculty members and students also did the necessary work to operate the farms and the campus.

As organized knowledge and theory replaced practical experience and know-how, and as faculty members found these chores increasingly time consuming and demeaning, the faculty gradually withdrew from farm and campus tasks. The hours of practical work required of students likewise decreased. Maintenance of the farms and campus could be delegated to nonacademic workers. So could much of the demonstration, advice, and noncredit activities offered under the extension label. As the Ph.D. research and lecture model and the departmental disciplinary syndrome developed, most of the faculty of the land-grant institutions viewed their roles and obligations as no different from those in other public and private universities.

The extension of the public service mission into personal development and human values and the solutions of social problems abetted this tendency. Social problems, in their complexity and magnitude and in their almost immediate alternatives under close scrutiny, are not readily resolved. Studies of social problems are typically laden with data, long on hypotheses, heavy in vocabulary, and short on solutions. On campus, they transcend disciplines and arouse anxieties, and off campus they arouse opposition rather than acceptance.

### SHIFTS IN FOCUS AND LOYALTY

Along with these changes in faculty orientation, the loyalties of the administrators and faculty were shifting. In the early land-grant college their loyalty was to the people of the state, and they viewed the institution as existing to serve the people's needs. Departments were small. Interactions, and even interchange, among departments and disciplines by individuals were commonplace. The prevailing concern was with identification and solution of problems and with the education of the people involved. Activities were diverse, but there was a unity in them which gradually faded as strong degree programs were developed in the arts, social sciences, and natural sciences.

Likewise, programs in social work, nursing, business, hotel administration, and other fields took on more of a national orientation. As faculty members entered these vocational areas, they continued to view the university as an agency to serve society, but many also gradually came to regard it as an organization to promote career, departmental, and ultimately professorial reputations. The shift in emphasis from practical problem solving to organized knowledge and theory became even more evident. The faculty now viewed itself as part of a worldwide learning community—a collection of scholars—rather than as a group of people devoted to helping others. Disciplines and subdisciplines were stressed rather than the supra- or multidisciplinary approach required to deal with the real world and its problems.

The service focus of the land-grant institution was itself changing. It was dealing with a much wider range of ever more complex problems to which solutions were not readily found. The extension worker became a resource linker rather than a problem solver. Attention to the farm and the farm home shifted to industry and business as indicated by the new term *agribusiness*. It also shifted to towns, cities, and suburbia as the growth in these areas and the greater range of communication lessened the isolation of the farm homes.

After World War II, attention was being focused on new groups—minorities, women, disadvantaged, aged—and generally on the problems of groups and organizations. Though individuals within the group were not ignored, it was recognized that an effective and well-focused organization constitutes one of the most significant ways by which people become able to help themselves. One simply could no longer assume that every member of the faculty was interested in or competent in dealing with practical problems or in disseminating knowledge to individuals and groups of people who would use that knowledge to improve their living. Evaluation of extension activities and Experiment Station research was also becoming more difficult as the range and type of people served multiplied.

The increased productivity and increased income that had often flowed quickly out of some of the earlier extension and research activities were not readily demonstrable when organizations were assisted to improve their operations and programs or when cultural events such as lectures, plays, or music were channeled to various sections of the state. Extension was at once becoming both a broader concept in respect to clientele and a more limited one in regard to programs offered. New forms of communication displaced some earlier extension activities.

### CURRENT PROBLEMS
### WITH THE EXTENSION CONCEPT

Agricultural cooperative extension made significant contributions to the development of the nation in the period 1870 to 1960. The most apparent contribution was the marked increase in productivity per acre. Agricultural productivity increased nearly ten times (1,000 percent), while productivity for the United States generally was less than half that. In the same period of time the productivity of the individual worker in agriculture was two to three times that of the industrial worker.

However, the number of farm workers or owners decreased. Nationally nearly 60 percent of the population was employed in farm pursuits in 1900. This figure was roughly 6 percent in 1964. This change confirmed the agricultural productivity but also reflected the transfer of vast human resources from rural to urban areas. Obviously extension and research had not successfully met the needs of all of rural society since the land-grant colleges dealt with the relatively prosperous rather than the marginal farmer. The research and technological developments supplied to agriculture by Experiment Station and extension workers were major factors in enhancing productivity.

The success of cooperative extension in the rural areas was a result of several conditions not present in the urban areas. Extension activities were educationally oriented and relatively long term. Both research and dissemination of findings required effort over time. Changes in seeding, cultivation, or fertilization called for planning ahead. Generally in the dissemination and demonstration of results, extension personnel could contact individual farmers and farm families and thereby gain their confidence in new procedures. Changes, on the whole, were not radical. People learned to do better something they were already doing. By increasing productivity and quality through better seed, cultivation, storage, and distribution, everyone benefited.

Urban problems were and are entirely different. They are of a range, complexity, and magnitude far beyond the rural problems that had earlier involved a majority of the population. The problems of rural areas had been solved, in part, by the increases in urban population. Many urban dwellers had no resources, no jobs, no skills, and no hope. They required assistance on a vast scale before they could attain a status in which they could even begin to help themselves. Many lacked knowledge, ambition, and ability to use what they did have. They had no patience with scholarly problem-solving and gradual change but expected or demanded immediate assistance and improvement rather than promises and prospects.

Housing, water pollution, racial conflict, poverty, mass transportation, health care, crime, and unemployment are problems of such magnitude and are so interrelated that attempts to alleviate them have required vast sums of money and the efforts of many agencies and people. Alleviation rather than solution was inevitable. Moreover, the possibility of immediate gain has influenced political policies and encouraged overt and violent crime and less apparent corruption. Sheer ineptness in planning and management has also resulted in misuse and misdirection of funds. The attempts to solve large-scale problems became problems in themselves and created still others. The experience was not without precedent. During and since World War II it has been evident that the peace, health, and prosperity we seek are not to be attained solely by dollar expenditures.

David C. Nichols remarks, "Seldom is it known that many land-grant institutions unsuccessfully sponsored urban extension even before 1900."[2] Then, as now, the clientele for urban extension was either elusive or adamantly resistant to academic efforts. In the 1950s the Ford Foundation gave $1 million to each of eight universities to develop consulting services to urban organizations. In reviewing these projects, it was concluded that it is not possible to reduce urban problems to a manageable number and precisely define them. The attempt to study or resolve them with limited funds, limited insight, and lack of unanimity as to what constitutes a solution is analogous to throwing

---

2. In *Land Grant Universities and Their Continuing Challenge*, ed. by G. Lester Anderson (East Lansing, Mich.: Michigan State University Press, 1976), p. 226.

a small amount of water into concentrated sulfuric acid. The immediate result is an explosion rather than a solution.

Title I of the Higher Education Act of 1965 represented an effort by U.S. President Lyndon Johnson to create a great society by declaring war on poverty. Johnson noted that 70 percent of the U.S. population resided in urban areas. He proposed an urban extension service to do for urban America what the agricultural extension service had done for rural America. The funds allocated under Title I were to be used to bring university resources to bear on housing, poverty, government, recreation, employment, youth opportunities, transportation, health, and land use. The total yearly allocation was about $10 million, and the largest amount allocated any state was $500,000. The net reactions to Title I were a combination of indifference, based upon the futility of attacking major problems with such a pittance, and of suspicion of misuse and waste of funds.

Long-existing conditions, no matter how sordid, can be turned into personal benefits by some people. Attempts to improve conditions will be resisted or, if possible, turned to further advantage by those who thrive on human miseries. Major projects involving large sums, several years of effort, and many developers and contractors are especially subject to corruption. Universities are poorly equipped and staffed to cope with such venality, and many are not entirely free of that vice in their own operations. Our universities and colleges have offered no ready solution to this problem.

In the summer of 1967, another attempt was made to enlist universities in revolutionizing urban America. The tentative plan called for special attention to urban schools and the designation of a national system of urban specialists. Disagreements on the respective responsibilities of various federal government agencies, a widespread doubt that urban problems were amenable to the applied research and extension approach, and the suspicion that the earlier Title I funds had been dissipated with no positive impact were difficult to overcome. Shortly thereafter, the expenses of the Vietnam War and resulting distrust and disillusionment effectively destroyed these second efforts.

The nature and extent of urban problems have caused colleges and universities everywhere to seek beneficial interactions with their immediate communities. For institutions in large cities, there is a changing and never-ending task as various groups demand what they consider to be due them from the institution. Some of their expectations for service from universities are reasonable and desirable, but someone has to pay for it. Even the use of the library by local teachers or students involves additional cost.

The results of effective service are likely to be cumulative rather than immediate. The impact of the land-grant institution on rural society has become apparent only after a lapse of decades. Money alone will not resolve urban problems in a few years, and any attempt to allocate vast sums through educational institutions or other channels could, if it has not already, become a boondoggle of such proportions as to imperil the future of American society.

The basic strength of the land-grant extension service was in its objective and scholarly approach to problems. The original justification for the land-grant college was based on confidence that the application of physical and biological science could increase agricultural productivity and improve rural living. Democracy and utilitarianism—amassing and applying relevant knowledge to improve individuals and society—were central values. But universities and colleges, especially those assisted by public monies, have become victims of their own success. They are even less able to control their development as they increase in size, clientele, and resources. They themselves have become major sources for funds and for employment. Institutional missions have become unclear, and balanced programs in relation to a unified goal are difficult to attain as resources are diverted to such extraneous and perhaps destructive matters as open admissions, remedial or developmental programs, fair employment practices, and time-consuming and expensive appeal practices. Tenure, salary, and fringe-benefit demands of faculty and staff result in public service being held hostage by employees' priorities.

## DIFFICULTIES IN MAINTAINING THE PUBLIC SERVICE MISSION

Full commitment to and pursuit of any well-defined mission require a clear definition and also a firm rejection of unrelated or conflicting missions. The more persons who are involved in or affected by a mission statement, the more difficult it becomes to define and maintain it. Self-denial—individually or institutionally—requires self-discipline. Denial of group, class, or political pressures for new services and programs requires objectivity, fortitude, and political finesse. Survival, acquisition of funds, and aspirations to excellence tend to determine an operational mission by altering and possibly corrupting the original one. Stubborn adherence to an archaic concept of mission, and to the programs generated in support of it, is as destructive of the service mission as is ready acquiescence to internal whims or external pressure.

The original land-grant institutions came into being to provide appropriate education for certain classes of people previously denied education beyond the elementary level but requiring further education to perform effectively as farmers, mechanics, merchants, and citizens. Thus, the land-grant mission was originally oriented to both class and competency. It met the needs of a rapidly developing society for the creation of professionals and quasiprofessionals to plan, direct, disseminate, and apply technological developments. But since an essential aspect of a democratic society is the value it places on the individual human being, the land-grant mission was shortly modified to include attention to personal development, family, and quality of living.

This broader conception of the land-grant mission soon emphasized the extension to rural youth of the opportunity for fuller personal development and for access to a full range of careers. The percentage of rural youth returning to rural areas after completing a land-grant college degree would become, for some years, a concern of legislators and of the rural supporters of the land-grant colleges, although the trek to urban areas was soon firmly established. That trend did not concern either the faculty or the students at land-grant colleges, which encouraged it by increasing farm productivity. Even the farmers with large families were pleased that some of their offspring could succeed in the city.

The original justification for the presence of the liberal arts and sciences, especially in newly created separate land-grant institutions, was based on their importance as foundation courses for integrated career and personal development. In the pragmatic American culture, selection of a liberal arts or science major at once evoked the question of its value in earning a living. Hence, the study of the liberal arts and sciences for their own sake, without regard for relevance to life or career, was not a part of the land-grant concept of education until the Ph.D. and the disciplinary department began to dominate the institutional structure and faculty organization. Although this development shifted attention from drawing upon a discipline for personal, social, and career development to concentration in a discipline, the career emphasis of the land-grant college still tended to attract undergraduate majors, graduate students, and even professors who believed that degrees at any level in any field would provide employable competencies.

The expansion of the land-grant mission to include individual and family welfare made the social sciences and the humanities seem fundamental rather than simply relevant to the land-grant curriculum. But the gradual proliferation of courses, departments, and colleges in these areas ultimately made the structure of the land-grant university much like that of the state or private university with or without a land-grant college. Whereas the early land-grant faculty selected content materials relevant to work, humanists and social scientists tended to select content on the basis of their views of the importance or quality of the works. Whether or not these materials were more conducive to personal development than others was and still is unknown, but that question has been considered to be both vulgar and irrelevant. However, the vast expansion in liberal arts departments and courses rendered the concept of liberal education essentially meaningless. Many institutions, such as Michigan State, sought a general education program that would provide in manageable form the essence of the liberal arts. But a generally educated faculty proved as difficult to find and maintain as a liberally educated one.

The land-grant college began with the mission of bringing to bear upon society's problems those ideas, concepts, principles, and modes of thought that might alleviate or solve the problems. The faculty was clearly to be a mediating agent by assisting individuals in acquiring knowledge and skills useful in resolving problems and in improving the quality of living. But it was not a role that appealed to the new faculties who viewed institutional stature as based upon the research productivity of professors and a large number of disciplines.

With some exceptions, this emphasis on research and discipline results in a faculty oriented to producing publications as a way of establishing their personal scholarly reputations. The belief in "publish or perish" has resulted in many relatively insignificant contributions. In spite of this, publication is encouraged on the assumption that continued scholarly activity keeps faculty members alert and cognizant of developments in their disciplines. Another argument is that only by encouraging research contributions from large numbers of people can we be sure that, in time, significant advances will be made. Although a similar argument could be made for awareness of problems and applications of basic knowledge to them, there is a tendency always to devalue research productivity that is interdisciplinary and closely related to practical problems.

Most real world problems have been found to be far more complex than recognized in early attempts at solutions. But applied research and experimentation are frequently the only ways in which that complexity can be understood. Mankind's progress is built as much on errors as on successes, and reflections on either random experience or planned experimentation can be enlightening. When problems dealt with immediate basic needs of food, clothing, and shelter, the knowledge and skills required to deal with these could be acquired by one individual and learned by others. This was especially true of technological developments in the late nineteenth and early twentieth century. When the focus of attention shifts to the impact and use of chemicals in the handling of waste or to the prevention of disease, it is clear that the problems are much more complicated and that the uses and effects of any new technologies and of human reactions to them become part of the resolution of a problem. The realization of this complexity is seen today in the way various individuals and groups react to any major proposal. The generation of electricity by atomic energy is a menace to the environment and therefore opposed by many persons. The development of offshore oil resources is criticized as a threat to coast and coastal waters. The complexity of the scientific issues related to any practical problem is equaled or even perhaps exceeded by the conflict of values and the complexities of human reactions generated by any proposed solution. Appeals to courts to make decisions always lead to appeals to higher courts, and perhaps the most complicated question of all has come to be "who decides?" Opposition to the death sentence means that murderers receive life sentences. In turn, the operation of parole procedures results in early release of prisoners under life sentence who are then free to murder again. Thus, a life sentence for one may well be a death sentence for another. Life sentences for many are also life sentences for the tax-payers, who in the end must provide the funds for the police, courts, and prisons. Law, as Hannah early decided, may indeed have little to do with justice.

The possibility of shifting medical care from curing or alleviating disease to maintaining health has received considerable attention recently. Health maintenance or disease prevention, however, necessarily delimits behavior and meets with resistance. For example, adverse reactions to and violations of vehicle safety ordinances such as helmets for bike riders, seat belts, speed limits and other restrictions are commonplace. Attempts to control or curtail use of cigarettes, alcohol, drugs, noise, air pollution, or sugar substitutes generate severe opposition and lead to expensive attempts at enforcement and punishment. Vaccinations or preventive inoculations are rejected by some as infringements on individual freedom, and fluoride treatment to prevent tooth decay continues to arouse opposition. The fact that some strongly opposed preventive services have been free demonstrates that the objection is not to the expense but rather to the imposition. It is difficult to implement health maintenance procedures when there are many dissenters. Formal education may ultimately effect change, but only over time. Much of its current emphasis has been on individualization. Perhaps more should be on socialization.

Continuing or Lifelong Education has suffered in its development because unlike Cooperative Extension and the Experiment Station, it has had, to a large extent, to be self-supporting. Whereas the early support of the land-grant institution emphasized service and applied research, similar support has never become available to most of the other departments and colleges in the university. Individuals can direct time on a voluntary basis to many types of research, but much of the research needed today requires a team effort which in turn requires administration, supportive organizations, and funding. Thus, fund availability and specific task assignments become determining factors in the activities of professors.

Public service, including problem-oriented research, is not a popular activity with faculties today, and funds for that mission are limited and (except for Cooperative Extension and the Experiment Station) not current from year to year. Public service activities dependent upon sporadic support are difficult to plan or staff and lack the security necessary to attract and hold faculty. Although there are other factors involved in rendering public service somewhat unattractive to faculty members, if continuous support were made available, there can be no doubt that institutions—land-grant or otherwise—would find rationales for accepting such funds. Commitment to the land-grant mission is essential to its success; but the availability of funds would attract many other institutions, not solely colleges and universities.

REESTABLISHING THE PUBLIC SERVICE MISSION

If the public service mission is to be reestablished as a primary and distinctive function of a university, the concept itself must be revived, elaborated, and supported. The governing board and the administration of the institution must seek support and take those actions essential for developing and maintaining an institution that will address the current problems and concerns of the people, the state, and the nation. This will require administrators, including departmental chairs, who accept the service mission and have at some time engaged in it. It will require the selection or development of some faculty members who accept as their primary role the task of applying their knowledge and skill in helping people and society. Maintaining an effective public service mission may also call for a reorganization of an institution. Depending upon how an institution defines its overall mission, this may necessitate the establishment of an alternative structure to the traditional colleges and departments such as institutes, centers, experiment stations, extension, and continuing education. An extreme reorganization might eliminate the departmental disciplinary structure and replace it with units more clearly related to the problems and needs of people.

An institution that intends to emphasize applied research and extension activities will need to budget accordingly, evaluate performance, and account to itself and to others for funds used in public service activities. There are also certain biases or dichotomies that must be abandoned by an institution that hopes to serve society and its needs successfully. Some of these are little more than faculty preferences or convenience. Others have some basis in maintaining controls to assure standards. None have a sound evidential basis.

One of these is the distinction made between campus and off-campus activities. For many years, state legislatures have traditionally regarded off-campus education as different from on-campus instruction. Despite the fact that land-grant colleges and state universities have generally argued that their campuses include the entire state, off-campus credit courses have often lacked the quality of facilities, materials, and instruction that is customary on campus. The campus/off-campus dichotomy is also closely related to the two categories of credit/noncredit and degree/nondegree. These concepts are further related to such terms as *nontraditional education* and *external degrees,* and to a variety of other educational offerings of uncertain meaning and indefinite quality. Many institutions offered programs of dubious merit that presume to meet an educational need but actually are planned to meet their own financial needs. The public-service-oriented university is obliged to meet a variety of educational needs with programs that are carefully defined and of demonstrable quality. Appropriate programs can be furnished in a variety of ways, and the concern should be with meeting needs by providing high-quality programs at reasonable prices rather than continuing to impose archaic requirements that reflect campus traditions but have no ascertainable relationship to either need or quality. Campuses do not present ideal learning sites for every type of person and program, and the faculties involved have seldom taken any responsibility for assuring quality.

A second dichotomy is that between liberal education and career education. Most educational institutions that currently attempt to provide a liberal education do so by requiring a distribution of credits. The requirement may be accompanied by a statement of objectives that relate to knowledge, understanding, attitudes, values, and other qualities that are never defined in detail and certainly never evaluated. Furthermore, no one has been able to demonstrate that the content of particular courses has much to do with those qualities. They are certainly not defined or assured by a credit distribution requirement.

Interpretations of the original land-grant theme always have emphasized the importance of a liberal education as well as attainment of career competencies. A human being and his or her career are inseparable, both in living and in the process of preparing for living. Knowledge of no use either for personal satisfaction or monetary return is simply useless. Yet it is strange that scholars who make their living from one or more liberal arts still insist that there is a meaningful distinction between liberal and vocational. Work can be enjoyed.

A third dichotomy is one between the disciplines of knowledge and the abilities to apply knowledge. The proliferation of departments and disciplines in the modern university have made the meaning of *discipline* itself uncertain. Furthermore, there is not necessarily a correspondence between the problems that individuals and nations confront and the disciplines into which we have organized knowledge. Much of disciplinary scholarship deals with trivia. The real significance of a discipline is, as the word itself connotes, a rigorous mode of thinking, acquiring, and organizing knowledge rather than the resulting body of knowledge. To those outside a discipline, its meaning is found in its contributions to broader insights. An institution that wishes to provide a meaningful education must emphasize the interrelation and integration of knowledge and its relationships to the tasks of the day rather than to some ultimate and probably vain hope to attain truth. The pragmatic view is underlined when one realizes that, were a truth to be discovered, it could not be neatly assigned to some disciplinary category to which scholars attempt to confine their efforts.

The several dichotomies embodied in such concepts as the lecture, discussion, teaching, learning, teacher, and student confuse and interfere with the educational process. Learning conducive to value commitments and behavioral change is what really counts when one evaluates educational experiences in reference to their benefits to individuals and society. An excellent lecture in Latin to students who know no Latin is clearly not a significant learning experience. An excellent lecture in English may not be a worthwhile learning experience even to an audience who knows English well. The public-service-oriented institution must insist that the efforts of its faculty be consciously related to and judged in regard to the worth of the learning that takes place. The question "What difference do my efforts make?" must be repeatedly asked of and by the faculty members and the people they serve. If the answer is "not much," then either the content or the educational procedures should be changed.

An institution and faculty that are committed to scholarship, defined as the search for knowledge, presumably serve not just the professors but others who also seek knowledge. In that sense, the same question above must be asked and answered. But whereas a university dedicated to seeking knowledge may well view its efforts solely on a cumulative long-term basis, an institution that aims to help individuals deal more effectively with the immediate must ask, "What difference does this make right now?" Thus, the service-oriented university cannot limit its instructional and extension services to predetermined periods of time and to rigid sets of experiences that add up to a degree. People looking for a haircut do not want a course in barbering. Research may ultimately produce cures for cancer, but alleviation of pain and enhancing the quality of life are also worthwhile immediate objectives.

Another confusing dichotomy is that of concentration in a single discipline versus breadth of learning across several disciplines. Any significant problem or question deserves to be looked at both in depth and in breadth. Whether in regard to our natural resources or our international relations, it is evident that the failure or inability to look at alternative decisions and actions in terms of possible immediate and long-term results for humankind is a fault that we must attempt to correct through education. Discipline-based course requirements are unlikely to help.

Also destructive of the public service mission is the confusing use of such words as *objectives*, *goals*, and *accomplishments*. Distinctions among these are arbitrary but necessary. *Objectives* usually indicate those learning outcomes that relate to student gains in knowledge, thought processes, scholarly skills, and appropriate attitudes and values. If stated at all by departments or colleges bent on achieving excellence, objectives often create only a facade behind which the faculty may seek such actual goals as becoming a first-rate, widely known college or university; receiving high salaries and small teaching loads; becoming one of the top ten research universities; attaining state-of-the-art plant, facilities, and research equipment; achieving world status in various departments and disciplines; and winning faculty-dominated governance. These goals are not undesirable. They may even have some limited connection with student learning objectives and public service, but they have more to do with faculty selection, accomplishments, and the reputation of the institution. The emphasis, appropriately for an elitist university, is on accumulating and organizing knowledge. Immediate and direct concern for public interest probably would not be denied in such an institution, but the public interest is unlikely to be much in evidence as a criterion for internal budgetary allocations.

The public service mission emphasizes people, their problems, and the provision of programs to resolve or alleviate them. This requires a variety of services and a flexible means to deliver them. Salaries, scholarly stature, facilities, and resources are certainly relevant; but attention must be shifted from a faculty concentrating on disciplinary research to a people- , problem-oriented staff. The programs offered must generally be planned and carried out in cooperation with those experiencing the problem. Accountability to external agencies in relation to effective and efficient use of time and other resources is essential. The approach to problems must be experimental in the land-grant tradition rather than based upon definitive research. The ultimate criterion should always be pragmatic: Does it work? Does it alleviate or resolve the problem?

Consonant with the experimental approach, public service efforts must recognize that complications, human fallibility, and unanticipated events are likely to render any proposed solution to a problem less effective in impact and less durable in time than desired. Hence there must be continuing interaction between extension public service personnel, the public, students, and campus-based programs. The next problem to be faced is likely to be implicit in the solution to the last one.

A university that would highlight public service—including instruction, demonstration, and applied research—must have faculty members of stature who maintain familiarity and competency in the various problems involved and who also possess sufficient breadth of knowledge and experience that they can collaborate with colleagues and others in analysis and study of problems. For this purpose faculty work loads, leaves, and sabbaticals should be flexible enough to permit any type of assignment that is relevant to the service performed.

To be effective, the administrative structure (personnel and organization) and faculty personnel policies (selection, task assignment, evaluation, and reward systems) must be rather different from the usual departmental discipline structure with its focus on graduate instruction and research. Viewing a discipline as a source of problems and of methods of handling them requires much more knowledge of the structure, concepts, and methodology of other disciplines and of their actual or potential relevance to analyzing and resolving problems than is true of the relatively narrow doctoral research now encouraged by departments and their graduate faculties.

As attention shifts from disciplines to individuals, to their personal and career development, as well as to the insights and skills provided to society by increasing knowledge, it becomes evident that those persons who accept and effectively perform public service must be accommodated in a structure that assists and rewards such service. Otherwise public service, like undergraduate teaching—itself a major public service mission—will be ignored or its resources diverted to support the research mission perceived by departments.

## ORGANIZATIONAL ALTERNATIVES

Although organizations and particularly reorganizations are frequently regarded as a means to change the character of an institution or to encourage some particular type of renovation or innovation, it is probably true that administrative organization or structure is far less important to the quality and emphasis of the academic unit than the individuals and commitments involved. As Michigan State was changing from an institution in which the primary purpose of various departments was to provide courses for home economics, engineering, and agriculture, the departments continued for some time to emphasize the service role despite the appearance of research-oriented faculty. Deans and department heads, supported by John Hannah, still held to long-existing service traditions and hired new faculty who were at least sympathetic to or tolerant of the public service and intrainstitutional service mission. So long as this type of service was counted as part of an individual's load or was, as often was the case before World War II, accepted as a not unpleasant additional chore, there was no problem about reward. But as deans and departmental chairs were brought in with the announced intention of upgrading the quality of the faculty and the departments, it became more and more evident that research productivity and publication were the payoffs rather than service.

Conceivably it would be possible, in an institution with a strong central administrative leadership extending to the departments, to modify the emphasis on research so as to give public service and applied research reasonable attention. It is not a change that can be made easily because faculty members prefer deans and chairs who are themselves eminent researchers or at least have demonstrated their support of research as a major activity.

Attempts to resolve the deficiency in the service function by assignment of unproductive teachers or researchers might incur as much ill will in the state as in the institution. Assignment of able researchers to public service is likewise risky. An example of this problem is found in departments where grants or contracts have been obtained for reshaping courses and teaching in disciplines at the elementary and secondary level. Outstanding research faculty have frequently worked poorly with these teachers, and their conceptions of what is appropriate from their discipline at this level may be completely erroneous. Typically the activities—and the interest—have ceased when the funds have been expended.

Just as agriculture, by the early twentieth century, had an extension service and an experiment station with separate funding and with individuals appointed to these units, colleges and universities in more recent years have set up centers for continuing or lifelong education. Many institutions have a vice-president for research, possibly conjoined with the office of the dean of the graduate school. In the university a vice-president for extension and continuing education and a vice-president for research may be assigned to coordinate those functions just as a vice-president for academic affairs, or provost, is assigned to coordinate instruction and degree programs. The vice-president for research has usually been justified in modern times because of the need for careful scrutiny and coordination of the extensive grant and contract funds coming to an institution. Although many of these grants or contracts primarily concern research, along with a very limited amount of formal instruction, doctoral dissertations are often involved.

A cursory examination of state and land-grant university organizations revealed such titles as vice-president (or vice-chancellor) for services, for extension, for records, for public service, and for continuing education. Implicit in some of these titles is the recognition that public service is a total institutional mission and one to be coordinated at the central administrative level. In a coordinated state system or a single state university, there may be coordination of public service across all campuses. This coordination has some advantage in reducing competition, but it also tends to sever the close cooperation and personal relationships that can develop between campuses and the groups served. Public service must not become bureaucratic.

Looking internally into institutions, it is possible to view the various colleges and units of a university as having responsibilities for extension activities and applied research that would justify an appointment (assistant or associate dean, perhaps) in each dean's office for coordination of these functions. The vice-president for public services is then the institution-wide administrator for these missions just as the vice-president for academic affairs administers the on-campus academic program. This organization assumes that most, if not all, extension and service activities are ultimately performed by departmentally assigned faculty. It is not a pattern that works well with all the public service tasks, most of which transcend departmental and even college programs. The departmental commitment to public service appears to remain strong in home economics and agriculture, but elsewhere it is not likely to be given a priority equal to instruction and research. If the public service commitment is restrengthened and staffed, departments will almost surely assert that the budget and staff should be assigned to them. One may doubt that the result will be effective performance of public service.

Most institutions in the last twenty or twenty-five years have found that a number of centers, institutes, or other nondepartmental units have been useful in obtaining funds and carrying out studies and contracts that transcend departmental and college lines. Such units have commonly been regarded as competitors to the traditional college departments. Colleges and departments prefer that the funds of such units be restricted to grants or contracts and that the faculty status be determined in the appropriate department. But such centers or institutes may be highly desirable units within the public service university, and within colleges of the university such units would enable faculty members to carry on studies transcending the departmental structure. Centers or institutes at the college level could even be the preferred college unit for public service and applied research, perhaps conjoined with some instructional responsibilities.

But since public service projects are likely also to transcend colleges, it would seem that extension and applied research require coordination at the university level with the possibility of rewarding individuals on the basis of service, a function that would be ignored or deprecated by the traditional departmental organization. Both centers and departments can coexist, each autonomous in selecting and rewarding faculty, including the award of any form of tenure or job security that may emerge from a reappraisal of priorities. Tenure as a safeguard of academic freedom or tenure as a hazard to institutional flexibility and quality? However *tenure* may be redefined, it should be granted for meritorious performance of assigned roles, and not solely for research and publications.

The matter of tenure must be addressed in developing and maintaining a strong public service mission. If colleges and departments will not accept the responsibility, then an alternative organization must be found, whether parallel to or completely supplanting the disciplinary department. The utilitarian focus is already apparent in career-oriented colleges. Faculties in the arts and sciences may find it difficult to accept, but—when programs and majors are closely examined—they are in fact more practical than is often realized, especially if advanced graduate study is regarded as career preparation. The substitution of a public service unit for the traditional department is not that outlandish an idea.

To achieve equity in support of public service, it may also be necessary to plan the budget accordingly. For example, had not specific budgetary allowances been assigned to agriculture and home economics, they could easily have been weeded out. One may recall at this point Hannah's early decision to make extension and Experiment Station appropriations line items, thereby assuring that they would not be assimilated into other programs by administrators having little interest in them. Budgetary appropriations to colleges and departments divided into three parts—for the three missions of teaching, research, and public service—and requiring separate accountability for each would greatly complicate the operations of these units. Experienced and slightly cynical administrators would expect some manipulation of the three-part budget in accordance with the values of the deans and department chairs. Internal auditing would be necessary.

There is another problem with identifying allocations for research and public service: a tendency on the part of state budget offices and legislatures, when funds are tight, to view instruction as the mission that the state primarily supports and to regard extension and research activities as things that can be cut or suspended for a time. In fact, suspension of a research or service program for a year or two is far more serious than suspension of some courses. Most legislators and budget offices involved in setting institutional allocations are intelligent enough to realize this, but almost any rationale will serve when the primary motivation is to reduce an appropriation request. In a sense the answer to this dilemma is very simple. If the public service mission of a university cannot be sold to the legislature and the public by demonstrating its worth and justifying continuing funding by one or several sources, then the decision to curtail that mission has been made outside the university.

Hence, keeping the public informed and maintaining public enthusiasm for support of the public service role is a major task. Research-oriented faculty members are not usually much interested in interpreting what they are doing for the general public. Unlike their predecessors in the land-grant institutions, they are not willing to spend time with people and their organizations to learn what the problems are so that their own scholarship might be directed to have some relevance to them. Yet if the public does not understand the services of the land-grant institution and see some value in these services, it cannot be expected to support the institution. And legislators, taking their cue from the people, will not support the public service mission.

A related problem is the fact that public service is, in a limited sense at least, a function of every university. Special and separate funding for for agriculture and home economics is a tradition. Legislative allocations for research have generally been avoided by regarding research as a necessary accompaniment of graduate instruction and a partial explanation of its cost. But direct support of public service and applied research by the state would irresistibly impel all state-assisted institutions to acquire "a piece of the pie." Politics would assure that they would succeed. The total sum then required would call into question once again the wisdom of separating public service from instruction. As this is being written, the Michigan legislature, urged by the governor, has allocated funds for research related to improvement of the state's economy. Although four major research universities have been identified, all state-assisted universities will receive some of the pie. But there is a question of whether or not there will be continuing support for research. Also, the intention to require that the research projects be reviewed and approved by a state commission or committee would be a direct threat to institutional autonomy.

There is an alternative to separate funding of public service projects: the assignment of similar if not identical teaching loads to all professors in a department, regardless of individual research productivity. Some do not produce and could be assigned to other tasks. The difficulty is that this determination is made too late to build a departmental faculty balanced across the three missions. And a department is justified for seeking such a balance. A university that would serve the people must be in constant touch with the people and must continually assure itself that it is providing them with a worthwhile and valued product although not necessarily that which individuals and various groups first sought.

The major component of public service is education. Colleges and universities have for years criticized the public schools, but their faculties have displayed no enduring interest in improving them. They would rather disparage the education faculties for concentrating on methods, social problems, administration, and evaluation to the neglect of content. Meantime, the former colleges of education, originally created to integrate substance and process for public education, have become obsessed with becoming universities and have abandoned their original mission. The revision of public school education is one requiring concentrated and continuing attention by our best minds.

Only those universities that view teacher preparation as a major social problem transcending all disciplines are likely to make a significant contribution to its improvement. Surely one of the major concerns of a university committed to public service should be the public schools, both elementary and secondary.

There is great need to redefine the appropriate content for the various levels of public education. It does not seem entirely appropriate to organize courses around disciplines as they are viewed in the research university. In various national attempts to revise science and social science curricula, many mathematicians or scientists have become more enamored of providing materials and experiences that deal with the fundamental nature of disciplines than with those facts, principles, and modes of thought that are appropriate and even essential in everyday living. In fact, in viewing some of the results of such projects, one could almost conclude that at present the university with a land-grant mission should avoid departmental organization and seek an organization more relevant to the problems of the real world. Perhaps the most fundamental contribution that a university could make to improving teaching at lower levels would be to reshape and improve instruction in the university.

SUMMARY

A few final words are appropriate about the implications and possibilities of restoring to a group of institutions the commitment to focus their major efforts on helping people, municipalities, states, nations, and the world to define their problems and move more expeditiously to solutions. If one believes, as John Hannah always has, that the aim of education is to help people help themselves, the task is relatively clear in concept but very different in execution.

Nevertheless, those who are aware of the great impact that the land-grant, public-service-oriented university has had over the years on American society feel that there is a need and a place in the United States today for educational institutions that direct their knowledge and activities to helping people and organizations to make improvements now, rather than deferring them until some indefinite and possible nonexistent future. One thing that seems evident after examining the Hannah years at Michigan State is that the public university's governing boards, which presumably are selected to represent the interests of the people, cannot be altogether trusted to do so—in part because the considerations involved in selecting them may have nothing to do with the nature of their tasks. The institution that would serve the public must educate the public to demand that service.

The public service university must assist its students and the general public to become aware of such problems as the cost and availability of energy; environmental protection and management; natural resources conservation; adequate nutrition; health protection and disease prevention; agricultural policies, laws, and regulations; trade and international relations; consumer protection; and human relations. Only when a majority of our citizens understand the nature and complexity of these problems, the priorities among them, and the possible solutions, can resources be mobilized to alleviate them. Even so, the measures taken will inevitably fall short of perfection and alter our priorities for the next stage. Whether in esoteric scholarship or in real life, the challenge is in the search rather than in attainment.

In asking that some universities direct attention to people and their current problems, one need not question the desirability of colleges and universities that see the primary mission of the institution as that of increasing knowledge. Ultimately the achievement of the full potential of human beings lies first in knowing the full potential of the human being. Such institutions are needed, though obviously knowledge may be destructively misused and may generate major difficulty even when a beneficial purpose is intended. But we also need institutions that focus on the immediate needs of society. The public service mission of the land-grant institution is indeed far more difficult to fulfill than is that of the more remote institution that pursues the expansion of knowledge untrammeled by society's problems. In reference to the problems of our society and the future of humankind, the public service mission is also more critical.

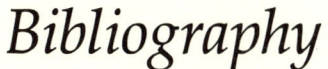

*Bibliography*

# Bibliography

BOOKS

Allen, Herman B. *Open Door to Learning: The Land-Grant System Enters Its Second Century.* Urbana: Ill.: University of Illinois Press, 1963.

Anderson, G. Lester, ed. *Land-Grant Universities and Their Continuing Challenge.* East Lansing, Mich.: Michigan State University Press, 1976.

*Degrees Conferred, East Lansing Campus—1960–1981 through Spring Term 1983.* East Lansing, Mich.: Michigan State College Press, 1955.

Dressel, P.L., ed. *Evaluation in the Basic College at Michigan State University.* New York: Harper and Brothers, 1958.

Eddy, Edward D., Jr. *Colleges for Our Land and Time.* New York: Harper and Brothers, 1956.

Edmond, J.B. *The Magnificent Charter: Origin and Role of the Morrill Land-Grant Colleges and Universities.* Hicksville, New York: Exposition Press, Inc., 1978.

Eklund, Lowell R. *Century of Service: An Historical Analysis of the Service Function of a State University.* Ann Arbor, Mich.: Michigan University Microfilms, 1955.

Fuller, Dunaway W. *History of the Pennsylvania State College.* State College, Penn.: Pennsylvania State University Library, 1946.

Garfinkel, Herbert. *An Experiment in Undergraduate Education.* Dubuque, Iowa: William C. Brown Company, 1968.

Hamilton, Thomas, and Blackman, Edward, eds. *The Basic College of Michigan State.* East Lansing, Mich.: Michigan State College Press, 1955.

Hannah, John A. *A Memoir.* East Lansing, Mich.: Michigan State University Press, 1980.

Kellogg, Charles E., and Knapp, David C. *The College of Agriculture: Science in the Public Service.* New York: McGraw-Hill Book Company, 1966.

Kuhn, Madison. *Michigan State: The First Hundred Years, 1855–1955.* East Lansing, Mich.: Michigan State University Press, 1955.

Morrill, Charles C. *Veterinary Medicine in Michigan: An Illustrated History.* East Lansing, Mich.: Michigan State University, College of Veterinary Medicine, 1979.

Olstrom, Einer, and Miller, Howard. *Plus Two Score: The Cooperative Extension Service in Michigan 1940 to 1980.* East Lansing, Mich.: Cooperative Extension Service, Michigan State University, 1984.

Phillips, Ione. *The Added Dimension: State and Land-Grant University Serving State and Local Government.* Washington, D.C.: National Association of State Universities and Land-Grant Colleges, ca. 1977–78.

Raper, Arthur, et al. *Rural Development in Action: Comprehensive Experiment in Action.* Ithaca, N.Y.: Cornell University Press, 1970.

Ross, E.D. *Democracy's College. The Land-Grant Movement in the Formative Stage.* Ames, Iowa: Iowa State College Press, 1942.

VanderMuelen, Joseph. *The Kellogg Bird Sanctuary Story: The First Fifty Years 1927–1977.* Augusta, Mich.: Kellogg Bird Sanctuary, Michigan State Unviersity, Kellogg Biological Station, 1977.

JOURNAL ARTICLES AND BOOK CHAPTERS

Beaman, John H. "A Botanical Inventory of Sanford Natural Area. I. The Environment II. Checklist of Vascular Plants. *Michigan Botanist* 9 (1970).

Berg, Herbert A. "The Reorganization of Michigan Cooperative Extension Service." *Michigan Service,* United States Department of Agriculture, July 1941.

Blackman, E.B. "Residence-Hall Instructional Programs." *Journal of Education* 35 (March 1965).

_____. "The Living-Learning Program at Michigan State." *University College Quarterly* (January 1965): 10–13.

"Cost of Private Higher Education." *Journal of the Association for Institutional Research* 18 (1983).

Dressel, P.L. "Evaluation." In *The Basic College of Michigan State,* edited by T. Hamilton and E. Blackman. East Lansing, Mich.: Michigan State College Press, 1955.

Dutton, Frederic B., and Brandou, Julian R. "The Science and Mathematics Teaching Center: A Retrospective View." In *Proceedings of the Conference Marking the 20th Anniversary of the Science and Mathematics Teaching Center,* Michigan State University, May 17, 1977, prepared and edited by Richard Brandenbury and James Joseph Gallagher.

Hoffer, Charles R., and Dove, James. "Organizations for Health and Health Care—A Survey of Jackson County Michigan." *Agricultural Experiment Quarterly* 42 (August 1959):200.

"John N. Winburne and the Development of Academic Counseling." *University College Quarterly* 19 (May 1974).

Kennedy, Donald. "Government Policies and the Cost of Doing Research." *Science* 227 (1984).

Kennedy, Theodore R. "The Department of American Thought and Language." *University College Quarterly* 20 (November 1974).

_____. "Enrolling Non-Preference Students." *Basic College Quarterly* 1 (Spring 1956).

Madsen, David. "The Land-Grant University: Myth and Reality." In *Land-Grant Universities and Their Continuing Challenge,* edited by G. Lester Anderson. East Lansing, Mich.: Michigan State University Press, 1976.

Molloy, John D. "The Department of Social Sciences." *University College Quarterly* (Janaury 1975):36–46.

Muse, W.V. "If All the Business Schools in the Country Were Eliminated . . . Would Anyone Notice?" *Collegiate News and Views* 36 (Spring 1983).

Olson, L.A. "Living-Learning Units, as Seen by the Faculty." *Journal of Higher Education* 35 (February 1964).
_____. "Student Opinion on the Coed Dorm." *University College Quarterly* 8 (May 1963).
_____. "Student Reactions to Living, Learning Residence Halls." *Journal of College Student Personnel* 6 (October 1964).
_____. "Students Live and Learn in Residence Halls." *College and University Business* 38 (March 1965).
Quill, Laurence L. "Some Problems of the Department of Chemistry in State-Supported Universities." *Journal of Chemical Education* 22 (February 1945).
Quimby, Robert S. "The Department of Humanities." *University College Quarterly* (January 1975): 50–57.
"Remedial Education in College: The Problems of Underprepared Students." *Issues in Higher Education* (Southern Regional Education Board) 20 (1983).
Winburne, John N. "Student Personnel Services." In *The Basic College of Michigan State*, edited by T.H. Hamilton and E. Blackman. East Lansing, Mich.: Michigan State University Press, 1955.
Wittwer, Sylvan H. "U.S. Agriculture in the Context of the World Food Situation." In *Science, Technology, and the Issues of the Eighties: Policy Outlook*, edited by A.H. Teich and R. Thornton. A report prepared for the National Science Foundation in support of the Second Five-Year Outlook for Science and Technology. Boulder, Colorado: Westview Press, 1983.

MICHIGAN STATE UNIVERSITY DOCUMENTS
*A boldface* **A** *indicates that the document is in the MSU Archives and Historical Collections.*

"Academic Freedom for Students at Michigan State University." A report of the Faculty Committee on Student Affairs to the Academic Council, 1967. **A**
"Adult Education; Michigan State College Summary Report—1947 to 1950 and Forecast." **A**
"Annual Report of the President to the State Board of Agriculture, the Governor, and the Citizens of Michigan, on Teaching, Extension and Research for the Year Beginning July 1, 1956 and Ending June 30, 1957." **A**
Baldwin, Robert J., and McDonel, Karl H. "History of Cooperative Extension Work in Michigan 1914–1939." *Extension Bulletin* 229. Michigan State College, Extension Division, June 1941. **A**
Barlowe, Raleigh. "Resource Development at Michigan State University: A History." 1984. **A**
Beal, William J. "History of the Michigan Agricultural College and Biographical Sketches of Trustees and Professors." Michigan State University Library and Archives, 1915. **A**
Berg, Herbert A. "Reorganization of the Michigan State College Cooperative Extension Service." 1945. **A**
Blosser, H.G. Speech presented at the inauguration of the National Superconducting Cyclotron, Michigan State University, 1982.

"Building Data Book." Physical Plant Division, Michigan State College, 1981.

Cole, G.E. "The Objective of the Justin Morrill College as Perceived by Its Members." Ph.D. dissertation, Michigan State University, 1967.

College II Planning Committee. "Report to the Educational Policies Committee on a Proposed Program for Lyman Briggs College." 1967. **A**

Committee on the Future of the University. "A Report to the President of Michigan State University." 1959. **A.**

Cooperative Extension Service. "Report of Committee on College Extension Organization and Policy Extension Reorganization." 1945. **A**

——————————. "Organization Flow-chart." 1954. **A**

Dutton, Frederic B., and Elliot, Jane E. "The Origin and First Six Years of Lyman Briggs College 1967–1973." 1982. **A**

Eckert, Fred W. "Proposal for the Eppley Center for Graduate Study in the Service Industries at Michigan State University, East Lansing, Michigan." August 21, 1959. **A**

"From the Ground Up: 75 Years of Progress in the Agricultural Engineering Department at Michigan State University, 1906–1981." 1982. **A**

Frost, Gary J. "The Building of an Academic Community: James Madison College." Ph.D. dissertation, Michigan State University, 1971.

"Geographical Distribution of Students from U.S. Possessions and Foreign Countries by First Year in Attendance, East Lansing Campus, 1855–1981." Office of the Registrar.

Gilchrist, Maude. "The First Three Decades of Home Economics at Michigan State College 1896–1926." n.d. **A**

Hannah, John A. "Annual Report of the President to the State Board of Agriculture, the Governor, and the Citizens of Michigan on Teaching, Extension and Research for the Year Beginning July 1, 1956 and Ending June 30, 1957." **A**

——————————. A statement by John A. Hannah, 1963–64 MSU Catalog, Vol. 57, No. 9, February 1963, p. 9. Extracted from "We Believe. . . ."

——————————. Statement from the *State Journal*, Vol. 114, No. 288, Feb. 9, 1969. Comments on John A. Hannah's personal philosophy.

Harden, Edgar L. A letter to _____, May 10, 1983. Enclosure: paper written by Edgar L. Harden, "Continuing Education at Michigan State College, 1950–1955." **A**

Haydn, Rose. "Report on Feedback to Michigan State University as a Result of Overseas Technical Assistance Project Involvement." 1971. **A**

Hill, Russell G. "History of Department of Resource Development. 1976. **A**

"The Honors College of Michigan State University." Honors College Committee Report, November 12, 1956. **A**

Houk, Wallace E. "A Study of Some Events in the Development of Entomology and Its Application in Michigan." Ph.D. dissertation, Michigan State University, 1954.

Hurder, Donald F. "Selected Affective and Cognitive Characteristics of Students in the Lyman Briggs College and the College of Natural Science at

Michigan State University." Ph.D. dissertation, Michigan State University, 1969.

"Improving Undergraduate Education." The Report of the Committee on Undergraduate Education. 1967. A

"International Role of the University in the Eighties." Proceedings of the Michigan State University International Year Conference, April 25–27, 1982. East Lansing: Michigan State University International Studies and Programs, 1982.

Kennedy, Theodore R. "Recollections of Theodore R. Kennedy, July 1983." Comments on his experience as a member of the Basic/University College Faculty. A

——————————. "Monograph on Academic Advising." University College Student Affairs Office, 1966. A

King, Herman. Recollections of Herman King, personal communications.

Lautner, H.W. "An Oak Opening: A Record of the Development of the Campus Park of Michigan State University." In 2 volumes. A

Lee, Chao Chang. "My Contributions to Michigan State's International Program." Unpublished paper. A

Meador, N.F. "History of Agricultural Engineering Department, Michigan State University 1906–1964," n.d. A

"Michigan Farm Economics." No. 332. Department of Agricultural Economics, September 1970.

Michigan State College. University Catalogs (1920–1984 inclusive). Office of the Registrar.

"Michigan State College 1855–1955—Centennial Wolverine." A

*Michigan State University Alumni Association Magazine.* Michigan State University Alumni Association, Summer 1980.

"Michigan's Upper Peninsula Rural Resource Development Program." Michigan State University U.P. Extension Center, Marquette, Mich., 1959. A

Moore, B.F. "The Michigan State University Counseling Center Origins and the Development of Current Functions and Services, 1946–1971." 1974. A

"The M.S.U. Centennial: Its Planning and Execution." 1956. A

Noll, Victor H. "The Preparation of Teachers at Michigan State University." College of Education, 1968. A

Paul, Wilson B. "Capsule History of the Lecture-Concert Series," n.d. A

Paulsen, Harold W. "Physical Education at Michigan State College." *Spartan Messenger Newsletter* (Department of Health, Physical Education and Recreation, January 1955).

Pettit, Lincoln C. "The General Studies Program at the Univeristy of Nigeria: Its Origins and Development 1960–1967." Department of Natural Science, University College, 1969. A

Pierson, Merrill R. "The Endowment Fund That Was and Wasn't." Unpublished paper, September 1983. A

——————————. "The Glowing, Growing Years of Michigan State College. Growing Pains." Unpublished paper, September 1983. A

"A Proposal to the Eugene C. Eppley Foundation." College of Business and

Public Service, n.d. **A**

"Publication List." W.K. Kellogg Biological Station, Michigan State University, Hickory Corners, Mich., 1982.

"Publications of the Faculty of the University College: A Bibliography." 1966 and 1969. **A**

"Recommendations of the University Honors Programs Committee for Revision of Legislation Governing the Honors College at Michigan State University." A report to the Academic Council of Michigan State University, 1969. **A**

Reeves, Floyd. "Recollections of Floyd Reeves." **A**

"Rural Resources Education at the W.K. Kellogg Biological Station." A proposal for program and facilities development from Michigan State University, 1980.

Rust, James. "Impressions of an Ombudsman." Unpublished paper, n.d. **A**

Ruswinckel, J.W. "Growing Pains." College of Business, June 1973. **A**

Sheedy, Joseph W. "Academic Survey of the First Basic College Class." 1944. **A**

_____. "A Report on Credit by Examination at Michigan State University." Fall 1949 through Spring 1953.

"Sponsored University Programs for Research and Education." Publication No. 12. Office of Research and Development and the Graduate School, 1971.

*The State News.* Michigan State University, 1935 to 1975.

"Thirty-Second Annual Report of the Division of Extension Work in Agricultural Home Economics to the State Board of Agriculture," 1946. **A**

"This Is Michigan State University: 1982 Facts Book." Compiled by the Division of University Relations, 1982.

Turkey, Harold. "Memorandum for James Denison Regarding my Relations with John Hannah." July 1971.

"Twenty-five Years of Music on Michigan State University Television WKAR-TV 1954–1979." **A**

"University College Self-Study. A Review and Assessment of General Education and the University College." A report to the provost of Michigan State University from the University College Coordinating Committee, College of General Education, 1977.

Van Ness, M. "Not with Tears, But with Flags Flying, 400 Wellwishers Pay Tribute to Departure of MSU President and Mrs. John A. Hannah." *Michigan State News*, March 18, 1969.

"What Can Colleges Do About Traffic Problems." October 1957. **A**

Wright, Jonathan W., and Rudolph, Victor J. "The W.K. Kellogg Experimental Forest: 50 Years of Progress." Agricultural Research Throughout the State, Special Report 7. Michigan State University Agricultural Experiment Stations, Department of Forestry, Field Stations, October 1982.

Yantis, Joseph E. "Communication Arts at Michigan State University before 1955—A Brief History." April 1966. **A**

MISCELLANEOUS DOCUMENTS

Association of State University and Land-Grant Colleges. "University Transportation and Accident Prevention Centers." A study conducted by the Traffic Safety Research and Education Committee of the Association with the assistance of the National Commission on Safety Education of the National Education Association, Washington, D.C., 1962.

Cooperative Extension Service, Committee on Organization and Policy. "A Statement of Scope and Responsibility, The Cooperative Extension Service Today." Washington, D.C., 1958.

Ford Foundation. "Urban Extension: A Report on Experimental Programs Assisted by the Ford Foundation." New York, 1966.

Hoffer, Charles R; Gibson, Duane L.; Loomis, Charles P.; Miller, Paul A.; Schuler, Edgar A.; and Thaden, John F. "Health Needs and Health Care in Michigan—Report of a Statewide Survey." Michigan Agricultural Experiment Station Special Bulletin No. 365, June 1950.

Knoblauch, H.C., et al. "State Agricultural Experiment Stations: A History of Research Policy and Procedures." Misc. Pub. No. 904. U.S. Department of Agriculture, Washington, D.C., 1962.

National Science Foundation, National Board of Graduate Education. "Summary Survey Report." Washington, D.C., June 1975.

"The Place of the Land-Grant College in the Public Educational System of the Future." Speech presented at the Land-Grant Association meeting, Chicago, Ill., October 25, 1944, in the MSU Archives and Historical Collections.

Sommers, Lawrence M. "Some Characteristics, Problems and Trends in the Evolution of Geography Graduate Study in the United States: The Example of Michigan State University." Paper presented at the First International Conference of Latin Americanist Geographers at Paipa, Colombia, August 8–12, 1977.

Songe, Alice H. "An Historical Bibliography of the Land-Grant Movement and the Individual Land-Grant Institutions." Legislative Reference Service, Library of Congress, Washington, D.C.

Tower, James D. "History of the City of East Lansing," 1933.

True, Alfred C. "A History of Agricultural Extension Work in the United States, 1785–1923." Misc. Pub. No. 15. U.S. Department of Agriculture, Washington, D.C., 1928.

University of Maryland. "The Post-Land Grant University." A report of the University. Office of University Publications, University of Maryland, Adelphi, Md., 1981.

U.S. Department of Agriculture and Association of Land-Grant Colleges and Universities. "Joint Committee Report on Extension Programs, Policies, and Goals." U.S. Government Printing Office, Washington, D.C., August 1948.

Van Alstyne, Carol, and Coldren, Sharon L. "The Costs of Implementing Federally Mandated Social Programs at Colleges and Universities." Special Report. Policy Analysis Service, American Council on Education, Washington, D.C., 1976.

Wittwer, Sylvan H. "The Michigan Challenge: Adjustments in Agricultural Research to Meet a Balanced Economy." Paper prepared for the annual meeting of the Agricultural Research Institute, Fort Worth, Texas, October 6, 1982.